LATIN
OR THE EMPIRE
OF A SIGN

LATIN
OR THE EMPIRE
OF A SIGN

From the sixteenth to the twentieth centuries

♦

FRANÇOISE WAQUET

Translated by John Howe

VERSO

London · New York

This edition has been published with the financial assistance of
the French Ministry of Culture

This edition first published by Verso 2001
© Verso 2001
Translation © John Howe 2001
First published as *Le latin ou l'empire d'un signe*
© Editions Albin Michel 1998

Paperback edition first published by Verso 2002
© Verso 2002

1 3 5 7 9 10 8 6 4 2

Verso
UK: 6 Meard Street, London W1F 0EG
US: 180 Varick Street, New York, NY 10014–4606
www.versobooks.com

Verso is the imprint of New Left Books

ISBN 1–85984–402–2

British Library Cataloguing in Publication Data
A catalogue record for this book is available from the British Library

Library of Congress Cataloging-in-Publication Data
A catalog record for this book is available from the Library of Congress

Typeset by The Running Head Limited, www.therunninghead.com
Printed by Biddles Ltd, www.biddles.co.uk

Contents

Introduction

"What can the public of today understand of Malatesta who lived with Cicero, and of Mother Agnes who lived with Jesus? They spoke a dead language", Montherlant wrote, before being reduced by this lack of comprehension to dropping, one by one, a number of Latin quotations that had appeared in the first draft of his essay *Malatesta*. These "crossings-out" give concrete measure to the break that had occurred between contemporary culture and classical culture, of which the growing ignorance of Latin – "a tongue not understood by the greater number" – was the most obvious symbol.[1] This observation could lead to despair and the lofty pose of the "last of the Romans", or to nostalgic dreams of restoring a Virgilian universe. But Latin can also be considered as a "historiographic object" and studied as such: perhaps even more easily now that the utilitarian hypotheses have gone. Now that the vernaculars reign in the Catholic Church, now that "the Latin question" has been superseded in schools by many other matters of greater urgency, there is a place for a book that is not a pamphlet or an exercise in special pleading, but resolutely historical.

Behind this book, along with earlier researches, lies recognition of the "Latin dimension" of the modern West. While historians generally harp on the emergence of the vernacular languages[2] and, with it, the differentiation of states and the constitution of nations, my own research on the Republic of Letters disclosed a different reality: that of a unitary intellectual Europe in which, until a relatively recent date, learning was expressed in Latin.[3] But that was nothing (if I can put it that way) compared to the enduring predominance of the old language in the schools and the Church: here childhood memories took over, and there came back to me the memory of a time – not so very long ago – when Latin was a part of people's lives. On all of that, however, historiography has little to say. Or to put it more precisely, despite numerous but narrow and dispersed studies, it has not come up with anything that casts any long-term light on this Latin past of the West as a whole.[4] Nor did it produce any answer to the question that had come to embody all the others: why, when the fate of Latin had been definitively sealed by recognition of the vernaculars, had the language maintained such a strong presence, some would say a tyranny? The imposing bibliography offered by neo-Latin studies made the question even more pressing; it recalled the abundance and vitality of works written in Latin well after the humanist restoration and up to the seventeenth century at least, displaying mastery of the ancient tongue at the highest level and, through it, the appropriation of a range of styles, genres and forms;[5] however, not only did it offer little by way of answer to the question under discussion, but it also gave glimpses, once the seventeenth century was past, of a world gradually ceasing to write in Latin. Moreover, as the history of ideas proves again and again, although a deep interest in ancient authors persisted, and some of the most "modern" philosophers and writers maintained a fertile commerce with the works of the great writers of Antiquity,[6] classical authors including Cicero, Livy, Lucretius, Seneca and others were being increasingly published in vernacular translations in which they were probably read by all but a narrow circle of specialists. The "time of translations", to use Henri-Jean Martin's expression for an editorial tendency seen in Paris in the middle years of the seventeenth century, was not a passing fashion, but the definitive adaptation of the product to the market.[7] For all that, however, the Latin which people hardly wrote any longer, and read less and less, still had a fine career ahead of it. For three more centuries it coloured the Western world so strongly that attempts to "mess with Latin" invariably unleashed passions out of all proportion to people's knowledge of the language. These reactions raise a small doubt: was the "Latin question" in the modern West a purely linguistic matter that should be seen solely in terms of competence and performance? Might it not refer to a more complex order of things, crystallized around the status attributed to this language by the people of the time? If so, Latin may have derived its authority and duration not so much from what it said or could say, but from what it wanted to say: from what it *meant*.

These are the considerations that lie at the heart of this work. It does not aspire to be encyclopaedic: to say (or at least refer to) everything, to detail developments on the destiny of Latin in the different European countries, to list the typographical details of Latin impressions, to describe the infinite variety of pedagogic methods used over the centuries to stuff Latin into children's heads. What I have tried to write is a cultural history of Latin in the modern era, retracing and analysing the uses made of Latin and the discourses concerning it; their content, but also the volition that drove them and the strategy that supported them. To this end, a historical record has been assembled which is primarily a statement: a record of the presence of Latin in the modern West. A massive presence, springing from school, the

"Latin country" par excellence, from that "stronghold of Latin" the Catholic Church, from the aptly named *Respublica litteraria*; one might even call it an impregnation given that Latin, present everywhere, has come (despite its otherness) to seem a familiar universe. That was the object of the first part of the book. At this point it became tempting to consider the question – which has hardly ever been formulated,[8] perhaps for fear of the answer – of the real levels of knowledge that scholars, academics and churchmen had of Latin: what degree of competence did they achieve? What sort of Latin did they write and speak? This investigation of performance fills the second part, which constitutes, in a sense, a counter-proof to the first. The contrast between them leads, in a third stage, to a change of perspective, adopting the viewpoint of men of the time who did not regard Latin solely as a language to write and speak, but as an instrument meant for other uses, as a sign invested with other meanings. That will complete the full circle, for the massive presence of Latin in modern society has depended on the uses that have been made of it, and these uses have given the Western world a Latin coloration . . . at any rate until the moment, fast approaching, when society starts to say and do the same things differently. Then the world will lose this coloration, and will have finished with Latin, at least with the Latin whose history I have tried to write.

Allow me to end by detailing the time and space limits of this work. The sixteenth and twentieth centuries were unavoidable: in the first, classical Latin was introduced into schools following the humanist restoration and the decision taken at the Council of Trent to choose Latin as the liturgical language; and in our own time measures have been taken to put an end "officially" to Latin in schools and the Catholic Church. These cut-off points are nevertheless slightly arbitrary: at one end of the time-scale, in Italy, pupils taught by Guarino of Verona were already emeritus Latinists when their young contemporaries in the northern countries were still "barbarians"; at the other, also in Italy, there developed in the 1930s what can only be called a "pan-Latinist" movement, while ten years earlier the Bolsheviks had abruptly abolished Latin from Russian education. There is however a broad period of some five centuries which appears to have an unarguable unity under the sign of Latin, covering the greater part of the Western world, the territory we are examining. This is an immense area, from Russia to the United States of America. A supranational perspective of this sort is inevitable, given that we are considering a language that postulated universality, while anything to do with the Catholic (literally, Universal) Church must necessarily cross state frontiers. However, this did not mean that I have always said something about every country under each heading – I have already rejected the encyclopaedic approach as inadequate – but rather the equally difficult task of choosing material and situations that would form a coherent whole, while being representative of the problems that arose and the solutions supplied to them.[9] This "aerial view", covering a wide space over a long period, was needed so that the focus would not be drawn into local situations and specific events, but would grasp significant overall tendencies and, through them, the continuity of practices and discourses that give Latin a fundamental place in modern Western civilization.[10]

During the four years I have spent working on this book, I have been helped in many ways, and I would like to thank all those who have made my work easier: the institutions that have opened their doors to me, the Herzog August Bibliothek at Wolfenbüttel, the Mission Historique Française en Allemagne, and the Wissenschaftskolleg in Berlin; and the colleagues and friends who have found or procured documents for me. I am greatly indebted to those who have taken the trouble to discuss this work and pass their observations on to me: in particular I would like to thank Olivier Christian, Etienne François, Daniela Gallo, Elena Fasano Guarini, Anthony Grafton, Bruno Neveu, Gilles Pécout, Philippe Sénéchal, Orest and Patricia Ranum, Mario Rosa, Daniel Roche, Jürgen Schlumbohm, Raymond-Josué Seckel, Bonnie Smith, Alain Supiot, Nancy Struever, Rudolf von Thadden and Natalie Zemon Davis. Special thanks go to Philippe Boutry, who not only helped me with advice but agreed to publish this book in the collection of which he is director. Lastly, the book owes a great deal of its polishing and editing to Perry Anderson, its first reader and first critic: I hope he finds it an adequate testimony to my gratitude for his patience, generosity and frankness.

Berlin, July 1998

Part I

"The European Sign"

CHAPTER I

"Latin Country": School

Any inventory of the traces of Latin in Western civilization has to start with school. Until the 1960s the world of education was closely associated with Latin, when not actually confounded with it. The "Latin quarter" of Paris, for example, is that part of the left bank of the Seine where educational establishments were clustered for centuries.

For obvious reasons of convenience, this long history has been considered on the basis of the French example. Over the half-millennium we are covering, three phases are clearly apparent: the Latin monopoly associated with the Ancien Régime, the royal grandeur it enjoyed in the nineteenth century, and finally an increasingly piebald period with the status of Latin shifting from the norm to an option. Studies of the history of education in different countries – from Russia to the US – confirm the validity of this chronological picture across a wide area.

Broadening the outlook in this way has revealed that, behind the common historical timetable, there existed a number of practices which were employed everywhere. This observation again underscores the deep-seated unity of the Western educational world under the sign of a Latin language forcefully – and uniformly – present.

1 France

The monopoly

"What is learned in the sixth grade? Latin. In the fifth? Latin. The fourth? Latin. The third? Latin. The second? Latin . . ." This terse observation appears in the *Plan d'éducation* published by Abbé Coyer in 1770.[1] Despite its polemical charge, however, it is an incomplete description of the educational reality under the Ancien Régime. For one thing, it was written when the monopoly of Latin had already been attacked and partially breached; for another, it refers only to the situation in college, leaving aside the first apprenticeship that confronted the child: learning to read.

For at that time the young child was taught to read in Latin; only when he had mastered reading in that language did he move on to French. Schooling started with Latin spelling books, with the child learning to recognize the letters and assemble them into syllables; then he worked on reading books, very diverse but always consisting of religious texts in Latin (prayers, psalms, verses and responses from the mass, liturgical offices and so on). While this choice of texts fulfilled the obligation of schools under the Ancien Régime to provide religious instruction, from the teachers' point of view it was dictated by a different sort of imperative that justified the use of books written in a language the child did not understand: acquiring facility in the pronunciation of Latin or, more precisely, matching the pronunciation to the spelling. Claude Fleury, writing in 1686, explained it thus: "We teach reading in Latin to start with, because we pronounce it more as it is written than we do with French". In the same period, however, attempts were made (at the Oratoire in Port-Royal, for example) to set up a system of learning to read using French texts. Jean-Baptiste de La Salle (1651–1719) argued for this system by pointing out that the children who attended his "Christian schools" would not have lengthy schooling, being from modest backgrounds and needing to earn their living from an early age. The trials failed in some cases – the small schools in Port-Royal for instance – and the case for this reform met widespread resistance, so much so that the traditional practice survived into the beginning of the eighteenth century. After that priority shifted to the vernacular, first as a Parisian phenomenon and then in other towns; in rural schools, the presence of Latin in basic literacy teaching persisted until the very end of the Ancien Régime, as can be seen from the account assembled by Abbé Grégoire's correspondents in 1791.[2]

When he went to a college the child entered a deeply Latin world, as he could see from the word *Collegium* over the establishment's entrance and classroom doors labelled *sexta, quinta, quarta* (sixth, fifth, fourth), etc.[3] In fact, Latin reigned there as exclusive master of the terrain. It was the spoken language, the one in which the teacher delivered his lessons, commented on the texts, gave explanations; the one the child spoke, in class but also in recreation time: there were "spies" whose function was to report any infraction of the rule.[4] Unsurprisingly it was also the language of punishment: in the early eighteenth century a pupil guilty of some fault would be invited with the phrase "*Porrige manum*" to extend the back of his hand for the ferule. Latin was, of course, the language in which teachers corrected the pupils' work. For example, at the Louis-le-Grand college in the 1720s, the word *palmas* was used to praise the best Latin version and the phrase *non potest legi* ("unreadable") was scrawled across the tissue of absurdities comprising the worst.[5] And it was used for comments on the pupils by the teachers, for example at the Oratoire de Troyes college where, in the mid-eighteenth century, the fathers sometimes played on their charges' names: a boy called Daniel Vilain was briskly described with the phrase *Non solum nomine, sed re* ("Not just by name, but in fact"); of the young dullard l'Étang (*étang*: shallow stagnant pool) it was written that *Instar stagni revera dormit* ("Just like a puddle, he really sleeps"); and an idle fellow called Lachasse (*la chasse*: hunting) was dismissed with *Dum lepores venatur, scientia evanescit* ("When he chases hares, knowledge vanishes").[6]

These usages resulted from the educational status Latin had at that time. It was the main subject – Greek faded away early, from the second half of the seventeenth century, and French was not taught – and the sole mode of access to other subjects like history, geography, rhetoric or philosophy.[7] Over the ten years it took to complete a full curriculum, the collegian consumed a terrifying quantity of Latin. He had been prepared for it – rather more in the eighteenth century than the seventeenth – by some basic teaching at a school or from a private tutor; he thus already had some rudiments, the declensions, the conjugations and rules of grammar, and could be set to work on numerous graduated oral and written exercises: these included explanations of texts, called *prélections* by the Jesuits, daily recitations of text learned by heart, debates between pupils or *concertations*, speeches in public, theatrical performances, compositions in prose and verse, and translations into French. Naturally the text and reference books were in Latin, whether grammars or works (like the *Gradus ad Parnassum* for verse and the *antibarbari* lexicons for prose) designed to help the child with composition.

This picture holds good, with minimal adjustments, until the 1750s (and, in colleges run by the Jesuits, until their expulsion in 1764). It is also the case, however, that at Port-Royal they had taught in French, composed a grammar in French, reduced the amount of spoken Latin, given French composition priority over "themes" (Latin composition) and reduced the emphasis on Latin verse. The "small schools" experiment was short-lived; but the ideas of the Port-Royal masters reappeared during the next century, first in that monument of French pedagogy, Charles Rollin's *Traité des études* (1726–28), and later in plans for educational reform and in various attempts at "modernized" teaching.

Back in the seventeenth century, the Latin monopoly had been challenged by the planned royal college at Richelieu (1640)[8] and, much more concretely, in the teaching practices of the Oratoire; from 1640, Fr Condren supplied the pupils at Juilly with a Latin grammar in French; the vernacular was used for teaching and it was not compulsory to speak Latin in class until after the third year of Grammar (equivalent to the fourth grade today).[9] The rhetoric course, which in the mid-seventeenth century had been taught in Latin, a century later took place in French, with most of the examples in French and ancient texts quoted in translation. Latin – and Greek too – nevertheless retained an honoured place at Juilly, and was used there until the end of the Ancien Régime for ceremonies such as prizegiving. Within the Oratory congregation, however, the situation varied between establishments. At Effiat, founded in 1724 and made into a royal military college in 1776, Latin was retained, but was supposed to "limit itself to giving them [the pupils]an understanding of all the texts by classical authors", for it was felt to be "pointless to push it too far".[10] There was a similar attitude at Sorèze, which became another royal military college in 1771.[11]

The Protestant colleges that existed in France at the beginning of the seventeenth century provided an education that, from our point of view, hardly differed from the one supplied by Jesuit establishments. Latin took up the majority of school time; pagan "classical" authors formed the bulk of the curriculum; the same textbooks were used. There were also differences, however: the children learned to read in French (to facilitate their religious instruction); in the academies, which combined all three stages of education and whose main purpose was the training of ministers, the choice of ancient authors was wider than in Jesuit colleges and the two other biblical languages, Greek and Hebrew, were taught in addition to Latin. Nevertheless the resemblances are more striking than the differences: the same humanist approach predominated in both systems, and the differences became even less marked over the century as the study of Greek and Hebrew declined in the Protestant academies.[12]

Over and above the practices specific to individual establishments, the eighteenth century saw a general decline in the use of spoken Latin. "Among us, in our better colleges, both the secular ones and the proper ones," Abbé Pluche commented in 1753, "it has at last been recognized how inconvenient it is to be perpetually speaking a language people do not know and the custom has been dropped".[13] Rhetoric and mathematics courses were given increasingly in French, especially in the second half of the century. In the seventeenth century, properly constituted colleges had aimed to turn out a pupil who could speak, write and read Latin; but this ambition was scaled down over time, until all that was required was comprehension of written texts. The exercises set reflected this evolution, with "versions", French translations from Latin, tending to take the leading place from "themes", Latin prose compositions. Textbooks went the same way: grammars and other manuals made increasing use of French, and at the same time word and phrase compilations gradually fell out of use, while *Selecta* – specially written pieces designed for translation by collegians – appeared in increasing numbers.

In the second half of the eighteenth century, then, the monopoly of Latin in the schools was being eaten away by the use of French for teaching, with its status tending to shrink to the scale of the written language alone. The development was not linear, however, and did not always go uncontested. So while the compulsory use of spoken Latin caused a pupils' revolt at the

Oratory college of Saint-Omer in 1754, another Oratory establishment at Avesnes was still using it in 1763, even for games. Sometimes half-measures were tried: at the Cambrai Oratory, the decision was taken in 1765 to speak French in the morning and Latin in the afternoon; an analogous solution was found at the Amiens college in 1776, when the philosophy professor, who wanted to teach in French, was permitted to use the vernacular for experimental physics, but had to continue in Latin for philosophy itself.[14] The fate of Latin could have been sealed with the closure of the colleges and the expulsion of the Jesuits; for there followed what amounted to a rash of educational theories, many of which, like one of the best known – La Chalotais' 1763 *Essai d'éducation nationale* (National Education Experiment) – attempted to "give the lead to the mother tongue". Nothing concrete emerged from these efforts; indeed, the competitive examinations through which schoolmasters were recruited were still based entirely on Latin tests in 1766.[15] In the end, even the pedagogic establishment's severest critics did not wish to do away with Latin, but merely to reduce its role, as emerges for example from D'Alembert's comments in the "college" article in the *Encyclopédie*:

> I am very far from disapproving the study of a language in which men like Horace and Tacitus wrote: such study is absolutely necessary in order to know their admirable works, but I believe we should limit ourselves to understanding them, and that time spent composing in Latin is time wasted. This time would be better spent in learning the principles of our own language.[16]

Conservatism, moderation, half-measures: might they not be expressions of a prejudice acquired at school, during long years spent under the tutors' lash? "All of us," wrote Frain de Tremblay in 1703,

> spent our childhood having nothing but the great merit of the languages taught at college pounded into our ears . . . So that invariably the whole of our early youth is spent in admiration of these languages, with nothing ever being said in favour of our own. They might have been content just to say nothing about it; but they praised other languages daily to its detriment, giving us an infinitely lower view of it than of them.[17]

These debates and reforms hardly touched the universities: to the end of the Ancien Régime it remained profoundly Latin, both for lectures and examinations. An attempt to teach in the vernacular at the Collège Royale failed, and in 1684 it was forbidden to "state or explain in French"; the ban lasted throughout the eighteenth century, and the curriculum was printed in Latin until 1791. Only special courses, like the ones given by the Comte du Buffon in the Jardin du Roi or those given at the end of the Ancien Régime by the School of Docimastic Mineralogy (mineralogy and assaying), the School of Mining or the School of Engineering at Mézières, were in French.[18]

On the eve of the Revolution, Latin still retained a solid presence in the schools, even if it no longer enjoyed a monopoly. It was still – by a long way – the main subject. French had worked its way into schooling, but neither its grammar nor its literature was yet being taught. The collegian still spent the best part of his time "doing Latin".

Royalty

The Revolution saw a backlash that reiterated and amplified the reformers' proposals and added to the vehemence of complaints from those most directly involved; they had argued for teaching in French, sometimes openly as at Château-Thierry, sometimes more timidly as at Essonnes, where it was proposed to cut the working day in two, with French used in the morning and the afternoon reserved for dead languages.[19] The succession of plans for organized public education presented before the assemblies, and the schemes thought up by "adventurous" pedagogues, were unanimous in calling for the suppression of what remained of the practice of teaching in Latin. But although everyone agreed on the need to "loosen the yoke of Latinism", there were differences of opinion on the relative roles of French and Latin in the new teaching. Although there was close and widespread interest in the education issue, a law covering public education as a whole was not voted until the closing days of the Convention. The organic law of 3rd Brumaire, year 4 (25 October 1795) confirmed the creation of the central schools that had been instituted by decree on 7th Ventôse, year 3 (25 February 1795). They were establishments of encyclopaedic ambition, in which the humanities took second place to the sciences and Latin had become just one subject among others, limited moreover to the first section alone.[20]

The Consulate, in the law of 11th Floréal, year 10 (1 May 1802), abolished the central schools, reconstituted the secondary schools and created thirty *lycées* as a third stage of schooling. Here Latin regained much of its lost ground: article 1 of the Decree dated 19th Frimaire, year 11 (10 December 1802) stipulated that the *lycées* would teach "essentially . . . Latin and mathematics". The creation of the Imperial University (1806–08) aggravated the "Latinist" revival of year 10: regulations and curricula gave Latin an increasingly important place in the *lycées*, leading Jean-Louis Burnouf to announce at the prizegiving after the general examinations of 1812, "So the tongue of the Romans is being reborn".[21]

School reverted to being the "Latin country" of the years before 1789. Jules Simon described the college of Vannes, where he had been a pupil from 1828 to 1831, as a "college of the Ancien Régime", and his account of the content of the teaching there recalled the words of Abbé Coyer: "What did they teach us? Latin and still more Latin. In the fifth grade we went from the *Epitome* to *Cornelius Nepos*; in the fourth, from the *Metamorphoses* to the *Bucolics*, and so on.

In the second grade, we started to discover the French language . . . but we always came back to Latin as the main – almost the only – subject."[22] A schoolchild's entire life was spent under the sign of Latin. The Comte de Larmandie recalled in his autobiography "this language Latin, that sank all its claws into me on my arrival at the Gymnasium",[23] and Victor Hugo described the end of his school career in these words:

> When I left college, and themes
> and Latin verses . . .[24]

The Revolution had been a parenthesis: no sooner open than closed again. The only change from the Ancien Régime was that all instruction was now given in French. Small children would henceforth learn to read using texts in the vernacular: although Ferdinand Brunot has produced examples of the use of Latin dating from the 1860s, it seems to have become rare except, apparently, in Catholic establishments for girls.[25] Within the new system, however, some individual masters retained the old habit of using Latin in class, including the one who caused such suffering to the young Léonce de Larmandie:

> [he] affected to use nothing but this language on orders from Above. Even our Christian names were Latinized: I was addressed as Leontius, my rival as Petrus. And as a whole choir we were known under the gracious epithet ingenui adolescentes. What torture to the ear and to the spirit is the interminable audition of this obscure idiom.[26]

In fact Latin even recovered an official place in education for a while: from 1821 to 1830 it was brought back into use for philosophy classes.[27]

Educational historians agree on the major place occupied by Latin in secondary education until as late as the 1880s.[28] This "uncontested royalty", as Françoise Mayeur calls it, can be seen in the timetables: in the year 1880, "sixth-graders" did ten hours of Latin, out of a total of twenty-four hours a week spent in class; and the whole school irrespective of age spent on average a third of its class time on ancient languages. This proportion rose to 40 per cent with the reforms of 1884 and 1890.[29] The *baccalauréat*, set up in 1808, confirmed the dominance of Latin in French nineteenth-century secondary education; the subject was compulsory for all candidates until 1882, when the *baccalauréat de l'enseignement spécial* was instituted. After that, it was possible to take the *baccalauréat* without Latin; but not until 1902 did the "modern" *baccalauréat* secure official equality with the "classical" one.[30] So it is hardly astonishing that after its reorganization in 1808, for the rest of the century the École Normale Supérieur, that "extension and crown of the French educational system", gave the leading role to the classical humanities: in 1850 they constituted more than half the content of the competitive entrance examination (four papers out of seven), Latin getting the lion's share with an unseen translation into French ("version"), a Latin verse composition and a speech. This profile survived until 1885 when Latin verse was dropped, the speech in Latin persisting until 1904 when it was replaced by a "theme". Until 1896, lastly, science candidates were set the same translation paper as those in humanities.[31] In higher learning, the universities retained Latin for the subsidiary thesis until 1903; the Faculty of Catholic Theology taught exclusively in Latin, at least in those subjects deemed most important, and until its abolition in 1885 required doctoral theses to be supported in Latin.[32]

It is clear from all this that, just as under the Ancien Régime, pupils spent long years slogging through endless Latin exercises, versions and themes, compositions in verse and prose. There was in consequence a most abundant output of textbooks of all sorts: primers, grammars, dictionaries, lexicons, books of exercises and selected fragments; Latin schoolbook publishing was an extremely dynamic sector throughout the century, with the number of new publications averaging more than 200 in each decade.[33] The caricaturist Grandville's representation of a young collegian as a Strasbourg goose being force-fed with Latin versions through a funnel is hardly an exaggeration.[34] And of course to the Latin in the curriculum must be added the Latin administered as punishment. Flaubert, who made Charles Bovary conjugate "the verb *ridiculus sum* twenty times", had himself in adolescence "copied out a hundred times . . . as an imposition" some cantos of the *Aeneid*; his friend Maxime Du Camp had never forgotten the day when, "banged up like a malefactor" in a dungeon at Louis-le-Grand, under threat of returning there the next day, he had had to copy "1,500 or 1,800 lines of Latin verse"; Victor Hugo, in his prosecution of college and its "pedlars of Latin", does not forget the punishments that rained down on young rhetoricians:

> Sunday in detention and five hundred lines of Horace!
> . . .
> Twenty times the ode to Plancus and the epistle to the Pisones.[35]

This predominance of Latin was strengthened if anything by the fifteen educational reforms that punctuated the nineteenth century. Every attempt by innovators to secure a wider role for the sciences in particular, but also for living languages, not only aroused impassioned opposition but elicited very concrete responses from the traditionalists who, on their return to influence, campaigned to restore the classical humanities to their former primacy and sometimes (as in 1884 and 1890) to even more privileged status. Scientific humanism remained in a position of inferiority throughout the century, and the failure of the bifurcation attempted in 1852 – the creation of parallel streams for humanities and science from the third grade to rhetoric – had grave consequences. Throughout the life of this reform, which lasted until 1863, those pupils who had branched off into the sciences were despised by their contemporaries. "As a humanities pupil," wrote Anatole France, "I espoused the prejudice of my class and took pleasure in jeering at the lumpish and inelegant minds of the scientists."[36] The "sacralization" of Latin was only intensified by the appearance of a secondary education that did not include Latin. This began in earnest between 1863 and 1865, with the establishment of the "special secondary education" designed by Victor Duruy, in answer to the growing demand for literate labour in agriculture, commerce and industry. It was less the competitor of its prestigious model than a sort of makeweight, whose implicit devaluation could only accentuate the *de facto* supremacy of the classics.[37]

Being regarded, moreover, as the "basis of education" in the *lycées*, Latin exercised a profound influence even over teaching of the vernacular. The intention was not to turn out Latin rhetoricians and poets but to achieve something very different: to produce, by imitation of Latin, facility with a written, literary French that Michel Bréal called "a sort of Latin". Hence the exercises aimed at saturation with Latin, like the classical mode of recitation revived by Villemain in 1839; hence the study of the great texts of French literature in tandem with the masterpieces of Antiquity; hence, too, the narrations leading pupils to echo not just turns of phrase but whole texts from classical Latinity, by writing compositions in French on "classical" subjects well known to the pupils. Thus, the French taught in the *lycées* did not appear to be "a language apart, but like a derivative of Latin" and the strength of the model remained so great that "to write in the strong sense, the intransitive sense, [was] to write Latin in French".[38]

From compulsory to optional

Latin had nevertheless been declining throughout the nineteenth century, faster in the second half. Latin verse was dropped in 1872 by the Minister of Public Instruction, Jules Simon, and the attempt by his successor Batbie to restore it bumped along inconclusively; in 1880 Latin composition and the Latin speech were dropped from the *baccalauréat* and the *concours général* (examination for teacher recruitment), then, in 1902, from the *lycée* curriculum; Latin composition had already declined and the exercises set for pupils were virtually becoming restricted to translations for Latin.[39] The reform of 1902 brought the uncontested reign of Latin in secondary education officially to an end: in the two successive cycles then inaugurated there were two sections without Latin, B (from the sixth to the third grade) and D (second and first); they were descended, as it were, from the heritage of "special education", but were now fully integrated into the secondary system and theoretically equal to the other streams. The phrase used was "unity in diversity".

Things were rather different in reality. Even the designation by letter of the different sections seemed to confirm the hierarchy based on the classical humanities: thus, the first cycle was split into A (with Latin) and B (without Latin), the second into A (Latin–Greek), B (Latin–Languages), C (Latin–Science) and D (Science–Languages). Its lowly positions on the chart did not augur well for the "modern side" which was regarded, in effect, as second-rate, both because of its pupil intake and because in most respects it functioned like a "copy" of the classical side.

This "congenital inferiority" was to endure. The many reforms of French education during the Third and Fourth Republics – no fewer than fourteen in the latter period – proved powerless to impose equality for the modern sector, and this failure boosted the prestige of the Latin sections. The reorganization of 1902 was even partially overturned by the Bérard reform of 1923, suppressing the modern section in the first cycle and making Latin compulsory for all in the first three years of *lycée*. The measure was short-lived and the modern section was re-established with the decree of 9 August 1924; a new reform, the decree of 13 May 1925, went even further by reducing the second cycle from four sections to three: A (Latin–Greek), B (Latin–Science) and C (Science–Languages), dropping one of the Latin sections (the old B, Latin–Languages, whose popularity and performance had been mediocre) and by the same token increasing the proportion of science (which was also given more teaching time in its own sections). All the same, the equal standing for science that was being pursued in these reforms very soon met with new difficulties, most notably the overloading of curriculums and consequent overworking of pupils, but also the growth of the school population with the commencement of completely free secondary education between 1928 and 1933. As a result, in 1941, Carcopino returned to a system broadly similar to the one launched in 1902. Not only had the attempt to unify secondary education on a scientific basis failed: there had been no success even in unifying the teaching of French. In 1925 the so-called "amalgam", which was supposed to bring pupils from the different sections together for common French lessons, had been established. One of the aims of this measure was to promote the modern sector by creating an autonomous discipline of French. "The failure of the amalgam," Antoine Prost writes, "confirmed the historical inferiority of the modern section" and, by implication, the superiority of classics. The way in which the only really modern education that then existed – education for girls – evolved can be seen as another tribute to classical superiority. In 1924, when it achieved equal status with education for boys, it was drafted on the classical model, with the result that (as we shall see) gaining access to Latin could then be presented as a feminist victory.

Even after 1945, Latin continued to play a central role in the debate on the organization of schooling, especially when the growth of the student population and the social inequality of sixth-grade entrants led to proposals that the transition from primary to secondary school should include one or two years of "observation", after which the children would be guided to make the best of their capacities. This idea of a "common trunk", launched by Jean Zay in 1937 and taken up again after the Second World War, most notably in the celebrated Langevin–Wallon plan, had no concrete result. It "came up against Latin". A common trunk was meaningless unless it was going to be truly common, and that meant delaying the start of Latin for one or two years. Bitter wrangling over this point lasted until the Fifth Republic (whose voluntarism in educational matters and unparalleled freedom of action have been widely emphasized), when the decree of 6 January 1959 established a common trunk, but one that lasted only three months: differentiation between classical and modern pupils was simply put off until the beginning of the second term in sixth grade.[40] Latin was still standing its ground, and Jean Guéhenno remembers it in those days as the "central column" of education, the "pillar" around which even the way the *lycées* used their time was arranged.[41]

Adverse signs were becoming apparent, however. In 1956–57 around half the children entering the sixth grade chose the modern section, and the numbers doing classics thinned out steadily all the way through school: while in the sixth grade the classicists very slightly outnumbered the modernists, by the first grade they were only half as many, and only 30 per cent of those who started out as little Latinists in the sixth grade sat the classical *baccalauréat*. This striking rate of attrition revealed a real decline in classical studies. Moreover, although the curriculum remained ambitious, the timetable had already been reduced quite substantially: the average was less than 125 hours a year, or a total of some 750 hours for a complete schooling (the weekly hour and a half of Latin and Greek was optional in the final year), compared with 1,400 hours before the 1902 reform and 1,260 after it. This state of affairs was sanctioned up to a point in 1959 with the establishment of an *agrégation des lettres modernes*[42] in which Greek was replaced with a modern language and Latin, while still compulsory, reduced to subsidiary status.[43] Cries of alarm arose from teachers and professors of ancient languages: words like "crisis" and "decline", but also impassioned advocacy of the "case" for classics, were often seen in the educational reviews and other media. The deep anxiety felt in classical circles can be seen from the title of a 1954 article by Eugène de Saint-Denis, professor of the Faculty of Arts at Dijon: "Are we about to see the death of Latin studies?"[44]

In view of what happened later this question looks prophetic. Following the events of May 1968 the Minister of National Education, Edgar Faure, established for the sixth grade a genuine "common trunk", without Latin and based on the famous "three languages": the mother tongue, modern mathematics and a living language. To speed the decision, he settled the question with a simple edict, dated 9 October 1968, setting the timetable and curriculum for the sixth grade. Latin did not appear in them.[45] So it was not with a bang, so to speak, but a whimper, that Latin lost its prestigious status and central role in education. What seemed worse, in a way, was that "this terrible blow" was delivered by a member of a conservative government who paradoxically justified the measure by reference to the "egalitarian spirit" of '68, declaring that compulsory classical studies were now acting as a "brake to democratization".[46]

This measure ending a secular tradition aroused violent protests. Professional associations and learned societies – including the Société des Etudes Latines, the Association des Etudes Grecques, the Association Guillaume-Budé, the Association des Professeurs de Langues Anciennes de l'Enseignement Supérieur, the Société des Professeurs de Français et de Langues Anciennes, and others – made their voices heard, published open letters in papers and journals, signed petitions, held press conferences, lobbied the authorities. A specific umbrella association appeared, explicitly named the Association for the Defence of Latin. The cause was supported by the Académie des Inscriptions et Belles-Lettres as well as many well-known personalities. Parliamentarians argued the case in the National Assembly (28 and 29 October 1968) and the Senate (29 November 1968), but in vain: the minister not only confirmed the measure of 9 October but announced his intention to put Latin off for another year, until the fourth grade. In that year, he went on, a new basic subject, technology, would be added to the "three languages" for everyone; but alongside these compulsory disciplines there would be complementary options, one choice being between Latin and another modern language. Somewhat grudgingly, the minister conceded that during fifth grade children might be given "some basic grounding in elements of the humanities" or, in other words, "a certain acquaintance with Latin". The edict putting Latin off until the fourth grade was signed on 9 July the following year. Later, in a debate on education in the National Assembly (14 and 15 April 1970), Edgar Faure, now a mere deputy again, defended his reforms vigorously and even caused a slight flutter by adding darkly: "Perhaps it would be no bad thing to delay the teaching of ancient languages until the second grade".

Years of deepening gloom were ahead. Pupil numbers plummeted: by 1975, candidates in Latin for the *baccalauréat* were a third of the number they had been in 1968.[47] Moreover, although curriculums were still heavy, timetables had melted away – by two thirds in the fourth and third grades – and the classes were often very badly placed in comparison with other subjects.[48] In 1992 the secretary of the Association Guillaume-Budé made a report on secondary education that could hardly have been more pessimistic. "The situation of classical studies, in reality," he noted, "is no longer just worrying, as people have been saying delicately for years; it is, in many respects, dramatic." As for the "theoretically large number of pupils who, in the fourth and third grades, do Latin and Greek", it was nothing but a decoy: nearly all of them dropped these subjects in the second grade, having little reason to continue with them in view of their trivial importance in the *baccalauréat*.[49] The consequences of this alienation were being felt in higher education, now granting no more than about 450 degrees in classics each year.[50] The accelerating decline can also be seen in Latin academic publishing: while between 1900 and 1987 an average of 114 new titles appeared in each decade, the whole period from 1970 to 1987 produced 130, with only 34 of those appearing after 1980.[51] Decline and lack of interest accentuated one another. In 1994 there appeared from Editions Nathan a *Dictionnaire encyclopédique de l'éducation et de la formation*, in which one could search in vain for any entry under "Latin", "Ancient languages" or "Classical languages". Times had certainly changed since 1960 when the *Encyclopédie pratique de l'éducation en France* devoted a long article to ancient languages, packed with historical information and pedagogic viewpoints. And apart from all that, Latin is no longer an object of study for the body charged with educational research in France, the Institut National de Recherche Pédagogique: none of its current programmes concerns the teaching of ancient languages.[52]

However, with the "new contract for school" put in place by François Bayrou, Latin had its right to exist from the fifth grade onward restored. This measure, tried out on the 1995 entry and generalized in 1996, was received better than expected: instead of the 20 per cent estimated by the Direction des Lycées et Collèges, a third of the pupils chose to do Latin.[53] But any optimism engendered by this Latin comeback should be tempered by awareness of the status given to Latin under the Bayrou reform: an option, pure and simple.

2 Elsewhere in the West

Monopoly, royalty, option: these three states characterizing the academic destiny of Latin in France from the sixteenth century to the present recur, with similar chronologies, throughout the Western world: the empire of Latin was deeply rooted and enduring, successfully resisting antagonistic forces and only collapsing very recently. While this general picture sometimes needs minor adjustment to take account of specific inflections and nuances, these differences in detail do not cast doubt on what amounts to a unitary history.

"Latin school"

The term "Latin school", used in some countries in the modern era to designate what we now call secondary education, is a perfect expression of the weight of Latin in the school world.[54] In the sixteenth century it was omnipresent. In London it reigned over St Paul's School, founded by the humanist Colet in 1509, which became the model for the English grammar schools. Before starting to read texts, pupils were given a solid grounding in

grammar which soon came to be based on Lily's *Grammar*, the textbook that
a decision taken by Henry VIII in 1540 imposed throughout the kingdom as
the "Common" or "Royal Grammar". The child was expected to acquire
mastery of spoken as well as written Latin: conversational training took the
form of dialogues, recitations, grammatical debates, frequent exercises in
translation and composition in both prose and verse.[55] A similar pattern was
followed in Venice, where small children – six or seven years old – started
their apprenticeship with grammar, usually working not from a humanist
textbook but a manual dating from the Middle Ages, still printed in Gothic
characters. Initially they "Latinized according to the rules", then went on to
compose short sequences. At the next stage they moved on to exercises in
written Latin, for example translating letters from Italian into Latin. Reading
of texts had begun with the collection of moral examples in Cato's *Disticha*;
and at around twelve years of age, when the boy was about to enter humanist school, he was able to read Cicero, Virgil, Terence and Horace.[56] At Liège,
under the Frères de la Vie Commune, the emphasis was on the spoken language, and children could make themselves understood in Latin from about
the age of seven. This was because they had learned it as a living language,
largely through the use of collections of "colloquies" written specifically for
their use: these textbooks, in effect, were scripts that took the children
through discussion of problems appropriate to their age in simple, correct
Latin, but sprinkled with more sophisticated quotations from classical
authors. The emphasis on spoken Latin, even in games, did not exclude a
solid grounding in the written language, here too in prose as well as verse.[57]
In Brunswick, school had been defined in the decree of 1569 as a "truly Latin
school". The children were immersed in Latin from the start: the letter-book
on which they learned to read was in Latin and the first text they deciphered
was the *Paternoster*. After that, alongside the learning of grammar which occupied about a quarter of the timetable, the pupils (who after third grade were
no longer permitted to speak "barbarian") worked on the rapid acquisition of
a wide vocabulary. Latin in effect was the vehicular language of the school
world, the language the masters spoke to the pupils. It was also its distinguishing sign: a ruling of 1562 had ordered pupils to use "Latin in all places,
that their discourse may distinguish them from the ignorant populace and
bear witness that they are scholars". Application exercises, written and oral
(in the form of dialogues), punctuated the working day, and Latin in its different forms represented between 67 and 77 per cent of school activity.[58]

These few examples depicting a uniformly Latin world are nevertheless
taken from countries with different religions. The Reformation had not given
the vernacular the same boost in its schools as in its temples: quite the contrary in fact. In German-speaking countries, reformers who at first had
attacked church and school indiscriminately adopted a more constructive
position with the arrival of Luther and, more particularly, Melanchthon: the

latter, nicknamed the "preceptor of Germany", led the reform of the schools
and universities, trained a large proportion of the teachers for the new school
system and produced textbooks, most notably a Latin grammar – in Latin of
course – which was immensely successful in the Lutheran countries. The
result for the German academic world was a deeply rooted unity characterized by the close link between religion and humanist culture. Returning to
the Brunswick example, ancient languages were given priority so that Christians, ministers in particular, would have direct access to Biblical texts;
however, Greek and Hebrew had a much smaller role than Latin. As with all
humanist schooling, classical authors who had been dropped during the
mediaeval period returned in force, with Cicero, Terence and Virgil in the
front rank. German played no part in the syllabus and its use was even forbidden to scholars who knew Latin; at most, the master might correct the
German in his pupils' translations from Latin and give them a few letters to
write in that language. The reformed schools gave an important place to religious instruction, and Luther's catechism was written in Latin as well as
German. With the exception of religion (and that only in matters of detail),
schooling in Brunswick and, it seems, throughout Lutheran Germany, was
very similar to its equivalent in Catholic countries. The situation hardly
altered in the seventeenth century. Under the great decree of Duke August
the Younger (1651), the school curriculum gave priority to religion, which was
now supposed to be taught in the vernacular: the reasoning behind this combined a desire for efficiency – "fear of God is inculcated in the children more
firmly by explaining the catechism in German" – with a purist argument: the
classical Latin that the schools were trying to instil into the pupils might be
contaminated by the more bastardized versions found in religious works.
Masters nevertheless continued to explain the catechism in Latin. And in any
case the more advanced classes, whose pupils were approaching theology
through study of Hutter's *Compendium*, used Latin. It retained the leading
place in real schooling, and took up the bulk of the timetable; it continued to
be the language of communication between masters and pupils, except in the
youngest classes; but the many complaints of Inspector Schrader suggest that
the use of spoken Latin might have declined in the second half of the seventeenth century. During this period, it is true, the vernacular made a timid
appearance: German schools taught in German and even taught German as
a subject; but it is also true that the same schools always had a handful of
pupils who could stumble through the Latin primer.[59] Still in the Lutheran
world, the Gymnase Sturm (1538) at Strasbourg used a curriculum based on
classical languages, starting with the usual solid grammatical grounding
in Latin; by the eve of the French Revolution German was used in teaching,
but Latin was still the official language of the establishment and of most of
the books given to the pupils.[60]

Similar situations prevailed in the Calvinist countries. In Lausanne, the college that prepared students for the Academy, and thus for the ministry, taught in Latin in compliance with a ruling of 1547. In the youngest class, the seventh grade which accepted children of six or seven, the basic disciplines – spelling, reading and writing – were taught in Latin, the only use of French being to provide translations of the basic vocabulary. The elements of religion and morals were imparted in the vernacular; nevertheless, after the fourth grade, the catechism was explained in Latin. The ruling of 1640, a century on, expressed the continued dominance of Latin: the college was to train pupils to be able not only to read and write Latin, but speak it as well; to this end the students' association, the General Senate, was expected to "encourage the use of Latin to be practised". The only exception was exercises in preaching, which were in French; but the textbooks used in preparing the sermons were still in Latin.[61] In the United Provinces of the Netherlands the classical languages, far from being banished, had official standing, given that the schools were called "Latin". These establishments were regulated by an ordinance of the Province of Holland in 1625, a ruling that remained in force until 1815. Latin, written as well as spoken, had the leading role every year, for example, during ceremonies that accompanied the examinations, the pupils of the school at Amsterdam made public recitations in one of the town's churches, their speeches hardly differing at all in either style or content from the ones composed in the Catholic world.[62]

Catholic or Protestant, seventeenth-century schoolboys throughout Europe all did Latin. And so of course did their Orthodox contemporaries. In Peter the Great's Russia there appeared schools copied from the Jesuit colleges, like the one in Kiev which offered a classical curriculum; the academy in Moscow was reformed following the same model at the beginning of the eighteenth century, when schools like those at Chernigov in the Ukraine, Rostov and Novgorod were also established. By 1750 there were twenty-six colleges in the Russian empire offering an education based on a Latin curriculum.[63]

Latin was not only the daily bread of collegians in Europe, but in the New World as well: the school system established in the American colonies was modelled on what was done in England. The first transatlantic "secondary school" to be founded, the Boston Latin School, derived its pedagogic approach from the English grammar schools, and ancient languages – Latin to the fore – formed the essence of the education given there.[64]

All these children, who started on Latin very young, sometimes even when learning to read, had to absorb – and churn out – truly stupefying volumes of Latin over the period of their schooling; and the task was every bit as gruelling in the English grammar schools as in the Jesuit colleges of Catholic Europe. Sir Simonds D'Ewes claimed that as a pupil at Bury St Edmunds early in the seventeenth century he had composed more than 2,800 Latin and Greek verses; William Lilly recalled that as a schoolboy in Ashby-de-la-Zouch "he could make Extempore Verses upon any Theme; all kinds of Verses,

Hexameter, Pentameter, Plaleuciacks, Iambicks, Sapphicks &c".[65] A century later, a Turin youth called Vittorio Alfieri competed with a college friend in the recitation of Latin verses; to his great shame he was regularly beaten by his rival, who could recite "up to six hundred lines of Virgil's *Georgics* at a time, without getting a syllable wrong, while I couldn't even do four hundred, and not as well either".[66] Many other performances with numbers of this sort could be quoted, but they would be no more eloquent than the astonished reaction of little John Waldegrave, aged seven, on his arrival at Eton: he judged it a "very odd place . . . full of boys and Latin".[67]

But Latin also had competition and was contested everywhere during the eighteenth century. Loyal to the principle of *Ratio studiorum*, the Jesuit college at Bologna in the years between 1675 and 1680 was still applying the rule that children had to address their masters in Latin: "When answering a Father publicly in school, one always speaks Latin," noted Pietro Antonio Adami in his journal, "and anyone speaking the vulgar gets a bad mark".[68] But with time this obligation was observed less and less. In England, the teaching of Latin as a spoken language declined throughout the eighteenth century, to a point where the textbooks designed for that purpose gradually disappeared from the grammar schools.[69]

As one would expect, the vernaculars worked their way into the classroom. At the Lausanne college, a Latin grammar written in French was introduced at the beginning of the eighteenth century; by 1721 the tutors were being required to explain Latin authors "in good French terms and turns of phrase".[70] At schools in Prussia and Wurtemberg, explanations were given increasingly often in German. But this did not mean that the vulgar tongue was being properly taught; in fact, the literary worth of German was not acknowledged until considerably later than that of French (let alone Italian). In German-speaking countries, as elsewhere, German was learned – discovered, even – via Latin. This experience is described, in a late eighteenth-century setting, as it applies to the eponymous hero of the psychological novel *Anton Reiser*. When in the second grade, the young Reiser was conscious that he spoke

> that language more correctly than German. For in Latin he knew how to make deliberate use of the dative and the accusative. But it had never occurred to him that in German mich, for example, was an accusative and mir a dative, or that it was just as necessary to decline and conjugate in his own language as it was in Latin. In unconscious fashion, however, he was absorbing a number of concepts at this time that he was later able to apply to his mother tongue.[71]

Competition from the vernacular languages was strengthening, however, with their growing claims to be taught as subjects in their own right. In Italy the Italian language was introduced in the 1750s, even in Jesuit colleges, although only as a subsidiary.[72] As in France, the expulsion of the Jesuits gave encouragement to educational reform plans that often included demands for the vernacular to be given priority; thus Gasparo Gozzi, in his plans for the schools of Venice, put Italian first and limited the Latin requirement to comprehension of the written language. Most of these reforms stayed on paper, though, and the only new elements in a pedagogy that retained the essential features of Jesuit schooling were the greater importance given to translations from Latin and the presence of vernacular composition exercises.[73] Even in the American colonies, where classics were enjoying their "golden age", voices were being raised against the pre-eminence of ancient languages. Opposition began in the 1750s and reached a peak in the last quarter of the century, when it was expressed not just in pedagogic works but in newspaper articles. The authors of these writings claimed that to promote "useful learning" Latin should be eliminated from the school curriculum, or at least have its role greatly reduced. They gave priority to teaching the English language and those disciplines – technical or scientific – that they judged essential to a new nation.

> We want hands . . . more than heads [cried one]. The most intimate acquaintance with the classics will not remove our oaks: nor a taste for the Georgics cultivate our lands. Many of our young people are knocking their heads against the Iliad, who should employ their hands in clearing our swamps and draining our marshes. Others are musing, in cogitation profound, on the arrangement of a syllogism, while they ought to be guiding the tail of a plow.

Some sought to reconcile classics with science, like the Rev. William Nixon who, in 1789, proposed that books dealing with scientific subjects should be written in Latin, thus satisfying both traditionalists and modernists at the same time. But the demand for "useful learning" achieved nothing concrete beyond some impassioned pleas and an assortment of projects a good deal more rational than Nixon's; at the end of the eighteenth century the curriculum was unchanged, and the classics still reigned supreme in American schools.[74]

So Latin was surviving well, and the failure of reforms further strengthened its position. In Poland, the Commission on National Education, set up to reform an education system falling into decadence, had ended the monopoly of Latin with its rulings of 1774. These banished the ancient language completely from parish schools – so that small children would henceforth learn to read in Polish – and made it a subsidiary subject in the Palatinate schools, with Latin coming not just after Polish but after natural ethics, law, political economy and science, and no longer learned as a spoken language. The vigorous opposition to this reform included the withdrawal of children from school by some families and, of course, the continuing use of the old methods by some teachers. In 1788 the Commission made a complete about-turn and restored the use of spoken Latin in the schools; in the senior classes the professor of rhetoric was even required to speak nothing else.[75] Piedmont offers another example of the tenacity of Latin and the assistance given to it by the vernacular. While the Revolution had resulted in priority being given to the Italian language, annexation by Napoleon imposed French, at first alongside Italian, later in first place: the children, most of whom spoke local dialect at home, were confronted at primary and secondary school with three foreign languages: French, Italian and Latin. Not very surprisingly, their results were poor. This mediocre performance, the suspicion aroused by the breakage of a secular habit and a certain amount of political opposition came together in the name of Latin: the measures to reduce the share of the ancient language had all been setbacks and had – all of them – to be repealed. So in the early nineteenth century, as in France in the last years of the Ancien Régime, children in the Piedmont countryside were still learning to read using Latin texts.[76]

Latin may have resisted victoriously in the schools, but its position was even stronger in the universities, which remained Latin to the core until at least the 1750s. The oft-cited exception of Thomasius teaching in German at Halle in 1687 proves the rule: the very frequency with which it appears makes it emblematic of the major – and official – place occupied by Latin.[77] This was as true in northern countries as in southern, in Protestant countries as in Catholic ones. In eighteenth-century Spain, royal ordinances invariably insisted on the exclusive use of Latin within the bounds of the universities; and not until 1813 was Castilian declared the language of teaching.[78] Latin also reigned by law in Italian universities: it was the language in which Galileo taught at Padua; it was used a century later (and somewhat despite himself) by another defender of the rights of Italian, the physician Antonio Vallisneri; even as late as the 1760s Father Beccaria, Professor of Physics at Turin, gave his famous course on electricity in Latin.[79] In Sweden, the University of Uppsala stayed loyal to Latin into the 1840s; the first thesis in a language other than Latin had been presented at the University of Turku (Finland) in 1749, but made little impact on a tradition that still had a long life ahead of it.[80]

It was as the language spoken within the universities that Latin gave way first. Neither the rules in place nor repeated calls to order were able to arrest the decline. At Oxford, the obligation for students to speak Latin among themselves and at table was included in the statutes laid down in 1636 by the then Chancellor of the University, Archbishop Laud, statutes that remained in force until 1854; in practice, though, Latin was no longer being spoken "in hall" by the eighteenth century. The same code required degree candidates to demonstrate fluency in Latin, an obligation reiterated in the examination statutes of 1800.[81] The masters therefore expected their pupils to address them in Latin, but the true decline of spoken Latin is suggested by the embarrassing experience suffered by one Robert Foulke at Christ Church in 1725. On demonstrating that he was incapable of stringing two words of Latin together, Foulke received the following rebuke – in Latin, of course – from the Professor of Rhetoric: "*Abi et disce latine loqui, non est meum in hoc loco audire aliquem nisi latine loquentem*" ("Go away and learn to speak Latin. It is not for me in this place to hear anyone who does not speak Latin.").[82]

Attempts to introduce the vulgar tongue into teaching became more frequent as the eighteenth century lengthened. It is interesting to note that the vernacular tended to be adopted for new or "technical" subjects; that sometimes there was hesitation in choosing between Latin and the local idiom; that Latin kept some rights even among adepts of modern languages. In 1754 the philosopher Antonio Genovesi, who had previously taught metaphysics and then ethics in Latin, was given the chair of commerce – the first of its kind in the Italian peninsula – and began lecturing "in good Italian language".[83] At Valence in the second half of the eighteenth century, the faculties of mathematics and physics were excused from observing the royal decree of 1753 (upholding the exclusive use of Latin), as they were held to be practical disciplines for careers in agriculture, industry and commerce.[84] The Lausanne academy hesitated between Latin and French. Jean-Pierre Crousaz, who taught philosophy there in the second quarter of the eighteenth century, gave his lessons in each language alternately; his colleague Barbeyrac gave the course in Roman law in Latin, but used French for natural law and history. In 1788 a new ruling stipulated that lessons in natural law should be in French or Latin, that French was compulsory for physics and history, and that the philosophy professor must teach mathematics in French but stick to Latin for metaphysics and logic.[85] However, teaching in the vernacular did not imply total abandonment of Latin. The philosopher Francis Hutcheson, teaching in Glasgow in 1730, launched the course he was giving in English with an inaugural lecture in Latin; similarly the first holder of the chair in natural history at Pavia, Lazzaro Spallanzani, began his course, delivered in Italian, with a Latin *Prolusio*.[86] From these few examples it emerges that although in the eighteenth century – the second half in particular – Latin as the language of university teaching had to face competition from the vernaculars, it retained a virtual monopoly for formal occasions like inaugural lectures. And this too was an enduring tradition; even in 1863 the historian Ranke delivered his inaugural lecture on history and politics in Latin.[87]

The humanist "revival" of the nineteenth century

The opposition to classics that arose during the eighteenth century seemed to suggest their probable withdrawal from secondary education in the next era.

Not only did this fail to happen, but there was, on the contrary, a substantial humanist revival: the ancient languages were honoured everywhere, and everywhere they were the distinguishing mark of educational establishments for the elite.[88]

They predominated, for example, in the Prussian *Gymnasium*. Although Greek had had the leading role at its foundation in 1810, Latin's share quickly increased until, by 1837, it had become the main discipline: under the syllabus established in that year the pupils did eight to ten hours of Latin a week, representing nearly a third of the whole timetable; Greek accounted for six hours a week for the first four years, only four hours after that. German had to make do with the leftovers: two hours a week for the first four years, four hours in the last two. Given the enduring nature of this situation – 46 per cent of school time was still being devoted to teaching classics in 1890 – it is not difficult to understand Kaiser Wilhelm II's plea to the conference on pedagogy in the same year to stop training young Greeks and Romans. But despite this heavyweight support, the efforts of lobbyists for modern education did not meet with much success: by 1892 the share of Latin in the *Gymnasiums* had declined from seventy-seven hours to sixty-two, and that of German had increased from twenty-one to twenty-six hours; Latin composition remained a compulsory part of the *Abitur*, which was still essential for entry to university. And after 1900, when Prussia, followed by the other states, admitted candidates from the *Oberrealschule* and the *Realgymnasium* – secondary establishments without Latin – to the universities, the *Gymnasium* was able to follow its classical predilections to the full, most notably by increasing the amount of Latin in the timetable.[89]

In united Italy, while Latin seems to have disappeared from basic reading exercises – let us recall nevertheless that small children in Milan were still learning to read in both Italian and Latin as late as 1839 – it continued to be the basis of the *Gymnasium* and the *lycée*, along with the national language and Greek. Nor was this model of a classical culture limited to nostalgic conservative opinion: the first Minister of Instruction Michele Coppino – a man of the left – confirmed the presence in the 1867 syllabus of a Latin verse paper in the final examination of the *quarta ginnasiale*.[90]

In England, where the cult of the classics reached a peak in the nineteenth century, ancient languages came to represent half or even three quarters of the timetable at some public schools. At Eton, admittedly one of the more conservative institutions, 26 masters out of a total of 31 were wholly devoted to teaching them in the 1860s; half the teaching staff were still classicists in 1905. In the lower forms, boys spent their time largely on Latin grammar in the so-called "gerund grind", an expression denoting both the method – wearisome repetition – and the material, Latin grammar named for its main singularity, the gerund. Then they moved on to the principles of Latin verse: the very names of the classes at Eton – Scan and Prove, Nonsense and Sense

– designate successive stages in mastering Latin versification, from the rules of scansion and prosody to the writing of pieces of verse, passing through poetic exercises in which meaning was ignored but the rules of rhyme, metre and scansion observed. This was accompanied by assiduous reading of Latin poets and the learning by rote of hundreds of lines of verse. At the end of the nineteenth century, not only had the teaching of classics hardly changed in the public schools, but the expansion of the public-school system meant that more boys were doing intensive classics in 1900 than in 1800. In addition, there appeared during the century a new category of preparatory schools (to prepare boys specifically for public school) where, under the lash of "grinders", the pupils were given high-pressure grounding in the ancient languages. When Henry Montagu Butler left Eagle House at the age of twelve, for example, he had already finished reading Cicero's *De Amicitia*, a good part of Virgil, a book of Horace's *Odes* and a small amount of Livy, had written a number of prose compositions and had been turning out sixteen hexameters a week (and that was just the Latin). Of course the predominance of classics at Eton, Winchester, Charterhouse and other elite establishments was helped by the late and timid appearance of the sciences, and by the fact that the study of English, regarded as "common", did not enjoy academic favour. The grammar schools pale into insignificance beside these prestigious institutions. An inquiry by the Taunton Commission, in 1864, found that more than half the grammar schools were no longer teaching Latin or Greek; among the 43 per cent that did offer Latin, the teaching was often far from satisfactory and sometimes purely symbolic (in one London school, pupils in the top class fulfilled the terms of the founder's charter by reading the beginning of the Latin grammar aloud for an hour a week, without any explanation or, of course, comprehension). The alarming findings of this commission led to corrective action, ensuring that, in the grammar schools, too, the situation for the classics was better at the end of the century than it had been at the beginning.[91]

Perhaps the most eloquent example of the royalty of Latin is provided by Czarist Russia. In a country where secondary education was just taking its first tottering steps at the beginning of the nineteenth century, Latin carved itself out a surprisingly prominent place considering that it was an imported phenomenon. Russian "classicism" reached its peak under the ministry of Count Tolstoy, who visited Prussia to observe the German education system at first hand. The plan he presented in 1869 was for two levels of secondary school: on one hand, establishments giving practical training to children destined for local functions; on the other, classical *Gymnasiums* channelling more able pupils towards the university and the civil service. With the revision of 1871, classical subjects – in practice mainly Latin – took up 41 per cent of the *Gymnasium* syllabus against 14 per cent for mathematics, 12 per cent for Russian and 10 per cent for modern languages. Although, after the minister's fall from grace in 1882, the Latin timetable was reduced and more time given to Russian, literature and geography, the *Gymnasium* still retained its dominant position over the *Realschule* on the eve of the October Revolution, and Latin was still its main subject.[92]

On the other side of the world, in the United States of America, the situation was more variable: the calls for "useful knowledge" had developed into equally earnest pleas in favour of applied science and professional training from the country's new leaders, many of them self-made men from the frontier or the business world. But classics teaching endured, and Latin still had an enviable place in the secondary schools in 1900, being studied by half the pupils (only algebra was more popular).[93]

So Latin continued to rule the secondary schools and with them, the lives of their pupils. As in the previous century, people inhabited a universe with a strong Latin coloration, and the feelings of the young Strindberg on his first arrival at school cannot be attributed solely to natural pessimism. The gloom that overcame him at the sight of the building deepened still further "when he saw the long line of classrooms marked with Latin names, ending with the *quinta*, through which he would have to pass over a period of years, before having to drag himself through another line of classrooms at the *lycée*".[94]

Humble pie

But that universe was drawing to a close nevertheless, and the 1960s and '70s marked a major caesura. In some cases the collapse was advanced or retarded by political events. Thus, the fall of Latin came earliest and most suddenly in Soviet Russia, where it symbolized the old pedagogic régime and was removed from the syllabus by the first Bolshevik reforms in 1920. In fascist Italy, by contrast, the idealization of Romanness led to a wave of what can only be called pan-Latinism in the schools (which incidentally outlived the Mussolini régime).[95]

The retreat started in the United States. Between 1910 and 1928 the proportion of high-school pupils doing Latin fell from just over 49 per cent to under 22 per cent; in the year 1928–29 Latin was still being studied by slightly more pupils than all the other languages put together; for the next twenty years it was the language studied by the largest number of pupils, being eventually overtaken by Spanish; then in 1961–62 it was first equalled, then overtaken by French as the second most studied language, before collapsing completely over the next few years. The 702,000 American high-school pupils doing Latin in 1962 had fallen to 170,000 by 1984, after a low point of only 150,000 in 1975: the slight increase in 1984 may result from a revival of interest in Latin, or it may reflect an increase in the school population.[96]

In Europe, secondary-school Latin has seen a similar steep decline in numbers since the sixties; and this has been accompanied by a reduction in the amount of time devoted to the subject. In Sweden, the number of hours spent on Latin, by those still doing it, has been reduced by 30 per cent. In Holland the reduction has been more drastic still: after 1968 pupils in the top form at the *Gymnasium* only did five hours of Latin a week, when Greek and Latin had previously occupied more than half their time (18 hours out of 35). In Belgium, the so-called "renovated" education system has reduced the number of Latin lessons by half, or even more in some classes: in the first grade, for example, nine hours of Latin a week have been reduced to two.[97]

In fact, Latin kept its importance in secondary education so long as it remained compulsory for entry to higher education. When this ceased, Latin went into free fall. In the United States, the decision taken by Yale University in 1931 not to require Latin from applicants, soon adopted by other establishments, was followed (as we have seen) by the collapse of classical studies in the high schools and a sharp decline in the number of school Latinists. This decline then affected colleges and universities, so that by 1995 the total number of Latinists was only 25,870; this places Latin seventh on the list of foreign languages studied in US further education, far behind Spanish, German and French, but also trailing Japanese, Italian and Chinese; what is more, the figure for Latin had dropped by 8 per cent in the five years since 1990.[98] Some thirty years after the US – the process dates from the dropping of Latin as a condition for entry to Oxford and Cambridge universities in the sixties and seventies – classics suffered a sharp decline in England and became an option.[99] In Germany, on the other hand, where Latin remained obligatory for entry to many faculties, Latinists have remained more numerous (and more ardent) in secondary education: 35 per cent of the Federal Republic's *Gymnasium* pupils were still doing Latin in 1990, for a minimum of three years and up to nine years for those choosing the full Latin option. Latin moreover was long recommended for entry to scientific faculties, and even today medical students are required to take a semester of Latin and sit a paper in the subject.[100]

3 A Community of Practices

From the Renaissance to the middle years of the twentieth century, from old Europe to the New World, schooling shared a common destiny under the sign of Latin. Everywhere, its predominance was profound and enduring; everywhere, its fortunes followed a similar chronology. This history, which unifies the Western educational landscape, is accompanied by a community of practices: adherence to the same canon and wide circulation of similar models, textbooks and teaching methods.

Behind the pedagogic particularities

An observer's attention may nevertheless be drawn initially to the many apparent differences. How can one fail to notice, on opening a Latin primer, that the paradigm for the first declension is not always and everywhere the famous *rosa*, adopted in France not so very long ago to replace the traditional *musa*? Although Italy and Spain use *rosa* too, in the United States and Canada pupils practise on *puella*, in England and Holland on *mensa*; in Germany, where schoolchildren use *agricola*, the textbook for medical students at Göttingen has *vena* as its model, while the one used at Münster gives *lingua* as its archetype.[101]

Less anecdotal are the divergences stemming from the different teaching systems of different countries, which can be demonstrated by comparing the German *Gymnasium* with the French *lycée* during the 1960s. The dosage of Latin was markedly bigger in Germany, with 20 per cent of the timetable against 14.5 per cent in France. Latin prose compositions had virtually disappeared there in favour of reading, translation and commentary on original texts. In these exercises great attention was paid to recitation, pronunciation, the rhythms of verse: a young German of the time must surely have been disconcerted in a French classroom, where he would have heard a mixture of disparate pronunciations and where ignorance of accentuation and syllabic quantities was virtually total. He would have been even more surprised to see his French contemporaries rootling ceaselessly in a monumental dictionary, since he himself did not always possess even a lexicon. And he would have been no less astonished to see them dissecting twenty lines or so an hour, when he himself, thanks to a larger basic vocabulary and the entirely authorized use of existing translations (or cribs), would have charged through several pages of text in the same time. Lastly, he would have been puzzled by the issues of syntactic construction and vocabulary raised by any piece of Latin, when at home he was used to hearing the teacher expatiate on moral, aesthetic and psychological questions.[112]

The Paris Universal Exposition of 1900 was an opportunity to compare teaching methods in the classics through the tests and exercises, school books and other *realia* from the world of pedagogy that were exhibited there. The comparison suffers from the absence of Germany, especially as countries where classics education was still strong – Switzerland, Austria, Spain, Belgium, Holland – showed nothing in this area and other (Scandinavian) countries showed little, preferring to emphasize their progress in technical and professional training. On the basis of the exhibiting countries – United States, Britain, Canada, Hungary, Italy, Portugal, Russia, Sweden, Norway and of course France – there emerged

two major methods for studying ancient texts: one, grammatical and formal, in force in Britain and Russia; the other, historical and archaeological, prevalent in the United States, Canada, Hungary and Italy. Under the first, Latin and Greek authors are read in order to learn Latin and Greek; under the second, to learn about Greek and Roman history. The method towards which the University of

France is increasingly drawn at the present time, a method that is moral and philosophic but also literary, a method concerned less with forms and facts than with ideas and sentiments, is very little represented anywhere else.

On the matter of exercises, the copies exhibited enabled the originality of Hungary and France to be underlined: in Hungary, the scholars made "analyses in Latin of explained pieces, résumés of Roman history after Livy or Sallust, improvised exercises, midway between themes and compositions proper, which are found nowhere else apart from our own country".[103]

In the middle years of the nineteenth century one of the most famous names in English education, the inspector of schools Matthew Arnold, made a number of visits to the continent to gather information and useful ideas for educational reform in his own country. The reports he presented to the School Inquiry Commission are predictably structured around comparisons with the English system. While some of his assertions are perplexing (for example his attribution of the high level of discipline in the *lycées* to innate French qualities of "military precision" and "exactitude"), his meticulous descriptions of teaching practices do highlight particularities in the different education systems. In the case of France the dominant impression was of similarity, with equal fluency in composition of both prose and verse; Arnold was impressed, however, by the amount of homework French children turned out, owing to the freer use of anthologies and a purely mechanical grounding in grammar. In Prussia, he was intrigued by the use of spoken Latin among teachers and pupils (although he noticed that the practice was in decline): young Prussians possessed enviable vocabulary and fluency, which also enabled them to read very extensively; but their composition, by contrast, lacked the elegant classical style that their French and English contemporaries were taught to reproduce, the finish that the abler pupils from the better public schools could give their Latin verse. He believed nevertheless that "the great superiority of the Germans" was based on greater mastery of *Altertumswissenschaft* and on a historical and philological approach to classical authors in the secondary schools. While the *Gymnasium* in Switzerland was based on the German model, it had a specific feature which could hardly escape the attention of a former Rugby pupil: although a Latin prose composition was set once a fortnight (as a purely grammatical exercise), there was otherwise a total absence of compositions, even in prose.[104]

In practice, the pedagogic particularities of which these examples provide a sketchy typology hardly affected the fundamental sameness of schooling throughout the West. Some are clearly minor, others are hangovers from the past, and the singular features are outweighed, in any case, by the many similarities. The similarity is the consequence of the very early adoption in all countries of the same range of choices and practices; and in more recent times particularities have been diluted by the wide circulation of certain text-books, the copying of techniques and the generalization of methods.

A universal canon

When scanning the syllabuses from all parts of the modern West that are reproduced in educational histories, one is struck by the way in which generations of schoolchildren everywhere have been set to labour over the same authors, the same works. In the syllabuses that have been unearthed covering Holland and the Principality of Liège in the sixteenth century, Cicero (mainly the *Epistolae*) emerges as the leading author, followed in order of importance by Virgil, Ovid, Terence and Horace, and then, a long way behind, Cato's *Disticha*, Aesop's fables in a Latin translation, Caesar and Sallust.[105] In Brunswick during the same period, half the works mentioned in the study plan were of Cicero, Terence and Virgil; again, the main work was Cicero's *Epistolae*. A century later, after the edict of 1651, this trio had become even more dominant, with pupils spending nearly two thirds of their reading time on them alone: 31 per cent on Cicero, 20 per cent on Terence and 13.4 per cent on Virgil.[106] In France during the seventeenth and early eighteenth centuries, the most frequently mentioned text for the first two classes was Cicero's *Ad Familiares*, accompanied by Ovid's *Tristia*, Cato's *Disticha* and, among Protestants, Cordier's *Dialogues* and Erasmus's *Colloquies*. Later, Cicero having been judged too difficult, Phaedrus's *Fables* and the *Histories* of Cornelius Nepos were adopted as the basic texts, with the addition of Eutrope or Aurelius Victor in Jesuit establishments. In the middle levels of school, the pupil invariably read one of Cicero's moral or philosophic treatises, usually *On duty*, *On friendship* or *On old age*; he would also take in extracts from Ovid's *Tristia* or *Metamorphoses*, a chunk of Terence and Virgil's *Eclogues* or *Georgics*. In the eighteenth century some works by classical historians – Justin, Caesar, Sallust, Quintus Curtius – were introduced on these levels. In second grade and Rhetoric, Cicero's oratorical works occupied a good deal of time, and a historian would be studied in detail (Livy was the obvious choice, sometimes followed by Tacitus); in poetry, the pupils always read Virgil, but just the *Aeneid*, and Horace, usually the *Odes*. Other authors are certainly to be found, but very rarely.[107] These were the works used in the 1750s at the college in Limoges, as a glance through the records of one of the town's booksellers reveals: in a shop not inappropriately named "The Ciceronians' Room" were stocked Cicero's *Ad Familiares*, *Selected Letters*, moral treatises and speeches; Ovid's *Tristia* and *Epistolae ex Ponto*; Virgil's *Eclogues* and *Aeneid*; and Horace's *Odes* and *Art of Poetry*.[108] On the other side of the Atlantic, grammar school pupils of the eighteenth century would read at some time in their schooling Cato's *Disticha*, Ovid's *Metamorphoses* and *Tristia*, Cicero's speeches, letters and treatise *On duty*, Florus (or Eutrope or

Justin), Virgil's *Aeneid*, Terence and Horace, authors who (along with one or two others reserved for "college") made up what James Madison – later to become US president – described in 1785 as "the common list of school classics".[109]

Many of these authors still figured in the French secondary-school syllabus at the end of the 1950s: Phaedrus (some of the *Fables*) and Cornelius Nepos in the fifth grade; in the fourth, Caesar (*Gallic Wars*), some moral works by Cicero and Ovid's *Metamorphoses*; in the third grade Sallust (the *Bellum Catilinae* and the *Bellum Jugurthinum*) and Virgil (*Aeneid*, first three books); in the second, Cicero (including notably *On old age* and the *In Catilinam* orations), Livy, Virgil (*Eclogues* and books VI to VIII of the *Aeneid*) and Tacitus (*Agricola*); in the first grade Cicero's moral writings, Virgil with the *Georgics* and the last part of the *Aeneid*, Horace, Seneca and Tacitus (*Annals* and *Histories*); and in the final year Lucretius, Tacitus (*Orators' Dialogue*) and Cicero's treatises on rhetoric and philosophical works. These texts, it is worth pointing out, were seen only in the form of extracts; so that, what with inevitable gaps in the programme under pressure of school reality, the average pupil could easily form the impression that "Latin literature is a rag-bag of rather sorry authors in which two giants – Cicero and Virgil – tower above the rest".[110] One could also add Caesar, whose reign only lasted a year but was so absolute that fourth grade used to be called "Caesar year".[111] With minor variations, the same syllabus was prevalent throughout the Western world at that time.[112]

The pedagogic canon was not only almost unvarying, but remained very narrow throughout: indeed, if Dominique Julia is right, it became even narrower (at least in France) between the seventeenth century and the eighteenth.[113] The reduced *corpus* of texts handed down from Antiquity was further culled for pedagogic reasons – a wish to concentrate on authors with the best Latin and avoid boring or difficult texts – as well as moral ones (keeping "unsuitable" texts away from children). A small range of authors and works, a number of extracted highlights, were promoted everywhere to the status of "true classics", became the daily grind of generations of schoolchildren and, through long years of assiduous absorption on all sides, federated the entire Western educational world across time and space.

The same textbooks

Children did not just work on the same classical texts; even in acquiring basic Latin they sometimes used the same textbooks, particularly in the sixteenth century when several of these had an international circulation. René Hoven has listed these best-sellers of Latin schoolbook publishing. The uncontested all-time winners are the various works of Jean Despautère (the first appearing in 1506), which in original or adapted form saw more than a hundred new editions published in Antwerp, Basle, Cologne, Louvain, Lyon, Paris,

Venice, Vienna, Wittemberg and elsewhere. Erasmus also had considerable success with his *Colloquia* and *De copia verborum*; the second of these, originally published in Paris in 1512, was reprinted more than 180 times in twenty-five towns including Alcalá, Basle, Bruges, Cracow, Deventer, Heidelberg, London, Sélestat, Venice and Vienna. Mathurin Cordier's *Colloquia scholastica*, which first appeared in Geneva in 1564, saw new editions in Amsterdam, Antwerp, Berne, Cambridge, Dantzig, Leeuwarden, Leipzig, London, Lyon, Montbéliard, Paris, Rostock and other towns: a total of 117 complete editions and fifty-five abridged editions have been traced. Similar international success smiled on Peter Schade (*Mosellanus*) whose *Paedologia*, after appearing in Leipzig probably in 1517, went through more than sixty editions in twenty towns including Paris, Lyon, Antwerp, Augsburg, Cracow, Deventer, London, Louvain, Smalkalde and Zürich. These are only the more successful of the books that could invariably be found in sixteenth-century syllabuses and school desks.

The examples listed show once again, from their places of publication alone, that religious frontiers hardly counted; when necessary a few minor corrections would render a Protestant work perfectly acceptable in a Catholic country, and vice versa. There were however a few textbooks that had considerable success but were restricted to a confessional bloc: one example is Melanchthon's grammar, which appeared in no fewer than 248 editions between 1526 and the eighteenth century, but was only used in Lutheran regions. Similarly, a number of pedagogic works published by the Jesuits, although used in more than one country, would only be found in colleges run by the Society.

This internationalization diminished with the passage of time, but was still perceptible in the seventeenth century, when many reprints of the books mentioned above were published.[114] It was also in the seventeenth century (1659 to be exact) that the famous *Gradus ad Parnassum*, that indispensable tool of all school versifiers, made its first appearance. Originally the work of an anonymous Jesuit but attributed to a fictitious "Father Chastillon", then reattributed to the German Jesuit Paul Aler in the early eighteenth century, the manual enjoyed enormous success which can be deduced from its very complex bibliographic history. By the end of the eighteenth century it had been published in Paris, Cologne, Frankfurt, Prague, Buda, Bamberg, Amsterdam, Milan, Venice, Antwerp, Rouen, Lyon, Bois-le-Duc, Poitiers, London and other cities. It is true, however, that the book had been adapted and revised over a century and a half, in particular by being translated into the different vernaculars. Thus in the Deville brothers' edition of 1742, published in Lyon for the Iberian market, the explanatory text appeared in Spanish translation and the second volume carried a sort of lexicon as an appendix, listing all the words used in the *Gradus* in Spanish and Latin. The wide popularity of this work brought longevity as well, and editions were still appearing in the nineteenth century (in Edinburgh, Paris, Avignon, Lyon and Buda among other cities).[115]

The increasing role of vernacular languages in teaching was accompanied by the "nationalization" of textbooks, in practice either the composition of original works or the adaptation of foreign ones (as with the 1742 edition of the *Gradus*). But it also happened, even in the middle of the eighteenth century, that books written in another time and for another place were sometimes used without the slightest modification. Alvarez's Latin grammar, the one favoured in the Polish schools, was used in Poland like that until 1773, when a new edition at last addressed a number of irreducible differences between Latin and Polish, notably the tenses and aspects of verbs.[116] Incidentally, the Alvarez grammar was another work of wide and enduring popularity: in 1868, when it became possible to study Latin once again in Japan, scholars returned to a textbook that had been written nearly three centuries earlier by a Portuguese Jesuit.[117]

So athough schoolbook publishing became increasingly national with the passage of time, the practice of straightforward importation did not vanish completely. As recently as 1980 Peter Wülfing gave the examples of "Holland, some of whose schools use the Cambridge Latin Course", "Germany where certain establishments have imported a very good Dutch textbook, *Accipe ut reddas*", and "Greece which, with a deplorable lack of prudence, has imported textbooks from Western Europe, France in particular".[118] One of the more interesting recent examples of this sort of borrowing emerges from the introduction of computerized aids to the teaching of ancient languages in the form of the CD-ROM *Perseus*. Conceived in the US, this offers on one platform not just classical texts, but maps and plans of ancient sites, pictures of sculptures, vases, coins and so forth, and a simple multi-choice search system giving the sort of prompt responses and correlations that set researchers dreaming. This first-rate instrument nevertheless carries the mark of its origin: the texts have been taken from the Loeb edition, with an English version alongside the original; and experience shows that French schoolchildren who have worked on *Perseus* use the language of this translation somewhat more readily than Latin.[119]

A moral component

The moral imperatives mentioned earlier did not lead merely to the exclusion from the school *corpus* of any work thought unsuitable for children and the expurgation from the works chosen of anything that might be seen as offensive to modesty, but also to a certain amount of sometimes rather hurried rewriting. A representative example of these many "chastened" (or "bowdlerized" in the English nineteenth-century expression) editions is the version of Horace's *Odes* published in Angers in 1689: odes XI, XII and XXI are omitted from book I, while among the textual changes is one in which the final strophe of ode VI, where Horace celebrates his muse's role in singing of love and pleasure, is replaced by a celebration of the simple joys of country life. This was another durable practice, still current in schoolbook publishing at the end of the nineteenth century. When the new French school syllabus introduced Plautus's *Aulularia* to the Rhetoric class in 1874, a so-called "classical" edition, produced by a Versailles teacher, suppressed a dozen verses concerned with the rape and secret confinement of the young girl and altered gratuitous vulgarities elsewhere; the resulting text was perfectly "suitable" but had become, in places, more or less incomprehensible. Similar adjustments were apparent in school editions from the first half of the twentieth century. And needless to say the anthologies of selected pieces, the books written in Latin by academics "in the style of" Latin authors, and the other pastiche-type works which always played a large role in Latin teaching – think of Lhomond's *De viris* – were always irreproachable from the moral point of view.[120]

Collections of adages – often the first book children faced at school – were admirably adapted to the double objective towards which most pedagogues leaned: imparting the basics of Latin while teaching morality. Hence the widespread success of Cato's *Disticha*, Erasmus's *Adages* and (to mention a lesser-known work) the *Viridarium* compiled by the Flemish humanist Vander Cruysen.[121] The same is true of the colloquies, textbooks intended for use in oral situations, helping schoolchildren to acquire fluency in spoken Latin while fortifying their moral health. An activity natural to children – play – could be used in these manuals to inculcate Latin and the rules of conduct both at once, as in the case of this brief dialogue from a German pedagogue called Herrmann Schottenius:

"Ho there! You're playing dice."
"Is that your business?"
"It's not a game for schoolboys."
"Who is it for, then?"
"No-goods, wastrels, scoundrels."
"I've seen plenty of schoolboys playing it nevertheless."
"It didn't make them any better."
"Do you think it made them any worse?"
"By Hercules! Not just worse, but worse and worse!"[122]

Behind the expurgations, rewriting of texts and careful choice of extracts, the teaching itself had a moral basis. It drew generally on ancient writings that exalted virtues and condemned vices, and on historical narratives celebrating exemplary behaviour and anathemizing bad actions. The teacher's commentary inevitably drew attention to the sort of conduct that should be emulated and actions to be avoided. The subjects of the compositions set for the pupils had the twin objectives of exercising their Latin and inculcating certain values and principles: generations of collegians toiled everywhere, in verse and prose, to extol the virtues of duty to others, filial obedience, devotion to one's country, the benefits conferred by hard work.[123]

The widespread and enduring concern with the moral content of education caused some people to question the formative role being given to pagan authors in a Christian society, and to suggest that texts describing the adventures of the gods of Antiquity were acquainting children with unsuitable material. In England, an attempt was made in 1582 to replace pagan authors like Ovid in the kingdom's grammar schools with a modern Latin poem by Christopher Ocland: an official instruction was issued to this effect, but does not seem to have been followed. A suggestion along similar lines was made in 1650 by William Dell, Master of Gonville and Caius College in Cambridge: he urged that basic Latin should be learned using Christian authors to avoid the dangers of contact with pagan writings "full of the fables, vanities, filthiness, lasciviousness, idolatries and wickedness of the heathen".[124] The same criticisms were made in puritan America where reading the classics was felt to be damaging to morality and religious faith. Mythology, filled with absurdities and misbehaviour, but also history, dominated by wars, betrayals and acts of violence, presented serious risks to young minds: so thought Thomas Paine, and so, in the last decade of the eighteenth century, thought Benjamin Rush.[125] In pietist Germany, the tendency was to replace the works of Virgil and other classical authors with Christian texts that would enable Latin to be taught without exposing children to bad thoughts.[126] In France, the most impassioned debate on pagan authors in education took place in the mid-nineteenth century, after the publication of Abbé Gaume's book *Le ver rongeur des sociétés modernes* ("The woodworm of modern society"). Starting from the principle that "Christianity should be substituted for paganism in education", this prelate suggested that in the teaching of ancient languages pagan authors should be replaced with Christian ones, starting with the Fathers of the Church. In his campaign he received support from Louis Veuillot who thought the authors of ancient Rome lay at the roots of modern rationalism, and saw Cicero as the linear predecessor of Voltaire.[127]

These criticisms had little practical effect, and teaching continued to be based on pagan authors deemed "classical". On one level expurgation, rewriting and "selection" had produced a uniformly anodyne set of texts; sometimes Christian religious principles were observed by using an uppercase initial letter for *deus*. In addition, the master's commentary gave him an opportunity to point out the errors of the Ancients and emphasize differences between their world and a Christian one. Thus for a Jesuit pedagogue of the 1730s, Cicero, Horace and Virgil ought to be denounced as pagans "who had not the slightest wish to use the enlightenment they had acquired to glorify God and thus earn eternal happiness"; and he invited his audience to despise the fables with which their works were stuffed in these terms: "Only see the vanity, discover the folly of men who have corrupted the sacred stories to forge gods as wicked as themselves, an immodest Jupiter, a cruel Mars, a thieving Mercury, in order to justify through an impious cult their most shameful faults".[128] In this way a pagan text, carefully chosen and judiciously presented, became in the classroom a source of Christian wisdom and morality. It was an enduring phenomenon. Until very recent times, the curriculum has given a lead role to tirades by Cicero and Seneca on human virtues and vices, courage in facing the death of relations and friends, the duties of friendship, magnanimity in responding to offence. And in addition to all this, the grammars which (as we shall see) were the very armature of Latin teaching used examples designed to illustrate the rules of the language through a lesson in morality, advantageously combining the Latin course with civic instruction.[129]

"Grammatical hypertrophy"

As a result of being used in this way, as well as through their constant presence in syllabuses and timetables, the works of Antiquity came to acquire a purely pedagogic coloration, heightened still further by the way Latin was taught: with grammar playing the leading role and texts used essentially in support of grammatical exercises. In any case that is the view some children had of the pieces they had to study. Sophia, the London schoolgirl depicted by Lionel Hale in *A Fleece of Lambs* (1961), did not even begin "to connect the words on the printed page with anything that ever really happened. Men marched, camps were struck, winter quarters were gone into; but to Sophia the Latin language did not concern men, camps, winter quarters and cavalry. It existed to provide Subjunctives, and Past Participles, and (oh golly!) Gerunds."[130]

Latin teaching nearly always included a massive dose of grammar, and learning its rules was generally the child's first contact with the language of the Ancients, as we have seen from the description of school under the Ancien Régime. Change was extremely slow in coming, we learn from the memoirs of Walter McDonald, who had been a pupil at St Kyran's College in Kilkenny, Ireland, during the 1860s: "We were set, daily, so many pages of Latin or Greek grammar to learn by heart, so many lines of a Latin or Greek author to translate – and parse, so as to be able to define all the names and adjectives and to conjugate all the verbs, giving the rule of syntax, whereby each case or tense was governed".[131] This grammatical tendency was further accentuated in the last decades of the nineteenth century by the prestige of German philology, which arrived rapidly in countries like Russia with weak or non-existent classical traditions, but had more difficulty penetrating those with a different way of working – aesthetic in France, for example, or rhetorical in Italy – although there too it made its mark.[132] This led to some first-rate achievements in the field of textual analysis but also, especially in secondary education, led to a pre-eminence of grammar that eventually degenerated into what can only be called "grammatical hypertrophy".[133] It is hardly surprising therefore that grammar should have become the scapegoat for the decline of Latin studies: "prime responsibility for the Latin crisis," wrote Jean Cousin in 1954, "lies with the authors of grammars".[134] Nor is it at all surprising that the solutions tried – "Living Latin", the reading of texts, a new concentration on ancient civilization and even their daily lives – relegated grammar everywhere to a subsidiary (if still not exactly minor) role.[135] In its death-agony, as in its days of glory, Latin pedagogy retained a unitary dimension.

CHAPTER 2

The "Latin Stronghold": the Church

Although the expression "stronghold of Latin" was used by Ferdinand Brunot, from whom I have borrowed it, in reference to the eighteenth century alone,[1] it possesses nevertheless a wider validity: Latin remained the liturgical language of the Catholic Church, in which it performed the sacrifice of the mass and administered the sacraments, until the Vatican II council. It was the inheritance of a historical situation, an ancient practice which had been ratified at the Council of Trent. During the four centuries that separate these two assemblies, Latin was seen as a distinctive characteristic of the Catholic Church, both by its members and by its detractors. During that period, every attempt to make room for the vernaculars not only failed but became an opportunity for the consolidation and extension of the arguments and apologia for consecrating Latin as a sacred language. That is the subject of this chapter which, after describing the long reign of Latin, will examine the "turning point" represented, on this and other issues, by the Vatican II council. As a counterweight to an excessively Roman view of events, a brief digression through the Protestant world will remind us that the Reformation was not just a matter of introducing the vernacular.

1 From a Custom to the Rule: The Tridentine Codification

The establishment of Latin as the Church language

In Antiquity, and during the Middle Ages, Latin alone did not rule the life of the Church; several different languages were used for writing liturgical books and the celebration of offices. Without going back to the first Christian community in Jerusalem, which probably celebrated the liturgy in Aramaic, we can say that the spread of Christianity inside the Roman empire would have been accomplished in the language that was known everywhere: Greek. Latin did not replace it even in Rome until quite late, after the Greek language had fallen from use, probably at some time during the third or fourth century. During these early times of Christianity, other languages – Coptic, Amharic, Armenian – were also used for liturgy, but only on a limited, local basis. The adoption of Latin by the Church of Rome should not, however, be interpreted as a concession to a language associated by the founding Fathers with a pagan culture that they rejected. The prime reason was to ensure communication by using the common language of the Empire; another, as Vittorio Coletti points out, was "the need to establish the religious discourse in a stable and reliable form, so that the linguistic aspect [would be] appropriate to the sacrality of its content and practice".

The Latin that shaped the liturgy was in a run-of-the-mill, popular register, remote from the classical tongue; but it was also, from its beginnings, a literary language, different from the one generally spoken. The difference was self-accentuating: the language of the sacred text became a language of culture and acquired a patina of archaism that ended by placing it outside time and withdrawing it from common intelligibility. In this development characteristic of liturgical languages – the growing differentiation of the cultural language from common speech, accompanied by a strong tendency for the former to become fixed and immutable – Latin became the property of a clerical elite. A number of factors, religious and cultural, combined to bring this about. The establishment of a clerical hierarchy within the Church brought a new relationship with the faithful, and the distinction between clerics and faithful grew more marked over time. It was accompanied by a radical divergence between the two cultures – learned and popular – reflected in the contrast between a minority of *litterati* who had received formal education, generally in Church institutions, and knew Latin, and the majority of *illiterati* or *idiotae* who did not know it, being wholly dependent on oral tradition and reduced, from about the seventh century, to the vulgar tongue alone.[2] In this way Latin became the language of clerics, although many of them were far from accomplished Latinists (St. Boniface, for example, was uneasy about a baptism he had seen administered *in nomine patria et filia et sanctus spiritus*).[3]

This predominance of Latin raised the issue of vernaculars at a very early date. The evangelization of peoples whose languages were profoundly different from Latin led to examination of the question and attempts at an answer. In the ninth century, the two brothers who converted the Slavic world to Christianity, Cyril and Methodius, organized a Slavonic liturgy; Rome hesitated for a while over this initiative before finally condemning it in 885, when Pope Stephen II theatened Methodius with anathema if he used Slavonic for the mass, authorizing him only to translate and explain the epistle and gospel in Slavonic for the edification of the faithful. Two centuries later, Slavs seeking permission to translate the liturgy into their language received a refusal from Gregory VII, explained as follows: "It is not without reason that the Almighty has desired holy scripture to remain secret in certain places, for had it been clear to all it might perhaps have been less respected or more easily ignored; or again badly interpreted by persons of mediocre culture".[4] In fact the Church took an extremely cautious view of the use of the vulgar tongue for the liturgy, and later sectarian moves in this direction by groups like the Waldensians and the Lollards aroused its resistance to such a point that the vulgar tongue and heresy were seen as "the two terms of the same binomial". Always circumspect in its attitude to vernaculars, its position did vary according to the different levels of religious life: very reserved – closed, even – on anything to do with the liturgy or sacred texts, more open where lay devotions were concerned. Within the Church, a difference of attitude was apparent between the hierarchy, deeply distrustful of vernaculars, and the mendicant orders based in the towns, in direct contact with the faithful, who employed the vulgar language in their sermons to impart religious education to the masses.[5] By about 1500 the situation was roughly as follows: vernaculars were widely used for preaching; translations of the Bible and of liturgical texts were in circulation; but Latin, and Latin alone, remained the language for celebrating the mass and administering the sacraments.[6] No normative text had been issued to regularize this *de facto* state of affairs.

The missions that followed the discovery of the New World naturally solved the linguistic problem in a similar way, although in their case it was further complicated by the need to choose between Castilian and indigenous languages. The earliest missionaries, who did not know the local languages and had no interpreters, started by using Latin. They first approached children, especially those of the more important Indians, teaching them in Latin to make the sign of the cross and recite the *Paternoster*, the *Ave Maria*, the *Credo* and the *Salve Regina*; then they turned to the adults and taught them to say prayers in Latin. To make the process easier, they resorted to chants and various mnemonic techniques. The mediocre results – the Indians did not understand what they were saying and retained their own religious practices, a situation the missionaries were unable to correct – soon led to the abandonment of all-Latin evangelizing. A fruitful apostolate seemed impossible without some knowledge of indigenous languages, and the missionaries settled on Nahuatl – already established as the official language of law and commerce – out of the eighty-plus languages and dialects spoken in the Aztec empire. The next task was to inject new notions unknown to the Indians; and this was done by introducing European words into the indigenous language. There was thus (in principle at least) no risk of heterodoxy or confusion with non-Christian ideas. In consequence, some of the texts written in the indigenous language are scattered with Latin and Spanish words, sometimes "creolized" or wearing, as it were, local clothes. But although the missionaries used indigenous languages for teaching and preaching, they stuck to Latin for mass and the sacraments; and here, exploiting the Indians' taste for pomp and ornaments, they introduced more music into the ceremonies and trained the Indians to sing hymns and prayers from memory, in Latin.[7]

Arguments in favour of the vulgar tongue and attacks on Latin

The predominance of the old language was threatened in the first half of the sixteenth century, when attacks mounted by the reformers resulted in the swift "dethronement" of Latin in the Protestant churches. Although the writings of the first reformers do not contain much material on the linguistic question, it went without saying that the religion ought to be celebrated in a language the faithful could understand. This assertion was based on the theological argument that the Christian religion is based on the word; and a cult of the word cannot be properly celebrated by a community unless that word is understood by the community, which means that it must be expressed in the language of the country. Adoption of the vernacular was accompanied by complaints that Latin prevented conscious participation by the faithful.[8]

The Protestant reformers' linguistic line and virulent attacks on the Latin stranglehold should not be allowed to obscure the fact that, until the 1540s, calls for the use of the vernacular were being made inside the Church itself by advocates of the renovation of religious practice. A *Libellus* to this effect was addressed to Pope Leo X in 1513 by two Venetian Camaldules, Paolo Giustiniani and Pietro Quirini. They suggested reforming the Latin education of the clergy, since many of its members were incapable of fully understanding the rite of the mass; they pleaded for translation of the Bible into modern languages and a vernacular liturgy, as ways of giving the faithful a more conscious body of belief and a more authentic practice.

The same views underlay Erasmus's call, made in 1516, for the Bible to be translated into the vernacular; he too was contemptuous of a religiosity that could only be superficial and mechanical when "uneducated people and women in the manner of parrots mumble their psalms and Lord's Prayer in Latin, without understanding what they are saying". This was a thinly-veiled indictment of the Latin liturgy. In France, "evangelicals" were striving to familiarize the faithful with the scriptures by giving them translations of the sacred texts; by 1523 the theologian Lefèvre d'Étaples had produced a French version of the New Testament, and Bishop Guillaume Briçonnet of Meaux was holding readings in the vernacular at his cathedral. But the advance of Luther's ideas, and his excommunication, were making the Church authorities increasingly suspicious of translations. The Sorbonne condemned them in 1526, at the same time reasserting the incompetence of laymen in religious matters and the absolute need for mediation by the Church. "Authorized" preaching was the only permitted form of religious instruction for the people, and the lay population only had one right: the right to listen. It mattered little, the Sorbonne added, that the faithful did not understand the words of their prayers, as their meaning lay not in the text but in the way the Church used them; for the Church was sole guarantor of the meaning of the rites and of their result.

In Italy the repression did not begin until the 1540s. In 1530 the Florentine humanist Antonio Brucioli had produced an Italian version of the New Testament, reprinted in 1532 with a translation of the Old Testament. In a *Commento* published in 1542, Brucioli justified this work by arguing that the Christian religion, unlike pagan ones, had nothing to hide: Christ wished his word to be known to all, and so it should be available in language accessible to all. There was nothing wrong, in fact, with "a woman or cobbler speaking sacred words and understanding them while reading them"; what was scandalous was that "women and the majority of men mumble their psalms and prayers in Latin or Greek, without understanding anything they are saying". Two years later, one of the haughtiest guardians of orthodoxy, Ambrogio Catharin, came out against assertions of that sort and condemned translation of sacred texts into the vulgar tongue, making much of the existing order of society: "If there are doctors, and thus something that they teach, it follows that there must be others who listen and learn". Similar ideas had already been put forward by the Spanish theologian Alonzo de Castro whose *Adversus omnes hereses* (first edition 1534) attacked translations, linking the vulgar tongue with heresy in a way that was already traditional, but sharpened by recent events: the very difficulty of reading and interpreting sacred texts reserved these activities for competent persons; moreover, when the learned themselves had been known to stumble, or even stray, what might not become of the general run of believers? If vernacular translations were to lead to such practices being permitted, the established order would end by being overturned, with women becoming doctors.[9]

Some twenty years earlier the Flemish humanist Josse Clichtove had arrived at broadly similar opinions from a starting point of clerical reform. In his view, a priest's sacrificial function made him "a being apart", different from other men, alone in enjoying the plenitude of religion. The pastoral functions inseparable from the priesthood necessitated qualities of intellect and a measure of learning; and Clichtove was scandalized by the promotion to holy orders of "ignoramuses and illiterates . . . who can neither read nor speak Latin". Like other humanists, Clichtove not only called for improved training for priests, with a deeper knowledge of scripture and the Fathers of the Church, but pleaded for better understanding of the liturgy. For he had noticed that priests did not always know the meaning of the words they recited or the actions they performed. In 1516, to remedy this situation, he published the *Elucidatorum ecclesiasticum*. The third part of this work, dealing with the mass, carried a warning that it should only be read by clerics; and in case any lay person should be tempted nevertheless to read these pages, Clichtove took pains to make his explanations of the rituals and texts used in the mass as obscure as possible to the uninitiated. While hostile to any idea of mass in the vulgar tongue – he argued this point vigorously with Luther in 1526 – he also wanted "simple people" to have no direct contact with scripture: in 1515, well before the Reformation, he was already opposing vernacular translations of the Bible, arguing that they would inevitably contain inaccuracies, ambiguities and errors, all the more dangerous in that they would be read by people wholly lacking in the training needed to make the necessary readjustments.[10]

The voices of simple believers were raised alongside those of theologians and churchmen, although (given the attitudes sketched above) they were not likely to be heard. Between 1546 and 1548 the Florentine Giambattista Gelli rebelled against the hegemony of Latin in the name of the vulgar tongue, which he was cultivating in the Accademia Fiorentina. Gelli, a prosperous artisan, wrote a series of *Capricci del bottaio* emphasizing the dignity and richness of the vernacular and, in consequence, its adequacy to deal with any and all learning, which would thus be made accessible to greater numbers of people; at the same time he attacked the monopoly of Latin, which he saw primarily as defending the privileges of a minority of adepts who were duping the people by making out that nothing could be learned without mastering the language of learning. The vernacular was perfectly appropriate for translations of the divine offices and the liturgy; such translations would increase the faithful's respect for holy things, and thus deepen their devotion. At this point Gelli, whose doctrinal orthodoxy was unquestionable, advanced arguments that had already been used by the reformers. His complaint that the recitation of psalms in Latin sounded like "the croaking of rooks or squawking of parrots" might have come from Erasmus or Brucioli. And in the mainstream of Protestant reform, he underlined the equality of Christians in the Church: Latin, the property of clerics, was just a priest's expedient for keeping the ordinary believers in a subordinate position. The *Capricci* were censored, and Gelli, to escape punishment, had to make some changes: among the passages he had to withdraw were those demanding translations of the scriptures and the liturgy, as well as those in which he attacked supporters of the Latin monopoly.[11]

The demands of clerics, as well as the ordinary faithful, had caused theologians to advance a number of arguments in support of Latin, and at the same time to spell out an ecclesiology separating the simple from the adept, the lay from the clergy. The Reformation had had its influence on the positions adopted during this process: any sign of interest in the vernacular automatically aroused distrust or even suspicion of heresy. The decisions that were taken at Trent could not be unaffected by these developments.

The Tridentine canon

The Council that began in Trent in 1546 debated language questions on several occasions, most notably when dealing with the issues of translating the Bible into the vernacular and the celebration of mass. Translation of the Bible was discussed from the first sessions, and especially in March 1546. There were two opposed groups of prelates, those who thought it appropriate to counteract Protestant bibles by producing Catholic ones, and those resolutely against all concessions. The geographical origins of the priests, and their functions in the Church, have both been suggested as possible reasons for this split. Those coming from zones deeply affected by heresy, essentially the Germanic region, favoured Catholic translations to answer the demand from the faithful and dilute the impact of the Protestant versions; those who lived in areas far from heresy – mainly Spanish prelates and members of the Curia – were hostile to anything that might resemble a concession to Protestant ideas or a relaxation of Church prerogatives. The first group included a number of men exercising pastoral functions, the second consisted more of theologians and monks. Debates on the "vulgarization" of the Bible were broadly conditioned by the perceived relationship between translation and heresy: while some saw translations accessible to uneducated people as carrying an inevitable risk of error, others emphasized the right of all men to know the scriptures, recalled that error is usually the fruit of ignorance, and pointed out that heresies had nearly always been generated by the learned, not by simple men of the people. In these discussions, Latin was seen as a means for defending the Church's authority and control over the faithful; nobody, not even the most determined opponents of "vulgarization", advanced the argument that the language possesses some sort of sacred character. The problem of translating the Bible raised the further problem of achieving a correct edition, and thus led to a philological and theological examination of the Vulgate. As V. Coletti has shown, if the version produced by St Jerome was found to contain imperfections, they could only be explained by recalling that the Vulgate was already a translation, which would make it difficult to forbid new translations. If on the other hand the Vulgate was found to be without defects, it would be possible to regard it as a sacred text whose immutable, authentic character, conferred by the saintliness of its author and the weight of tradition, excluded all translation. The discussions that ensued resulted in a prudent solution, embodied in the decree of 8 April 1546: the Vulgate was retained in its existing form and the hope expressed that a more correct version would be prepared, the question of translations was not mentioned, and the publication of unauthorized writings on the subject was forbidden.[12]

The decree of 8 April 1546 inevitably influenced what was said when the fathers were discussing the language used for mass: the linguistic issue was at no point considered in isolation but always with the mass in mind. A first

series of talks took place in December 1551/January 1552. They began with
a definition of the differences with Protestant doctrine on the issue; but the
interruption of the Council prevented publication of the document on the
mass that had been discussed. When the Council met again ten years later it
had to start again at the beginning, in a different context: 180 participants –
more than twice the previous number of seventy – met in an altered religious
situation, with the advancing tide of the Reformation leading to more
entrenched positions. The debate on the language of the mass began on 19
July and ended on 17 September. The discussion was centred on the sacrificial dimension of the eucharist: the mass is not a memorial of Christ's sacrifice, but a sacrifice itself, and one that operates independently of human
dispositions; the priest alone has a need to understand; he alone is the guarantor of comprehension, the holder of the faith, which can therefore be
expressed perfectly well in the language consecrated by tradition: Latin. The
theologians taking part agreed on rejecting the use of the vulgar tongue, as
demanded by the Protestants: there was absolutely no need for lay people to
understand the text of the mass, all they needed was the unity in faith that it
provided. While admitting that there was nothing to forbid use of the vulgar
tongue, they insisted that the Church should keep Latin for reasons of convenience. The dignity of the liturgy required a fitting language: Latin, the
most literary of languages, answered this elevated need; moving into the vernacular would be an impoverishment. It seems probable, moreover, that to
these men Latin did have something sacred about it, having for centuries
expressed the supernatural verities. The theologians also pointed to the difficulties inherent in translation, the risk of introducing errors; the Reformation
with its linguistic innovations was the best illustration of this; and besides,
adopting the vernacular would look like a concession or even a capitulation
to the heretics. Echoes of these discussions are perceptible in the summary
presented to the Council on 6 August: it affirmed the *maxima congruitas* of Latin
for the mass – respect for the holy mysteries might be lessened if they were
celebrated in the vulgar tongue – and emphasized the great peril that might
arise from translations. This part of the dogmatic exposé corresponds to the
following canon: "If anyone says that the mass should be celebrated only in
the vulgar tongue, let him be anathemized". Recognizing, however, that the
readings and the gospel ought to be understood, this draft suggested that
explanations be given to the faithful during the ceremony.

These suggestions were discussed between 11 and 27 August, and were criticized from two different angles by the nineteen prelates who spoke in the
debate. Those of Roman culture wanted a stronger case to be made for
Latin; but there was another group that felt unable to accept the dogmatic
arguments in its favour, not because they opposed Latin as the language of
the Western liturgy, but because these arguments purported to cover too
many disparate situations – they referred to the Eastern Churches and their

privileges – and because they contained implicit disapproval of the vulgar tongue. A new draft was completed on 5 September. It proclaimed that the holy mass *contains* a precious doctrinal treasure; here the Council was taking issue with the Protestants, for whom it *is* just a teaching. Although the mass was rich in doctrine, the Council did not say that it should be celebrated in the vulgar tongue; the Church had never favoured this tendency. There was agreement on endorsing existing practice, as it had been maintained over the centuries, and it was stated that an explanation would be given to the people in the vulgar tongue. This new version was submitted to the prelates on 7 September, raising little debate and being passed by vote at the twenty-second session, on 17 November. Chapter VIII, "on the doctrine and canons of the most holy sacrifice of the mass", stated:

> Although the mass contains a great teaching for the faithful, nevertheless it has not seemed good to the fathers that it should be celebrated here and there in the vulgar tongue. That is why, although keeping everywhere to the ancient rite proper to all Churches and approved by the holy Roman Church, mother and mistress of all Churches, in order that Christ's sheep may not die of hunger and the little ones may not ask for bread and be given none, the holy Council commands priests and all those who have charge of the soul to give frequently some explanation, during the celebration of mass, themselves or through others, based on the texts involved in the mass and, among other things, to throw light on the mystery of the sacrifice, especially on Sundays and feast days.

But canon 9 in the following chapter warned: "If anyone says that the mass should be celebrated only in the vulgar tongue . . ., let him be anathemized". The same principles were applied to the sacraments: they were to be administered in Latin and explained in the vernacular.

The text approved on 17 September differed from the earlier discussions and draft documents in making no reference to those arguments for Latin that attribute special qualities to it: treating it as a sacred, universally used language whose stability and dignity guarantee conservation of the treasure of faith. The Council's task had been to define the doctrinal value of the mass as a real sacrifice; the linguistic question was only involved at all to the extent that it was grafted into the dogma on the mass. The value of the teaching contained in the mass seemed insufficient to justify changes to the traditional ritual, but it was agreed that explanations should be given so that such teaching value would not be neglected. Although the mass was not linked in absolute fashion with any one language, and although no link between heresy and the vulgar tongue was established, defensiveness in response to the Reformation played a determining role in the retention of Latin. This circumstantial element counted less later on when justifications were advanced for Latin that had not figured in the final text and when the vulgar tongue was alleged to carry a risk of heresy in itself.[13]

The decisions reached at Trent clearly expressed the hierarchy's anxiety to take charge of the religious instruction of the faithful, monitoring the process in order to avoid any deviation or error. The Council also paid close attention to the character of the priest, and to his training with a view to the fullest performance of the role of mediator between God and the Christian populace, to prepare him for the supervision of his flock. For this purpose it decided to create seminaries which, with some local variations, were all characterized by the emphasis given to Latin. This promotion of the clergy and the recognition of a contrasting laity established in the Catholic world a hierarchical and static conception of society, with the holders of knowledge on one side and passive recipients of instruction on the other, each remaining in their respective conditions.[14]

2 Orthodoxy and Apologetics

The decisions taken at Trent remained in force in the Catholic Church until the Vatican II Council. Any "novation" was resisted and, when authorized, amply justified. As time passed, a body of arguments in support of Latin was built up, amounting in fact to an apologetics to which clerics and faithful subscribed alike.

The reign of Latin

The restrictive position reached by the Council on "vulgarization" of the Bible happened to coincide with an existing secular suspicion of vernacular languages. The way the Tridentine decree was applied in France is enlightening. It strengthened the position of the Sorbonne doctors and other authorities, who had started condemning translations in the first half of the century. It is hardly surprising that they should have pressed their advantage. In 1548 Esprit Rotier, the Inquisitor of Toulouse, published a dissertation with the utterly unambiguous title *De non vertanda Scriptura Sacra in vulgarem linguam*: a treatise of theological type, it employed well-known linguistic and literary arguments comparing the poverty and instability of the vernacular with the majesty and permanence of Latin; the very origins of the Bible, its elevated status as a text inspired by God, postulated a language on the same scale, which could only be Latin. Laymen too defended the position adopted at Trent, like Montaigne who sat, of course, in the parliament that ordered the seizure of the Psalms in 1556. "It is not without good reason, it seems to me," he wrote in his *Essais*, "that the Church forbids the promiscuous, reckless and indiscreet use of the holy and divine songs that the Holy Spirit has recorded in David. We should only involve God in our actions with reverence and attention filled with honour and respect." He went on to mark the distinction between clerics and laity, in much the same way as the Council:

It is not the study of every man. It is the study of persons who are dedicated to it, whom God has called to it; the wicked, the ignorant are made worse by it; it is not a story to tell, it is a story to revere, to fear and adore. What absurd people, to think they have made it accessible to the populace, just by putting it in popular speech! . . . I also believe that freedom for all to dissipate such religious and important words in all sorts of idioms, is far more dangerous than useful.[15]

Translations of the Bible, or of the New Testament alone, were nevertheless circulating among French Catholics, although these versions were distinct from the so-called Louvain Bible. The Louvain translation was not faultless, either in content (although its authors had striven to make it conform to the Vulgate) or form (despite efforts to improve on a rather archaic and awkward style). Between 1620 and 1630, when it seemed necessary to make the sacred text accessible to people who, although ignorant of Latin, still had strong spiritual needs, paraphrases were produced that provided an orthodox interpretation while evading the questions and polemics that would inevitably be raised by a translation. The success of these publications did not stop people from hoping for a Catholic Bible in French, one that would supplant the Protestant versions and bring heretics back into the orthodox fold. Towards the end of his reign Louis XIII authorized a translation, and it was published in 1643 with the approval of the doctors of Poitiers (those of the Sorbonne having reserved their judgement); at about the same time, Richelieu had entrusted three theologians with the task of preparing another translation. Richelieu's death followed by that of the king brought a halt to these enterprises, although over the next few years the appearance of several versions of different books of the Bible gave the impression of a general movement in favour of unfettered access to the scriptures.

But in 1650 the Archbishop of Paris, Cardinal de Retz, issued a pastoral letter reiterating the traditional restrictions and banning the reading of the Bible in the vulgar tongue without permission; and the following year, under de Retz's aegis, the "king's adviser, almoner and preacher" Nicolas Le Maire published a fat book with the significant title *Le sanctuaire fermé aux profanes ou la Bible défendu au vulgaire* ("The sanctuary closed to the profane or the Bible forbidden in vulgar speech").[16] Its proposition, spelt out in the preface, was to "uphold one of the most important practices of the Church and one of the main maxims of the religion, which is to hide the mysteries from the unworthy and keep the profane out of the sanctuary" thus showing "that scripture should not have been rendered common and vulgar at all, both because of the reverence due to the word of God and because of the submission that is owed to the oracles of the Church"; or putting it more concretely, the "book of Religion that the saints themselves never opened without trembling" should not be treated as "the plaything and pastime of artisans". In the first part of the book, Le Maire demonstrated that holy scripture is obscure, difficult, perilous to the ignorant and the weak, and that not every sort of person should be permitted to read it, before concluding logically that "what belongs to priests should be left to priests" and hinting at the dangers that would arise from the interruption of an order supported by Providence. The second, historical part showed that "reading the Bible had never been common or vulgar". The third part established that "the general licence that some people want to establish concerning the reading of the holy Bible is contrary to the Church's wishes and all the rules of prudence and good judgement". The nature of the biblical text itself, the secular tradition of the Church and its successive decrees all pointed to a ban on reading the Bible in the vernacular. At this point, Le Maire raises a question which is of great interest to us:

> Why has the Church only forbidden reading the Bible in the vulgar tongue and why has it allowed it in both Greek and Latin, as if a man had greater capacity as a result of understanding and speaking these languages, as if that strengthened his faith or made him more intelligent about scripture, or again as if such reading could not be harmful or perilous to scholars and the learned as well as to the ignorant and weak, seeing that ordinarily they have more vanity and less humility than others?

For many heretics were, in fact, educated men. Did the languages of learning, including Latin, promote error, or did they do the opposite and protect against it? The second, evidently: for "the use of these languages places a man apart from the mass of the people"; it trained his judgement and tempered him, protected him against common errors and being carried away by first impressions; what was more, knowledge of ancient languages enabled him to compare translations with the original texts and thus unmask the errors planted by heretics; knowledge was fortifying against error, and the reason why Calvin had fallen into heresy was not that he was learned but that he had a "vindictive and self-seeking" character. In this way, in addition to the dividing line between priests and the profane, Le Maire traced another line, not so much theological in character as cultural and social, separating the learned from the ignorant. This second line consisted, once again, of Latin.[17]

The Council of Trent had not placed an absolute embargo on translation of the sacred texts or on the reading of such translations, but had made both subject to permission from the ecclesiastical authorities. At the end of the seventeenth century, the versions produced by Amelote and Le Maistre de Sacy had made the whole of scripture accessible to French Catholics; at the time, moreover, new converts were presented officially with copies of the Bible in French.[18] But although this represented a decisive advance – even a victory – for the national language, and some translations, for example the so-called Mons New Testament (1666), were very successful (the Mons Bible sold 5,000 copies in six months), direct contact with sacred texts remained very limited in the Catholic world, especially when compared with Protestant practice.

The liturgy itself remained exclusively Latin, any exception being accompanied by justifications. Tradition, the historical argument based on enduring secular practice, was bolstered over time with proofs of cultural and religious type brought to bear on those advocating use of the vernacular. The struggle over the Chinese liturgy is particularly revealing here.[19] Those citing the local situation in support of introducing the vernacular, mostly Jesuit missionaries with some support from their colleagues in the West, met determined opposition from the authorities in Rome, theologians and members of the congregations, who maintained that Latin had irrevocable rights. The conflict lasted more than three centuries and was not finally resolved until 1949. But the rival positions became entrenched very early, crystallizing around a few arguments which were subsequently repeated *ad nauseam*. It is not our concern here to list every detail of this prolonged controversy, further complicated by inter-order rivalries in the Far East, anti-Jesuit campaigning in Europe, and the connected differences over ritual and terminology; apart from describing the general context, we will restrict ourselves to the main episodes and principal decisions.

The Jesuit missionaries settled in China quickly realized – and the conviction grew stronger with time – that if that country was going to be won for Catholicism it would be essential to create a local clergy: "China will not be converted, unless by the Chinese," noted Fr Jean Basset, like others before him, in 1702.[20] There was to be much prejudice and bureaucratic obstruction directed against what was after all a foreigners' religion; and the persecution the missionaries endured on several occasions only served to strengthen their views. The problem then arose of choosing candidates for the priesthood. The socio-cultural situation in China was not at all helpful, placing serious obstacles in the way of training young people. No respectable parents would ever allow their children to waste time unprofitably learning Latin, a foreign language, especially at the cost of their Chinese literary education, the sole route to an honourable career. The missionaries could easily procure children of humble birth, but when they became priests these men would still have no social prestige whatsoever, to the great detriment of their religious function. The rule of celibacy was a further obstacle to the recruitment of young candidates. There were of course some older, widowed literates among the converts who, if ordained, would be capable of effective evangelizing; but these were kept from the altar by what seemed an insurmountable difficulty: they were too old to start learning Latin. And on this point Rome would not give an inch, not even to authorize a Chinese liturgy as a temporary measure.

The argument in fact was concerned less with knowledge of Latin than its pronunciation. Missionaries and apostolic visitors to the Orient all agreed on the inability of the Chinese to achieve a correct pronunciation; their letters, memoirs and reports were filled with proofs to this effect, referring knowledgeably to the peculiarities of Chinese phonetics, lacking in several of the sounds corresponding to Latin letters. The main examples were the vowels a and e and the consonants b, d and r in the initial position, which became respectively *ya, nge, pe, te* and *lle*. It was also impossible for the Chinese to end a word with any consonant other than m or n, so that *vos amatis* would be pronounced *vosi yamassissi*. And they did not have sounds corresponding to l and g, so that *ego*, for example, would be pronounced *nheco*. There was also their inability to pronounce two conjoined consonants or a double consonant without introducing a mediating vowel: *sanctam* would thus become *sanketam* and *ecclesiam* an almost unrecognizable *ngekekelesiam*. Even this absurd cacophony for a single word was as nothing compared to what became of whole sentences and phrases such as *Ego te baptizo in nomine Patris et Filii et Spiritus Sancti, Te absolvo a peccatis tuis* or *Hoc est corpus meum*, which became: *Nghe ngho te bapetiso in nomine Patelisu nghe te Filli te Sepilitusu Sanketi, Nghe te yapesolva ya pekiatisu tuisu* and *Hocu yesutu colpusu meum*.

This pronunciation was thought ridiculous by the fathers, who filled their pleas for change with examples to this effect and pointed out that even Chinese audiences laughed on hearing such jargon. Worse still, it was unintelligible; not only were common words going unrecognized and phrases losing all meaning, but word-endings for different cases and conjugations were no longer being respected. A Fr Buglio noted of the Chinese in 1678 that "Not only do they speak like parrots without understanding anything, but they cannot even pronounce words that parrots can pronounce".[21] There was nothing to be gained by representing the sound of Latin words in Chinese characters; the pronunciation remained as defective as ever, with the additional complication that literate pagans suspected sorcery when they saw a series of Chinese characters without coherent meaning. Fr Intorcetta gave the meanings of the Chinese characters for the phonetic rendering of the Latin consecration as: "breath, old, lord, function, rule, handsome, sleep, each, road, flee, affair, reflect, prairie".[22]

Behind the picturesque details – plentiful in the surviving texts – loomed a problem of major importance. The phrases quoted above are the sacramental formulae for baptism, absolution and the eucharist. Turning them into mumbo-jumbo in this way, and more generally the Chinese inability to master Latin pronunciation, raised fears that they might also change or omit some essential word of these sacred pronouncements, and thus administer the sacraments invalidly. This fear led the missionaries to baptize newcomers a second time, worried as they were by variants of *batino* and *batito* in place of the authentic *baptizo*.[23]

The extreme gravity of these difficulties led the Jesuits to press Rome for an authorized Chinese-language liturgy. Their demand, we must remember, was entirely circumstantial: its aim was the rapid formation of the much-needed local clergy, and it was a purely temporary expedient to this end.

At first the Jesuits got what they wanted. In 1615 Pope Paul V granted a privilege giving permission to translate scripture into literary Chinese, and allowing future Chinese priests to celebrate mass, recite the breviary and administer the sacraments in their own language. This was only a provisional measure, however; it was planned to set up a seminary, after which things would resume their normal course. And in fact this privilege had few concrete results: translation of scripture into Chinese came up against formidable problems of terminology, while the ordination of priests was put off until later, partly because of the small number of candidates and partly because of the urgent work of conversion that preoccupied the missionaries. The problem of the Chinese clergy was expressly raised again in 1658, when apostolic vicars were sent to the Far East to ordain indigenous priests. In Rome, where a Chinese liturgy had its supporters and opponents, the latter were eventually brought by the difficulties Latin presented for the Chinese to make a concession embodied in the Bull *Super cathedram* (9 September 1659). Alexander VII gave the apostolic vicars being sent to the Orient the ability to ordain as priests Chinese postulants who could read Latin, even without understanding it. A few Chinese were ordained as a result. Subsequently the missionaries, and their allies in Europe, renewed their pleas for a Chinese liturgy – reiterated after every persecution – and, failing that, for extension of the privilege granted by Paul V; but in vain. Young Chinese were sent to the West to be trained in Latin, and a college was set up for this purpose by Matteo Ripa in Naples in 1732. Rome, exemplified in the position adopted by Benedict XIV in 1752, stayed with Alexander VII's Bull. Some timely help arrived from China in the shape of the Chinese priest André Li who came out against even that text, maintaining stoutly that Chinese priests ought to master Latin perfectly, not just to avoid the scorn of European missionaries but to draw directly from Latin sources the knowledge required for their ministry. In 1784, after yet another persecution, a Chinese liturgy was again considered as a means of ordaining a large number of local priests as quickly as possible; again the idea was not followed up. Then, for good or ill, the Latin education of young postulants was undertaken in seminaries in China, and during the nineteenth century Alexander VII's privilege fell out of use. The Chinese liturgy was discussed no more until 1949. On 8 March of that year the Holy Office, after examining the study of Latin by Chinese student priests and the use of literary Chinese for the liturgy, concluded on the

> need for the Latin language to be learned by all the members of the Chinese clergy. However, the study of Latin should leave young students the possibility of applying themselves to the difficult, long and laborious study of their own national language. At the same time, candidates for the priesthood should

acquire a knowledge of Latin at least sufficient to give them a correct understanding of the official language of the Church, especially in the liturgy and in
correspondence with the Roman Curia . . . As for the celebration of holy mass, a
missal may be produced for the Chinese nation, in which will be printed in literary Chinese all parts of the mass from the commencement to the start of the
canon and from the post-communion to the end of the mass. With regard to the
canon, it must remain in Latin with the exception of those parts that are recited
aloud (Paternoster, Pax Domini and Agnus Dei).

This decision, approved by Pius XII on 10 March 1949, brought the secular
controversy over the Chinese liturgy to an end.[24]

Apart from the privilege granted by Paul V – a temporary one at that –
Rome never gave way on the Latin question; its intransigence dated from
Alexander VII's Bull which, noting the difficulties Latin presented to the
Chinese, had nevertheless asked future priests to read a language they could
not understand. To tell the truth there was nothing so very extraordinary in
this, as the partisans of Latin indicated by pointing out that in Europe itself
– as we shall see – there were plenty of priests who could hardly understand
what they were reading.[25] Advocates of the vernacular could point to the concessions made in the old days to Moravians and the like, raise hopes of
Catholicism conquering China or even the whole Far East, emphasize the
eminent suitability of the literary Chinese adopted for the liturgy which
"would not be the ordinary speech of the people, but the language of the lettered, which is like our Latin here";[26] nothing worked.

Underlying the Roman position throughout the controversy was the fear
that granting a Chinese-language liturgy might lead to a schism; that even if
China did not fall into formal schism, communion with Rome would be
impossible owing to the ignorance of Latin. Any dispensation should therefore be refused; especially as the Chinese, unlike the Indians for example,
were in the words of a supporter of the Latin cause "very gifted and, apart
from the uneducated, continually occupied with study. It follows that young
people called to the priesthood can easily learn Latin, if not perfectly, at least
so as to be able to read it well enough."[27] Which was all that the Bull *Super
cathedram* required. Sometimes other arguments were advanced: during the
deliberations preceding the publication of that text it was recalled that in the
tradition of the Church, Latin alone, with Greek and Hebrew, was a language
of worship; it was emphasized that unity within the faith was accompanied
by liturgical uniformity, that the holy mysteries lost their dignity when celebrated in the vulgar tongue, that Latin, being a dead language, is more stable
than vernaculars and thus particularly suitable for the conservation of sacred
texts; and it was pointed out that if a favour was granted to China it could
not be refused to other countries. But over and above the special qualities
thought to qualify Latin expressly to say sacred things, what really carried the

day was fear of a schism; the celebration of the offices in the vulgar tongue
by heretics was frequently mentioned, and more specifically the fact that this
had been a demand of the Protestants; and at this point – but only at this
point – the Tridentine decree was cited.[28] Certainly the memory of the Reformation was still very much alive in these middle years of the seventeenth
century, and the Roman authorities could hardly fail to be influenced by it;
during the same period a new equation was emerging, one that would become
predominant with the passage of time: the equation of Latin and orthodoxy.

The linguistic question had been resolved in the case of China, a missionary country, by the victory of Latin. The same thing happened in old Europe,
although there the demand for the vernacular was based on very different
pastoral motivations. In France, the standard set by the Council was strictly
observed; the offices were celebrated and the sacraments administered in
Latin.[29] Among other things, this led to the production of Latin hymns of very
high grammatical and literary quality, some of the best written by Jean-Baptiste Santeul, better known today for his role in the famous quarrel over
inscriptions. A poet who deplored the "Latin gibberish" that was being sung
in the churches and the grotesque howlers with which old breviaries were
filled, he produced during the 1670s, at the request of the Archbishop of Paris,
several compositions in the highest order of Christian Latin poetry.[30] Few
voices were raised to deplore the exclusive use of Latin. A proposal that the
vernacular be used, put forward by the Bishop of Oloron in 1682, was entirely
circumstantial, aimed at making the conversion of Protestants easier.[31] Altogether different was the position of the Jansenists, who complained that the
faithful were prevented from joining their prayers and voices with those of
the Church during offices: this was the content of the three proposals by
Quesnel condemned in the Bull *Unigenitus* (1713). But while the Jansenist
Church of Utrecht – which had separated from Rome – never used anything
but the vulgar tongue for the administration of sacraments, in France the
practice was exceptional and caused scandal, in Metz for example, where
orthodox Catholics were shocked when the Jansenist priest Pierre Brayer gave
extreme unction and the last sacrament in French.[32] It was in another
Jansenist-influenced circle, the Parisian parishes of Saint-Médard and Saint-
Etienne-du-Mont, that a place was made – very timidly to tell the truth – for
the vulgar tongue: between 1726 and 1744 Vespers were sung in Latin and
French on alternate Sundays.[33] These are the rare exceptions to be found
under the Ancien Régime in a French Church that remained profoundly
Latin in matters of public worship.

Much the same was true of another large Catholic country, Italy, where
Muratori's thinking and the reforms promoted by Scipione de'Ricci brought
back the monopoly of Latin. Ludovico Antonio Muratori was not only the
editor of monumental collections of historical documents, but a man of letters
deeply involved in the life of his time, who took an active part in all the

debates that agitated the Italian peninsula. As a priest, he paid particular attention to the spiritual lives of laymen and tried to lead them towards a more authentic piety, battling vigorously against the superstitions and false legends that encumbered religious practice. In *Della regolata divozione de'cristiani* (1747), a collection of his thoughts on the subject, he deplored (among other things) the atmosphere that prevailed in churches during mass, with the sacrifice receiving "little respect or at least . . . little attention" from the majority of worshippers, who did not know Latin; in consequence, imitating what had been done in France, he went on to give an explanation of the ceremony and its stages. This, he specified, was intended solely to increase people's devotion, without detracting in any way from the majesty of a ceremony that the Church quite rightly continued to perform in Latin. In a later chapter he returned to the same subject, reporting that in the Tyrol the priest, after reading the gospel at the altar, came into the chancel and read it again in German, made the worshippers recite the *Confiteor*, gave them absolution with the *Misereatur vestri*, then went back to the altar and continued his mass. He noted that in Dalmatia, where mass was said in Latin, on feast days the epistle and gospel would be sung in Slavonian; he mentioned a similar practice in Moravia. The Church had good reasons for celebrating mass in Latin, he went on, before adding with some vigour that it would be no bad thing if priests were to explain the gospel to the faithful in their own language "as they are required to do by the holy canons"; it would appear from this that the pastoral obligation written into the Tridentine decree may not have been universally respected. And Muratori added that priests using the holy books as sources for their sermons were quoting a great deal of Latin as a result, so much that the spiritual nourishment to be derived from preaching was lost to the majority of those present. It seems probable therefore that the role given to Latin in Italian churches exceeded Rome's requirements.[34]

Muratori, even if some of his actions and ideas aroused the suspicion of the *zelanti*, never departed from orthodoxy; but it was a different story with the Archbishop of Prato and Pistoia, Scipione de'Ricci, who openly espoused Jansenism. This doctrine was a source of inspiration for the reforms launched in his diocese and endorsed during the synod he held at Pistoia in 1786. In books intended for priests, and in other publications, a major place was reserved for the vernacular in the makeup of ritual; more importantly, at the second session of the synod it was specified that one of the tasks of this meeting would be to examine whether it would be useful to "administer the sacraments in the vulgar tongue, to make even persons ignorant of Latin enter into the spirit of the Church's prayers". At the fourth session, entirely devoted to the sacraments, liturgy in the context of the eucharist was treated as "an act common to the priest and the people", and strong regret was expressed that it could not be "uttered in the vulgar tongue and aloud"; as second best, the pastoral imperative expressed at Trent was cited, and the

participants were urged to provide the people with books "in which the ordinary of the mass would be in the vulgar tongue, and thus bring the people
to accompany the priest".[35] Local protests and condemnation of the synod by
Rome, then the political developments agitating Tuscany, eventually got the
better of Scipione de'Ricci and put paid to his reforms, including use of the
vulgar tongue in the diocese of Prato and Pistoia.

What happened in Tuscany – and here we should bear in mind the support
that the Grand Duke Peter Leopold had given to de'Ricci – had an echo in
Germany. Under the influence of Josephism efforts were made to reform the
liturgy, to improve it in keeping with the new ideas, give it a community-
based character and render it more comprehensible and edifying. Karl Anton
Winter, a professor at the University of Landshut, produced studies to this
effect as well as drafts of masses and rituals in German. A few years later, in
the context of a more limited *Aufklärung*, J. B. Hirscher, a professor at the University of Tübingen, made some similar proposals: his view was that it was
possible, through the liturgy, to help people to rediscover their Christianity
provided they were given the means "genuinely to take part in the mass of
which they have become the mere audience"; the mass should become an act
"common" to the priest and the faithful. Hirscher, whose reforming zeal led
him to envisage communion in both kinds (bread and wine), public confession and the dropping of celibacy for priests, preached the celebration of mass
in German as one of the essential conditions for the restoration of Catholic
life in his country. His book expounding these ideas was promptly put on the
Index.[36]

In France, a few years earlier, people had become impatient with endless
wishes and proposals, and brought an experimental French liturgy into being
in the setting of the schismatic constitutional Church. First in lists of
complaints, then in statements to Grégoire's survey on dialects, and in
petitions to the Constituent Assembly, there had already been scattered calls
for the introduction of the vernacular, motivated not by any hostility to the
Church but by a concern to deepen the devotion of the faithful (who would
thus cease to behave as dumb "statues" or "parrots" mechanically repeating
words they did not understand).[37] These minority suggestions were going to
be reinforced by a current of support in the lower ranks of the clergy, and in
the hierarchy by the backing of Grégoire, Bishop of Blois, who also saw a
French liturgy as a means of spreading the French language. He was to play
a major role in the first Council of the Gallican Church in 1797, at which he
was chairman of the congregation on liturgy. Among other measures, it was
decreed that "prayers from the pulpit will be delivered in French in all
Catholic churches in France" and that "in the uniform ritual to be decided
for the Gallican Church, administration of sacraments will be in French: the
sacramental formulae will be in Latin". Ponsignon, the deputy bishop of
Versailles, who had been asked to translate the ritual, went somewhat further

than the Council's decision which struck him as a "half-reform" at best: in his *Essai de sacramentaire français–latin* (Draft French–Latin Sacramentary), published in 1799, he had translated the sacramental formulae along with the rest. Although he had Grégoire's support and his own bishop's approval, he encountered strong opposition from most of the other bishops, who responded stonily to his enthusiastic descriptions of the marvellous effect on the congregation of the many baptisms he had conducted in French. What they saw was a dangerous innovation that went beyond what the council had decreed, or even (as the Bishop of Dax put it) the "first step towards the destruction of religion, the first step towards general vandalism". Certain prelates had even launched vigorous protests immediately after the Council; the Bishop of Rennes had reiterated the arguments that adoption of the vernacular would break liturgical unity, that there would be many translations carrying many risks of error, that the abandonment of Latin would carry a danger of schism as many historical examples showed. Behind the bishops' opposition there also lay a fear that adoption of the vernacular might widen the rift between the Gallican clergy and those who had stayed loyal to Rome. The provincial synods of 1800 either passed over the linguistic question in silence or pronounced in favour of tradition and therefore of Latin. In practice, moreover, there were few actual attempts to introduce French, and enthusiasm soon waned even at Versailles where the movement had begun. The second national Council which met in 1801 buried the question.[38] Although even the first Council had only (as Ponsignon complained) taken half-measures, and there had never been any real question of a liturgy in French, this setback could only strengthen the cause of Latin.

The Tridentine decree thus suffered hardly any exceptions; nor did the way it worked in reality lead towards any degree of mitigation. The Council had insisted on the intellectual preparation of the clergy and thus on its training in Latin: the results in reality were well short of the recommendations. In France the level was particularly low at the beginning of the seventeenth century: during a tour he made in 1613–14, the Archbishop of Lyon found parish priests who could hardly read at all, understood very little Latin and did not know the formula for absolution or administering other sacraments. One curate, at the parish of Gorrod, "reads very badly and understands none of what he reads, could not even read distinctly the sacramental words for the blessing of the wine eucharist even after being made to repeat them two or three times". In 1668, the teachers of the Mission congregation were invited to assess Latin teaching by questioning the seminarians and making them speak a lot of Latin "so that [those] who do not know that language practise and improve in it"; the explanation of difficulties, the second part of the lesson, should be conducted "in Latin and in French to help those who do not have sufficient understanding of Latin". The standard would have improved in the eighteenth century with the generalization of an entry examination for seminaries. In places like Brittany, however, the requirements were not very exacting: in the diocese of Nantes, a ruling of April 1753 specified only that future priests should have "started Latin" and "shown some disposition to persist with it"; in 1771 the Bishop of Dol, himself a good Latinist, only required some "principles of Latin". Modest as they were, these conditions still represented a break with the earlier practice of accepting low standards in the hope that there would be some catching up later on. A far from isolated case in point is that of the unhappy acolyte of 1711, Mathurin Elie, who in 1715 was a sub-deaconate postulant for the sixth time: "he does not understand Latin at all and knows absolutely no philosophy", his examiners commented before giving him one more year on the understanding that he would be "exercised in everything". The fact is that apart from an elite educated in establishments of high intellectual calibre, the lower clergy seem to have had very modest knowledge of Latin.[39]

The Revolution did not improve matters, and may even have made them worse. Priests were still being trained in Latin, very much so: in a well-known passage of Stendhal's novel *Le rouge et le noir* its central character Julien Sorel is asked by the head of the seminary on his arrival: "*Loquerisne linguam latinam?*" ("Do you speak Latin?"). Young Sorel is able to answer in the affirmative and converse thereafter largely in Latin,[40] but some of his colleagues would have been severely embarrassed. The extreme case of the Curé of Ars comes immediately to mind: he was noted for the weakness of his school performance despite great application, and was incapable of mastering Latin grammar or easily translating rather simple passages. One witness at the large seminary in Lyon commented that "the result of his studies was nil, because he did not have sufficient understanding of Latin"; another noted that "He understood Latin badly and spoke it worse still". He was not alone: he had so many fellow-sufferers at the small Verrières seminary that eventually a special dunces' group of seven pupils had to be taught in French. It was piety rather than learning that earned Jean-Marie Baptiste Vianney his sub-deaconship.[41] Historical circumstances also lent him a hand. The "frightful famine of priests" after the Revolution – by 1813 only 31,870 secular clergy remained of the population of 60,000-odd parish priests and curates in 1789 – led to greater indulgence in assessing the intellectual qualities of seminarians; and until the 1860s, moreover, the aim was to produce saints rather than sages. So despite the efforts of some ecclesiastics to raise the intellectual level, the product remained for some time uneven to say the least. But poor knowledge of Latin, still the key to the whole training, was often deplored. The superior of the large seminary at Quimper grumbled that his students' ignorance of both Latin and French was going to "reduce their theology professor to giving his classes in Breton". The Archbishop of Bourges referred waggishly to his seminarians as "Palatins" (pronounced in French *pas-latin* = no Latin); thirty years later, in 1844, several students were judged "very weak in Latin" and considered for expulsion; similar situations were recorded at Lyon and Cambrai. One of the teachers at Bourges in this period gave his classes in Latin, but switched to French when he wanted to emphasize an argument, a practice denoting mediocre student Latin that was not unknown elsewhere. Even in the second quarter of the century, when some improvement was achieved, the standard of Latin was still the subject of complaint.[42] So it is hardly surprising that at a higher level, during discussions in 1856 between Paris and Rome on the future of faculties of theology, the Minister of Public Instruction should have shown some caution on the use of Latin in class, remarking that "The literary education of the clergy is still too weak for this rule to be established in absolute fashion"; an Italian source stated more baldly that "of all the professors, there is not a single one here in Paris who could teach in Latin".[43]

Judging by the calls for the use of the vernacular in training priests, the situation was little better in other countries. In 1896 the Rev. John Talbot Smith criticized the practice in force in American seminaries of teaching entirely in Latin: the students did not understand much and the Latin used was of deeply mediocre quality; the priests who left these institutions were ill-prepared for the real needs of their ministry; what was more, their English did not improve but actually deteriorated during the twelve years they spent speaking and listening to bad Latin which, as used in the seminaries, was "a solid obstacle to true culture and proper training". The prelate consequently hoped that the leading place would be given to English and that Latin, which ought to be maintained, would be relegated to second place.[44] Similar ideas were expressed a few years later by Walter McDonald, a teacher at St Patrick's College, Maynooth, which trained the Irish clergy. He too referred to the weakness of Latin among the future priests, and denounced it as a bottleneck, obstructing their progress in other disciplines, starting with theology. While not denying the need to maintain a "bond of union", he questioned whether that bond was still Latin; at present the Church was threatened not with schism but "excessive centralization". In fact the need for a common language as a "bond of union" was less acute than it had been, while the evils resulting from the exclusive use of a dead language were increasing by the day, to the great detriment of the quality of studies and the vitality of theology itself. In consequence, McDonald came out squarely in favour of using the vernacular for teaching in seminaries.[45] The proposals made by these two prelates were not just without effect; they were violently criticized.

The mediocre performance of the clergy and the decline of Latin studies throughout the West in no way inflected the position of the Holy See which, on the contrary, took measures to remedy the situation. In an "Encyclical Letter to the Archbishops, Bishops and Clergy of France", Pope Leo XIII in 1899 responded to the reduction of Latin studies in state establishments by urging the small seminaries to ignore "these innovations inspired by utilitarian concerns" and to "maintain the trust".[46] In an apostolic letter of 1922, Pius XI reiterated the bond of unity that Latin constituted for the Catholic Church and called for the way the language was studied in seminaries to be developed and strengthened; he deplored the priests' lack of interest in Latin literature and their neglect of the Fathers and Doctors of the Church in favour of recent authors with their seductive but dangerous novelties, when only knowledge of Latin, opening the way to further reading, could protect against the many errors these modern writings contained.[47] In 1924 he addressed the same warning to the religious orders.[48] In the same year he founded, within the Gregorian University, a Higher Pontifical Latin Institute, intended specifically to give priests a good mastery of the Latin language and help them acquire a Ciceronian style; he mentioned, in passing, the earlier measures taken by Leo XIII and himself in their constant concern to strengthen Latin in the seminaries.[49] Again in 1951 the Pope, this time Pius XII, addressing teachers of the Carmelite order, expressed regret that Latin, "the glory of priests", now had only "rare and timid practitioners"; and he exhorted them to develop its study. There should not be a priest anywhere who could not read and speak Latin easily and fluently, and he hoped that the Carmelites would even produce good stylists.[50] A glance at Joseph Rogé's book on "the simple priest" indicates pretty clearly that the pontifical rec- ommendations had little effect in France. On the training given in large sem- inaries, this author remarks that the culture imparted was superficial and its emphasis less on intellect than piety. He also felt — and here we might almost be listening to Talbot Smith or McDonald — that "one of the reasons for this is the use of the Latin language, to the extent that this practice is main- tained," for it "hampers and impoverishes the process of thought, even when it is a Latin based on French and even though the small seminaries are making a particular effort to improve the standard of Latin".[51]

Apologia for Latin as language of the Church

Although the French clergy was notably feeble at Latin in the early nineteenth century, an apologia for Latin was developing at that time, one that has become indissociably linked with the names of Joseph de Maistre and Dom Guéranger. Before they formulated their ardent demonstrations, however, there had appeared a literary text in which theology ceded its place to poetics and reason to emotion: Chateaubriand's *Génie du christianisme*, published in 1802. The author of this immensely successful work raised the question of crit- icisms of the Catholic religion for "using in its songs and prayers a language unknown to the people". His answer deserves to be quoted in its entirety.

> We believe that an ancient and mysterious language, a language that has ceased to change over the centuries, is pretty well suited to the worship of the eternal,

incomprehensible and immutable being. And since consciousness of our sufferings forces us to raise a suppliant voice to the King of Kings, is it not natural for us to speak to Him in the finest idiom on earth, the one used by grovelling nations to address their prayers to the Caesars?

After these literary and historical arguments establishing the elevated dignity of Latin and its special suitability for conserving the sacred trust, Chateaubriand went on to underline the emotional power of a language made all the more mysterious, for most people, by being unknown to them:

> Moreover, and this is something remarkable, orisons in Latin seem to redouble the religious feeling of the crowd. Might this not be a natural effect of our penchant for secrecy? In the tumult of his thoughts and the miseries that beset his life, man believes that by pronouncing words that are unfamiliar or unknown he is asking for things that he needs but of which he is unaware; the charm of the prayer lies in its vagueness, for his troubled soul, which hardly knows what it desires, loves to form wishes as mysterious as its needs.[52]

These arguments are also to be found in *Du Pape* ("Concerning the Pope"), a book published by Joseph de Maistre in 1819, defending the absolute power of the Pontiff against any autonomist tendencies on the part of national Churches, and upholding papal infallibility against any interference by the Council. With this single head of the Church there went a unique language, the object of his "digression on the Latin tongue". Like Chateaubriand, he starts with criticism of the Roman Church, made in this case by the illustrious Protestant objector Jacques Necker, for "using a dead language"; but his reply is very different. It begins with the universality of the Latin language, in scale with a universal Church. "From pole to pole", no Catholic is ever a foreigner anywhere, since he can hear the same offices and "mingle his voice with those of his brothers"; this common language helps to form "a mysterious bond of immense strength". De Maistre contrasts the resulting "brotherhood" with the dire consequences that always followed in the past when a pope authorized some special version of the liturgy. Latin had been the cement of unity and the best rampart against schism. And apart from being a bastion and proof of orthodoxy, Latin could call on cultural arguments of a high order in its support. "Nothing is equal in dignity to the Latin language," notes de Maistre, citing its perfection, its majesty and its illustrious history as the language of conquerors, from the emperors of Antiquity to the missionaries of modern Rome. Its uncommon destiny had made Latin the "language of civilization". A glance at the atlas proved it: "Just trace the line where this universal language falls silent: there are the outer limits of European civilization and fraternity; beyond it you find only the human kinship which happily is to be found everywhere". The conclusion was easy to draw: "the European sign is Latin". At this point, after recalling the "glittering privileges" that belonged to Latin and qualified it beyond argument to be the language of the Church, Maistre returns to the initial "vulgar" objection to Latin as "a language unknown to the people", sweeping it aside in terms at least as polemical as they are theological:

> The Protestants have repeated this objection a great deal, without reflecting that the part of worship we hold in common with them is in the vulgar tongue in both cases. For them, the main part and, so to speak, the soul of worship is the sermon, which by its very nature is delivered in the vulgar tongue in all religions. For us, the sacrifice is the real worship; all the rest is subsidiary: and what does it matter to the people whether the sacramental words, which are only pronounced in an undertone, are recited in French, German etc., or in Hebrew for that matter?

The unknown language objection is just as invalid for the office and scripture: Latin after all was not "Chinese or Sanskrit"; an "educated" man could "learn it in a few months" or, failing that, read the many translations and paraphrases available; everything was done in the ceremonies to ensure that "he is always in perfect harmony with the priest, and if he is distracted it is his own fault. As for the populace, in the true sense," de Maistre goes on, "if it does not hear the words, so much the better. Respect gains and intelligence loses nothing. He who understands nothing understands more than he who understands badly." Finally, after referring to the serious inadequacy of "a changing language" for the conservation and transmission of the sacred text of "an immutable religion" in all its purity, Maistre concludes with the solemn warning: "In every way imaginable, religion ought to be kept out of the human domain".[53] This plea brought little that was new: it owes more to the number of its arguments than to the intrinsic force of many of them or its overall organization; and it draws mainly on historical and cultural themes to establish Latin as the language of the Church, reducing the theological argument to the by now classic associations between heresy and vernacular, orthodoxy and Latin.

Dom Prosper Guéranger campaigned in a similar spirit of struggle against rationalism and for a return to Church tradition. Placing the liturgy at the heart of his concerns, he denounced the neo-Gallican liturgies being used in his day, which he saw as marked by the French errors of Jansenism and Gallicanism, and argued that their very multiplicity made them harmful to the unity of a Church centred in Rome. Hence the campaign he waged, with complete success, to get the integral Roman liturgy adopted in France. In parallel, he embarked on a large number of editorial projects to palliate the lack of religious training he observed in his contemporaries; but he only managed to complete three volumes of his *Institutions liturgiques* (1840–51). It is in chapter III (entitled "De la langue des livres liturgiques") of the last of these that he states his position on the language of the Church. The use of a liturgical language distinct from the vulgar tongue is a practice common to many Churches and in the Christian Church, in particular, a very ancient one, dating from the earliest times. The faith was not announced in all languages but in those said to be from the notice on the cross: Hebrew, Greek, Latin. While there have certainly been versions of scripture in various Oriental languages – Coptic, Amharic, Armenian, Persian and so on – these by no means represent all the languages of all the Oriental peoples; the same is true of the West; and in any case Rome has seldom favoured these versions and has always treated them with suspicion. "The privilege of sacred languages," valid for scripture, is equally so for the liturgy which is "largely composed of passages from holy scripture"; in fact it is all the more essential since, while scripture is subjected to "private" reading, the liturgy, by contrast, is a "solemn public reading"; in consequence it "should be grave and mysterious like the divine oracles; it should not be subject to variations of language, to prevent it from becoming trivial and common". Guéranger went on to give a series of definitions of the liturgy, underlining the absolute necessity of non-vernacular languages. The liturgy is a collection of formulae that accompany the celebration of holy sacrifice and the administration of sacraments, "all things that help to constitute the specific and incommunicable ministry of priests"; it is therefore more exclusively reserved for priests than scripture and should not be recited in the common tongue, if only to protect it from the "indiscreet and dangerous interpretations of the multitude". Liturgy is "the principal instrument of tradition" whose formulae are necessarily ancient and inviolable; living languages which change constantly are inappropriate for preserving these in all their integrity, unlike a fixed, stable dead language. Liturgy is "the bond associating Christian peoples": this definition postulates a single liturgical language, which also strengthens fraternity between Christian peoples and maintains "the idea of a single centre". "While it is important," Guéranger went on, "for the language of the liturgical books to be fixed and inviolable, and not to be purely national, it is also in its nature to be mysterious: so it ought not to be vulgar". Just as holy scripture is "a mysterious book" and will always remain so for "the vulgar" in spite of translations, so it is for the liturgy "in which the mysteries simply announced in the holy books are operated": hence the undertone in which the prayers of the canon are recited and the use of a non-vernacular language for the liturgy. At this point Guéranger counters the unknown-language objection by arguing, on the one hand, that "the simple . . . would not always understand the holy formulae even if they were delivered to their ears in the vulgar tongue", and underlining, on the other hand, the "marvellous effects" produced in pious hearts by the words of holy scripture. To the pious, he adds, "the liturgy, in any language, is always luminous, and the Amen that rises from their chests is always in full harmony with the prayers

the priest is reciting at the altar". Nevertheless the Church did not wish to
leave the faithful bereft of instruction, as it had clearly shown at Trent. While
it was forbidden for the priest at the altar, "in those fearful moments when
he is placed between heaven and earth", to use the vulgar tongue, he had a
duty, when in the pulpit, to make use of it to instruct the people, thus helping
to "illuminate their faith" and "put them in communication with God".
Guéranger ends by countering rationalist and Protestant arguments with the
defence of sacred languages offered by Chateaubriand and Maistre in the
name of sentiment, and shows in passing how the Church had applied the
principle of sacred languages in the liturgy and how Latin had been imposed.
He concludes by asserting that it was "the sympathy of heretics for the vernacular in the divine service" that had brought the Council of Trent to "pronounce a dogmatic definition in this matter which at first glance seemed only
to affect discipline".[54] A reading of Guéranger's "long chapter" on the question of liturgical languages (and therefore Latin) in the Catholic Church
impresses, once again, more by the mass of the arguments advanced than by
their originality. However, the interpretation of the Tridentine decree that he
gives in conclusion is striking for its baldness: the fathers had not taken a disciplinary measure but had given a "dogmatic definition" establishing Latin as
a sacred language and, *ipso facto*, excluding vernaculars from the liturgy of the
mass. In common opinion this became an absolute fact.[55]

A large part of this argument in support of Latin can be found in much
more concentrated form in two articles – "Lazio" (Latium) and "Lingua"
(Language) – in Gaetano Moroni's very official summary of knowledge on the
Christian world, *Dizionario di erudizione storico-ecclesiastica*. He reiterates the traditional arguments that use of Latin is an ancient, constant and reasoned
practice; then more specifically, in the second entry, refutes the Protestant
objection to worship conducted in a language unknown to the people, first
by recalling the Church's solicitude for the faithful as stated in the Tridentine
decree, then by asserting a real "participation" by the people: when "it unites
its voice with the priest's, in a language with which it is not familiar," the congregation "knows, at least in a confused way, the meaning of the prayers it is
reciting, and that is sufficient to feed its faith and its piety". He concludes
with this brief theological reminder: "It is very important to note that in
public prayer, it is the Church itself that offers adoration and supplication to
God in the name of the people, so that it is necessary only to be present and
concur with its intent to offer jointly with it an excellent prayer, even without
knowing the words".[56] The arguments stated by Moroni had certainly been
reformulated; but he presented them as forming part of a deliberate plan followed by the Church almost since its origin, to establish an order that would
be immutable for ever.

The answer that Rome gave in 1858 to the enquiry by France on the
possibility of teaching theology in the vernacular is enlightening in this area.

The request by the French authorities was motivated by the reality of a poor standard of Latin among young priests; the response was that nothing could justify "the creation of doctors of theology who were not in a fit state to understand the Latin of their offices"; and (not without good sense) it added that "fluency in languages is only acquired through practice . . . so dispensing with it is not going to produce any improvement". But that was not the core of the answer. "The unshakeable repugnance of the Holy See against consenting to this proposal" was based on a much more serious reason: "even the temporary substitution of the national language for Latin in theological teaching would only be opening the door to schism, a step taken on its responsibility down the deadly slope towards nationalization of worship". The same arguments used for clerics and theology would soon be recycled, and with more justification, for the people and the liturgy; if the first had been agreed to, it would have been difficult to refuse the second. The Holy See responded to the looming peril in the negative.[57] And the French ambassador in Rome, who passed on the reply, appended this comment: "Rome is treating this question as a dogmatic issue, in the sense that it considers use of the Latin language to be closely linked with conservation of dogma".

Until the Vatican II Council, the official position remained unchanged and the same arguments were repeated. They are stated in the *Dictionnaire de théologie catholique* (1925), in a long article on liturgical languages which deals with the "attitudes and thought of the Church of Rome" on the subject. Broadly based on the ideas of Dom Guéranger, whom it quotes several times, it contains a detailed exposé of the movements in favour of the vernacular that had appeared over the centuries, followed by an analysis of the Church's position. The near-exclusive use of Latin and the rarity of concessions on this matter showed that Rome based its position on "reasons that may be assumed *a priori* to be very serious"; however, they were not specified in any official document. At the Council of Trent, the article's author continues, Rome had stated its wishes in the matter, no more. So it was necessary to compensate for this silence. One of the first reasons would have been fidelity to tradition: the wish to pray "as our fathers prayed, using the same words, the same rituals, the same language". This was an expression of unchanging belief across the centuries, and with it a proof of the "fixed nature of the Church's faith". Any change was of extreme consequence. In practice, to make itself accessible to the people, the Church would not just have to modify its language but also write a new text in keeping with current attitudes; such a break with tradition would be the start of "a series of variations that would never stop". The second reason for keeping Latin stemmed from a concern for unity. Latin was on the appropriate scale for the Catholic Church, both being universal. Over and above the distance separating men from one another, it was the "striking symbol of unity of faith that rules minds, a symbol and in some sense a support, since prayer in its fashion is a form of teaching". It was also the bond that united the faithful dispersed across the world to their centre, in other words the "symbol . . . of the social unity that makes the entire Church a single body with Rome at its head". Introducing the vulgar tongue would therefore have baleful consequences, and the history of the Church demonstrated that abandoning Latin had "resulted, through the working of some unknown law, in the complete separation from Rome of most of the Churches which had been given the concession". These, for the writer of the article, were arguments strong enough "to justify the Church's position and show that it is not about to set aside its traditional language: the interests involved are too many and too serious".[58]

Where the liturgy was concerned, concessions were in any case rare and very limited, even though they were a way of showing that Rome's position was less intransigent than its adversaries claimed. In 1920, for example, Benedict XV allowed the "Czecho-Slovaks", recently united in a single state, to use the vulgar tongue in ceremonies under certain circumstances which were very tightly defined; but this permission was not promulgated in any way in the *Acta Apostolicae sedis*.[59]

The arguments we have been examining in the form advanced by men of the cloth were taken up and stated by the faithful in their own fashion. A collection of examples emerges from a survey on the use of Latin and the vulgar tongue in the liturgy conducted by the periodical *Témoignage chrétien* in the autumn of 1946. Readers had been invited to make their feelings known, and the 200-odd replies were said to represent "the Christian people in all its motley diversity". Most of those favouring Latin said that it was of great help in surrounding the liturgy with the necessary atmosphere of mystery. To many it appeared essential as the visible manifestation of the unity of the Church: through it, unity of worship and thus unity of belief had been conserved; numerous examples were given of international religious events in which people from everywhere pray together in the same language, of travellers far from home discovering a familiar world during Latin mass. Several respondents insisted that Latin represents continuity over time, sometimes adding a tweak or two to strict historical truth. "Latin," wrote one of them, "is the language . . . that takes us back to the origins of our holy religion, that puts us in communion with the thought and works of the Apostles and Fathers who codified our faith and creed into definitive texts". Some stressed the advantages of a dead language for preserving the purity of the faith and the integrity of its sacramental ritual. Then, with a wealth of historical examples, they recalled that heresy, schism and use of the vernacular very often went hand in hand. These pro-Latin responses, as people were quick to point out, revealed an extremely dubious level of liturgical culture; some were even (in the words of Mgr Martimort, who wrote a commentary) "theologically unacceptable". They were nevertheless the views of sincere Christians, sufficiently motivated to put pen to paper and give enthusiastic expression to their opinions.[60] It is not unreasonable to assume that the great mass of believers, unable to summarize their position so clearly or aspire to such "speculations", would still have seen the equation between the Church and Latin as something intrinsic to both: a lesson in the obvious dictated by custom, practice and tradition.

On the eve of the Vatican II Council, Latin still retained a strong position in the Catholic Church, although the exhortations of various pontiffs indicate that signs of disaffection had been discerned in the clergy. Concessions to the vernacular had been extremely rare and the arguments for Latin as the language of liturgy had been comprehensively internalized by the faithful.

3 The Turning Point of Vatican II

Pastoral work and the vernacular

New needs had already become apparent, however. The liturgical movement that developed in the twentieth century was marked by pastoral concerns; there was now a wish to make the whole congregation participate actively in the liturgy, to give all the faithful access to its spiritual riches. This led naturally to the linguistic question being raised. "It is certain," wrote Dom Bott, "that the barrier of Latin has helped keep the Christian people from active participation in the holy mysteries". In France, the Centre de Pastorale Liturgique, founded in 1943, played a particularly active role in the matter, notably by publishing a number of studies on the language question, and in 1947 devoted an issue of its review *Maison-Dieu* to "liturgical languages and translations".[61] Dom Travers, who wrote the introduction to this number, saw the problem as immense, touching on theology, history, linguistics, sociology and culture, going beyond the question of doctrine to lodge in "the drama of civilization" itself; and he invited readers to let themselves be guided by "the light of the Church's supernatural prudence" and rely on "the hierarchy, [the Church's] authorized interpreter". Even so, any solution would have to be preceded by some sort of basic liturgical and Biblical training, or disappointments would soon follow: certain groups, for example, "after adopting the French text of the psalms for singing Compline, . . . soon reverted to the Latin liturgical text, the French version of the sacred poems having proved in practice to be even more tedious and just as hermetic". On the theoretical level, Dom Travers noted that from the legal point of view there was no problem with liturgical language: "It will always be preferable for the Church to proclaim and express the word of God in the language of the ethnic and linguistic community it is addressing". In practice, it had gone differently, and one could not ignore certain background conditions including "the cultural situation" of the faithful: they were no longer an illiterate mass, but "a people that has been to school" and "wants to understand".[62]

The same survey contained an article that examined the problem in the light of experience in the Germanic countries, where the translation of liturgical texts was further advanced than in France. Its author, Felix Messerschmid, pointed out that words are used in a wide variety of ways in different parts of the liturgy and perform very different functions. Thus the *Credo*, a solemn profession of faith, implied an active participation by the community that was only possible if the words were in people's mother-tongue. But the canon was a completely different matter, being the very core of the eucharistic liturgy containing "the sacramental and efficacious word"; this last should be said in a language that was sheltered from constant fluctuations of meaning, not necessarily Latin, but an archaic language; which is what Latin was in the Latin ritual. After explaining the mystery of the eucharist ("a mystery that only faith can grasp"), the author recalled that the community played a part in it only indirectly, through the intermediary of the priest, and that its participation was "independent of any comprehension in the natural sense of the word". Latin was thus essential for this part of the liturgy: it proved that "the centre of eucharistic worship is totally independent both of the subjective character of the individual and of the inaccessible nature, or even the more or less perfectly executed form, of the act". In this context it also worked as a "guarantee against any tendency to the gradual falsification of this central point of the mass".[63]

The decline of Latin was thus marked very concretely in France by the publication of liturgical texts for the faithful, bilingual missals and trials, during the 1950s, of a new liturgy with some readings and prayers accompanied by vernacular versions, and so on. This explains why shortly before the Council, the bishops of twenty-four French dioceses, in answer to an enquiry from a preliminary pontifical commission, expressed the hope that use of the vulgar tongue would be extended in the liturgy.[64]

Nevertheless, translations and paraphrases still seemed "a facile solution" to some people who, from the same motive of enabling the congregation to take part, suggested a basic training in the Latin of the mass. One of them, the grammarian Anne-Marie Malingrey, published in 1951 a sort of primer for people who knew no Latin but "are desirous of understanding the Church's prayer in order to associate themselves with it consciously". At present the Christian

> hears [the language] spoken and even sung every Sunday. If he is a good parishioner he speaks it and sings it too, but without understanding much of it.
> However, the undeniable advance of liturgical life has left many of the faithful with a desire to give their prayer the accent of sincerity that only comes from understanding the text.[65]

This method had been the basis for adult classes in liturgical Latin held once a week at the Institut Grégorien in Paris, as well as a course for "Christian children aged seven to eleven".[66] And the survey by *Temoignage chrétien* shows that Latin still had enthusiastic advocates, with a number of correspondents on both sides of the argument favouring mixed solutions, using both Latin and French (combined in a wide variety of different ways) for liturgical ceremonies, the mass in particular.[67]

The Constitution Sacrosanctum Concilium

The linguistic question brought into prominence by the liturgical movement was the subject of impassioned debate during the Council.[68] A preparatory liturgical commission had been set up, containing a sub-commission *de lingua*. Represented to the Curia as anti-Latin, this was dissolved after a few months and its subject matter distributed among other sub-commissions; this explains why, in the constitution on liturgy, the decisions concerning language are not assembled in a chapter of their own, but dispersed across a number of articles in several chapters. When the Council started work opinions were strongly divergent; there was real fear of ending up with a modernist liturgy, and any attempt to shift Latin was interpreted as a step in the direction of a new schism. Supporters of the vernacular were considered "innovators". The defenders of tradition advanced two main arguments: the existing form of the liturgy expressed unity of faith, and it also expressed the mystery of faith. Neither of these arguments prevailed. The Eastern bishops asserted that the unity of the Church is not expressed even symbolically by Latin, and the Patriarch Maximos reminded the council that in the East "every language is liturgical".[69] To the non-Western prelates, Latin presented specific problems in itself. The Bishop of Krishnagar, India, said that "the use of Latin, which is inaccessible to the peoples of Asia, suggests to them a magical mentality"; Japanese and African bishops, in whose territories not even the educated faithful understood a word of Latin, wondered aloud whether it was permissible to sacrifice the spiritual progress of a people to an external idea of unity.[70] This question brought the Council back to the pastoral argument at the heart of the case put by partisans of the vulgar tongue: instead of Latin, which was just as incomprehensible to many faithful in the West, and which some saw as alienating people from religion, they favoured vernacular languages as a way of associating the people closely with liturgical celebration and encouraging active and aware participation. In the end the need to evangelize peoples, and therefore introduce everyday language, carried the day over fear of schism and the exclusive retention of the language of worship. But the arguments had been bitter, the opposition strong, and the intervention of Pope John XXIII on the side of Latin was not without influence on the Council.

On 22 February 1962, on the tomb of St Peter, the pontiff signed the apostolic constitution *Veterum sapientia*; the pomp surrounding the ceremony, its
location, the nature of the act itself, were eloquently expressive of a solemn
wish to maintain tradition. Since the wisdom of the Ancients represented a
dawning of the evangelical truth Christ was to bring to the world, it behoved
the Church to venerate these monuments of wisdom and particularly Greek
and Latin which are "like the golden cloak of its own wisdom". The Church
had accepted for the liturgy and scripture other "venerable tongues", at one
time widespread in the East and some still in current use. However, Latin had
been necessary for the diffusion of Christianity in the West. "It is not without
the intervention of Divine Providence," the Pontiff explained, "that this language, which for many centuries had united a vast federation of peoples
under the authority of the Roman Empire, became the language specific to
the apostolic See, and that, handed down to posterity, it became a bond of
unity between the Christian peoples of Europe." Latin had in fact every qualification to be the international language of communication inside the
Church: on the one hand, it was not the particular privilege of any nation;
on the other, it was imprinted with a nobility of style perfectly suited to the
matters it would have to deal with. It also possessed qualities of universality,
unchangingness and majesty in scale with its religious function. The Pontiff
added – and here there is a slight feeling of scraping the bottom of the barrel
– a reminder of the formative value of Latin on "the tender minds of adolescents". Like his predecessors, then, he was preaching the use of Latin, and
his answer to the controversies then surrounding it was to enshrine in "this
solemn document" not just his wishes in the matter, but measures to ensure
that "the ancient and uninterrupted use of Latin be maintained and restored
wherever it has fallen into virtual disuse". He insisted strongly on compulsory
Latin for the training of priests and teaching of the main sacred disciplines;
and finally, he envisaged the foundation of a "Latin language academy"
which would work to enrich "the living language of the Church" with specific and appropriate new words; this academy would supervise schools
charged with educating "in a more perfect knowledge of Latin, and its use in
an appropriate and elegant style", future professors for the seminaries and
bureaucrats to staff the Church's administrations.[71]

The Council's debates on liturgy took up fifteen general congregations
between 22 October and 13 November 1962. Of the prelates who spoke on
the issue, the remarks of Cardinal Montini, Archbishop of Milan and later
Pope Paul VI, were particularly noticed.

The use of the ancient and ancestral language, meaning the Latin language in
the Latin Church [he declared], must remain firm and unchangeable in those
parts of ritual that are sacramental and sacerdotal, in the specific and real sense
of the words. That is necessary for conserving the religious unity of the mystic

body in prayer and for the correct expression of sacred texts. But where the people are concerned, all difficulties of comprehension should be eliminated from the didactic parts of the holy liturgy to enable the faithful to offer their prayers to God in intelligible words.

And after recalling St Paul's teaching that "he who prays in a Church should understand what his lips pronounce", he defined liturgy as "the prayer of the Christian community"; then continued:

If we desire that this community should not desert the churches, that it should come to them willingly, to be trained in an internal spiritual life and in the worthy expression of its faith, then we must prudently but without delay or hesitation remove the obstacle of a language that is incomprehensible, or at best accessible to a few only, and that does not encourage our people to worship but on the contrary sends them away.

In support of this position he quoted St Augustine: "It is better to be blamed by philologists than not to be understood by the people".[72]

The Constitution *Sacrosanctum Concilium* was approved by 2,147 votes, against four, and promulgated by the Pope on 4 December 1963. The articles dealing with the linguistic question (principally 36 and 53) broadly reproduced the ideas put forward by Cardinal Montini, and in general expressed the pastoral orientation of the liturgical reform, the wish to encourage active participation by the faithful to the maximum. Article 36 stipulated:

1. The use of the Latin language, except with specific permission, will be retained in the Latin ritual. 2. Nevertheless, whether in the mass, the administration of sacraments or other parts of the liturgy, use of the language of the country can often be very useful to the people: it may therefore be given a wider role, especially in readings and Monitions, in a number of prayers and in chants.[73]

Thus, the Church did not renounce Latin – it is still permitted for any Catholic priest to celebrate mass in the language, provided the Latin used is that of the new *ordo missae* which in 1969 replaced the mass of St Pius V – but did admit vernaculars to the liturgy, where they made further advances. For the first two years after the Council the canon stayed in Latin, but experience soon showed that a celebration half in Latin and half in the vernacular was awkward; and the vernacular prevailed. Latin was retained as the language of the prototype editions of new liturgical books which, from 1964, were prepared under the supervision of an international commission, the *Concilium*; their translations into the different languages were to be approved by episcopal conferences, with confirmation from the authorities in Rome. In their origins as well as their effects, the Council's decisions were aptly called "a turning point (not theological, but practical)"[74] in the life of the Church.

Resistance and retreat

The reform that was progressively put in place was generally well received in the Catholic world, if France is taken as an example.[75] The faithful had been prepared for it to some extent by the development of the liturgical movement, and a traditional obedience reflex did the rest. The change was painful for some people, however; and of the elements that were dropped from Church practice Latin was probably the one that aroused the strongest reservations and the greatest regret, so strongly did many of the faithful identify the mass with Latin.[76] Moreover, the "local substitutes" on offer were by no means always of the best quality, and a lot of adults, even those who favoured French liturgy, complained that the ceremonies had been better – more elegant and convincing – in Latin. Some did not stop at grumbling, but organized in the name of tradition. The organization *Una Voce* was formed in Paris in 1964 "for the safeguard of Latin, Gregorian chant and sacred polyphony in the public prayer of the Church". Similar organizations were set up in several countries, and in 1966 formed an international federation. The members of *Una voce* were making it clear that the Council might have introduced vernaculars into the liturgy, but had certainly not suppressed Latin; and they could produce a number of texts originating from the Pontiff himself, the Roman congregations and other high Church authorities, that broadly agreed with them. They consequently asked, as an absolute minimum, for a certain number of spoken or sung Latin masses to be maintained everywhere, on weekdays as well as Sundays.[77] Latin became a war-horse for both progressives and traditionalists, but for the latter group it was part of a deeper desire to keep the Church as it had always been. In the accusations of "schism, heresy and scandal" that he hurled at Paul VI, Abbé Georges of Nantes wrote:

> You have broken secular tradition by changing languages. From being mysterious and sacred, it has become what you hoped would be intelligible and profane. Quoting St Paul, mistakenly as usual, you put the Church of all the ages in the wrong by taking the other view and denouncing its immutable law. Is that not schism?[78]

Only a minority of believers followed Mgr Lefebvre into his break with Rome; shortly before the schism, however, 27 per cent of practising Catholics approved of it, most often for psychological reasons. Although theologians like Fr Congar pointed out forcefully that Latin was not a problem from the viewpoint of dogma, and that the tradition invoked by Mgr Lefebvre and his supporters was in fact only a historical period, "the one that was sanctioned at Trent", this demonstration was unlikely to mean much to the large proportion of faithful whose theological and liturgical culture was limited. In any case, many French Catholics believed, in effect, that "Mgr Lefebvre wants to say mass in Latin and Paul VI won't let him".[79] Fr Congar was close to the truth when he wrote of the "enormous coefficient of irrational opposition to all novelty" animating Lefebvre's sympathizers.[80] The weight of ingrained habit, and the simplistic but sincere convictions of people who felt they "had not praised God properly by reciting these hollow formulae in everyday language",[81] seem to have played an important role.

In Italy, practical application of the liturgical constitution was attacked by insistent reference to the terms of the document itself. Thus Cardinal Antonio Bacci, a former Vatican secretary whose responsibilities had included "Latin letters and briefings to princes", fiercely denounced "the total and exclusive use of the vulgar tongue" which "not only [went] against the Council, but [was] also the cause of intense spiritual suffering for a large part of the people". He feared that Latin might "end by being totally banned, like a mangy dog, from the holy rites", and hoped that some Latin masses would continue to be celebrated.[82]

In Britain, where the vernacular liturgy was introduced in 1964, the bishops acted in voluntarist fashion without offering much in the way of explanation. They were only too well aware that Catholics identified English with Protestantism, when they did not regard it as the mark of heresy. And there was no point in presenting use of the vernacular as a tactic (the intelligibility of the mass bringing the faithful back into the churches) in a country whose magnificent Anglican vernacular liturgy had had no such effect on the Anglican population. The majority of Catholics accepted the change. But the bishops had to deal with the opposition, numerically small but extremely stubborn, of the Latin Mass Society, formed in 1965, which regarded the vernacular as a concession to human weakness and came out resolutely in favour of an all-Latin mass. The vernacular, associated with the triviality of everyday life, was not suitable for the expression of sublime mysteries; Latin on the other hand possessed a majesty that made it appropriate for saying holy things. Its unchangingness, its universality, made the mass a source of spiritual strength. To these arguments, found everywhere in the Catholic world, the Latin Mass Society added another, specific to a country where the Reformation had had some brutal moments: Latin was the language of the English martyrs, and to give it up would be to scorn their sacrifices.[83]

Something similar was present in the defence of Latin mounted in the same period by Anton Hickman, a professor at the University of Mainz:

Up to now, Latinity for us, at least sentimentally speaking, has been something, so to speak, essential to the professed faith itself. To a much greater extent than is felt in the linguistically Latin countries, for us, European Catholics, linguistically non-Latin, but all the more Roman religiously speaking, and thus Latin too, Latin, the language of our holy liturgy, has been a holy language. The very thought that it might be possible one day to interfere with it would have seemed a sacrilege. We certainly liked, and sang with enthusiasm, religious hymns in German . . . But liturgy in the strictest sense, the liturgy of the mass, in German . . . No! That was inconceivable. The debates of the Protestant Reformation were not after all so very long ago; nor had we forgotten that our ancestors once took up arms against the whole gamut of different Protestant princes and princelings to conserve the Latin mass, to maintain the "Romanness" of our faith, to prevent the religion from being "Germanized" . . . The Roman mass, in Latin, was for us the most splendid, the most eloquent manifestation and demonstration of the world-wide unity of our faith . . . Such was Catholicism: the entire world was our country.[84]

The role of Latin declined sharply following the Council. It remains nevertheless the official language of the Church, of its acts and administrations; but the Apostolic Constitution *Pastor bonus* (28 June 1988) and the Roman Curia's general ruling of 4 February 1992 stipulate that "the dicasteries of the Roman Curia in principle write their acts in Latin, but may however use the most widespread languages of today both for correspondence and, if the need arises, when writing documents".[85] Paul VI, following up on his predecessor's work, in 1964 established in Rome, under the Pontifical Salesian University, an Institutum Altioris Latinitatis to give training in fluent and elegant written Latin.[86] Using Latin in this way as a living language led to the coining of neologisms to express some contemporary realities, and a *Lexicon recentis latinitatis*, containing some 15,000 of them, was published between 1992 and 1997. Even in Rome itself, however, at the Gregorian University, the part played by Latin today seems notably reduced. According to one of its professors, the Rev. Reginald Foster, of the 3,000 students "perhaps a hundred have good knowledge of Latin"; moreover, for the last four years, teaching has been in Italian and English instead of Latin.[87] And with Latin surrendering even inside the Roman bastion, there is no longer anything surprising about the presence of Latin-free priests in the wider Catholic world.

The Vatican II liturgical reform, or to be more precise the way it was applied, appeared to some individuals to suggest a far-reaching plot aimed at "the murder of the ancient languages", an "international conspiracy" with Church and State both involved. Without going quite so far, there were many who, like Pierre Grimal, saw the decline of Latin in the schools as connected with the Council's decision: in the distinguished professor's view, "the most grievous blow dealt to Latin" had been the Church's abandonment of the language, and he added, with veiled meaning, that the change had been made "for reasons which are certainly not the ones the Vatican has tried to give out to the world".[88]

4 Protestant Latin

As the language of the Catholic Church, Latin came to be identified with
Catholicism itself. An eloquent illustration is the attitude of a group of Puritan
soldiers in Cambridge in 1643: they would not allow the sermon for the Easter
term to be delivered in Latin, as the statutes required, on the ground that it
was the language of Catholic liturgy.[89] The opposite was just as true: the vernacular meant Protestantism. The Jansenist priest Pierre Brayer (whom we
have seen at Metz giving Extreme Unction and the Viaticum in French) was
thought to be a minister who had arrived secretly from Geneva or Amsterdam on one occasion in 1724 when he had just given the last sacraments to
a new convert.[90] The common view was that Latin went with Catholicism
and the vernacular with Protestantism, but the reality was more nuanced: the
Protestant Church was not a world without Latin.

During the Reformation, the vernacular diffused gradually through the
Protestant world; the change was in no way brutal or radical. The German
mass that Luther produced in 1526 was meant to be celebrated only on
Sundays, with services during the rest of the week staying in Latin; Luther
originally intended to keep Latin in the mass for educated people and the
young, and, provisionally, at all times for certain parts of the liturgy until
prayers and canticles were available in German. While it is true that the vernaculars rapidly gained the upper hand, old habits die hard and even in
Calvin's Geneva it sometimes happened that persons called before the consistory to prove their faith answered by reciting the *Paternoster*, the *Ave Maria*
and the *Credo* in Latin.[91]

The reformers themselves, who were both pastors and humanists, used
both languages with equal facility in their works; in their correspondence
Latin was heavily predominant, to the extent of 80 or 90 per cent. Luther did
not abandon Latin for his own writings, and his *Table Talk* shows that the
absence of German terms for philosophic or theological realities sometimes
led him to switch from German to Latin even in informal conversation.
Calvin composed his *Institutio religionis christianae* (1536) in Latin, then translated it into French; before the second edition of either version, the author
amended the text sometimes in French, sometimes in Latin. The final text,
much augmented, appeared in Latin in 1559 and in French the following
year. Calvin explained his linguistic choices thus: "First, have put it in Latin:
so that it could be used by all people of learning, of whatever nation; then
afterwards, wishing to communicate any fruit that might come from it to our
French nation, have also translated it into our language". Other works by
Calvin – many of his theological treatises and his catechism, most notably –
were published in both languages. His correspondence was largely in Latin,
a language Calvin used even when writing to French churchmen. Pierre
Viret, who generally used French in his writings "in order to be accessible to

the ignorant", nevertheless had good mastery of Latin, which he used in about four fifths of his lectures and correspondence.[92] Latin translations of the Bible were another indication of the presence of Latin in a world too easily and too exclusively associated with the vernacular: no fewer than fifty-eight complete versions of scripture were published by Protestant editors and printers between 1521 and 1570.[93]

In the training of ministers Latin, along with theology, had a major role. In Württemberg immediately after the Reformation, young people training for the ministry were fed with Latin throughout their *cursus*, all the way from their *schola particularis* to the *Stift* in Tübingen: Latin was the language used in class, for examinations and in everyday conversation.[94] The Rhineland clergy in the same period received the same solid Latin training, so that after 1556–57, when the conditions for ordination became strict, cases of poor Latin were unusual.[95] Throughout the Ancien Régime in France, the academies responsible for training pastors gave an education in which Latin, one of the languages of the Bible, was very much present.[96] The same was true of the faculties of theology established in the nineteenth century. So the majority of pastors, then trained at the University of Montauban, were necessarily Latinists: the *baccalauréat*, which included Latin, was a condition of entry, and the five-year course included work on improving their Latin; those wishing to become theology teachers had to obtain a degree for which two theses had to be presented, one of them in Latin.[97] Although the minister performed his duties in the vernacular, he was still always a Latinist by training (and quite often a better one than his Catholic opposite number). However, Latin suffered competition from other disciplines in the theology faculties that reduced its role, apart from the fact that its decline in the schools was felt in due course in the Protestant theology faculties. At the end of the 1960s, the University of Uppsala dropped Latin and replaced it with a 30-hour course in terminology: Latin had come to be seen as a scarecrow, an added deterrent to the dwindling number of religious vocations.[98] It could also be said that under its waning star the Catholic and Protestant worlds had come to resemble one another more than ever before.

CHAPTER 3

Latin Scholarship

The conclusions of the first two chapters are well summarized in the *Encyclo-pédie* in these terms: Latin, the "language of the Catholic Church and of all the schools in Christendom" was an "indispensable necessity . . . as much for philosophy and theology as for jurisprudence and medicine; and it is, for that very reason," the entry continues, "the common language of all the scholars in Europe".[1] This view was current in the middle of the eighteenth century. Something very similar had been said in a speech made half a century earlier by Anton Maria Salvini to the Accademia degli Apatisti in Florence: "The world of the sciences learned in the universities has and will always have Latin as its own formal and natural language". The same author, who reserved the vernacular for literature alone, noted elsewhere that the sciences could only be written about in Latin, which for that reason had become "the common language of the learned".[2] These statements of principle were accompanied by recurrent thoughts along the same lines in letters and notes between scholars. In 1709 Gisbert Cuper urged his friend Mathurin Veyssière de La Croze to write his universal history in Latin, explaining that while the French language "is very widely understood and admirable for books that are slight and of the moment . . ., a work that is to be for intellectuals ought, I believe, to be published in Latin".[3] François Peleau, in a letter to Hobbes listing his "doubts" on the latter's *De cive*, confessed to feeling "shame" for "communicating with you in a language other than that of science" by writing in French.[4] Latin was a constituent part of the world of learning. The naturalist John Ray condemned an adversary in these terms: "He is so igno-rant that he cannot even write Latin without solecisms".[5] Christian Gottfried Hoffmann chided his learned compatriots for writing in German: that, he said, was writing like an ignoramus.[6] Pascal wasted no energy on explana-tions when, in a letter to Fermat on calculating probability, he abandoned the vernacular with the terse comment: "I will say it in Latin, for French is worth-less here".[7]

These quotations give some idea of the status Latin used to enjoy in the Republic of Letters, at least until the middle of the eighteenth century. They suggest that a survey of printed output would establish a more precise view of the role played by the old language in the intellectual world. What seems to be indicated is a chronology of Latin publications, highlighting favoured genres and perhaps some specific printings. These are concrete descriptive elements that will enable the function of Latin in writing, and in the very con-stitution of learning, to be understood, and throw light on the reasons for using this language, for its persistence and eventual disappearance. An inven-tory of the types of Latin used in intellectual work would not be complete if it did not, in addition to writing, cover oral modes for the expression of knowledge: political debate, diplomatic negotiation, juridical practice and so on.

1 The Lessons of Latin Publishing

Bibliographical statistics

Although the printed book is a good indicator of the relative importance of languages in the production of knowledge, bibliographical statistical data for such a long period and large geographical area are less plentiful and less precise than one might have wished. Moreover, in compiling historiographies, which are still national, researchers have paid a good deal less attention to Latin than to the vernaculars. A few examples will have to suffice.

In France, Latin predominance over the printing presses was of short dura-tion. The monopoly of the first quarter of the sixteenth century (of the eighty-eight books printed in Paris in 1501, only eight were in French; in 1528 the proportions were little different with thirty-eight books in French out of 269) was soon breached; in 1549, still in Paris, 21 per cent of printings were in the vernacular, and by 1575 the proportion had risen to about 55 per cent. In the whole kingdom, more books were printed in Latin than in French until the 1560s, but after that time the vernacular became increasingly predominant. A cross-section of the very end of the sixteenth century (1598–1600) shows the proportion of Latin titles as being under 25 per cent. The proportion then stabilized at around 20 per cent, according to an examination of French pro-duction in 1644 and a survey of Paris printings in 1660. But it fell steeply in the second half of the century: in 1699, 1700 and 1701 works in Latin repre-sented only 5.7, 12.2 and 8.5 per cent respectively of total Paris production. The decline continued into the eighteenth century, so that by 1764 publica-tions in ancient and foreign languages only accounted for 4.5 per cent of printed output in the kingdom.[8]

By this time Latin had declined everywhere in the western world, although the speed and pattern of the development were not always exactly the same as in France. The process was considerably slower in Italy. According to figures supplied by *Il Catalogo Unico delle Biblioteche Italiane*, Latin retained a dominant position throughout the seventeenth century with 51.8 per cent of impressions, registering a slight decline from 55.4 per cent in the period 1501–50 to 50.2 per cent in the latter half of the century. Analysis of the data in the *Catalogue of Seventeenth-Century Italian Books in the British Library* shows that the vernacular then became heavily predominant, with the percentage of Latin titles dropping below 30 per cent for the whole century. There were however wide differences between regions: Latin may only have represented 21 per cent of output in Venice, but was 50 per cent of the total in Rome and 56 per cent in Padua, owing largely to the presence of the Church in the first case and the university in the second.[9]

In Germany, by contrast, the decline of Latin began even earlier than in France, but the process was less linear. The vernacular made strong progress from 1520 onward under Luther's influence, and during the Reformation most publishing was in German. Subsequently, however, Latin regained much of the lost ground, and kept it for some considerable time: more than half the books exchanged at the Frankfurt fairs were in Latin until well into the 1680s. After that, Latin titles underwent a steady, but relatively slow, decline through the eighteenth century: their share was still 14.25 per cent in 1770, and only became insignificant in 1800 when it dropped below four per cent.[10]

In England, Latin impressions seem to have represented 10 per cent of printed output over the period 1530–1640. James W. Binns, whose estimate this is, stresses that this apparently low proportion needs to be seen in the context of the qualitative disparity between the English and Latin products: while the English titles included a large proportion of ephemeral publications, the "most brilliant minds" published their works in Latin.[11]

These figures, to be honest, are not detailed enough to give more than a general indication; no breakdowns by discipline are available. But Henri-Jean Martin's work does enable us to go into some detail where Paris is concerned. Despite its decline, Latin was used throughout the seventeenth and into the eighteenth century in these areas: theology, scientific works and schoolbooks. In religious publishing, Latin persisted mainly in theological treatises and works of holy erudition. This last category, in which first the Jesuits and then the Maurist Benedictines distinguished themselves, was not just one of the success stories of Paris publishing from the 1640s onward, but included a number of brilliant achievements in philology and sacred history. It is not surprising that some of these – including editions of the Church Fathers – were reprinted abroad, notably in Venice.[12] These works overlap with scientific and scholarly publishing, where Latin was present not only in works of erudition proper, but also in medicine – the turning point seems to have been about 1685[13] – and law, in the latter case despite a strong advance by French. However, the most solid and durable bastion of Latin was academic publishing: colleges and universities had a considerable output of theses and textbooks, dictionaries, grammars and other works for learning the basics of the language, and the exercises in translation and verse or prose composition that constituted the collegian's everyday diet. Obviously the printer-booksellers in provincial towns, and even in typographical centres like Rouen which had opted for modernity, did not neglect a thriving sector with the added advantage of relative immunity from market fluctuations. Some of these works enjoyed very large print runs: Père Pajot's *Dictionarium novum latino-gallico-graecum* was published at Rouen in 1651, 1653–54, 1655 and 1658 in editions of 5,200, 6,000, 7,000 and 6,700 copies in octavo and 2,500 copies in quarto; new editions were published in the same town in 1662, 1665 and 1666 at least. The greater emphasis on French in education that came with the pedagogic reforms of the eighteenth century, and the expulsion of the Jesuits who were among the most ardent defenders of tradition, resulted in a loss of influence for Latin, although the *lycées* remained "Latin country" apart from a brief eclipse during the revolutionary period. The nineteenth century saw a truly imposing output of textbooks and other teaching instruments, with no fewer than 200 new titles appearing in each decade. Some of these were reprinted many times: seventy-six were republished in editions spanning half a century, and Lhomond's *Eléments de grammaire latine*, originally published in 1780, appeared in sixty-three editions during the nineteenth century. These multiple reprintings are evidence of real and impressive success; one of the all-time best-sellers of French schoolbook publishing, Quicherat's *Dictionnaire latin-français*, for which precise print-run figures are available, was produced in 445,886 copies between 1835 and 1934.[14]

The "scholarly" character of Latin impressions emerges from the analytic description given by J.W. Binns for the 1530–1640 period: the old language was used at that time in all the higher forms of learning, from literature to law, from science to theology. Latin may have suffered a sharp decline in English printing after 1640, but it was still very much present in the output of Oxford University's presses at the turn of the eighteenth century: at least half of the books published between 1690 and 1710 were in Latin, mainly, it is true, titles concerning erudition and philology.[15] This last discipline kept the profile of Latin high until very recent times: indeed the publication of papal Bulls under the auspices of the International Diplomatic Commission, or of the *corpus* of Greek inscriptions procured by the Berlin-Brandenburg Academy of Science, is still accompanied today by a commentary in Latin.

To return to a period when Latin had not yet become a curiosity, namely the eighteenth century, the accounts given in the *Bibliothèque raisonnée des ouvrages des savants de l'Europe* between 1728 and 1740 give an idea of the share that the old language still retained in works belonging to the scholarly forms of culture: 31 per cent of the texts analysed by this periodical were in Latin.[16] It still had a far from negligible place in medicine at the end of the eighteenth century, judging by the (surely authoritative) opinions of publishing professionals like the bookseller Gosse who, in 1779, commented in Geneva: "Anything to do with medicine is generally good in Latin. Spain, Portugal, Italy, even France does not [*sic*] reject them".[17]

What makes this judgement seem so sincere and convincing is the fact that in earlier times intellectuals had often been annoyed by the reluctance of printers and booksellers to publish or sell books in Latin. A fairly typical example is the doctor and antiquarian John Woodward, who noted of London in 1711 that "our Booksellers care not to meddle with any Thing that is in Latin".[18] Although in steady decline, Latin publishing survived in the "scientific" domain through the role that fell to it, more or less by default, in early eighteenth-century Europe, where few of the vernaculars had yet acquired full literary acceptability, and where the scholarly readership was both small and geographically scattered. Within this specialized sector, the persistence of Latin is especially apparent in three practices: the publication of periodicals in that language, translations of works originally written in the vernacular, and bilingual editions.

Three types of Latin publication

Most learned periodicals including the very first, the *Journal des savants*, were in the vernacular, but some were in Latin. These seem to have been about 20 per cent of the category in the period between 1665 and 1747; in the second half of the eighteenth century, though, fourteen new Latin titles appeared between 1751 and 1760 and thirteen more between 1771 and 1780, in the Germanic world (admittedly in the broadest sense) alone. This region, in which the vernaculars took longer than elsewhere to gain acceptance in the world of scholarship, was where journals were most often published in Latin. Some of these periodicals were of universal interest, among them the *Acta eruditorum* that started to appear in Leipzig in 1682, the *Acta litteraria Regni Poloniae et Magni Ducatus Lithuaniae* whose first issue, bearing the double address of Warsaw and Leipzig, dates from 1755, and the *Acta litteraria Bohemiae et Moraviae* launched in Prague in 1744. Most were specialized, however, dealing with erudition, theology or science (principally medicine): one of the best known, not least for its longevity, was the *Miscellanea curiosa medico-physica* which was published, under a succession of titles but always in Latin, from 1670 to 1791. Many of these Latin periodicals emanated from learned societies or academies: the academies of Berlin, Göttingen, Turin and St Petersburg, the Institute of Science at Bologna and the Palatine Society of Mannheim, to name a few illustrious examples culled from the eighteenth century, all published their proceedings and memoranda in Latin for a more or less extended period. As late as 1793 a society of antiquaries in Utrecht made the same choice for its *Acta literaria.*[19]

While much attention has been devoted to translations from Latin into the vernacular and from one vernacular – especially Italian – into another, little interest has been shown in Latin translations of books originally written in the vernacular.[20] But many such were produced, especially in the seventeenth century and the first half of the eighteenth. That is the first observation to be drawn from a list of these publications compiled by W. Leonard Grant and completed by Peter Burke.[21] The tabulation of these "versions", starting with literary writings listed under their original languages, and then running through other products discipline by discipline, shows firstly that the practice was universal: works from every area of learning were translated into Latin, and it was done everywhere. That was the general picture, but there were local nuances and variations. Germany, the Low Countries and Switzerland played leading roles in this translating activity. The dynamism of the Dutch printing industry, the important mediating role of the Swiss book trade (with a pool of translators available from Geneva's Protestant exile community) and the presence of a market that was still largely Latin in Germany and Eastern Europe,[22] all help explain the concentration of the practice in that region; but another important factor was that living languages – French and Italian excepted – were still generally unknown outside their own frontiers at the end of the seventeenth century.

Grant's judgement on the style of these translations – "basically Ciceronian in rhythm, but eclectic in syntax and vocabulary" – is not surprising in view of the "advice to readers" sometimes added to translations of scholarly works: exactness of meaning was favoured over elegance of style.[23] This was certainly the reason why Francis Bacon turned down the draft translation of *The Advancement of Learning* offered to him by an excellent Latinist, Dr Playfere: despite the "superfine Latinity" of Playfere's text, Bacon insisted that the work be presented in a style that was "clear, masculine and apt".[24] The contrary view was adopted seldom, and always for a reason: the translator of Swammerdam's *Histoire des insectes* justified the stylistic improvements he had introduced by explaining that the author had only been prevented from polishing the work himself, and probably producing a Latin version as well, by a premature death.[25] The reason for these translations into what Francis Bacon called the "general language"[26] was to make the works accessible to a wider readership than they would have had in a vernacular. Some of them mention this hope of a wide circulation in their blurbs and forewords, when it is not included in the actual title. "Translated into Latin for the sake of foreigners", announces the frontispiece of the Latin edition of Descartes' *Passions de l'âme* (Amsterdam, 1656); "to serve for the use and curiosity of the greatest number" is the formula used at the front of the *Osteologia nova* (Frankfurt, Leipzig, 1692), originally written in English by the physician Clopton Havers. The same reasoning lay behind the translation of learned periodicals, thought to fulfil their function even more fully when put into Latin. Hence the extremely rapid translations of the two major periodicals of the Republic of Letters: *Philosophical Transactions*, published in London from 1665, appeared in Holland from 1670 onward under the title *Acta philosophica*, reprinted in 1675 at Leipzig, the source four years earlier of a Latin version of the *Journal des savants* which, it will be remembered, first appeared in 1665.[27]

Translations were occasionally produced by the authors themselves, Christian Wolf being one example; or they were vetted by the author, as Descartes did with the Latin text of the *Discours de la méthode*, making corrections and accepting responsibility for the sense, but not the style.[28] More usually these translations were done by another scholar, either spontaneously or at the request of a printer-bookseller; the resulting translation was sometimes accompanied by notes and observations, which could then come to be valued in their own right. An example is *The True Intellectual System of the Universe* by the Cambridge Platonist Ralph Cudworth, a work of 900 folio pages, which was translated into Latin and annotated by Johann Lorenz von Mosheim and published at Jena in 1733; a second Latin edition based on Mosheim's work appeared at Leiden forty years later, and that eminent theologian's notes and introductory essay were still thought sufficiently interesting after another half-century to be translated into English for the 1845 London edition.[29]

This example reminds us that Latin translations were sometimes reprinted. Grant noted of medical publications that in the seventeenth and eighteenth centuries, works in the vernacular had only one or two editions, while their Latin equivalents might have as many as eight or ten.[30] The same applied to religious polemics: the Latin version of the *Lettres provinciales* produced by Nicole (but attributed to the reassuring *nom de plume* Wilhelm Wendrock, theologian of Salzburg) had six editions between its first appearance in 1658 and 1700; Sainte-Beuve thought that "this translation truly popularized the victorious pamphlet in Europe".[31]

In fact some works and their authors owe any renown they may have outside their countries of origin to their Latin editions. The circulation outside the Italian peninsula of Galileo's *Dialogo dei due massimi sistemi* was achieved largely by the Latin edition of 1635.[32] Robert Boyle's success on the Continent is indissociable from the (extremely rapid) translation of his writings in Germany, Switzerland and Holland; moreover the first collection of his works, *Opera varia*, appeared not in England but in Geneva, published by de Tournes, who three years later brought out an edition augmented with later writings.[33] Cartesian physics was still being diffused in Newton's England thanks to Jacques Rohault's Latin translation of the *Traité de physique*, reprinted six times between 1682 and 1739 (it is true however that the comments of its editor Samuel Clarke become increasingly Newtonian in the later editions).[34] It could even happen that the Latin translation was the reason for a work's success. *La Città del sole* was hardly noticed in its original Italian edition; in fact this utopian text only became known through the Latin translation made by Campanella himself. From Latin, the work went into French, English, German and even back into Italian, the original edition lying forgotten until the middle of the nineteenth century.[35]

The Latin translations of works of fiction which still sometimes appear today (*Pinocchio, Bonjour tristesse, Asterix the Gaul, Winnie the Pooh*) are assertions of the established success of their originals, rather than contributing to it in any way; for who is supposed to be capable of reading them? But things were very different in the seventeenth and eighteenth centuries, when the old language made it possible for texts to be read, and ideas circulated, throughout the Republic of Letters.

This made the printer-booksellers firm allies of Latin, which they saw as a way into wider markets. In particular they favoured the old language for large-format books, printed on fine paper and ornamented with plates or engravings, magnificent but very costly products that, for obvious economic reasons, needed Europe-wide circulation; so they pressed authors to supply a Latin translation along with the text. Montfaucon spells the point out in his *Plan d'un ouvrage qui aura pour titre les monuments de la monarchie française* (1729): "The booksellers want me to put a Latin version at the foot of the pages, as in *Antiquité expliquée* and in the *Supplément*. They claim that this is necessary for a lot of foreigners, who do not understand French well enough." Thus, mainly in the eighteenth century, and more particularly its first half, especially on the subjects of archaeology, botany, zoology, anatomy and painting,[36] bilingual books were published, juxtaposing Latin and vernacular text in a variety of typographical layouts. One of the finest books I have had the pleasure of examining, the *Description exacte des principales curiosités naturelles du magnifique cabinet d'Albert Seba* (1734) – the title is no exaggeration – even had two different bilingual editions, Latin–French and Latin–Dutch.

This brief foray into the publishing world makes it pretty clear that Latin was seen as the essential language for learned writings until well into the eighteenth century. Could this be the reason why in the Germanic countries, where Latin survived longest, works written in German were sometimes given titles that began with a few words of Latin, a sort of label to indicate the learned, or anyway not mainstream, character of the contents?[37] Latin thus labelled the world of scholars and indicated familiarity with the highest spheres of learning. Such in any case, to stay on German soil, was the view of young Anton Reiser in the famous psychological novel that bears his name: called *Reiserus* by the head of the local secondary school, he

was not a little proud to see for the first time his name thus adorned with an "us". With names bearing this ending he had always associated the idea of great dignity and immense learning. In imagination, he could already hear himself being referred to as the scholarly and celebrated Reiserus . . .; he saw himself becoming an illustrious erudite like Erasmus Roterodamus [sic] and others whose biographies he had read and whose engraved portraits he had seen.[38]

2 Latin in Learned Writing

Despite the rise (and eventual predominance) of the vernaculars, Latin endured in the world of learning. Ferdinand Brunot, whose monumental history of the French language underlines every stage of its development and describes each of its major advances, recognizes that in Louis XIV's time, when a splendid French literature was in full flower, the progress of French in the sciences remained extremely slow.[39] Throughout the eighteenth century, quite large numbers of works continued to appear in Latin, including (to limit ourselves to major texts) Jacob Bernoulli I's *Ars conjectandi* (1713), Leonhard Euler's *Mechanica* (1736) and *Introductio in analysin infinitorum* (1748), Linnaeus's *Systema naturae* (first edition 1735) and Galvani's *De viribus electricitatis in motu musculari* (1791). In the following century the tradition was kept alive by the German mathematician Carl Friedrich Gauss, who published his work in Latin, and the Italian doctor Leopoldo Caldani – the "Vesalius of the nineteenth century" – who produced ten volumes of *Icones anatomicae* between 1801 and 1814.[40] Although by that time the sciences were generally dealt with in the vernacular, Catholic theology, academic theses and other university texts remained predominantly Latin (this has already been adequately covered in the earlier chapters on the Church and education).

The Latin context of "modernity"

A number of factors helped to maintain Latin as the language of learning, starting with the practice of teaching in it, which persisted until a late date; it was an obligation with which even devoted supporters of the vernacular like Antonio Vallisneri had to comply.[41] In this area, the statutes of the chair founded by Lord Lumley at Oxford in the late sixteenth century to give a proper training to surgeons – not especially Latinist as a group – constitute a very revealing half-exception: the professor was required to speak for three quarters of an hour in Latin, then for a quarter of an hour in English, "wherein that shall be plainlie declared for those that understand not latine, what was said in latine".[42]

Lecturing was really only one aspect, perhaps the most visible, of an environment in which Latin was pervasively present. Newton, who taught at Cambridge and wrote most of his work in Latin, had more books in Latin than English in his library, and annotated the Latin books he read in Latin.[43] This last practice would have come naturally to men who spent most of their time reading and writing Latin. Two good examples are provided by the notes Huygens scribbled in the margins of the *Acta eruditorum* and the ones that Swift, admittedly less an academic than a literary and intellectual "virtuoso", wrote in his copy of Baronius's *Annales*.[44] A striking and very special illustration of the intellectual world's easy familiarity with the old language is provided by the *Secunda scaligerana*, a collection of propositions advanced by Joseph-Just Scaliger, in which French and Latin are so closely interwoven that phrases sometimes start in one language and finish in the other, an undifferentiated use of language apparently governed only by the writer's passing convenience.[45]

Reading, writing and speaking Latin in the specific context of their specialities, intellectuals did not feel the need to use the vernacular for their scientific publications as strongly as we might expect today. Even when they were not considering classical texts, even when commentary and explanation gave way to hard experimental data, the force of established habit, the need for a specialized vocabulary, awareness of the readers' preferences, all help to explain why the vernacular was slow to impose itself on the world of learning. An interesting example is the excuse offered by the Chancellor of Paris University, Rollin, for writing his *Traité des études* (1726) in French instead of Latin; although he favoured "modern" pedagogy, he admitted that he was "more used to the latter language, to which he had devoted part of his life, than to the French language".[46] Another factor that naturally contributed to the maintaining of the old language was the major influence of certain works first published in Latin: the new concepts they contained were not always easily translatable, but were perfectly clear to the small number of scholars who would be dealing with them; that is why in eighteenth-century Italy, for example, the best writings on Newtonian physics were all in Latin.[47]

So the publication of the first widely quoted great works written in modern languages, Galileo's *Dialogo dei due massimi sistemi* and Descartes's *Discours de la méthode*, did not signal any significant decline of Latin; both authors, in any case, published some of their other writings (in Descartes's case the most important ones) in the old language. According to Descartes's biographer, Baillet, he "wrote on philosophical and mathematical subjects even more fluently in Latin than in French". Like many of his contemporaries, in fact, he could move easily from one language to the other and adapt his use of language to the proposition being discussed; Baillet notes of his *Meditationes* that "he did not think it appropriate to publish the work initially in French, as he had done with his *Essais*: but having written it mainly for scholars and in a style both elevated and new, he believed he should speak their language and express himself in their manner as far as possible".[48] The same attitude persisted in the next generation: Galileo's disciples, in the second half of the seventeenth century, used Italian as well as Latin depending on the nature of the work and its target readership. Torricelli wrote his *De motu proiectorum* in Latin, explaining that it was intended for mathematicians and not gunners; but his *Lezioni accademiche* were in Italian, being intended for a "literary and academic" readership. Borelli used Latin for works on mathematics, astronomy and mechanics, but the vulgar tongue for writings that might have a practical outcome, like the *Progetto per la bonifica della laguna di Venezia*. Malpighi wrote several of his works in the vulgar tongue, but all his writings addressed to the Royal Society were in Latin.[49]

These few examples show (among other things) the role of the intended readership in the choice of language. The fact is that while the potential readership for learned works, or anyway works of a lofty sort, remained limited, Latin kept a strong position: more than that, the vernacular did nothing at all to increase the circulation of these writings. This is particularly true of the "first wave" of modernity. In 1525, Albrecht Dürer published in Nuremberg his *Underweysung der Messung mit dem Zirckel und Richtscheyt*, a work in which he had assembled a body of geometric knowledge for the use of artists and artisans; with them in mind, he used German. However, the work was more widely read in its Latin translation (1532) and the readers were scholars, scientists and mathematicians: even in German, the mathematical notions in this work were still too abstract for the readers originally envisaged.[50] An inverse example is provided by Jean Bodin's *Universae naturae theatrum* (1596). The work had three Latin editions which were highly successful in France as well as abroad (Poland, England, Italy and Germany where two of these editions were published); the French translation of 1597 did not sell well, however. With the cultivated reading public still very limited in size, there was practically no one with an interest in natural philosophy who did not have good Latin; so the original edition covered the market adequately.[51] The same conclusion can be drawn from the failure, well into the eighteenth century, of attempts to translate the papers of the St Petersburg Academy of Science into Russian: the Czarist empire had not at that time a reading public educated enough to read such material, and what readers there were could read Latin.[52]

In the context of this example we should bear in mind that in some places, one of the factors favouring the retention of Latin was the absence of a vernacular fit for the expression of learning. While in some countries modern languages acquired literary dignity quite early on and were thought adequate to carry the thought of scholars, in others Latin survived until a late date in the absence of any other "language of culture". Finland was one of these. In the eighteenth century, when it was ruled by Sweden, the linguistic situation in Finland was as follows: the people spoke Finnish, while the aristocracy, clergy and urban middle class spoke Swedish; neither language was considered a language of culture. Under these conditions learning was inevitably expressed in Latin, and so the situation remained until quite late in the nineteenth century, when the only books published in Finnish were still religious works and writings with no great intellectual pretensions.[53]

The bibliographical statistics show clearly that things were changing in the seventeenth and eighteenth centuries; but the development was neither radical, nor linear, nor monolithic. While vernaculars had established themselves early on in works intended for a popular audience – the Middle Ages had not been uniformly Latin! – or those dealing with practical matters, the old language continued to be used for theoretical writings, exemplified in the second half of the seventeenth century by the disciples of Galileo cited above: treatises and "fundamental" studies, works intended for the author's peers, remained in Latin. The same observation holds true for medical literature in England between 1640 and 1660: English was used by amateurs and reformers with social aims, but university physicians who valued scholarly exchange with their foreign colleagues continued to use Latin.[54]

These remarks generally hold good for the juridical and political sciences. In the first half of the seventeenth century, thinkers like Hobbes, Lipse and Grotius were writing in Latin; their renown is what brings them to our attention today, but they were by no means isolated in their use of the old language. Naudé's *Bibliographia politica*, which appeared in 1633, lists under all aspects of political thought a number of authors who used Latin between 1600 and 1630.[55] Nor were they by any means the last to do so: Samuel Pufendorf springs immediately to mind. Moreover, these authors continued to be read, and in Latin: the curriculum worked out in 1722 for an academy to train French diplomats included the names of all the authors mentioned above.[56] Law shows a similar prevalence of Latin, illustrated by an analysis of Italian juridical publishing for the whole of the eighteenth century: of the 3,700 works printed between 1700 and 1800, 81 per cent were in Latin and 19 per cent in Italian; but the vulgar tongue gained ground in the second half of the century (31 per cent, against seven in the first half) and was used more for editions of laws and statutes (52 per cent) than in jurisprudence and doctrine (12 per cent); *a contrario*, Latin remained the language used in treatises, exegetic writings on the sources of civil law and sentences handed down by the supreme courts.[57] Even in juridical practice it retained a far from negligible role for much of the eighteenth century. In Piedmont, where advocates were still making their *allegazioni* in Latin in 1723, sentences continued to be pronounced in Latin until 1789. In the Kingdom of Naples an order was given in 1758 that the *scrivani* of the Sacro Reale Consiglio should know Latin, since the court's decisions were delivered in that language and Latin documents could be submitted during hearings.[58]

Specialized terminologies and vocabularies

Latin may have been losing ground in publishing – the bibliographical statistics are unambiguous – but this did not make it disappear from the world of scholarship: terminology itself was already being Latinized, something that was apparent in quite early vernacular translations of technical works. In England, the solution prevalent in the sixteenth century was to anglicize specific terms, either by adapting them and giving them an English ending or by translating them literally; failing that, in cases of Latin words with no English equivalent, the Latin word would be retained accompanied by an explanation, perhaps in a glossary at the end of the book. In this way Latin "untranslatables" were incorporated into scientific English.[59] Similarly, the French translation of the work by Bodin mentioned above contains a number of Latin borrowings: faced with lists of Latin names of birds and fishes without descriptions to identify them, the translator resorted to virtually direct transcription. Thus, *orphus* becomes "orphin", *sargus* "sargon" and *abramis* "abrame", obliging the reader to refer to natural history books in French, with remarks like these by way of justification: "otherwise the names may be confused in our language, if they are changed from their Greek and Latin correctness"; and again: "we retain Latin and Greek names as the most common and best secured".[60] It sometimes happened that the lack of vernacular equivalents was so marked that a scientific text was impossible to translate. Goethe had to resign himself to this in his work on the theory of colours; despite help from the philologist Friedrich A. Wolf, he ended by simply reprinting a Latin text by Antonius Thylesius on the etymology of terms used to designate colours. "We wanted to translate it," he wrote, "but quickly found that the etymology of one language cannot be dealt with in another language; and" (to avoid adding to the confusion already created by translations of texts on this subject) "we decided to leave it in the original language".[61]

Between Bodin and Goethe, nevertheless, quite a few specialized vocabularies were composed in the different vernaculars. Latin was often the basis of these: the anatomical nomenclature employed by an eighteenth-century French physician was "essentially Graeco-Latin". Along with the few terms "whose physiognomy [was] French", Ferdinand Brunot notes "an abundance of lightly-gallicized Latin words" and "others that are simply transcribed"; some of these names, moreover, definitively supplanted the French popular terms used previously, *abdomen* for example replacing *susventre* (now obsolete, meaning over- or outer-belly), *radius* replacing *rayon* (also obsolete in the anatomical sense, but derived from the Latin *radius* and still used for other senses of that word) and *sternum* replacing *bréchet* (meaning breastbone).[62] Italian medical, and more particularly anatomical, terminology bears the mark of a similar Latin influence, discernible in several chronological layers. In the fifteenth and sixteenth centuries, the systematic recasting of medical terminology on the basis of classical works of Greek medicine translated into Latin, and of forgotten Latin authors like Celsus, led to the borrowing of Latin terms; the old language was also the basis for the coining of new names for the many anatomical phenomena discovered through dissection, a practice which had been resumed after an interruption of more than a thousand years. In the seventeenth and eighteenth centuries, when medical terminology expanded greatly (particularly in anatomy and biology) as a consequence of the use of the microscope, there were new borrowings from the vocabulary of the Ancients: these were not generally technical terms but words chosen for their expressive quality. Although the vernacular gained much ground in medical writings, the specialized vocabulary remained predominantly classical. Even Antonio Vallisneri, who argued consistently for the use of Italian in the sciences, had to include these Latinisms in the dictionary entitled *Saggio alfabetico d'istoria medica e naturale* which he published in 1733. Even in the present day, Latin retains a place in the terminology with words that are almost all invented composites.[63] Similar conclusions have been drawn on medical English, whose classical heritage is an imposing one; even in the twentieth century new words were being concocted on the basis of Latin, or borrowed complete from the old language. The results, at a time when the medical profession knew a good deal less Latin (let alone Greek) than it once had, sometimes included strange efforts which, while clearly derived from Latin, displayed unfamiliarity with the most basic laws of morphology; John D. Dirckx has assembled an impressive anthology of errors of case and gender, along with basic misperceptions of the nature of words (for example, using an adjective as a noun or vice versa).[64]

There is one science that, in the modern era, established itself entirely in Latin (anyway so far as terminology is concerned): botany. In the sixteenth century it had shown a tendency towards vernacularization, with between a quarter and a third of all works published in France written in French. The utilitarian and practical nature of this discipline counted in the choice of the vernacular, also favoured by the adoption of locally-coined names for the plants then being identified in Europe and the New World. But this vernacularization led to a feeling that the discipline was being diluted, with a consequent return to Latin, especially marked in the seventeenth century.[65] Gaspard Bauhin tried to impose some sort of system in his *Pinax theatri botanici* (1623) by composing a descriptive phrase for each plant. So great was the need for order that these phrases, despite their considerable length, became widely used. But apart from the terminological jungle, leading botanists like Tournefort and Rivinus (to name two of the most eminent) differed so strongly on fundamentals that they used different names for the same plant. It is against this confused background, with each botanist more or less obliged to publish his own list of synonyms, that the reform brought about by Linnaeus should be seen. We do not need to dwell here on the binary system governing the new nomenclature, or on the speed with which it was adopted as a result of its great practical utility. Suffice it to say that the plant that Tournefort called *Gramen Xerampelinum, Miliacea, praetenui, ramosaque sparsa panicula, sive Xerampelino congener, arvense, aestivum, Gramen minutissimo semine* was henceforth to be known as *Poa bulbosa*. The success of this reform was also a success for Latin. Linnaeus was ruthless in purging "barbarous" terms and showed a clear preference for Latin names; but he was careful to preserve names of Greek origin in honour of the fundamental Greek contribution to the discipline. He Latinized these names, however, along with the names of eminent botanists which had become generic terms. Jussieu, who followed different criteria – a "natural method" – in his own work on the taxonomy of plants, also stayed faithful to Latin. Modern botany became such a Latin science that John Berkenhout could write in 1789: "Those who wish to remain ignorant of the Latin language, have no business with the study of botany". This botanical Latin, which has been called "a modern Romance language of special technical application", diverged from classical Latin in many ways; with the passage of time it fell out of use except for description and nomenclature, where it remains in force to this day.[66]

Linnaeus's reform served as a model for the efforts being made to give chemistry a systematic nomenclature. In this discipline, too, the confusion was great: different terms were used for the same substance, chemists differed on the use of some names, and to avoid ambiguity the practice had arisen of using long descriptive phrases that were more definitions than names. In the second half of the eighteenth century the need for system became acute, what with the discovery of new elements, the invention of new compounds and the appearance of "pneumatic" chemistry; a standardized nomenclature had become crucial to the very progress of the discipline. Between 1775 and 1784 a professor at the University of Uppsala, Torbern Bergman, devised a complete method for systematic nomenclature that included a vigorous plea for Latin: it was the traditional language of scholars with the added advantage that, being a dead language, it was protected against mutation; translations made from this common base would have consistent references, giving the *lingua chimica* uniformity in all languages. Bergman's approach is not difficult to understand: he was a professor who taught and lectured in Latin; his model was the classification (in Latin) devised for botany by Linnaeus, whose pupil he had once been; and his mother tongue, Swedish, was unknown outside Sweden and not regarded as a language of culture even there. This choice of language was a point of disagreement with Guyton de Morveau, who held out for the vernacular which in his case was French. In his contribution to *Méthode de nomenclature chimique* (1787), however, more specifically the dictionary of new French terms, he included the Latin equivalents: the old language was still a reliable vehicle for exchanges between scientists. When Berzelius, in the nineteenth century, first used abbreviated symbols for the elements, he based them on the Latin names, and was sharply critical of his colleague Beudant for adapting these symbols to the French names of the elements – E for tin (*étain*), M for mercury, O for gold (*or*), etc.; if this was done everywhere, Berzelius complained, all advantages of precision and ease of scientific communication would be lost. Bergman had also suggested that the Latin names of all metals should end in -*um*; the principle was adopted and remains in force to this day.[67] Only recently the International Union of Pure and Applied Chemistry gave the Latin, or to be exact Latinized, names of rutherfordium, dubnium, seaborgium, bohrium, hassium and meitnerium to the transuranian elements of the Mendeleyev table with atomic numbers from 104 to 109.[68]

A number of the names, works and processes mentioned above contradict the simplistic equation too often drawn between ancient and Latin, modern and vernacular. True, some of the authors emblematic of "modernity" campaigned for the vernacular and associated Latin with an obsolete sort of learning: for Thomasius, for example, it symbolized scholastic thought or, more generally, "the dead weight of modes of thought showing their age".[69] Nevertheless Latin survived, sometimes flowing from the pens of sages and scientists that historiography places among the most modern. The role played by the old language was one of which it alone was capable. Moreover it had adapted itself to changing needs by undergoing its own *aggiornamento*, as Maria Luisa Altieri Biagi's studies of the post-Galileo generation make clear. Behind the choice between Latin and the vulgar tongue, which these men made according to the type of work and the intended readership, the use of language remained the same in both cases: the Latin they used was functional, simple and elegant, closer to the Tuscan of their other writings than the Latin of the humanist tradition.[70]

3 Latin in Practical Science: State Administrations and Diplomacy

Apart from published writings, the far more colossal mass of stored archives attests to the long-term survival of Latin in the government and administration of the states of modern Europe. The date of transition to the vernacular varies between countries, but also between different regions and different administrative levels. We will limit ourselves to a few examples, first observing that Latin survived longest in the central part of Europe and in territories where more than one language was spoken; that even in these places, local administrations made the change to the vernacular earlier; and that elsewhere, official "proclamation" of the vernacular did not signify *ipso facto* that the bureaucracy had wholly abandoned the use of the old language.

There is no need to dwell on the circumstantial use of Latin in the English court of George I: the Prime Minister Robert Walpole addressed the sovereign in the old language because the former Elector of Hanover knew no English, while Walpole knew no German.[71] The Polish example is a good deal less anecdotal: that kingdom was enduringly loyal to Latin, and the lower nobility (from which the administrative class was recruited) remained strongly committed to its retention all through the eighteenth century. During the first partition of Poland in 1772, Prussia gained dominion over Silesian and Polish territories. In order to administer them the Prussian aristocracy (which, like its prince, really preferred French) had to retain Latin as part of its education. One of the King of Prussia's ministers stated in 1798 that Latin was "indispensable not only because of the Roman law, but because of the new Polish territories, where nearly all the educated strata speak Latin".[72]

"Royalist" Hungary, at that time part of the Austro-Hungarian Empire, offers a particularly complex and interesting example of the tenacity of Latin in administration. In the seventeenth century no fewer than five modern languages were spoken on its territory; it would have been an utter Tower of Babel, Cominius noted in 1652, had it not been for the presence of a sixth language, Latin, to serve as a *lingua franca*.[73] It is no surprise, then, that the central government should have used it for the acts passed by its diets – of course this does not mean that Latin was constantly spoken in parliament or ministries – and for correspondence with Vienna: the King of Hungary – in other words the Emperor – likewise used Latin in relations with his Hungarian subjects, as can be seen from documents issued by the two bodies most in touch with Hungary, the Hungarian Chancellery and the Chamber of Accounts. In local administration, however, Latin was far less predominant: the lower the administrative level, the more Latin was effaced by the various vernaculars. This situation persisted until the end of the eighteenth century when Joseph II – who knew Latin well and even spoke it – decided for practical reasons to Germanize the Hungarian administration by substituting German for Latin. So strong was the resistance that in 1790 he had to revoke his rulings on the matter, and his successor restored the old practice: "The language of the administration is again, until further notice, the Latin language".[74]

Also under the Hapsburg monarchy, and after the difficulties with Hungary, there arose the issue of relations with Croatia. The union between Hungary and Croatia, which lasted in one form or another from 1097 to 1918, was always unequal, but more or less worked until the early nineteenth century when relations started to deteriorate. The linguistic question lay close to the heart of the conflict: the Hungarians wanted to impose their language on the Croats, who used Latin in their own diets (and in the Hungarian parliament, where they were represented). The disagreement, limited to start with, became embittered in 1840 when Magyar replaced Latin as the language of the Hungarian parliament, and three years later when it became the official language of law, government, administration and education. Special measures were applied to the Croats, or more exactly the administrative class: they were given six years to absorb Magyar, after which the same rules would apply as in Hungary. By 1848, although Latin was still used in local administration and local courts, Magyar was the sole authorized language for communication with the Hungarian authorities. In another devastating blow to Latin, it was declared that speeches in that language delivered by Croatian delegates to the Hungarian parliament would be regarded as not having been delivered at all.[75]

Latin was used by the Hapsburg monarchy as a third language: an administrative tool essential for the government of a very linguistically diverse group of territories. That explains why the "Instruction" left by the emperor Charles V to his son Philip (1543) included earnest encouragement to diligence in the study of Latin.[76] The old language was used in a very similar way in diplomacy.

While the principle of equality between states implies that there is no "language of diplomacy" and that each state has the right to use its own language, Latin was widely used by tacit convention in the Middle Ages and the sixteenth century. In 1640, other governments managed their correspondence with France as follows: a number of states (including, of course, those whose populations spoke French) used French; others like the king of Spain, the Protestant Swiss cantons and the Italian states used their own languages; and others only wrote in Latin, including the Hapsburg Emperor, the Elector of Saxony, the imperial city of Augsburg, the Hanseatic cities and the kings of Sweden, Denmark and Poland. France itself ordinarily used French for diplomatic correspondence; but correspondence addressed to the Diet and the princes of the Empire, and to its component states addressed collectively, was written in Latin; so too, for example, was correspondence with the Chancellor of Poland. In audiences as well as negotiations, diplomats were extremely careful to respect linguistic convention, using either their own language or the customary bridging language, Latin. When the French, for example, submitted documents in French or containing French addressed to the imperial princes and deputies at a meeting in Münster, the imperial team protested indignantly that the imperial diets made it an inviolable rule to communicate with foreign powers only in Latin. Any departure from established custom was presented as an exception: at Utrecht, when an imperial envoy used French during talks, he was careful to warn that it should not be taken as a precedent "as the Emperor's ministers ought never to speak anything but Latin". Until the treaty of Rastadt (1714) which marked the advent of French as the language of diplomacy – the Empire having agreed to sign a treaty in French – diplomatic exchanges continued to use Latin extensively.[77] A number of treaties were written and signed in Latin even after that date, France being no exception despite the assertion of its language on international level: the Treaty of Versailles (18 September 1735) between France and Poland, on the subject of King Stanislaus, is in Latin. But use of the traditional language tended to diminish over the eighteenth century when it persisted mainly among the "powers dedicated to Latin": the Papacy, the religious orders and the Hapsburg Empire. It was also used in 1720 for a treaty of alliance between Sweden and England; in 1737 for a trade and navigation treaty between Sweden and the Sublime Porte; and again in 1756 for a similar convention between Denmark and the Porte. Similarly, it remained "very widely used" in the chancelleries of Europe; France was the only country writing regularly to the Pope in its own language by the 1750s. Poland, by contrast, still used Latin which was also the majority language in the imperial chancellery in Vienna; even at the end of the nineteenth century the Emperor was still writing in Latin to the King of Sweden.[78]

Good Latin thus remained necessary for the conduct of foreign policy until a late date. There were princes who knew it well enough to conduct negotiations properly, like Charles XII of Sweden who in 1701–02 dealt with the Poles in German but also in Latin.[79] *A fortiori*, the staffs of chancelleries, as well as ambassadors and other diplomats, had to have thorough training in the subject, and some were distinguished Latinists.[80] Milton's talents in this area earned him the post of Secretary for Foreign Tongues in 1649, a job which included translating letters between Cromwell's Council of State and foreign powers from English into Latin and vice versa, as well as acting as interpreter between the Council and visiting envoys.[81] The Comte d'Avaux, who led the French embassy in the negotiations over the peace of Westphalia, wrote and spoke such perfect Latin that he sometimes verged on purism: he crossed out the phrase *Sacra Majestas Christianissima* not because it was in any way unflattering to the King of France but because it was "not good Latin".[82] It is thus no surprise to learn that, during the negotiations over the treaty of Rastadt, Marshal Villars, who lacked confidence in his own Latin, summoned the rector of the Strasbourg Jesuits, explaining in a despatch to Torcy (dated 25 February 1714): "I will employ him so as to make no solecisms and so that there be no term that I cannot understand perfectly". The problem was not just a simple matter of Latinity, but of avoiding the use of any word whose interpretation might lead to later complications. Working in Latin called for extra vigilance and many precautions. During a negotiation at Utrecht, the French plenipotentiaries rejected the first draft of the treaty because "there were expressions in it to which we could not agree". Even after a treaty had been signed difficulties could arise; a letter from the Duke of Shrewsbury dated 24 April 1713, seeking further details on the "particular cases" mentioned in article 9 of the trade treaty, asks the English envoys to point out that "the clause of the 9th article should have been more precisely explained than it was in Latin". The vagueness had not in fact been unintentional, however: the four "particular cases" excepted from the customs tariff of 1664 could be interpreted very broadly.[83]

All of this helps explain why Latin was included in the training of diplomats until a late date, even in France where administrative and judicial acts had been in the vernacular since the sixteenth century[84] (and even when French was well on the way to becoming the established language of diplomacy).

Apart from the fact that some powers continued to issue instruments in Latin, staff capable of reading and understanding texts in the old language were needed for matters in which precedent or verification of old titles played an essential part. Hence the recommendations to that effect in treatises on the "perfect ambassador" at the end of the seventeenth century and the beginning of the eighteenth. François de Callières, in his *Manière de négocier avec les souverains* ("How to negotiate with sovereigns"), emphasized that all diplomats ought to have a good knowledge of Latin, a language "of which it would be shameful for a man engaged in public endeavours to be ignorant". Louis Rousseau de Chamoy explained that "Latin is absolutely necessary to him [the ambassador] because it is spoken almost everywhere, and may thus serve him up to a point in the absence of others [other languages]".[85] More concretely, in the political academy founded in 1712 on Torcy's initiative, future diplomats were trained in Latin for reasons as practical as they were obvious. "The pupils," stipulated the establishment's statutes, "will at least know Latin, and well enough to be able to translate the acts of countries where they are issued in that language, bulls, briefs and other similar documents, as also to extract from books in Latin the ancient and modern facts which are often needed for different matters, either to use in memorandums on various matters or to verify those produced by foreigners". This school disappeared after seven years of existence; in 1722, the plans for its projected re-establishment included Latin among the subjects to be taught; it was explained that "extensive" knowledge of Latin was essential "so as to be able to consult the originals if necessary".[86]

Nevertheless, as the eighteenth century advanced, Latin tended increasingly to decline in favour of French, which reigned for the whole nineteenth century before itself meeting competition from English. The diplomatic and political vocabulary of that language has retained a number of Latin expressions, enough to remind us of the major role Latin once played in relations between states.[87]

CHAPTER 4

A Familiar World

While admiring the city's monuments and palaces, do visitors to Rome notice the hundreds of Latin inscriptions placed there over the centuries, from Antiquity to the fascist period? Do they read this "written city"? Did their predecessors read it in times gone by?[1] In the eighteenth century the people of Provence, nearly all illiterate, used to mark the votive offerings they left in the churches with the Latin phrase *ex voto*, often badly written and deformed into *et voto* or – a by-product of local phonetics – *es voto*. This expression represents, "for many illiterate donors, a sort of ideogram indicative of the votive image"; but what impression did the ideogram make on its beholders?[2] On prints and engravings, the names of the artists are often followed by the word *delinavit* or *pinxit* (for the artist) and *sculpsit* for the engraver, sometimes abbreviated to *del., pinx.* and *sculps.* Are these Latin words read literally, or do they just work as indices or signs denoting the job of each artist? Did the Latin word *fecit*, which used to accompany the name of the architect on monuments, make literal sense, or had it become a mere "custom" (and one so deeply rooted, incidentally, that not even the French Revolution could get rid of it)?[3] In Italy, the Latinization of juridical language influenced journalistic style in the late nineteenth century, so that, especially in the political area, Latin – or Latin-derived – words and expressions were widely used.[4] Traces of this custom are still present: during the debate a few years ago on providing equitable access to television for the political parties, the expression *par condicio* was used in parliament and by the press. Again: was this expression recognized as Latin?

Shortage of data makes it impossible to answer this series of questions, but behind their specific formulations they are all really variants of a single issue: did the omnipresence of Latin render it, so to speak, "invisible", or (to put it more exactly) was it assimilated in spite of its otherness? Academic life and religious practice do, however, provide some elements of an answer to this problem, which in this context concerns symbolic appropriation rather than the extension of linguistic skill.

1 Latin and the Faithful: Taming the Unintelligible

There was no shortage of voices, either inside or outside the Church, to criticize the absurdity of ceremonies conducted in a language unintelligible to the faithful, whose role was thus reduced to that of "parrots", "automata", "statues" or (in less polemical terms) "witnesses", an "audience". The fact is that until very recently Latin reigned in the Catholic churches over worshippers who (to put it mildly) did not always know it.[5]

In the situation of communication (or rather non-communication) connoted by the epithets in the last paragraph, unintelligibility was further deepened by phenomena linked to the conditions of production of the message and the cultural situation of its recipients. Liturgical Latin was for many centuries a language more heard than read (although, after a certain date, the use of missals should not be underestimated). This predominant orality made exact reception of the words uttered by the celebrant far from easy. Part of the mass was said in an undertone with the priest's back turned to the congregation; some of the prayers – especially on Sundays and at high masses – were sung rather than recited. Before modern technical methods existed, moreover, the priest's voice (although practised) could not always reach the furthest corners of the church, often a huge and labyrinthine building with poor acoustics.[6] The faithful, for their part, generally lacked the means to reduce or bypass the linguistic obstacle. Their knowledge of the religion, more particularly its theology and liturgy, was very slender; and until quite recently the great mass of people lacked even the education needed to understand texts put in the vernacular for their benefit. The catechism, the sermon, the explanations the priest was supposed to give in the course of the mass, must have helped to make the ritual being performed seem less opaque, although many of the faithful probably never progressed beyond a stage of "confused" understanding (considered good enough, however, by the Church).[7]

Religious doctrine, the mysteries of the faith, were interpreted by uncultured laymen using the analytic instruments available to them, and recoded into representations rooted in a familiar universe, or at least one that they "understood". Studies of "popular" religion, which are generally very informative in this area, have not paid as much attention to language as to rituals and prayers. Where Latin has been considered, it has been defined as part of a power system, a mark of the oppression of the poor by the strong, in a manner reminiscent of the attacks by men of the time (like the miller Menocchio or Renzo in *I promessi sposi*): an interpretation not without its own effect in strengthening the negative image of Latin as something incomprehensible.

We shall return to this theme later.[8] At the same time, however, the ordinary faithful somehow domesticated a language which to the great majority was unintelligible or very nearly so. Liturgical Latin became a familiar object: not only did repetition create habituation, but here too the unintelligible was adjusted into some sort of intelligible terms when it did not make sense in itself.

The force of repetition

Until quite recently the Church ruled people's lives from the cradle to the grave. The regular cycle of Sunday and feast-day observances, with the return of the same words and the same sounds, helped accustom the faithful to a language they did not know and make something foreign seem familiar.

This familiarization with Latin could start very early, as can be seen from Bossuet's recommendations in his catechism for the very young, *L'Abrégé de la doctrine chrétienne pour ceux qui commencent* ("Abridged Christian doctrine for beginners"). "As soon as they are lisping their first words," he writes, "they should be taught to make the sign of the cross; it is also good to make them say it in Latin, so that they may be accustomed from the cradle to the language of the Church". Under the Ancien Régime, as we have already seen, this familiarization was further encouraged by the custom of teaching children to read using religious texts in Latin. Lastly, Sunday catechism was an opportunity for children to learn – generally by heart – the *Paternoster*, the *Ave Maria*, the *Credo* and the *Confiteor*, prayers that they heard at mass and learned to recite in their turn.[9]

Attendance at mass and other services was the setting for saturating with Latin believers who, in their overwhelming majority, were not Latinists in any other sense. The writer Marie Noël, who regarded herself as "ignorant" ("I know no more Latin than my mother, my grandmother and their servants"), gives an admirable description of this experience which was certainly not hers alone: "The words, many times repeated, of *Veni Creator*, *Miserere*, *De profundis*, *Magnificat*, *Te Deum* and all the others had become within us our family treasure". Her *Notes intimes* give a clear impression of what it was like to have contact with a language that – apart from everything else – was neither read nor spoken, but sung, and that was therefore inseparable from its musical coating: "The little girl of Auxerre will begin . . . on hearing Christmas carols, the moving monody of the *Stabat*, . . . to become aware of the power of words". Words, moreover, that resounded in the nave of a cathedral whose rich décor accentuated the impression they made.

> I had just turned nine. She [my grandmother] took me with her. For me it was the entrance to a sublime world, outside the other one, a world in which God and men exchanged unprecedented words that had no meaning in other

countries. On the evening of All Saints' Day, at six o'clock, the two of us made our way into the great Night of the Cathedral which at that hour, under its prodigious vaults, had neither beginning nor end . . . In the tower the knell tolled . . . that admirable knell of Auxerre Cathedral, a tragic group of deep bells that burst suddenly into sobbing – five or six heartbreaking notes – and then fell back into silence from which, after a few minutes of anguish, they would break out once more in sombre tears drawn from some unknowable well of suffering and fear . . . Nevertheless, we sang along with the priests.[10]

So for Marie Noël, as for many French people of her generation, Church Latin was both remote (being neither learned nor spoken) and close (because constantly heard, recited and sung). It was an unknown tongue, and a familiar idiom.

Eamonn Duffy draws similar conclusions from a study of private devotion in England on the eve of the Reformation, based on the primers of the period, books of hours that must have been extremely successful, since between Caxton's first edition and the first Protestant publications in 1530 they went through some 114 impressions. Such popularity must raise one or two questions: the primers were in Latin and their owners lay people, with little or no knowledge of the old language. They were nothing more than books containing prayers to be recited, and that is how they were used. Some of these prayers were far from unknown to the lay faithful, who heard them regularly during mass or other services, and were thus returning, in the privacy of their own devotions, to texts they already knew. In the hands of many of their users, who knew little or no Latin, primers were probably not so much read in the strict sense as used as "a set of clues to launch them on prayers they knew by heart from hearing and recitation". Through repetition, texts written in an unknown or little-known language had ceased to be totally foreign.[11]

Translation into intelligible terms

The very repetition of the Latin prayers of the mass made them familiar to the faithful. However, it did not necessarily give an exact understanding of the words recited and heard; but this does not mean that the "simple folk", unschooled in Latin, would have been a passive audience, obediently reciting and chanting to cues. In reality, whether reciting public prayers or responses to the priest, the faithful could sometimes be anything but dumb witnesses to an unintelligible ritual, or parrots mechanically repeating words they did not understand. In their own way, they participated actively in the ceremonies they were attending by interpreting the sounds they heard into familiar terms or words that seemed to make some sort of sense. At work here was a process which has always been quite common in human apprehension of reality:

reduction of the unknown to the known. Three examples should suffice to demonstrate it.

The first comes from Tuscany, where recitation of the *Paternoster* has given birth to a series of bizarre characters not to be found in the official records of the Church. *Sanctificetur* engendered Santo (or Saint) Ficè, *da nobis hodie* produced a mysterious lady called Donna Bisodia, and *et ne nos inducas* a being called Tenenosse, strangely contained in two crates (*in du' casse*). These creatures of fantasy may be products of misunderstanding, but are certainly not (as has been suggested) caused by an "absence of participation" among the faithful; what they express, on the contrary, is a wish – naïvely and awkwardly effected perhaps – to take part in the ceremony by translating into intelligible words a reality whose literal meaning the linguistic barrier has not just made inaccessible, but transformed into mere sounds.[12]

A similar process can be seen at work in words and expressions derived from the Bible and religious offices that were current in the dialect of Lucca at the beginning of the twentieth century. Although (to some people) they denote total incomprehension of the literal meaning, they do manifest the effort made to assimilate unknown words from an unknown language by adapting them to the familiar sounds of the vulgar tongue. Thus, *Homo natus de muliere* ("Man born of woman"), the opening phrase of one of the readings from Job, became a saying redolent of commonsense fatalism: *omo nato deve morire* ("the man who is born must die"); and a "poor woman" was reported to have interpreted the last words of the *Ave Maria, nunc et in hora mortis nostrae. Amen* ("now and at the hour of our death. Amen") as follows: *la'ncatenò e la morse e nostre amme* ("chained her up and bit her and our . . .?").[13]

The same phenomenon of appropriation can be seen at work in Pierre Jakez Hélias's description of Sunday services at his native village in Brittany. The people of Pouldreuzic who, in the 1920s, spoke only Breton, at Sunday mass had to cope with Latin, which was not just incomprehensible but spoken only by the priest and heard only on Sundays and feast days. But this unintelligible and superior language was in no way foreign; indeed its popular name, "Sunday Breton", conveys the effort people were making to assimilate an unknown or imperfectly understood reality, to make it their own by transposing it into their own language. Still more revealing is the attitude of the congregation during the ceremonies. "[They] give the impression of being well acquainted with this language," Pierre Jakez Hélias writes,

> since they respond to the celebrant in unison without ever faltering. So we [the children] try to link this church Breton with our everyday Breton through the occasional words floating on the Latin music that seem to be our own.
>
> That is why we give our total assent to the *Dies irae, dies illa*. In Breton *diêz* means difficult and we quite agree: all this is far from easy, we have every reason to repeat the word. Alas! The rest completely escapes us. From the catechism

and the Stations of the Cross, we know what a deplorable character the one called Pilate is. So in the sung *Credo* we bawl out the words *"Pontio Pilato"* to show our strong disapproval of his conduct. The grown-ups do the same. Why is it that this name Pontius Pilate always has a foreign ring to our ears when that of Jesus Christ slips into them as easily as if it was Breton? Perhaps because of *Kristen* (Christian) which we hear repeatedly in sermons, prayers and canticles. But *pilad* means overthrow in Breton. That accursed Pilate is the one who has brought Christ down . . .

But what a lot of problems remain to be solved when we have totted up our meagre store of knowledge! For example, we sing the *Kyrie eleison* with great fervour . . . But we still wonder what all those carts have to do with the celebration of mass. Our ears hear *Kirri eleiz 'so* (there are heaps of carts) but we never see the colour of a single one. Neither inside nor outside. Oh well!

Although "restoring" the language of the mass into Breton in this way caused a certain astonishment, and while the transposition thus effected was a long way from guaranteeing correct understanding of the liturgical text, the practice itself nevertheless expressed an active attitude on the part of the congregation, also apparent in the fervour of its singing, its responses to the priest "in unison without ever faltering". In marked contrast was the dissipation and boredom that settled over the same congregation during the sermon, even though that was given in the vernacular or "everyday Breton".[14] This example gives a glimpse of the other face of the problem posed by the participation of the faithful in religious life, when the question is viewed not from the theologian's viewpoint but that of the "simple", in other words the great mass of Catholic people. Reduction of the unknown to the known was one way of making a religion spoken and practised in the language of learning into something more familiar to the majority of the faithful; but it could also happen that the unknown was domesticated even without the need for this work of translation.

The charm of the mysterious

When she describes Auxerre Cathedral during mass as "a sublime world, outside the other one, a world in which God and men exchanged unprecedented words that had no meaning in other countries", Marie Noël was underlining the mysterious dimension that Church Latin possessed for many of the faithful. Of course this characteristic was considered propitious for the spiritual life of the Christian populace: mystery, respect and religious sentiment went together (remember the texts by Chateaubriand, Joseph de Maistre and Dom Guéranger quoted in chapter 2). While it is true that the development of a more feeling and emotional Church, in reaction against Enlightenment rationalism, gave this function of Latin a wider role, it had been recognized very much earlier. Without going back into the Middle Ages, we need only recall that some speakers at the Council of Trent had underlined the special reverence aroused by an unknown language, asserted that the Word of God is more efficacious when swathed in the respect given to things that are not fully understood;[15] and that in the aftermath of the Tridentine decisions, authors opposed to vernacular Bibles insisted on this link between Latin and the "reverence due to the Word of God", the language of the scholars shielding "the secrets of religion" from the "contempt of men who find it easy to ignore things that are familiar to them and common".[16]

Apart from all that, the very conditions of production of the Latin heard during church services exacted respect. It emanated, so to speak, from the extraordinary, in the literal sense of the word. In a village community, it was only ever heard on the lips of the priest – even the schoolteacher, his *alter ego* under the Third Republic, did not speak it[17] – during ceremonies that represented a break with the everyday, in an edifice whose scale and architecture distinguished it radically from most other buildings; and accompanied, moreover, by ritual gestures and movements imbued with solemnity, using objects and ornaments that would have seemed very magnificent to people of humble condition.

The respect thus commanded by Latin – the sentiment that moved the Breton peasants described by Pierre Jakez Hélias – harmonized perfectly with the concept of a "religion of mysteries", theologically erroneous but nevertheless the viewpoint of many of the faithful. The answers by supporters of Latin to the 1946 survey by *Témoignage chrétien* are unequivocal on this point. "I admired without understanding, just as we believe in the Holy Trinity," wrote one of Forbach's correspondents. Another mentioned "that air of mystery that goes so well with the mysteries of our religion". Yet another, writing from Avignon, listed the characteristics that he believed made Latin superior to French as "a more religious note, a more mystical soul, a more divine accent", and went on to compare the "rationalist" present, unfavourably from a spiritual viewpoint, with the "mystical" past:

> Our era, the daughter of the Renaissance, wants to illuminate everything, to understand everything. And that will be the death of it . . . It aspires to centre the liturgy on man, and not on God: what an aberration! Restore a sense of the sacred, of the infinite, give these people a taste of it, and they will grumble no more against Latin.
>
> Did not our ancestors pray in huge dark halls crowded with enormous pillars? But those were centuries of faith.

For its partisans, Latin was of great help in surrounding the liturgy with an appropriate atmosphere of mystery; they saw it as "a barricade of secrecy, a frontier raised before the intelligence to magnify the majesty of religion and the respect owed to it". Their many quotations and borrowings – not always appropriate or properly understood – from the writings of Dom Guéranger underline the force that these calls for a liturgy swathed in majesty, secrecy and mystery possessed for the faithful;[18] they deepened the reverence felt for holy things.

It is hardly surprising, therefore, that to some people a liturgy associated with secrecy and mystery should have acquired the appearance of an incantation: that words uttered by the priest in an unknown or little-known language – or even the language itself, in its difference from everyday language – should have been perceived as possessing an intrinsic magical power.[19] Although theologically quite wrong, this interpretation of Christian liturgy was common enough to be taken into consideration by Catholic writers on the language of worship. "The use of the Latin tongue by those who do not know it," writes Gianfranco Venturi, "may give rise to automatisms similar to those encountered in the magical world".[20]

Some very interesting examples of this are to be found in sixteenth- and seventeenth-century England. The pre-Reformation primers studied by Eamonn Duffy, books of prayers to be recited, also functioned as sacred objects. They certainly had that appearance for users ignorant of Latin: their bindings resembled those of the books used at the altar, they contained images some of which conferred indulgences on the viewer, and a good proportion of the texts they contained were the ones recited during formal services. The prayers were in the language used by the priest at the altar, the language of scripture, the language of God. Hence the intrinsic power attributed to these books, along with the inherent virtue contained in their prayers, further underlined by vernacular headings indicating that this or that precise form of words had been revealed as especially pleasing to God and the saints.[21]

These primers thus reflect a popular concept of the Church as a vast reservoir of magical power that could be deployed for secular ends. While theologians rejected this outlook, drawing a clear distinction between magic and religion, the "simple" tended to confuse devotional practices with magical ones, the use of an unknown and mysterious language making the assimilation easier and more natural. As Keith Thomas has shown, the Reformation represented a break with this tradition while being, on another level, a revealing exception to it. Protestantism emphatically rejected the magical view of the sacraments and other consecration formulae; with a view to establishing a direct relationship between the believer and God, it set out to eliminate all belief in the magical aspects of religion, and strove to abolish the idea that Church rituals had some sort of mechanical efficacy in themselves; and in order to reduce the incantatory aspect of formal prayer, it abandoned Latin for the vernacular. This break with a familiar order arrived, however, at a time when religion, for the populace, was more a matter of practice than belief, a set of rituals that structured everyday life and tapped into an infinite source of supernatural aid. Religion might change, but the problems that confronted people stayed the same; in such conditions, practices of magical type could not be expected to disappear overnight. Thus (to restrict ourselves to the role of Latin), the saying of Catholic prayers in that language was for a long time a standard feature of magical remedies for sickness; similarly, charms or amulets supposed to protect people or animals contained Latin fragments copied from Catholic prayers, and spells for the recovery of lost or stolen property might involve reciting such fragments.[22]

It is not unreasonable to compare all of this with some of the reactions to Vatican II which, four centuries later, altered the liturgy and launched "a new way to live Catholicism".[23] Some Catholics had difficulty in adapting to the consequent break with ingrained habits, and mourned the passing of a famil- iar world. "They liked ceremonies of which they understood little," wrote A- M. Roguet, "but which were familiar to them, which evoked childhood memories, which cradled their religious feelings. The ideal view of praying in church was that it was a refuge from the problems and anxieties of life."[24] Fr Congar, too, noted that an element in the believers' allergy to change was "the natural – and in itself respectable – need to seek security in religion".[25] For the faithful, this was to be found in "the ancestral practice of an uncom- prehended liturgy, . . . the use of a dead language, . . . [and] a sequence of gestures that, little by little, have lost . . . all meaning";[26] more in ritual, in other words, than in any belief. When the liturgy was uttered in everyday lan- guage, did it still possess its authority and power?

Not according to some of the replies to the 1946 *Témoignage chrétien* survey: these correspondents, while favouring translation of the prayers used in the sacraments, took an inflexible attitude on certain "essential" phrases – for example *Ego te baptizo* or *Dominus noster Jesus Christus te absolvat* – which they felt must absolutely stay in Latin. It was a view that aroused the uncompre- hending indignation of Mgr Martimort, who commented on the survey: "If there is one sacrament which nobody would dare to insist on having in Latin for the sake of form, it is that of marriage . . . Surely the knowledge that he is baptized in the name of the Trinity is, for a Christian, the decisive orien- tation of his whole life?"[27] He was missing the point that for some believers these Latin phrases functioned in the same way as magical incantations: heard as pure sounds, they were thought efficacious in themselves. Apart from sounding less solemn – itself not necessarily an improvement – would the same effects be produced in vernacular languages? Unintelligibility made sense. Translated into everyday speech, the liturgy (for some Catholics) had been stripped of one of its signs of authority[28] and lost its efficacy in the process. Apart from its anti-clerical tone, Georges Brassens's song *Tempête dans un bénitier* ("Storm in a holy water stoop") summarizes the feelings of a lot of Catholics in the aftermath of Vatican II:

Sans le latin, sans le latin,
Plus de mystère magique.
Le rite qui nous envoûte
S'avère alors anodin.[29]

(Without Latin, without Latin,
No more magical mystery.
The rite that holds us spellbound
Then turns out to be tame.)

The disappearance of Latin meant more than the interruption of banal habits, the replacement of simple mechanisms; it disarranged a mental universe in which that unintelligible language had been fully domesticated. For those faithful who had come to believe that, as Chateaubriand put it, "the surge of [their] prayer is what makes its charm",[30] the unknown words possessed an incantatory value – think here of what the sign of the cross in Latin represented – and helped in the realization of their wishes. Did not the reactions aroused by the vernacular liturgy include, apart from opposition to what some saw as its flat and awkward language,[31] a perception – perhaps confused – that a new relation with the sacred, paradoxically less intimate than the old one, was being established? Since "the problems and anxieties of life" remained, it is not surprising that some individuals devoid of Latin culture should have sought refuge in the familiar world of a Latin tradition.

2 Schoolchildren and Latin: Capturing the Monster

Until the 1960s, most children in secondary education found themselves faced with long years of Latin. Without going back to the Ancien Régime, when Latin and learning to read were the same subject, remember that even in the late nineteenth century a child was set at Latin at the age of seven and did not see the last of it until he left secondary school ten or eleven years later; for those ten years, moreover, it was the bulk of his diet in terms of the hours assigned to it and the number of translations, compositions and recitations required. Even when the old language began to lose its importance in education, it remained one of the fundamental disciplines of the curriculum; it was still usual to do six or seven years of it in the 1960s. For Catholic children, the prayers learned from the catechism and heard at mass helped engender an early familiarity with Latin: the subject they encountered on entering secondary school was not unknown and therefore alarming, but (in Mary McCarthy's phrase) "an old friend".[32]

The Latin that used to accompany adolescence did not show itself in a particularly attractive light, however. The teaching, dominated by a hyper-grammatical tendency and based on texts chosen for their linguistic and moral qualities, was generally very austere. The forbidding image that resulted was confirmed to some extent – we will return to this later – by the difficulty of acquiring the rudiments of Latin and the mediocrity of most people's performance in it.[33] It is hardly surprising that some of its peculiarities, without parallels in this or that modern language, have caused Latin to be imagined in strange or monstrous forms: the gerundive, whose function is baffling to an English speaker, was once caricatured as an exotic creature "attacking peaceful pronouns" before being captured by the emblematic Victorian grammarian Benjamin Kennedy.[34] In their own way, schoolchildren made the same gesture in symbolic fashion: by "capturing" the Latin they were taught, integrating it into their universe or adapting it to their needs, they made it more familiar or anyway less frightening.

"Contrary imaginings"

This expression is used here to designate the responses of schoolchildren to Latin as it was taught to them. We are not concerned here to evaluate their performance or calculate their standard, but to show how children, sometimes very young, experienced the teaching they were given by their masters and textbooks, and how they reacted to these authorities. In general they were far from passive recipients and far from accurate interpreters; they deciphered what they saw, interpreting it in terms that made sense to them and assimilating it into their world.[35] These procedures of decoding and appropriation helped them to absorb the Latin quite literally imposed on them, and at the same time rendered more bearable the feelings of fear, aversion and boredom that were (it seems) the common lot of schoolchildren.[36]

Games were an early response. The games played by the future Charles XII of Sweden included Romulus and Remus, and Caesar crossing the Rhine. For the latter game, his page recounted, "he would place a hurdle over the kennel of the palace court, and would storm at me for that I would not willingly fall in the water or mud when I was killed by his little sword"; that was one of the uses the young prince made of the Latin education he was given, an education largely based on reading ancient authors, historians in particular, with Caesar – studied in a way that emphasized what it was like to be in the field – featuring prominently.[37]

Most people learned Latin in a much more grammatical way, involving a major effort to memorize a large number of complex rules. Rhyme was felt by pedagogues to be an effective mnemonic technique, although it sometimes had the opposite effect, as in the case of Jean-Jacques Rousseau who inveighed against "those Ostrogothic verses that made me sick to my heart and could not get into my ear".[38] They lacked a certain musical quality that would have made them easier to remember. The children tried to supply it themselves by superimposing tunes they knew on the dry words of some grammatical rule. This helps explain the much more favourable impression Edward Hornby retained of the gender rule for nouns expressed in what he calls "little pearls of poetry":

> Third Nouns Masculine prefer
> endings o, or, os and er ;
> add to which the ending es,
> if its Cases have increase.

> Not great stuff you may say but listen to the mellifluous tones of some exceptions:

> many neuters end in er,
> siler, acer, verber, ver
> tuber, uber, and cadaver
> piper, iter and papaver.

> My favourite excerpt is this. A Rule followed by some beautiful poetry.

> Third Nouns Feminine we class
> ending is, x, aus and as,
> s to consonant appended,
> es in flexion unextended.

> We used to commit these to memory . . . while queueing to go to the . . . lav. after breakfast . . . We chanted them to the tune of Hymn No 520 "Love Divine all Loves Excelling".[39]

This musical foundation supporting acquisition of the rudiments of Latin is well illustrated by Jacques Brel's song about the *rosa* paradigm, which symbolized Latin to generations of French schoolchildren.

> C'est le plus vieux tango du monde
> Celui que les têtes blondes
> Anonnent comme une ronde
> En apprenant leur latin.

> (It's the world's oldest tango
> The one the fair-haired youngsters
> Drone like a roundsong
> While they learn their Latin.)

A childish "roundsong" dedramatized entry to the austere world of Latin grammar; the first declension became a simple refrain, sung here by a choir of children that accompanied Brel during the refrain:

Rosa rosa rosam
Rosae rosae rosa
Rosae rosae rosas
Rosarum rosis rosis.[40]

In these exercises where musical rhythm acted as a memorization aid, grammatical rules could end up as mere collections of sounds; in such cases accent or stress made the sense. For Thomas Thornely, for example, prepositions taking the ablative had a grave accent, those taking the accusative were pronounced with an acute.

Whose heart has not been stirred in early youth by the solemn chant of the Latin prepositions that govern the ablative?

A, ab, abque, coram, de
Palam, clam, cum, ex and e
Tenus, sine, pro and prae.

In this meaningless collocation of syllables we seem to hear the low rumbling of thunder of the Dies irae and are naturally led to contrast it with the light tripping of the banded prepositions that favour the accusative.[41]

In the same way that children tamed the rules of Latin grammar, they took hold of the Latin world and bent it to their own uses. In a lot of French establishments the principal was known as *Peto* ("I demand" in Latin) and the vice-principal Cato in memory of the famous Roman magistrate of that name; the dictionary, that permanent companion of the young Latinist, became the *dico*, an abbreviation that was also the Latin for "I say". At Chambéry, the top pupil in the class was known as the *mec plus ultra* ("guy *plus ultra*").[42] At the Laon college in Lavisse's time, the principal had been nicknamed *Dico* and the future historian, for an error in translating the story of Horatius Cocles, for a time bore the handle of this character from Antiquity.[43]

This last example also illustrates the familiarity created by the translation of texts – not very many of them – with famous episodes of Roman history and their heroes; but these texts could also be adapted and distorted. In *L'enfant*, Vallès's indictment of classical education, the name of the famous defender of Rome Mucius Scaevola is "deformed" and ridiculed by being changed to "Cervelas" (Fr. *cervelle* = brain).[44] The opening words of Cicero's first Catiline oration – *Quousque tandem*, a well-known landmark of the school world – has inspired a good deal of clowning. Thus the humorist Alphonse Allais:

Without going back so far, the tandem, that famous tandem that you worship as a god, was current (perhaps running would be a better word) in the old days of Rome.

One of the most sought-after makes at that time was the Quousque tandem, used to the exclusion of all others by the Catilina brothers' team.

When Cicero (see the first *Catiline Oration*) had mentioned the Quousque tandem to the Catilinas, he had said it all.

And he added, did Marcus Tullius *abutere patientia nostra*, which meant: "When are the Catilina brothers' team going to leave us in peace, them and their lethal Quousque tandem?"

In this piece of bravura Alphonse Allais (incidentally a good Latinist) was making a joke for cultivated readers possessing the same cultural references, and able to recall a shared past.[45] The parodied Latin speech introduced by Jules Romains in *Les copains* shares a similar inspiration: derision of – quite genuine – Latin learning combined with instruction, here by way of the tall story, in the best Ecole Normale tradition.[46]

The Latin learned in class was also, for pupils at colleges run by religious orders, heard in chapel and the refectory. Here too there was no shortage of plays on words and other jokes. Lambert, the narrator's friend in Claude Simon's *Histoire*, when serving mass for the prefect of studies would

> bawl at the top of his voice never missing a "Bite y est dans le caleçon" ("Prick is there in the drawers") instead of Kyrie eleison or "Bonne Biroute à Toto" ("Good Hard-on to Louse") for Et cum spiritu tuo, having for almost all the responses a version of that sort, many as forcible as "En trou si beau adultère est béni" ("In hole so fine adulterer is blessed") instead of Introibo ad altare Dei.

This "arsenal of puns and spoonerisms supposed, through verbal magic, to emancipate him from inherited beliefs and the lessons of the catechism" was also a challenge to the authority of the master; but the rebellion was conducted in a fully domesticated Latin.[47]

Like certain texts and words, the textbooks and other works used for learning Latin became parts of a familiar universe. The great majority of French collegians conceived a very strong attachment for Gaffiot's *Dictionnaire*, bearer of all their hopes. In English public schools at the end of the nineteenth century, idle doodling in class transformed the front cover of most school copies of Kennedy's *Shorter Latin Primer* to read "Shortbread Eating Primer"[48] or something of the sort, often showing considerable typographical artistry along with the adolescent preoccupation with food and aversion to Latin.[49] It sometimes even happened that the pupils used the Latin they had been taught against their masters by turning it into a sort of secret code; Montherlant wrote of a friend he remembered at college: "We quite often used Latin so that the masters would not understand us".[50]

Mistakes could cease to be regarded as shameful and become badges of glory remembered almost with pride. "A stranger to all that was said and done in class," wrote Anatole France when recalling his years at college, "ignorant of all useful precepts, unaware of essential rules, I produced compositions and translations far removed from that exactness, that elegance and concision. Everything that emerged from my pen abounded in solecisms and barbarisms, mistakes and mistranslations."[51] Verlaine shows similar complacency in an anecdote concerning his own early experience of Latin; when he had got as far as "the second conjugation of active verbs" he had this exchange with a teacher:

> "Verlaine, conjugate *legere*."
> "*Lego*, I read, *legis*, thou readest", etc.
> "Good. The imperfect?"
> "*Legebam*, I was reading", and so on.
> "Excellent. The preterite?"
> I was all fresh from the first conjugation.
> "*Legavi* . . ."
> "*Legavi?*"
> "*Lexi*," whispered a friend of mine, better than me at Latin, with the best of intentions.
> "*Lexi*, sir."
> "*Legavi! Lexi!*" the master literally howled . . . and a vigorously hurled bunch of keys struck the wall to the left of my head (now covered by both hands and sunk between my shoulders), soon followed by a Noël et Quicherat dictionary, almost the size of a Bottin, which smashed into the wall in question on my right.[52]

In this way the barbarisms and solecisms that punctuated daily life at school were transformed into trophies, or were at least referred to in affectionate style (in French colleges as *barbos* and *solos*) so as to dedramatize mistakes and make them seem less shameful.

The discovery of sexuality

The education given to children in modern Europe was characterized until quite recently by strong prudery. Politeness, seemliness and modesty conspired to draw a veil of discretion over a variety of anatomical and sexual realities, which were mentioned either not at all or, at best, only in roundabout fashion.[53] Ancient authors, by contrast, had written on these subjects with attitudes ranging from great directness to extreme crudity. No wonder then that some of these texts should have attracted the attention of adolescent collegians like the narrator and his friend in Claude Simon's *Histoire*, poring over the spicier passages from Apuleius's *Golden Ass*, lifted by the narrator from his uncle's library without permission.[54]

These readings exploring an unknown world were rendered all the more exciting by the whiff of the forbidden that accompanied the new discoveries.

Chateaubriand recalled the deep impression – "a revolution within my person" – that "an unbowdlerized Horace and an account of *Badly made con-fessions*" made on him. Soon afterwards the young boy was troubled by the episode of Dido in the *Aeneid* and Lucretius's poem "Mother of Aeneas's sons, pleasure of gods and men". Even more intense were the effects of a filched copy of Tibullus: "When I reached *Quam iuvat immites ventos audire cubantem* ("what a pleasure it is to hear the wild winds blowing when one is in bed"), these feelings of pleasure and melancholy seemed to reveal my own nature"; here the author implies without mentioning it the real reason for his emotion, found in the next line: "and tenderly embracing one's mistress".[55]

The young Chateaubriand had discovered sexuality by reading an un-bowdlerized Horace that chance had placed in his hands. For a very long time school editions were expurgated to remove any content considered unsuitable or shocking: crude or obscene words, anatomical details, sexual episodes. Cuts, rewritten passages and sweetened translations were therefore the common fate of Martial, Terence, Horace and Juvenal. These techniques, which we will describe in detail later, were intended to produce texts in keeping with the noble idea of Antiquity then current, texts that would rein-force the moral content education was supposed to have. Tender young minds should not be shocked, and they should certainly not be given wicked thoughts.[56] Of course these editions sometimes had the opposite effect, whet-ting adolescent curiosity to read uncut versions (which also possessed the allure of the forbidden).

> When I was at college in the late 1920s, [recalls Professor Olivier Reverdin] we were reading Horace in the Hachette edition, which is a school edition. In the account of the journey to Brindisi there is mention of a girl whom Horace awaits for a long time, but in vain; irritated by the delay, the poet ejaculates and soils his couch. This passage had been expurgated, but for reasons of candour or honesty the numbering of the lines had not been altered. When asked what the gap contained, the Latin master hummed and hawed and finally refused to tell us. So we procured a complete edition, with translation, and I should imagine that the expurgated passage is the only one, from the whole of Horace, that most of my classmates remember today.[57]

Some of these school editions accentuated the very temptation they were supposed to guard against, like the anthology of Latin poetry used at Harrow in Byron's time there. The expurgated passages had been moved to the end of the book; naturally it was to this appendix that the boys turned first. When this famous example was mentioned at a conference in 1979, Professor Arnaldo Momigliano called out: "In Italy, too, we used editions like that!"[58]

Like texts, the Latin-vernacular dictionary was the companion of adoles-cent fantasies. The indispensable instrument of the apprentice translator, it was also scanned and explored in the search for "crude and anatomical words". This is how the narrator of Claude Simon's *Histoire* remembers it:

> stirred to the depths to the very roots of my (inguinum: groin, lower abdomen) breathing the dusty and faded odour of the dictionary its corners dogeared and fluffy from being turned with a licked finger, seeking cheeks on fire (the hurried gasping breathing of the phrase present participles following each other, jostling, accumulating, panting breath, burning, lacinia remota impatientiam mea monstrans: lifting the skirt of my garment, pulling up my clothes, uncovering it, showing it, saying vides jam proximante vehementer intentus look how I the donkey's member raised painful blind unbearable oppido formoso ne nervus) finger running down the columns from top to bottom, the yellowed pages, among the words
>
> cubile
> flora
> formosus (well made, handsomely formed),
> nympha . . .

and a little later: "finger, its nail stationary below the fat-charactered word: *nervus*, tendon, ligament, virile member, nerve".[59]

The sweetness of memory

Latin came to be perceived through the prism of childhood and thus to evoke a time of happiness for an adult leafing through his past. That is the impression given by Jacques Brel's song *Rosa*, even though the future singer had not been the most exemplary of scholars:

> It's the time when I was bottom of the class
> . . .
> It's the tango of the time of the zeros
> I had so many of them skinny ones fat ones.

But the school years awaken an altogether different music in the memory:

> . . . it's the tango of the blissful time
> . . . it's the tango of the time we yearn for.[60]

Evocation of the paradigm of the first declension, both an emblem for Latin culture and the symbol of what remains when all else has been forgotten, brings back memories of college transfigured by the sweetness of recall. The American author T. Higginson had the same feeling on coming across his Latin grammar in a trunk in the attic, "my very dear old Latin book with the elderflower perfume of the springtime of my adolescence".[61] Mary McCarthy

in her autobiography recalled her adolescent's passion for Caesar and resulting interest in Latin grammar: "So that today," she wrote, "I cannot see an
ablative absolute or a passage of indirect discourse without happy tears
springing to my eyes".[62]

A number of works by so-called *nouveaux romanciers* have used Latin,
expressing a mythical childhood, as a backcloth to the narrative. It returns
ceaselessly to the adult's memory, at the mention of a word, on reading an
inscription, on looking at a photograph; even memories of a recent war are
mingled with other memories of much more ancient wars, battles from
Antiquity discovered during school translation exercises.[63] This presence
alone, like a continuous bass line, expresses the appropriation of a language
frequented for many years, a Latin which certainly became familiar although
not always known.

Part II

Standards and Ability

Introduction

From the Renaissance to the middle of the twentieth century, Latin was one of the characteristic features of Western culture, one of its common elements. Despite the many differences between countries, it can be said that Latin had the same lasting hold on the intellectual world in both Catholic and Protestant territory. Although, with chronological variations between regions, Latin gradually lost its early monopoly over the elaboration and diffusion of learning, it nevertheless retained a number of strongholds, education in particular remaining a solid bastion until very recently. Latin had its rivals there too, but was long predominant, its decline marked by determined rearguard action. This saturation with Latin engendered a solid familiarity with a language that formed part of the daily environment, for some individuals from the moment of first introduction to it; what was true everywhere for the educated elite was true in Catholic countries for the entire people. It is this omnipresence that made Latin "the European sign", to use Joseph de Maistre's felicitous expression.[1] It is tempting to investigate what the imprint's product was like.

It was certainly substantial, as we can see from a glance at the catalogues assembled by Jozef Ijsewijn.[2] They contain the names of hundreds – thousands – of scholars and men of letters who (after the humanist period) wrote in Latin. Those listed, moreover, are all what we now call "writers", or at least scholars on various subjects displaying some literary talent. Their considerable output included writings of every sort; despite a somewhat laboured imitation of classical models, these works often display remarkable virtuosity, and they include original efforts of the very highest quality.

These lists reveal the limitations of neo-Latin literature as well as its successes. The first catalogue, which is chronological, shows that after 1700 the output of these works decreased sharply under strong and increasing competition from works in vernacular languages. Although he observes in a general introduction that "the great period of neo-Latin literature stretches from 1400 to 1800",[3] Ijsewijn is compelled, in the specific discussion he devotes to the different countries, to revert to the *terminus ad quem* or proceed much more rapidly after the middle of the seventeenth century; as Latin writers became rarer the number of published works had declined, and – although virtuosity was still apparent – it seems that the time for masterpieces was over. By the turn of the nineteenth century a writer like Giovanni Pascoli was regarded as an exception; his Latin poetry in any case had only a small circle of admirers, and it is to his work in the vernacular that the "official poet" owed his renown.[4] The chronological limit that can be placed at around 1700 coincided with a sociological mutation. After that, Latin authors came from two main backgrounds: the world of school and university, and the Church with the Jesuits at the forefront (and, at the confluence of these two streams, the Society's colleges). This development was not without effect on the types of writing being cultivated: school theatre, university oratory[5] and poetry – with a predilection for the shorter forms – absorbed the largest numbers of talents.

The situation in France is emblematic in this area. Change took place in the second half of the seventeenth century. Early in the reign of Louis XIV Latin literature, especially poetry, was still being cultivated and attracting real interest: in 1662, for example, Chapelain included many neo-Latin authors in the list of people of letters who were to receive pensions from the King. However, the more substantial forms were hardly being practised any longer, most of the output consisting of epigrams, elegies, satires, tomb inscriptions and epitaphs. Twenty years later Bayle observed, in reference to what was being published at the time, that Latin poetry was "breathing its last". Even Boileau, an admirer of the Ancients, was irritated by Latin poets who merely "weave poems out of joined-up fragments" and denounced the "strange enterprise of writing in a foreign language when we have never had anything to do with its native speakers".

> How are we to know [he went on] on what occasions in Latin the substantive should come before the adjective or the adjective before the substantive? But imagine what an absurdity it would be to say in French mon neuf habit instead of mon habit neuf, or mon blanc bonnet instead of mon bonnet blanc, whether or not the proverb says they mean the same thing.

During this period, the major Latin poets – one of the greatest being Jean-Baptiste Santeul who produced many admirable Latin hymns – disappeared, never to be replaced. Only the Jesuits kept the tradition going, and they wrote mainly on pious or didactic subjects. The last hope was dashed in 1747 by the appearance of Cardinal de Polignac's *Anti-Lucretius*, a philosophical poem some 12,000 lines long which had been eagerly awaited for the past thirty years: alas, the masterpiece was received with the most extreme disappointment. After that, Latin poetry fell into the hands of the colleges, where until the turn of the twentieth century it engendered a colossal mass of Latin verse, the best of which is more notable for technique than for original inspiration. In the nineteenth century – outside the school world – Latin verse was the hobby of amateurs, who cultivated forms derived from the neo-Latin tradition and educational practice, didactic or descriptive poetry and "occasional" verse. These poets could show off their talents at the international competitions either organized to mark special events (like the birth of Napoleon I's son in 1811 or the coronation of Pope Leo XIII in 1882) or held annually (like the *Certamen Hoeufftianum* held in Amsterdam from 1843 to 1978). Two journals willing to publish their efforts – *Hermes romanus ou Mercure latin* and *Apis romana, journal de littérature* – still existed in the first thirty years of the twentieth century.[6]

Give or take a few adjustments of chronology, the same remarks hold good elsewhere.[7] The altogether exceptional case of Croatia, which still harboured remarkable Latin poets well into the nineteenth century, can be explained by the official status that the Latin language enjoyed there.[8] Generally speaking, neo-Latin literature – nearly all of it poetry – was now no more than a minority pursuit,[9] even though Jozef Ijsewijn has still been able to list quite a lot of names. Their reputations have remained obscure, however, except sometimes in other zones of endeavour: if Miguel Antonio Caro is remembered in history it will be as President of Colombia, rather than as a Latin poet.[10]

So what became of this Latin revival when its literary output, instead of measuring up to the ubiquitous and enduring presence that we have noted, shrank after a certain – and rather early – date to miserable proportions? Perhaps the resurrection of Latin was out of the question, when even someone like Boileau thought that "if Terence and Cicero came back to life, they would roar with laughter over the Latin works of people like Fernel, Sannazar and Muret".[11] Or perhaps the answer should be sought elsewhere, on the more everyday terrain of written and oral standards that failed to live up to the orator's or writer's ambitions. That is the purpose of the next two chapters.

CHAPTER 5

Written Latin

"Oh! How I would love it to be in Latin! Perhaps if I wrote it in Latin first
. . . I think much better in Latin. I'll translate it afterwards." That is how the
hero of Jules Vallès's novel *Le bachelier* proposes to deal with the correspondence of the commercial firm that employs him. In that respect at least he is
a perfect product of the French secondary education which, in the first half
of the nineteenth century, gave more training in Latin than French. If his
wish had been granted, though, would he have been up to writing a business
letter in Latin as if it had been his native language?[1] The question may be
purely hypothetical in his case, but it is quite legitimate when examining the
mass of Latin impressions in the context of European publishing in general
and scholarly and religious publishing in particular. What sort of Latin is
found in these works and how, therefore, do we rate the linguistic competence of their authors?

1 Scholars' Latin

We should come clean at the outset and note that, although Latin may have
been praised to the skies as the language of learning, studies in this area are
extremely rare. Almost more paradoxical is the fact that the works of scholars – a colossal output that neo-Latin specialists cite to prove the continuing
relevance and vitality of Latin in modern intellectual life – should have
received so very little attention. Not being "literature", they have tended to
be excluded from the field of enquiry; and the few exceptions become even
rarer once the glorious times of Humanism and the Renaissance are past.
Historians of science, while interested in the choices between Latin and the
vernacular made by authors whose works they were analysing, have paid virtually no attention to their heroes' "Latinity", making at best a few general
observations. And the existing bibliography provides only the thinnest of data

on the kind of Latin scholars wrote, outside a small number of individual cases.

Given all of this, the indications that James W. Binns has derived from a study of Latin publishing in England between 1530 and 1640 are infinitely precious. Knowledge of and ability in Latin increased throughout the sixteenth century, and people tended to conform to classical models in syntax, vocabulary and style. Despite inherited spelling mistakes and the survival of constructions crudely adopted from English – *quod* meaning "that", for example, intruded into a sentence where one would expect only a Latin infinitive – the improvement over the mediaeval version of the language became increasingly marked. The Latin written in England was nevertheless not as fluid as that produced on the continent (France and Italy to be precise) at the same time. And J.W. Binns concludes on a sober note: in general this Latin cannot be mistaken for classical Latin.[2]

Similar observations apply to the theses submitted to Swedish universities between 1611 and 1716, dissertations on theology, philosophy, law, history, medicine and the sciences. These texts represent the point of intersection between a linguistic practice maintained by university teaching, with roots going back to the Middle Ages, and a stylistic ideal of humanist origin based on imitation of classical authors. The result is an "eclectic" Latin, but one rendered distinct from mediaeval texts by its greater concern for correctness. Vocabulary is a useful indicator. The compilers of thesauruses, lexicons and other *antibarbari* intended for the use of those wishing to write correct Latin generally adopted a moderate position on *stylus philosophicus* (scientific style). The authenticity of a word was supposedly dependent on the authority of an *auctor probatus* – itself a criterion of variable validity – but they accepted that *vocabula artis* (technical terms) and *res novae* (modern phenomena) justified a fairly wide interpretation of the classical norm. However, they seem not to have adhered very closely to this system. Although the vocabulary of these publications is consciously biased towards the "classical", it still contains a number of non-classical words, some of them mediaeval: for example the word *medium* is frequently used in the sense of "means" or "instrument", although this is a barbarism identified even by a tolerant grammarian like Cellarius, who wanted it to be replaced by *subsidium*. There is no shortage of neologisms and – contrary to the wishes of purists – ancient words are used in new meanings, while non-classical ones are not just seen in specialized terminologies, but often reappear in the general vocabulary. Grammar is also affected by the prevailing eclecticism. Spelling is often inconsistent, with classical and mediaeval spellings coexisting, sometimes in the work of the same author; understandably, however, as grammar textbooks contained very few rules on this point, while dictionaries, and editions of the classics as well, included forms that were not classical. While the morphology is entirely satisfactory, the syntax by contrast contains a lot of constructions not found in the works of Cicero and his contemporaries. A reduction in the time spent on learning grammar and the practice of learning syntax while reading texts could help explain the relatively high frequency of non-classical constructions; and among these thesis-writers they also result from the influence of the vernacular, sometimes copied too closely.[3]

This defect could also be seen in authors of a different stature, if the judgement of one "expert" – the philologist Gilles Ménage – is accepted. "M. de Balzac's Latin is very pure," he wrote,

> nevertheless, it seems to me to have a French turn of phrase. I said so the other day to a man of great merit, and he replied that he had the same feeling, and that this reason often deterred him from reading the prose and verse of our moderns. Broadly speaking, I said to him, setting aside a few of our people such as, among others, M. de Valois, M. Huet, M. Petit, Madame Dacier and some others the Roman elegance of whose works almost equals their erudition, most authors are full of Gallicisms, Teutonisms, Anglicisms and all the other European idioms. Among foreigners, there are some who can certainly be regarded as exceptions, among others M. Cuper who at present is in the Sovereign Council of the States of Holland, M. Graevius of Utrecht, M. Carpzovius of Leipzig, M. Fabretti in Rome, Fr Noris in Florence, M. Spanheim and some others whose writings do honour to the Republic of Letters.[4]

So only a tiny minority seems to have managed a purely classical use of Latin. The rest, even among the learned elite, wrote a grammatically correct language in which clarity and precision of expression generally triumphed over any great concern with style. Descartes was among them. "If he had never composed in French", wrote his biographer Adrien Baillet, "his Latin would have been held up as embodying the best possible style for a philosopher and mathematician . . . He applied himself far less to beauty of expression than to the appropriateness of the words; but he did not neglect it either, and carried exactness to the point of trying to purge his Latinity of any appearance of Gallicism."[5] The same observations apply to Latin translations of works originally published in the vernacular. An instructive example is the long preface that Pierre Nicole, using the pseudonym Wilhelm Wendrock, placed at the beginning of his Latin translation of Pascal's *Lettres provinciales*. He begins by confessing his inability to convey the "singular and Attic brilliance" of many passages, to equal in Latin the author's "elegances". A more adept translator could have been chosen, but there was a risk that he might be less well versed in theology, that the style might be improved to the detriment of the content. Nicole refused to sacrifice the smallest part of the content of these letters or their profound truth, and accepted in advance that he would not be able to convey the texts in all their original beauty. None of this prevented him from coping with the banter in imitation of Terence, or from displaying solid Latinity (admittedly containing a few Gallicisms).[6] Other translators also mentioned the problems encountered in producing these Latin versions (including the transposition of modern idiomatic expressions), and justified in their various ways the approach that was generally adopted: giving up the idea of literary elegance and striving for a clear and exact translation that would render the meaning perfectly.[7]

It is hardly surprising, therefore, that exhortations to write in the mother tongue should have become frequent after the seventeenth century. Historiography has often chosen to interpret these in national terms, or as expressions of a wish to "democratize" learning. In reality the greater convenience of the vernacular in use, asserted openly by men of the time, was just as important. Vocabulary alone constituted a major obstacle, one emphasized in the *Encyclopédie* edited by Yverdon, who deplored the poverty of the Latin language in "modernisms":

> it lacks words to express the new inventions and discoveries that have been made in all areas since the decline of the Romans . . . Anyone who doubts the truth of this explanation has only to read the efforts skilled Latinists have made to write political gazettes for our time in the Latin language: they will see both the torture undergone by these authors and the poor success of their efforts.[8]

The problem was not simply a matter of finding Latin equivalents for (to use the *Encyclopédie*'s examples) words like "cannon", "perruque" or "coat-button"; for an author, it was much more a question of finding correct and faithful expression without having to achieve a *tour de force*. Voltaire's mockery of the Sorbonne theologians writing the decree condemning the views of the Abbé de Prades shows the depths of perplexity in which Latin "authors" sometimes foundered:

> When the question arose of saying in Latin that the said thesis had been printed too small, the Faculty could not get out of the hole: they all said they could not express a thesis printed small in Latin, and they sent a deputation to Sieur Le Beau, the Professor of Rhetoric, to ask him how this phrase should be rendered in Latin.[9]

Much more seriously, anyone can understand why scholars would have argued for the "easy solution" offered by the vernacular; as Antonio Vallisneri pithily put it, what was the point of beating one's head against a dead language?[10] In the draft statutes of the academy he proposed to call the "Literary Republic of Italy", Muratori declared his preference for Italian as "easier and more convenient".[11] Lazzaro Spallanzani advanced almost the same argument: "It is incomparably easier for us to explain ourselves with clarity, precision and elegance in the language we speak, owing to the familiarity we have with it, than in the Latin language whose strength, savour and graces cannot be grasped so easily, because it is dead".[12] Nevertheless neither of these men was a declared enemy of Latin, and what is more they were both good Latinists: Spallanzani's lessons were in a Latin that was "flowing, limpid and elegant";[13] Muratori not only published a great deal in Latin, but was able enough to re-edit the mediaeval chronicles included in his *Rerum italicarum scriptores* into Ciceronian Latin.[14]

Although scholars made increasing use of the national languages after the eighteenth century, some academics continued to write in Latin, exclusively so in some disciplines (botany for example). But the Latin used was very remote from the language of Cicero: botanists' Latin is virtually an artificial language, its syntax unencumbered with grammatical subtleties, its carefully-defined vocabulary nothing more than a nomenclature.[15]

The universities were the last area of the world of learning where Latin was required (as it were) by law. The Patristic theses submitted in France between 1870 and 1906 constitute an interesting sample for assessing the Latin written by people who, while not *stricto sensu* specialists in the language, had consistent experience of it through their subject. In the main these texts are more or less correct. "What is lacking," notes Brigitte du Plessis who has studied them, "is not really knowledge of grammar . . ." But they give an "impression of unease" and are "themes that are not always well put together": the Latin phrases ought to have been constructed differently, some of the combinations of words should have been avoided, along with terms and expressions not found in Cicero.[16] These remarks raise the question of the sort of Latin that would be produced by thesis-writers in subjects a good deal more remote (than Patristics) from the world of Antiquity. A sort of answer is provided by Louis Couturat and Léopold Léau: "It is no secret from anyone that a lot of candidates manage by translating (or getting someone else to translate) work they have written in French. Thus, most doctors of letters are unable to make fluent use of Latin".[17] Not much of a funeral eulogy when the second thesis in Latin was on the point of disappearing!

Only the Catholic Church maintained the exclusive use of Latin for its acts and documents until very recently. On several occasions since the end of the nineteenth century, however, the papacy has felt compelled not only to deplore the decline of Latin in the Church, but also to take measures to train Latin writers of quality. Thus in 1964 Paul VI, continuing the work of John XXIII, founded (under the Salesian University) an institute meant to give its students a good practice of written Latin, teaching them to write the language "rapidly, purely and elegantly".[18] At that time the Curia still included Latinists of the first order, starting with Cardinal Bacci (Secretary for Latin Letters and Briefs to the Princes) who wrote a Ciceronian Latin; these men were not unaware, however, that many ecclesiastics, when confronted with encyclicals and other documents written in a style worthy of the Renaissance cardinal and poet Bembo, would exclaim: "Letters from the Sovereign Pontiff, oh! How difficult and complicated their Latin is . . . Best to wait for the vernacular translation."[19] And these days a glance at the *Acta Apostolicae Sedis* is enough to show that the time of elegance is over in the Vatican's dicasteries; the Latin used in the acts of the Church is a simple vehicular language, grammatically correct and rich in neologisms. *Mutatis mutandis*, J.W. Binns's opinion of Latin output in England between 1530 and 1640 applies again here: this Latin cannot be mistaken for classical Latin.

These necessarily brief observations leave aside whole areas of Latin output from the modern era. We know nothing of the Latin in which bureaucracies and judiciaries drew up documents, in some cases until very recently. It seems reasonable to assume that it would have developed no differently from elsewhere, that the vehicular role assigned to Latin would have favoured clarity and precision of expression without giving much time to stylistic elegance. Paul Claudel, as a consul in China at the turn of the nineteenth century, had sometimes to correspond in Latin. One of his messages reads:

> Venum = datus est ager Thien-cho-tang pretii quinque millia patacarum – Lis composita est – Irruperunt satellites in Petrum catechistam cum fustibus et scolopetis – Comperi cito advenire quamdam navem vapoream Gallicam munitam viginiti quatuor tormentis bellicis

> (Sale = the field of Thien-cho-tang has been sold for five thousand cash – The matter has been settled – Guards have attacked the catechist Peter with cudgels and blunderbusses – I have heard that a French steamship armed with twenty-four guns is about to arrive[20])

We do not know whether this correct but stiff Latin represents administrative prose in general. But it does show the sort of thing that a former top pupil of Louis-le-Grand used to be able to manage without undue exertion.

2 School Latin

Throughout the West, and until the end of the nineteenth century at the very earliest, all children receiving the education we would now call secondary used (as we have seen) to get through a great deal of Latin. They started on it very young, at seven or eight, and kept it up for ten years. So they had already read large numbers of texts while still children; we should bear in mind that private education (at home, with tutors) was at one time relatively common among rich or well-connected pupils and produced some impressive examples, among them Giosuè Carducci who, by the age of ten, had translated many of Cornelius Nepos's *Lives* and all of Phaedrus, and John Stuart Mill who read the whole of Latin literature before the age of thirteen. Although in France, by the 1960s, syllabuses were not ambitious, Latin, by then just one subject among others, still loomed large in the classics section at *lycées*, whose pupils spent much time on it between sixth grade and the *bac-calauréat*.[21] Latin teaching has been exhaustively described, its textbooks analysed, its methods detailed; far less interest has been shown in the end result. Efforts to assess the knowledge acquired from it are rare, and statistical studies based, for example, on class records, were almost non-existent until the present day. We are therefore obliged to resort extensively to narrative sources, the remarks of teachers and the memories of former pupils, to get some sort of answer to a simple but very legitimate question: what did the children learn in the course of this long schooling in Latin or, more exactly, what level did they reach?

Virtuosity and amusement

Some collegians achieved very satisfactory results. The examination papers found by Marie-Madeleine Compère and Dolorès Pralon-Julia show that there were pupils at Louis-le-Grand in the 1720s who could translate the Latin text set for them competently, and even with fluency; some managed not only to avoid mistakes and mistranslations but to express themselves, as was expected of them, in elaborately elegant French.[22] The thousands of Latin poems churned out by English public schoolboys, and the pupils of French *lycées*, from one end of the nineteenth century to the other reveal at least the assimilation of a certain technique; some individuals even displayed considerable facility, with Harrow, Eton and Shrewsbury all producing boys who could improvise Latin verse; at Winchester (according to one Wykehamist) "many of us would turn out thirty or forty lines of passable Latin, either in prose or verse, per hour".[23] A number of French writers were first "recognized" as Latin poets. Alfred de Musset, Sainte-Beuve and Baudelaire all made the roll of honour for their Latin verse in the *concours général*; Rimbaud distinguished himself on several occasions in competitions between the collegians of the Douai Academy; Stendhal and Vallès were both prizewinners at their schools.[24] Jules Simon, now remembered as the minister who dropped Latin verse from school classics curriculums, had shown some talent for it himself when a pupil at the Vannes college: "I could write Latin verse almost as easily as prose," he wrote in his autobiography.[25] We do not know whether the pupils of the Liceo Niccolini in Livorno showed equivalent levels of prowess, but the course in prosody and metrics given by their professor, Giovanni Pascoli, in 1894 presupposed extensive grammatical, literary and historical knowledge; the basics of prosody and metrics were thought already known: "The quantities of endings are no mystery to you; some of the elementary rules of prosody – vowel before vowel, vowel before two or more consonants, vowel before a mute letter or liquid consonant, synaloepha . . . – your ears are full of them. How a hexameter is constructed, at least basically, you all know". In the lesson Pascoli used the terms "choriambic", "Ionic *a minore*", "Bacchic", "palimbacchic", "Pyrrhic" and "molossus" to designate certain words as well as metrical feet or groups of feet, but did not explain these terms as they were known to the pupils.[26] The *agrégation de lettres* registered excellent standards at the beginning of the twentieth century: performance in the 1903 examination was judged "good" by the jury chairman Maurice Croiset, who noted that results overall were satisfactory and better than in previous years. In 1905, recalling the eighteen years of his chairmanship, he noted a real improvement in the candidates over this long period. Latin composition – due to disappear in 1907 – showed noticeable improvement, as did the Latin translation. The oral tests – improvised Greek or Latin explanations – had given "the best results ever obtained, at least in overall standard. Really bad explanations, which were quite common when this test was instituted, are becoming increasingly rare".[27] On the more modest level of the fourth grade, at a time – 1976 – when expectations had dropped considerably, a survey carried out in the Paris region announced "satisfactory findings", and the inspector added: "the best papers are virtually perfect; . . . overall the results are good, one might say very good; . . . exercises show quite a good familiarity with the language".[28]

Success in learning Latin could be accompanied by the sheer pleasure of using it: for some it was an agreeable subject, even an amusement. That is how Lord Berners remembered his first steps in Latin at the age of seven, under a master who presented Latin grammar as "an acrostich or word game".[29] This impression was shared by the young Lavisse when he started Latin at eight: "I declined *Rosa, the Rose*, and was pleased and amused by the changes of ending, like a game, the only game I wasn't bad at".[30] Miguel de Unamuno too was fascinated in childhood by the first declension, especially the heavy sonorousness of the genitive plural, *rosarum*.[31] Much more recently, teachers have noticed the lively interest, "great joy" or "enthusiasm" shown by sixth-grade youngsters on discovering the new discipline of Latin at the *lycée*; they attributed this to "the amused curiosity awoken (in the child) by pictures and travel" or by his "liking for puzzles and enigmas".[32] Even quite complex exercises delighted some children. Chateaubriand, when a pupil of the college at Dol, used to await "the time for Latin lessons with a sort of impatience, as a rest from my numbers and geometric figures".[33] Isaac Williams, the future Cardinal Manning and Henry Montagu Butler, who were at Harrow, all took real pleasure in composing Latin verse, and Butler said that he and his friends had also enjoyed reading the prizewinning poems (transcribed into a book) and commenting on them.[34] Valery Larbaud, about to enter third grade, said that the time spent translating a letter from Pliny had been "the two best days we spent in the long holidays"; he had daydreamed about being a philological scholar preparing the definitive edition of the Latin author's works.[35] For some, pleasure and fulfilment were early rewards of learning Latin.

"The standard is lower than it ought to be"

In the memories of former schoolchildren and the comments of their teachers, however, the predominant impression is very different. While a small elite may have been successful, even brilliantly so, the mass seems to have dragged itself painfully along, eventually arriving after huge effort at a depressingly mediocre level.

There is no shortage of defeated stories about the pathetic results of lengthy application, from as early as the first half of the seventeenth century (as can be seen from the writings of Jean Cécile Frey, Comenius or Milton).[36] A few years later, Antoine Arnauld was contrasting the eight hours of Latin a day stipulated by the regulations of Paris University with the "extreme ignorance" of the undergraduates: "We know from experience that most of the people leaving college at present do not understand Latin".[37] Much the same opinion emerges from the entry on "college" in the *Encyclopédie*: "A young man after spending ten years at a college . . . leaves it with very imperfect knowledge of a dead language".[38] Helvetius went even further: this slight knowledge was forgotten "immediately after leaving the classroom".[39] These attacks on a prolonged and sterile learning effort became more virulent still under the Revolution. The lawyer Raymond de Varennes rolled all the accusations into one when he exclaimed: "After ten years of Latin principles, Latin themes, Latin verse, Latin speeches, Latin arguments and reading and translating Latin authors, they come home stuffed and bloated with unintelligible Latin and very ignorant about everything else".[40]

The cruel precision of a number could make a diagnosis seem even more pessimistic. "Out of seventy or eighty boys, there may be two or three from whom something can be dragged," Antoine Arnauld wrote. "The rest just kill time, or torture themselves without achieving anything of value".[41] Estimates were not much higher a century later, the author of the *"études"* entry in the *Encyclopédie* asserting: "With constant application on the part of the schools and the masters, hardly one in three of the pupils manages to become competent in it: I mean even among the ones who complete their schooling, for I am not talking about the infinite number of others who lose heart in the middle of the race".[42] This takes us back to the observation of Abbé Coyer who exclaimed after an examination of the school curriculum: "Look, after such a lot of Latin, I can pick a hundred of your pupils at random, and open Cicero, Livy, Horace, Juvenal: I won't find ten of these Latinists of yours who can understand them".[43] Louis Sebastien Mercier used the same estimate in the chapter headed "Collèges, etc." in his *Tableau de Paris*: "Seven or eight years are taken up with learning the Latin tongue; and out of a hundred schoolboys, ninety leave still not knowing it".[44] Verlac, a professor at the Ecole Royale de la Marine (Royal Naval School) in Vannes, was only slightly more optimistic: after eight years of study in a college, he thought, there were not 20 per cent of pupils who "might be up to managing a conversation in Latin, or explaining a single author".[45]

Similar complaints were heard throughout the nineteenth century: long years of study in most cases resulted only in mediocre performance. Weak Latin was even a subject of complaint at the Ecole Normale Supérieur (in this case perhaps because too much was expected).[46] In the colleges Latin verse, which was still a compulsory exercise, required an apparatus of literary knowledge and aptitudes that (in Cournot's opinion) could only be expected from "one schoolboy in a thousand".[47] Success in themes (Latin prose composition) was greater, but still far from impressive: "six or seven pupils out of sixty," according to Michel Bréal, "may get some benefit from this exercise".[48]

At the beginning of the twentieth century, when reform of secondary education was under discussion, the general view was that for a start, "where the mass of pupils is concerned, the standard is lower than it ought to be".[49] This observation became a commonplace of pedagogic literature. "The weakness of Latin studies in our secondary education is incontestable," noted a teacher at the Puy *lycée* in 1904.[50] Henri Bornecque's slightly more optimistic judgement that Latin teaching suffered from "relative weakness" was shaken by his experience as an oral examiner for the *baccalauréat*:

> With very rare exceptions (one in thirty at most), they start by reading, or rather mumbling, the text they are given until they are asked to stop; then they re-read the first part of the phrase and go through it agonizingly word by word . . ., then move on to the next part, and so on, and smugly finish off with a translation into gibberish or pidgin, of similar quality to their reading and word-by-word deciphering.[51]

Pessimism had now become *de rigueur*. "Our secondary school pupils know less and less Latin," wrote a teacher at the Limoges *lycée* in 1927, and added: "On this point everyone is agreed".[52] A colleague at Pau felt that "the mediocrity" or even "nullity" of the results of Latin studies was a patent fact "apart from a few exceptions, perhaps ten per cent".[53] Two surveys during the 1950s – one in France in 1954 among classics teachers, the other in 1957 in a wider Unesco context – reached similar conclusions.[54] More generally, the teachers questioned said they felt "devastated" by results thought alarmingly poor and deplored the "very low level of student knowledge in this field".[55] Some even went so far as to call Latin teaching in secondary schools "bankrupt".[56] Judgement had been passed by Paul Valéry in 1943 with the terse comment: "Pointless to teach Latin, if four fifths of those taught cannot then *fluently* read and understand a text from Cicero or Virgil".[57]

A glance at the pupils' work tends to confirm their masters' pessimism, or anyway disenchantment. We have already seen that there were boys at Louis-le-Grand in the 1720s capable of translating a Latin text with ease; but they were at the top of the class. Behind them came the "average" pupils, whose awkward and vague translations suggested that the sense had been at least partially grasped, even if it was not well expressed. No such illusion was possible with the efforts from the bottom of the class. This is how a youth called Coulombier rendered a translation exercise based on a famous episode in Roman history, Horatius's murder of his sister:

> His sister horatius crying the death of one of the curiatii the condolence of his
> sister irritated a great courage in his victory and with so much public dagger thus
> he killed her with a naked sord that was seen to the senators and to the people
> as a cruel action and horatius was already being led to tortur his father embrac-
> ing his son said he how you see this triumphant you can see a victer in the
> middle of tortur a lictor does he dare bind the hands with chains which not long
> before they acquire the empire of the weapon to the roman people to whom all
> the people was so agitated that the oration has finished.

The spelling of the time and the absence of all punctuation add an extra surreal level to Coulombier's word-by-word rendering, filled with mistakes and mistranslations, in which he has followed the Latin word order closely, apparently untroubled by the resulting tissue of absurdities. We will have more to say on this attitude later; for the moment, suffice it to say that Coulombier was not bottom of his class and that there were several other wretches whose work was just as bad.[58]

These apprentice translators had a descendant in the narrator of Claude Simon's novel *La bataille de Pharsale*. The child is remembering a homework episode, a version of a few lines of Caesar on that same battle.

"Me sitting in my room lining up an incoherent sequence of words looked up in the dictionary," the passage begins. Then, "rough-work book in my hand", he knocks on the door of his father's study, to show his work as much as to seek help.

> I sat down placed the open book on the papers I'm listening I cleared my throat
>   dextrum cornu ejus rivus quidam impeditis ripis muniebat I stopped
>   well?
>   rivus: a river
>   impeditis ripis: with obstacle banks
>   obstacle banks what does that mean explain it to me
>   I went quiet
>   you might perhaps take the trouble to look beyond the first word you find in
> the dictionary how much time did you spend preparing this version?
>   I kept quiet
>   good very well impeditis ripis: with steep banks doesn't that seem better?
>   yes
>   he waited a moment looking at me I didn't raise my eyes from my page of
> rough work Eventually he said Very well continue

muniebat: sheltered

he started to laugh Sheltered have you ever seen anyone sheltering in a stream are we talking about Julius Caesar or the village idiot

I was still keeping my head down

he expelled smoke from his cigarette blowing it through his tight lips

Come on be brave

dextrum cornu: the right horn

horn?

I waited

again he made the same noise expelling his smoke

Then

ejus: of him

and?

I kept quiet

and quidam?

quidam?

where did it go?

I kept quiet

good if your teacher asks you for word-by-word you'll manage you'll explain to him that the quidam fell in the river with obstacle banks doubtless it was a jockey what do you think?

I was still looking at my page of rough work

come on let's get it over otherwise we'll be dining at nine you might think sometimes of the pain you give your mother write A river with steep banks protected his right wing.[59]

This passage recalls many memories of school and home life. But beyond that, it embodies an accurate description of the ordinary *modus operandi* of French collegians, making blindly systematic use of the dictionary and not being overly troubled by the incoherence of the resulting translation. In this respect the passage is emblematic of the errors denounced in pedagogic literature, in particular enslavement to the dictionary.[60] It is also an example of a profoundly mediocre effort with an easy Latin text. This brings us back to the conclusions of the survey carried out in the Paris region in 1976. Although the fourth-grade beginners managed "good" results, in later stages, the third grade and especially the second, when confronted with "authentic Latin texts", they lost ground; two-thirds of the pupils failed to achieve an average mark, and the examiner remarked that although there were "some good versions", other efforts were "heartbreaking" and appeared to be "out-and-out tissues of meaninglessness and error".[61]

Performances were, it seems, no better elsewhere: the same disparity between a long apprenticeship and mediocre output was apparent everywhere. English grammarians and educational reformers during the first half of the seventeenth century saw it as a patent fact.[62] A few years later Morhof, whose *Polyhistor* adopted a Europe-wide perspective, noted that the usual method of teaching Latin gave disappointing results: despite their extreme efforts (*summo labore*) the children were leaving school with weak (*exigua*) and imperfect (*imperfecta*) knowledge of the language.[63] The Jesuit Bandiera, who taught in several colleges in the Italian peninsula in the mid-eighteenth century, discovered by experiment that the pupils were incapable of understanding a text in Latin, and thus *a fortiori* incapable of writing in it.[64] In the newly independent United States, a main argument of adversaries of the classical languages was that very superficial knowledge – "a smattering of the dead languages" – was all that was gained from seven to ten years of study.[65] Things were no better in nineteenth-century England. "Most boys", concluded a study of secondary schools, "never attained the fluent reading of literature, despite years of study, or could recall more than a few phrases shortly after leaving school".[66] Matthew Davenport Hill noted that "not two boys out of three," after undergoing the usual course of instruction in Latin, "ever become able to read even the easier classic authors with fluency".[67] Latin verse composition, which took up a good deal of time, gave results out of all proportion with the effort expended on it: from among the hundreds of children slogging away at verse in the public schools, only "a dozen composers" emerged each year; the rest, "after hundreds of hours spent in verses and correction of verses, are perfectly unable at the end to write one single tasteless and hobbling line without making two or three errors in it".[68] The level of success in the United States seems to have been even more discouraging: John Adams, who thought Latin and Greek "indispensable" for a proper education, accepted that "not one in ten thousand of those who study them at schools and colleges ever make any great proficiency in them".[69] In 1917, during a conference at Princeton on "the value of the classics" in a liberal education, the speakers were again obliged to refute the perennial argument that mere snippets of classical learning were being too dearly acquired and too quickly forgotten.[70] A survey conducted in 1924 revealed that only six out of a thousand children who had started Latin in secondary school were capable of reading a little of it a year after finishing their schooling.[71] Although not supported by statistics, the assessment of classical studies made by a Belgian professor in the 1950s exuded a similar pessimism: classics, he wrote, "no longer produces as much fruit as one is entitled to expect", before going on to use words like "crisis", "decadence" and "bankrupt".[72] In Italy, where the classical *liceo* still retained its primacy in the period following the fall of fascism, the philosopher Guido Calogero violently attacked the sterile "panlatinism" that reigned there:

> Depending on his school cursus, the young Italian . . . studies Latin for three, five, eight or twelve years, sometimes even more than twelve years when he is fuori corso at the Faculty of Letters owing to repeated failures in the Latin examination. But when, after a course like that, you put him in front of, I won't say Horace or Virgil, but the Bible, say, or a simple inscription that you might find

in a church, it is extremely rare for him to be able to read and understand it with the same decent rapidity that any good hotel porter shows in understanding a tourist who addresses him in English or French.[73]

In 1995, another professor at the University of Rome noted sadly that pupils at the *ginnasio* and even the *liceo* were now incapable of "understanding ten lines" of an easy text; he admitted, however, that his own generation which had gone through the *liceo* thirty years earlier was "not a great deal more expert". His feeling was that one would have to go back to the turn of the century to find people capable of reading Latin straight off the page.[74] They too would probably only have been a minority: an official commission had been appointed in 1893 to examine the reasons for the "poor return in Latin" from the *ginnasio* and *liceo*, and suggest remedies.[75]

When considering the efforts of their pupils, masters did not ignore the question of standards. Here we will restrict ourselves to the case of France, where there were frequent investigations in this area from the beginning of the twentieth century. The general conclusion was that standards were declining. When the reform of secondary education was being discussed in about 1900, with unanimous agreement on the mediocre performance of schoolchildren, a number of teachers asserted that "over the last thirty years, the decline of classical studies has steepened".[76] In 1913, analysing the decline of classical studies from the vantage point of the Sorbonne, Jules Marouzeau noted that, while the crisis "had raged almost uninterrupted for several generations", it had become "more acute" after the recent reforms of secondary and higher education (1902 and 1907 respectively).[77] In 1951 Paul Crouzet, Inspector General of National Education, admitted that "our young sixth-graders are not worth as much as those of earlier times".[78] In 1954, during a large-scale survey among classics teachers, it was admitted that "our pupils these days know almost no Latin at all . . . They are obviously no longer capable of reading Latin authors. Only the best can manage, with great effort and the indispensable aid of a large dictionary, to translate a not-too-difficult text correctly."[79] In 1960 an article in the *Encyclopédie pratique de l'éducation en France* showed that the standard had declined steadily during the first half of the century. The instructions issued in 1925, it was recalled, had noted "a retreat by Latin"; in 1959, practising Latin teachers with many years of experience had been unanimous in recognizing that they could no longer set the exercises of thirty years earlier. Their view was that the bulk of pupils left school having almost reached the level of third grade, but that the majority still lacked the grammatical knowledge stipulated for that class in the syllabus. These pessimistic assessments were broadly confirmed by *baccalauréat* results.

All the examiners marking Latin translations attest that only extreme indulgence enables them to give an average mark (10 out of 20) to more than a quarter of the papers. It is not unusual to receive a bundle of 120 papers in which twenty or

more deserve a zero mark, papers that are just a tissue of nonsense with no relation to the text or anything else.[80]

Could the decline in "standards" be a recent phenomenon, dating from
about the end of the nineteenth century? Some would argue that it is not:
during the discussion of educational reforms in 1900 it was claimed that "the
weakness of the pupils is no greater than it used to be".[81] The same opinion
was expressed in 1954 by a *lycée* teacher who, after noting the "mediocrity,
even nullity" of the results of Latin studies, added: "It seems always to have
been like that".[82] Changes in the exercises being set appear to confirm these
remarks. During the eighteenth century, as we have seen, the "version" –
translation from Latin to French – gradually took the first place from the
"theme" (in the sense of Latin prose composition). During the final third of
the nineteenth century, several exercises characteristic of the classical curriculum were dropped: Latin verse was dropped in 1872; in 1880, Latin composition and the Latin speech disappeared, first from the *baccalauréat* and the
concours général (examination for teacher recruitment), then in 1902 from the
lycée syllabus; the "theme" (by now in the sense of translation into Latin of a
French text) had already gone, and the "version" became the main – and
eventually the sole – test that the Latinist collegian had to face.[83] These developments, ratifying the long-term mediocrity of results, represented an effective lowering of standards.

So what really happened with standards? A confident answer on this point
is impossible. Not only are statistical studies rare, but a number of other
factors that have to be taken into account have changed over time, for
example the amount of time devoted to study, the proportion devoted to
other subjects, the school population and the level of effort demanded by
teachers; moreover, the best and worst pupils are better known than the
average ones, and there is a strong tendency to be dazzled by the one group
and appalled by the other. But it does not seem unreasonable to suppose, in
the light of opinions expressed by teachers and the results registered by pupils,
that overall standards have probably never been very high. Nor is it unreasonable to suppose, looking at school exercises, that these same standards
declined over time, and that in the last years of compulsory Latin, just before
1968, children knew less Latin than their forebears at the beginning of the
twentieth century. Does this mean that the contemporaries of Hugo and
Lamartine were worse Latinists than those of Voltaire and Diderot? Person-
ally I would not say so.

A cross children had to bear

Mediocre though it generally was, this performance still cost children much
pain and torment, something that emerges consistently from memoirs, auto-

biographies and other narrative sources touching on school Latin. "It was my most difficult subject and one in which I never made much progress," Rousseau wrote in his *Confessions*. "With time and effort, I came eventually to read Latin authors fairly easily, but never learned to speak or write in that language."[84] Many other children could have said exactly the same, and some could have added that they had forgotten almost everything soon after leaving school.[85]

Learning the rudiments of Latin presented a spiky mass of difficulties, essentially the memorization of a large number of rules, starting with those regulating the declension of nouns and the conjugation of verbs. Latin declensions were trying even to Germans and others whose own languages used them. Heine, who had great difficulty remembering the exceptions to third-declension parisyllabic nouns, came as a result to grumble generally about the extreme complexity of Latin, remarking that "the Romans would not have had much time left to conquer the world if they had had to learn Latin first"; he felt this interpretation to be confirmed by the "horrible difficulty" of irregular verbs.[86] Even Goethe, who became a good Latinist, jibbed on his first acquaintance with Latin grammar which seemed to him "an arbitrary law; the rules seemed to me to be ridiculous, because they were demolished by a thousand exceptions which I had to learn separately; and if it had not been for the *Latinist beginner in rhyme*, things would have gone hard with me".[87] It is hardly surprising that even learning the rudiments defeated some children, those with little gift for memorization for example, whose exhaustion sometimes threatened their health. "The words left absolutely no trace in my head," wrote Marmontel,

> and getting them to stay there was as difficult as writing in shifting sand. I tried to compensate for the weakness of my organ with determined application; the work was beyond my strength at that age, and my nerves were affected. I became as it were a somnambulist: at night, fast asleep, I would sit up and, eyes half-open, loudly recite the lessons I had been learning. He'll go mad, my father said to my mother, if you don't make him stop that miserable Latin; so the subject was suspended.[88]

Once past the first hurdles the young Latinist was confronted with others, a good deal more forbidding, on a path that was beginning to look like a calvary. In the memory of Miguel de Unamuno, the initial enthusiasm awakened by *rosa* very quickly gave way to the "extreme torment" of having to learn by heart "the interminable lists" of irregular verbs; but the child was able to bear that, as well as grammatical analysis – "turn this into the passive", "put that in the gerundive" – in the expectation that in the next year he would be reading the Latin classics of whose "exquisite beauties" the teacher spoke with such conviction. But the second Latin course was harder and more arid than the first. How many times had I to endure "first take the subject with all its dependent phrases, then the verb with its adverbs", and so on and so forth. How many fine afternoons I wasted, burrowing in that paving-stone of a Raimundo Miguel dictionary until I could hardly see. My friend Mario and I exhausted our minds on the accursed dictionary. For each Latin word that huge book gave an abundance of Castilian terms, four, six, even ten or twelve, in no genetic or logical order and without explanation or examples. We looked up all these vocables and understood absolutely nothing of the text we were supposed to be translating . . . We were told we should first construe and then translate, a major meaningless instruction . . .

The texts generally translated, Cornelius Nepos, Sallust, Julius Caesar, are intolerably dry from a child's point of view. Of all that we translated, the only thing I remember anything about is the grateful lion.

All of this led me to form a very singular idea of Latin writers. I imagined them writing straightforwardly, expressing their ideas in the same order as we would, and then amusing themselves by dislocating the phrases, dissecting the sentences, scattering the words here and there with capricious abandon, simply to annoy us, the children of future generations, and force us to cogitate . . . The reason for this, I believe, was that I had heard mention of natural order, logical order, inverse order and other stylistic trivia, but could not conceive of anyone wanting to express his ideas in a different order from the one I would have expressed them in myself.[89]

This text gives some idea of the difficulty that a child, even a gifted one as in this case, could experience in dealing with Latin, and why such words as "punishment", "servitude" and "torture" were so often employed.[90] The suffering endured by other children, as with the young Unamuno, was intensified by their perplexity with a language they found baffling in itself. "Without understanding" and "by heart" – what Stendhal called privately "stupid by heart" – are among the commonest descriptive expressions for school Latin.[91] Some examples will illustrate what this apprenticeship was really like. When Churchill started Latin at the age of seven, his master handed him a grammar and asked him on the first day, without any other explanation, to learn "words in a frame of lines", the first declension, written as follows:

Mensa	a table
Mensa	o table
Mensam	a table
Mensae	of a table
Mensae	to or for a table
Mensa	by, with or from a table

What on earth did it mean? Where was the sense in it? It seemed absolute rigmarole to me. However, there was one thing I could always do: I could learn by heart. And I thereupon proceeded, as far as my private sorrows would allow, to memorize the acrostic-looking task which had been set me.

After half an hour the puzzled child was able to recite this text and, encouraged by his performance, asked the master to explain, being intrigued by the fact that "mensa" could mean both "a table" and "o table". The explanation of declensions and cases being long and arduous, the master, to be brief and to the point, said:

"O table – you would use that addressing a table, in invoking a table." And then seeing he was not carrying me with him, "You would use it in speaking to a table."

"But I never do," I blurted in honest amazement.

"If you are impertinent, you will be punished, let me tell you, very severely," was his conclusive rejoinder.

Churchill never became a good Latinist; his Latin marks, in the three examinations he sat for entry to Sandhurst, started below average and became steadily worse.[92]

Many other children plodded methodically through the exercises set without understanding much, like the young Gibbon who at nine "painfully construed" texts by Phaedrus and Cornelius Nepos that he had been given to translate but whose meaning he could hardly discern.[93] The work of construing often engaged the whole strength of the tyro translator, at the cost of any real understanding of the sense and, *a fortiori*, of any literary interest in the text. A master at Marlborough observed of his pupils: "They laboriously toiled at the scaffolding and never built the house".[94] Some would dive straight into the dictionary without taking the time to try to understand. "You would rummage your way through the dictionary," Michel Butor wrote in *Degrés*, "the text never appearing to you in its continuity, but as a succession of words each of which demanded a tiresome effort".[95]

To deal with exercises that resembled difficult and pointless puzzles or acrostics, children deployed a wide range of strategies, starting with seeking help from others. As the Claude Simon text quoted earlier reminds us, some would ask their father for help with homework; and it could happen that the father, out of lassitude or exasperation, would end by doing the whole translation. Stendhal had the help of an affectionate grandfather with his first exercises as a Latin poet, who "did my verses while pretending to help me".[96] Dunces leaned on brighter pupils, terrorizing them when necessary: Vittorio Alfieri recounted having to do the homework of an older and stronger classmate, under threat of a couple of clips over the ear and the simultaneous promise of two footballs.[97] Similarly, in the English public schools, "big boys of lazy or bullying habits" got their Latin verse composition done by clever pupils, compelling them to oblige by threats of violence.[98]

Children also developed resources of their own, making full use of the school books available to them. Jacques, the central character of Jules Vallès's *l'Enfant*, did well in Latin verse and speech; but by his own account, everything had been lifted from authors and dictionaries, phrases and expressions taken from here and there and cobbled together end to end:

> I search for adverbs and adjectives in the Gradus, and I just copy down what I find in the Alexandre . . . I suffer when they cover me with with praises that I do not deserve; I am seen as a bright student, really I am just a simple pickpocket. I steal from left and right, gather rejected material from the corners of books.[99]

This quotation is an example of the dubious practices of borrowing and cheating that existed alongside the accepted use of the *Gradus* and the dictionary. English public schoolboys sometimes owed their success with Latin verse to a "tradition" (in the etymological sense) described by Thomas Hughes in his classic of school literature *Tom Brown's Schooldays* as it was practised at Rugby. The subjects set for Latin composition by the masters were limited in number; the boys kept exemplary compositions or *vulgus* in books passed from hand to hand down the generations; so that the more popular boys, who might acquire several of these books, were in a position to cope with everything. The only real risk was that "the successions might have become confused" and two boys would produce the same composition. But even this danger was reduced by the way the books were used. Tom Brown himself, who had inherited two of these books, "picking out a line here, an ending there", would put the "pieces" together and with the aid of the *Gradus* produce the required minimum of eight elegiac lines, before finishing off with two moral lines extracted in their entirety from one of the two books.[100] In the same way, for prose composition, there were "Keys" that contained "corrected" versions of the exercises given in Matthew Arnold's *Latin Composition*;[101] and until very recently, there also existed "cribs" that made the lives of apprentice translators easier by providing the English text of the Latin passages most often set as unseen translations by the masters. While "cribs" as such had no exact French equivalent, French children used similar practices, copying from an available translation of the text and taking good care to sprinkle it with a few convincing mistakes. Marcel Pagnol recalls that in the fifth grade, thanks to his friend Lagneau, he came into possession of a French translation of Caesar's *Commentaries* with the Latin text printed at the bottom of the page, a small book

> that was going to be as useful to us as the handrail on a staircase.
> I must say, without undue modesty, that I was able to make skilled use of it.
> After finding the chapter from which our week's Latin version had been taken, I would copy out its translation; but to avoid arousing Zizi's (the Latin master's nickname) morbid suspicion, I would render our homework credible by inserting some errors.
> For Lagneau, two mistakes, two mistranslations, two "infelicities". For myself, one mistake, one error involving a dative taken as an ablative, three "infelicities".[102]

But although such practices helped to make the daily school grind less uncomfortable, not many children retained the happiest memories of their years of Latin. The sadness felt by Miguel Unamuno was a very moderate reaction compared to the much more negative ones displayed by other children. "Boredom" is the word used by Vittorio Alfieri to sum up his first acquaintance with Latin, explained as follows:

> We were translating Cornelius Nepos's Lives, but none of us and perhaps not even the master knew who the men were whose lives we were translating, or where their countries were, or in what period or under what government they lived, or even what a government was. All the ideas were either limited or false or confused; no systematic purpose in the teaching; no interest among the taught.[103]

Similar feelings are recalled by Lavisse who, in second grade, had to cope with Latin verse and a master he thought "lazy, ignorant and affected"; and by Otto Jespersen for whom "the lessons were only concerned with correct translation and the use of grammatical and metrical rules".[104]

Despair could overcome some children and many tears were shed over unseen translations and Latin compositions; there was good reason for Salomon Reinach to call his textbook published in 1914 *Cornélie ou le latin sans pleurs* ("Cornelia or Latin without tears"). Samuel Johnson recalled his anxiety while learning to conjugate verbs under permanent threat from the strap or the back of the teacher's hand; "silent tears" had flowed.[105] Gibbon only mastered Latin syntax "at the price of many tears and a little blood".[106] The classical tongue and corporal punishment ended by becoming inextricably entangled in the children's imagination. Thus Johan, the central character of Strindberg's autobiographical novel *The Son of a Servant*, from the age of seven associated Latin" with "rattan" (the cane) and "when he was older, skipped all the passages in books that mentioned memories of school and avoided books dealing with the subject".[107] Where children were not put off classics by slaps and canings, Latin impositions were just as effective. At the age of nine Maxime Du Camp, a pupil at Louis-le-Grand, was put in a cell and made to copy out 1,500 to 1,800 lines of Latin in a day. He commented: "The school authorities who inflict such brutalizing punishments on children do not realize that they are inspiring a horror of the very poems they are supposed to teach them to admire".[108] Some children were so overwhelmed by the work and terrorized by the perpetual threat of punishment that they even called on Heaven for help. Tom Tulliver, hero of George Eliot's *The Mill on the Floss*, being little given to abstract thought, found learning the first elements of grammar a terrifying ordeal. Defeated by the attempt to memorize the supines of the third conjugation, the little boy determined to ask God for help and slipped the following petition into his bedtime prayer: ". . . and please to make me always remember my Latin".[109]

Boredom, fear and despair could lead to extreme reactions. Some children would avenge themselves on the instruments of their "torture", like the young Scapin in *Gil Blas*.

> I sat under a tree at the side of the main road; there, to amuse myself, I pulled my primer out of my pocket and looked through it idly; then, happening to remember the strokes of the ferula and whacks on the side of the head it had got me, I started tearing its pages out, saying angrily: Ah, you dog of a book, you won't make me shed any more tears! I savoured my vengeance to the full, scattering declensions and conjugations all about me on the ground.[110]

Others took refuge in derision. Offended by the Latin speech – a speciality of French educational practice – Jacques Vintgras, Jules Vallès's *Enfant*, reflects sarcastically:

> The subject we were given the other day was Themistocles haranguing the Greeks . . . "I hope that's a good subject, eh?" the master said. "Put yourself in Themistocles's place." They always say you should put yourself in this or that person's place . . . and they're always generals, kings, queens! But I'm fourteen, I don't know anything about what Hannibal or Caracalla ought to say, or Torquatus either.[111]

Strindberg's character, Johan, retreats into silence. At the age of ten, the child finds the teaching method applied to him "absurd".

> Half the year was devoted to explaining the life of a general in Cornelius Nepos. The teacher had a way of complicating the business by requiring the pupil to be capable of discerning the construction of the sentence. But the teacher never explained how this ought to be done. It seemed to mean that the words of the text should be read in a certain order, but what order? No one ever said. It did not coincide with the Swedish translation and after making a few attempts to understand how it held together, without succeeding, the boy undertook to remain silent.[112]

Rimbaud's revolt against the classics was somewhat more radical. "Why learn Latin at all?" he demanded. "No one speaks this language," and he developed the idea still further: "Who knows if the Latins existed? Perhaps it's just some forged language."[113]

It may not be inappropriate to see, in the feelings of disgust and hatred sometimes aroused by Latin, echoes of a wider critique of the kind of teaching given;[114] and it is worth remembering that some of these "rebels" – Rimbaud among them – were good Latinists at college, while others (like Flaubert, Giordani and Trollope) rediscovered the Latin they had hated at school with great pleasure in later life.[115] It does seem, however, that Latin, or more precisely the way it was learned and the exercises required, may have been beyond the reach of most children. Paul Valèry had a point when he concluded "Latin, Greek – enjoyable at 40".[116]

Making Latin "easy"

Experienced masters, who of course had also been pupils in their time, witnessed children's struggles and deemed the acquisition of basic Latin very arduous for them, never very effective and all too often doomed to failure. From the seventeenth century onward this was a commonplace of pedagogic literature.

> What a cross to bear, what torment for a mind born to the finest and greatest things, to burden and overwhelm it with a chaos of barbarous rules more obscure even than the sybilline oracles [wrote Du Tertre in 1650]. How many commentaries by Béhourt does it take, how many line-by-line interpretations, then repetitions, applications and explanations, to discover the literal meaning of this gibberish which only manages to repel children, give them an aversion to study, blight the flower of their youth, overload their memories with bad verse that might as well be anathema and execration . . . And which anyway is useless for scholarship, as most of them do not retain one word of it.[117]

Torment, ignorance and aversion: these words and their synonyms were now part of the standard vocabulary used to describe Latin schooling and its results. They are found in the education plan that Diderot drafted in 1775 at the request of Catherine II; on the basis of the results produced by French colleges, he relegated Latin to the top class:

> Young students know neither the Greek nor the Latin that they have so often been taught . . . The most able are forced to study them again on leaving school to avoid being ignorant of them for the rest of their lives, and the suffering they have endured explaining Virgil, the tears in which they have soaked the pleasant satires of Horace, have given them such an aversion to these authors that they cannot look at them without quailing.[118]

Identical ideas were current in nineteenth-century England: "How many years of life are spent in learning Latin!" wrote Matthew Davenport Hill. "How much labour, pain and imprisonment are endured by the boy! . . . How much disgust of literature is engendered! . . . In short, how much misery has been produced, is being produced, and will continue to be produced, in teaching and learning the Latin language?"[119] This gloomy prediction was confirmed in the next century when the generally-perceived "Latin crisis" was described in similar terms. Although syllabuses were supposed to lead the child in a harmonious, gradual sequence to a good knowledge of the language and of classical civilization, the reality in most cases did not correspond with this idyllic design: results were mediocre, both in terms of what was learned and more generally in terms of intellectual gain, judging by *baccalauréat* papers. "What obscure massaging of the text," wrote P. Paillet in 1954,

> what incoherent alchemy could have spawned those awkward, tortured phrases, strung together without even an elementary attempt at logic, cobbled up out of the dictionary, those phrases of which one sometimes wonders with dismay how a sane individual can write them down without flinching? It is as if in the presence of a Latin text the laws of thought were abolished and every form of delirium became legitimate . . . To that can be added a total ignorance of Latin civilization and literature . . . When the examination is over, the adolescent closes his Latin books never to open them again; and in all probability he will never have the desire even to read translations.

Terms of this sort were being used to describe the attitudes and performance of pupils until the end of the 1960s.[120]

In official circles, even as early as the eighteenth century,[121] it was sometimes suggested that Latin instruction was beginning at too early an age, as well as that some (if not most) pupils were not able enough.[122] But the most consistent criticism was levelled at the pedantic teaching, for a long time itself given in Latin (explaining "the unknown by the unknown"),[123] that made things even more difficult for children already struggling with dry texts and exercises beyond their ability.[124] In the remedies suggested, the main theme was promotion of simplicity and rapidity: the methods and textbooks used should make acquisition of the rudiments easier, thus ensuring greater success at smaller cost. The mere fact that this slogan is still being repeated today would seem to indicate stubbornly mediocre results.

Criticisms were concentrated on grammar, whose study effectively consumed a very large proportion of the children's time and energy; already true under the Ancien Régime, this continued to be the case until very recently, owing to the lasting influence of German philology after the last third of the nineteenth century. Grammar and its rules were denounced incessantly as formidable obstructions: they were an ordeal for the children, they discouraged their efforts, delayed their acquisition of the rudiments, gave them a permanent aversion to study. The pedagogic literature has resounded with these reproaches since the Renaissance. A few examples will suffice. Erasmus himself advised against too prolonged a study of grammatical rules, judging that it caused excessive and pointless delay in reading classical authors. In England, Thomas Elyot warned in his *Governour* (1531) that such an approach so "mortifieth his (of the lerner) corage" that by the time he is introduced to the texts themselves "the sparkes of fervent desire of lernynge is extinct with the burdone of grammar, like as a lyttel fyre is sonne quenched with a greate heape of small stickes; so that it can never come to the principall logges where it shuld longe bourne in a great pleasaunt fire".[125] In less figurative terms,

Comenius in his *Janua linguarum* (1631) deplored "the first cross" that had to be borne by young people "retarded, or rather tormented, for a number of years by rules of grammar that in general are diffuse, muddled or obscure, and quite often useless as well".[126] The misdeeds of grammarians were catalogued some hundred years later by Facciolati: they had

> accumulated rules, appendices, commentaries in such quantity that the very sight of them frightens some tender children, and their immense weight overwhelms minds that are still unformed. That is the origin of this aversion to study, these feigned illnesses, this impatient desire for holidays, these stratagems for dodging classes and satisfying their laziness and love of idleness.[127]

Diderot thought grammar too abstract a subject for a child of eight or nine. "How can you expect him to take care that the adjective agrees with the noun in gender, number and case, any more than he could imagine such a thing? All these scholastic terms can do nothing but frighten him and put him in despair."[128] While Latin grammar was often compared to a "dark forest", in Italy it was naturally associated with the "wild, bitter and thick forest of Dante's Inferno", further deepened with images of a "labyrinth", sometimes spelt out as "Daedalus's", but "without Ariadne's wool". The nineteenth-century pedagogue Niccolò Tommaseo, in a violent Philippic on the rules of grammar, called them "instruments for destroying the memory instead of exercising it, training a population of parrots, a labyrinth, a dungeon, a sack in which children must run blindfold and if they do not run straight, they are clouted enough and more".[129] Similar polemics were launched in England: the three first rules of the Eton Grammar – *Propriae quae maribus*, *Quae genus* and *As in praesenti* – were likened to "a three-headed monster worse than Cerberus", and the textbook itself, "one long rosary of anomalies", was accused of having "caused more human suffering than Nero, Robespierre or any other enemy of the human race".[130] In the 1960s, when teachers had taken to lamenting the "grammatical hypertrophy" of Latin teaching, they still deplored their pupils' "grammatical atrophy"; the poor results were accompanied by boredom in class with the constant repetition of the same rules, and by "vague terror" that "it would never end", that there would always be new forms and new rules to learn, new traps to watch out for.[131]

These criticisms – four centuries of variations on the same complaint – had two concrete results: the production of simplified textbooks, and the formulation of teaching methods that laid less stress on grammar, or reduced its importance. Works meant to simplify the study of Latin started to appear very early. The intention was printed on the frontispiece of the books, and there are countless examples of titles including the magic words "simple", "easy" and "quick" (or their synonyms) to suggest a smooth and fruitful acquisition of Latin rudiments. The famous Port-Royal grammar of 1644, *Nouvelle méthode pour apprendre facilement et en peu de temps le latin* ("New Method for Learning Latin Easily in Little Time"), is just one distinguished example of the extremely abundant output of textbooks promising quick and easy success that has continued to this day.[132]

In fact, the most varied means were always tried in the effort to make learning Latin easier: starting with use of the vernacular, including rhymes and jingles to help with memorization of rules, and the use of tables and diagrams.[133] Anything seemed worth trying if it seemed capable of pushing in a bit of Latin and making it stick: like the "Declinograph" of the 1950s, in which "a system of tabs, windows, arrows, brackets [and] discs . . . disclosed panels in different colours" to help the pupil find his way through the declensions and conjugations.[134] These procedures were not always as effective as was hoped. Teachers at Port-Royal, and especially Pierre Nicole, thought tables and diagrams created more difficulties than they solved "because the colour linking the words together is not a natural link that sits comfortably in the memory and stays much in mind. If there were only two things to remember, perhaps this method could help; but as there is a very large number of them, the mind is confused and dazzled."[135]

Grammar textbooks outbidding one another in simplicity did not always live up to their promises. Melanchthon wanted his grammar (1525) to be an instrument enabling good Latin to be written in a short time; this led him to avoid the use of technical terms, with the result that the meaning of a rule sometimes seemed ambiguous. One example is the one expressed as *"Substantiuum cum substantiuo genitiuo casu iungitur"*: Janus Dionysius Jersinus, later to become Bishop of Ribe in Denmark, confessed that he had not understood which of the two nouns should be put in the genitive.[136] The Port-Royal grammar, which among other things embodied a critique of Despautère's grammar, was intended to be a "small book" explaining the rules in a simple way. "In Despautère's country, all was displeasing to children," Lancelot wrote in support of his scheme to "change an irksome obscurity into an agreeable light and enable them to gather flowers where before they had found only thorns". A century later Abbé Le Chevalier, in his *Prosodie latine*, ridiculed the rhymed formulation of rules found in the Port-Royal method (e.g. *"La voyelle longue s'ordonne/Lorsqu'après suit double consonne"*) and asserted that a simple and clear prose formulation was better: "A vowel followed by two consonants is long".[137] A splendid example of this large gap between declaration of intent and concrete achievement is supplied by Kennedy's *Public School Latin Primer*, published in 1866. It had been written by a master at Shrewsbury as an answer to the "grammatical anarchy" believed to be prevalent at the time; although its success was immediate (and enduring), the primer encountered strong criticism. Kennedy underlined the concern he had had to facilitate the acquisition by "young minds" of a solid grounding in Latin; that was why he had used a specific vocabulary of terms that "belong to grammar as a science". These terms gave rise to the most virulent of the criticisms. The most popular targets were "trajective", "prolative" and "factitive", and the glossary Kennedy had put at the end of the primer was attacked as a supplementary source of confusion. A master at Harrow complained:

> "Trajective words take a dative", p. 98. Turning to the glossary to discover what "trajective words" are, I find this lucid paragraph: "Trajectiva (trajicere, to throw over), verbs and adjectives which take a dative. Pure trajective verbs have a dative alone (cui verbs); trajective verbs transitive (cui-quid verbs) have accusative and dative", p. 162. I could give hundreds of similar instances of rules needlessly obscure, of explanations which explain nothing, and of definitions in which nothing is defined.

Then, setting about the "bizarre terminology" used, he demanded indignantly why "innocents of 12 or 13 years will have to acquire familiarity with 'factitive or *quid-quale* verbs', 'trajective, transitive or *cui-quid* verbs', 'prolative relations', 'circumstantive relations (!)', 'proprietive and receptive relations', 'oblique complements', 'receptive complements', 'sub-oblique causes', and Heaven knows what".[138] Almost a century later in the 1950s, when recognition of falling output had made ease and simplicity *de rigueur*, the Besançon University professor Jean Cousin attacked the "pretentious" grammars used in the *lycées*, "thick volumes stuffed with second-hand pseudo-scientific considerations, printed in small characters no under-sixteen is going to read", in which the explanation of every rule turned into a dissertation and the anxiety to say everything, the fear of not being comprehensive, caused exceptions to multiply and the pupil to be overwhelmed.[139]

The mediocrity of Latin results after an arduous learning process was contrasted by pedagogues and other educational theorists with the simple and fruitful way a mother tongue or living foreign language is absorbed. This was a common observation after the second half of the seventeenth century. It is made by John Locke in *Of Education* (1693): the child learned English perfectly well without master, rules or grammar, simply by hearing it spoken; an English girl could learn French in a year or two from a French governess who spoke it to her. The same method would work with Latin. The best solution would be to employ a master who spoke to the child in Latin; failing that, a pleasant book, like Aesop's *Fables*, would be the best way to start: it should have "the English translation (made as literal as it can be) in one line, and the Latin words, which answer each of them, just over it in another. These let him read every day over and over again, till he perfectly understands the Latin; and then go on to another fable." In the process he would acquire a knowledge of elementary grammar without it ever becoming predominant.[140] From this text there arose a learning method – usage – and a technical procedure – interlineation – both of which were to gain widespread adherence in the eighteenth century.

Although not everyone approved of the method – the pedagogues of Port-Royal, for example, thought it led to people learning the same thing a hundred times over – and teachers like Fleury and Rollin retained grammar, a growing suspicion of rules supported schemes for mechanical acquisition of Latin, through repetitive usage rather than a rational or structural approach. These included Du Marsais's "routine" and Pluche's "mechanics". Du Marsais popularized both this teaching method and the technique of inter-lineation which, let us remember, was not new. The text being studied was presented on four levels with different type faces and sizes. At the top came the original Latin text, then the Latin text presented in logical (i.e. French) order, then the literal translation, and finally the translation in "good French":

> Veneris mater Dione fuit, filius, Cupido . . .
> Dione fuit mater Veneris, Cupido fuit filius ejus . . .
> Dion was the mother of Venus, Cupid was son of her . . .
> Venus was daughter of Dion and mother of Cupid . . .

Beginners used only "the construction line and the literal translation line" for which "all that is needed is the ability to read, it is unnecessary to know how to decline and conjugate"; in the process some vocabulary was acquired, and the children disposed to learn declensions and conjugations before moving on naturally to syntax. "The main purpose of these interlinear versions," Du Marsais explained, "is to lead to the pure text which appears above, but chil-dren should not be taken there at first, for fear that they may be put off by the awkwardness of Latin inversion; they get used to it unconsciously out of curiosity and vanity." The method's great success lasted into the nineteenth century. From the very start, however, objections were raised, mainly by those like Pluche or Chompré who could not accept the re-ordering of Latin words. Chompré even claimed that "construction" was really "destruction", taking the view that Latin words should be taken in the order that occurs in the text:

> Urbem Romam a principio reges habuere
> The city of Rome at the beginning kings had

While the "encyclopaedists" (Du Marsais, Beauzée), who were heirs to the Port-Royal tradition, took the opposed view that it was essential to use analytic construction, or even put the words in natural order, more or less the same order as French, they were not unanimous. Beauzée disagreed with Du Marsais on the nature and importance of the role given to "routine" or intuitive practice; his view was that recourse to "routine" at the beginning was useless, even dangerous as a way of training the mind, and it was appropriate right from the start to give a predominant place to grammatical logic; that after all was the essential rational basis for teaching not only Latin but all languages.[141]

The debate between "rules" and "usage" still had many years ahead of it. In the 1950s, when a grammatical method inherited from the nineteenth century reigned in the *lycées*, the approach was attacked as sterile; the "preliminary and methodical study of theoretical grammar" was compared unfavourably to "a grammar of experience gleaned from the texts", the reading of classical authors was urged, and improvised Latin dialogue was suggested as an important class exercise.[142] The "Living Latin" movement placed emphasis on acquisition of vocabulary through oral practice of the language as well as reading the authors; this implied a reduction of the role given to grammar, although Jean Bayet's presence as head of the commission charged with producing a simple and rational textbook – there was talk of a thirteen-page grammar – calmed the fears of the traditionalists.[143] Some of these were very reserved if not hostile towards methods based on "overall comprehension" of the text, which invited the pupil to translate after a first reading and before attempting any analysis; they condemned "intuitive Latin" on grounds of its poor results and its dubious effects on mental discipline. Against the excesses of intuition (even "divination" according to some) they favoured a return to reason, to analysis . . . and to grammar.[144] Perhaps the secular debate between rules and usage has found its solution with the adoption of recent teaching methods which, to "save" Latin, have sacrificed knowledge of the language itself to the study of Roman civilization:[145] linguistic performance is no longer an issue.

Most of the children made to learn Latin never reached a very advanced level. This was not through any lack of effort on their part. Nor was it through deficiencies of devotion or ingenuity in their masters. Techniques of every sort were tried, and "recreational" methods[146] had proved no more effective than traditional themes and versions. Perhaps genuine success was not really possible. Even in 1686 Claude Fleury had no illusions: "We still need to cure ourselves of the erroneous belief that it is possible to learn Latin or any other dead language perfectly". No less a person than D'Alembert observed in the next century: "Latin being a dead language almost all of whose subtleties escape us, those who are thought today to write best in that language perhaps write it very badly".[147] There is nothing surprising about "realism" or derision, since even in the glorious days of Humanism some pupils of Guarino of Verona and Pomponio Leto found it difficult to follow the master, writing while he was talking and making mistake after mistake; the *pannicum* scribbled down by one of them instead of *Phatniticum* – one of the mouths of the Nile – is an eloquent expression of the pupil's state of disarray, but also symbolizes a basic learning process that seems never to have been easy and a success that seems always to have been very limited.[148]

CHAPTER 6

Oral Latin

In the middle years of the sixteenth century, the French naturalist Pierre Belon contrasted the closed world of the peasant with the infinite universe of the sage, the essential difference being mastery of the old tongue. "A community of village men," he wrote in his *Portraits d'oyseaux, animaux, serpents, etc.,* "a Breton, a Basque, a Scotsman, would not understand one another, as their languages are foreign one to the other. But if they were lettered men and spoke the written language which is used in their religion, then each would understand the other's speech. How great therefore is the advantage of the lettered man over the mechanical."[1] Latin traced the dividing line between the Babel of the ignorant and the unitary society of the educated. But how, in reality, did those who "understood one another's speech" (in Belon's expression) speak Latin? Did they really understand one another perfectly?

Setting aside declarations of principle (or allegations that Latin has some kind of inherent communicative virtue) it would seem necessary to examine a range of situations involving oral communication in Latin. Two questions spring immediately to mind: what was the quality of the language spoken? And what was the level of comprehension? The information we have is inevitably incomplete (not surprisingly, in a retrospective assessment of the oral apprehension of a language). Apart from that, sources are much rarer here than they are for written discourse, and the quest is difficult and unpredictable; the thinness of the bibliography on the subject makes this clear in advance.[2]

1 Speech

There used to be no shortage of opportunities to speak Latin, given the important role the language once had in the schools, the Church, the sciences and in the everyday practice of law, politics and diplomacy. Demand for a knowledge of oral Latin remained strong until well into the eighteenth century. But it is no less true that from the seventeenth century onward, the frequency of calls to order seems to indicate a decline of the spoken language in the academic world; in the next century, as the vernacular entrenched itself in education, oral exercises started to give way to written ones. This change in initial instruction had inevitable effects of its own, at a time when the vernaculars were gaining the upper hand in oral exchange.[3] From that time onward, Latin was spoken less and less. Paradoxically, this is an area where printed books provide excellent evidence. During the sixteenth century, the practice had grown up in typography of accentuating Latin texts, using acute and grave accents, circumflexes and diaereses to distinguish homonyms and homographs and at the same time give guidance on pronunciation. These diacritical signs, which served to indicate the length of a syllable and the location of the stress, disappeared in the first quarter of the eighteenth century, partly as a result of critical attacks on a system deemed complex and incoherent, but because their usefulness had diminished as Latin evolved irremediably towards the status of a written and read language.[4]

Nevertheless, spoken Latin still had its defenders, mainly because of its role as a language of communication, even in the middle of the Enlightenment century, and even among men who were ardent advocates of the vernacular. Diderot, in an education plan put forward shortly after the suppression of the Jesuit order, advised the study of Latin in the following terms:

> The point is to know Latin, not for the Latin itself, but for the useful things written in that tongue, and to speak it, not to become a praetor or a consul, but to be understood by foreigners who want nothing more than to understand us: so it is appropriate to exercise accordingly and oblige schoolboys [he meant children of ten or eleven years of age] to speak Latin among themselves and with their master.[5]

The Catholic Church, of course, until very recently presented Latin as its "living language", its "instrument of universal communication";[6] for proof, it will be recalled that the two ecumenical Vatican Councils were held in Latin, and that the pupils at the Institutum Altioris Latinitatis in Rome, founded by Paul VI, were still speaking Latin in 1970.[7] And it could happen that people who did not know one another's languages might use Latin to start a conversation. There is no lack of anecdotes to illustrate this, but it is worth quoting Primo Levi's moving example: after his liberation from Auschwitz, while still in Cracow and living in the greatest poverty, looking for a public soup kitchen for food, he made enquiries of a priest who, although benevolent looking, did not know French, German or Italian. Levi writes that "for the first and only time in my post-school career, I made use of my years of classical studies to engage, in Latin, in the most extravagant and disordered of conversations", beginning with the words: "*Pater optime, ubi est mensa pauperorum?*"[8] It is also apparent from this example that the urgency of a situation might lead people to turn to the old language; thus the troops of the British General Whitelock, defeated by the Spanish during the assault on Buenos Aires in 1807, negotiated surrender terms with the victors in Latin, as none of the officers on either side spoke the enemy's language.[9]

There may have been a strong obligation to speak Latin, and opportunities for its use may not have been lacking, but the sources offer very little evidence on the quality of this spoken Latin: what, for example, was the level of Latinity among orators in the Hungarian parliament during the 1840s? A certain level of linguistic competence was expected from university teachers and diplomats until at least the middle of the eighteenth century, and among prelates of the Catholic Church until very recently indeed: but in what class of Latin did they teach, negotiate or confer? Biographers have emphasized the fact that their heroes spoke Latin: but how well? Various personalities referred to their own use of Latin without giving any further information: one would have liked to know the exact Latin in which Descartes talked to Beeckmann on the occasion of their meeting at Breda.[10] Sometimes, admittedly, there is some documentation to satisfy our curiosity. According to the Venetian ambassadors, King Philip II of Spain "spoke Latin very well for a prince".[11] Goethe, more usually celebrated for his talent as a writer in German, displayed a precocious "facility" with both written and "babbled" Latin, and in his *Memoirs*, recalling his time at the University of Strasbourg, relates that he spoke Latin "fluently" at that time.[12] Such eulogistic references are rare, however. Usually the sources refer to speech which is incorrect, awkward or ridiculous, and describe situations in which communication is approximate at best, often difficult, sometimes impossible. The existence of a small number of superior talents does little to temper this dominant impression of very mediocre performance.

For example, the form used by Primo Levi when talking to the priest in Cracow, *pauperorum* instead of *pauperum*, is not very classical. Much earlier examples of sub-Ciceronian Latin are not in short supply. President de Brosses, who was obliged to resort to the old language at Genoa in order to converse with the very learned Father Ferrari, had few illusions on the quality of his remarks, noting that it must have been "utterly ridiculous to overhear me speaking here, like Merlin Coccaïe, a macaronic jargon made up of Italian, Latin and French".[13] Lord Byron had an analogous experience in Lisbon, speaking "bad Latin to the monks, who understand it, as it is like their own".[14] Horace Walpole admitted that the Latin he had had to speak on one or two occasions was in fact, at least where verbs were concerned, "Italian with Roman terminations".[15] The impression of mediocrity given by these examples is further accentuated when we look at the two domains where we might expect to find the most perfect speakers: the Church and the schools.

We have already observed that the Catholic clergy was not always very Latinist, although the Curé of Ars who "understood Latin badly and spoke it worse still" is probably an extreme example.[16] While the language spoken in seminaries has hardly been studied at all, it is not unreasonable to suppose that it must often have been that "very miserable" and "rocky" Latin that Fr Stanislas Breton mentions in his memoirs.[17] So it is not at all surprising that extremely feeble Latinists were to be found even at the highest levels of the Church. By no means all of the seven hundred-odd prelates who attended the ecumenical Vatican Council in 1869 were Latin orators of the first order: "not all spoke (Latin) with the same facility", was the mild comment of Leon Dehon, whose role of stenographer made him pay close attention to the linguistic quality of the speeches. Even the Italian and Hungarian priests, distinguished as they were by relative fluency in the old language, were far from perfect. The opening address given at the first session by Mgr Puecher Passavalli, Archbishop of Iconio, was judged "fine" although he displayed "some unevenness in his Latinity" and the "joins" were sometimes noticeable. More serious, though, was the case of the three Italian cardinals initially chosen to chair the assembly: none of them was capable of improvising in Latin. Of the prelates from other countries, the French in particular showed themselves as rather weak Latinists. "They did not shine either in the elegance or the correctness of their Latinity," noted Dehon of his compatriots, before naming two examples: "Mgr Vérot, Missionary Bishop of Savannah, and Mgr Bravard, Bishop of Coutances, permitted themselves numerous shameless barbarisms". Later, he noted that the first prelate spoke "kitchen Latin" and the second displayed a "poor" Latin "studded with barbarisms and solecisms". Mgr Dupanloup, who entered a vigorous plea for the role of the classical language in education, wielded a Latin described as "passable", but also as "poor" with "some words of French escaping the orator whenever he becomes animated".[18] There does not seem to have been any improvement at the Second Vatican Council, where a lack of fluency was again apparent in the responses; Fr Congar admitted his awkwardness in a lecture given in Rome at about that time: "I speak about ecumenism in Latin. Latin gives me a lot of trouble in the nuances, to which it does not really lend itself, even on the lips of those who know it better than I do."[19] The deficiencies that can be noted at the very top of the Church, at a time when Latin was in retreat, can be found just as easily in much earlier periods, when very poor Latinists were to be found alongside distinguished humanists. A case in point is Ferdinand de Medici, a prince who, before becoming Grand Duke of Tuscany, had been a Cardinal in the Church of Rome. He was a child of thirteen at the time, not much given to letters, and it had been extremely difficult to get him to absorb the Latin necessary to his condition. After ten years of study his knowledge was still of the flimsiest, despite all the different means employed by his masters, which included the use of carriage journeys to talk to him in Latin.[20]

The picture in the schools was no better. In the eighteenth century, men like Daunou were denouncing the "semi-Latin jargon of our schools";[21] others, like the Abbé Coyer, were severely critical of colleges where children spent "ten or twelve years [learning] to speak Latin badly";[22] still others, like Diderot, complained that the mediocrity of pupils often originated with masters who spoke "barbarous Latin".[23] Although this observation might be thought slanted by reformist zeal, it was far from new. A French pedagogue called Du Tertre pointed out in 1650 that many young people, on leaving Rhetoric (the top form) at the age of eighteen or twenty, could only "speak Latin very indifferently, having no sound and genuine taste for that beautiful language".[24] Observations of this sort were not restricted to France. In six-teenth-century England, where the grammar schools initially aimed to teach children to speak Latin, results were equally disappointing. Roger Ascham, author of the famous *Scholemaster*, observed that even in the best schools "for wordes, right choice is smallie regarded, true proprietie whollie neglected, confusion is brought in, barvariousnesse is bred up in so yong wittes, as after-ward they be, not onelie marde for speaking, but also corrupted in judge-ment".[25] In Poland, after the introduction of Polish as the language of education had failed at the end of the eighteenth century, spoken Latin was restored in the schools, but there were few illusions on the quality of Latin that could be expected. The Education Commission, which had ruled that "Latin, even if incorrect, is needed for juridical matters and by men of Law", gave permission for Latin to be spoken in class and for pupils to learn to speak and understand it "as with living languages", albeit "in a less pure fashion".[26]

Leaving school for the higher spheres of learning, from the seventeenth century onward we find scholars who did not have "the facility they wished in speaking Latin". In support of this observation, Guy Patin produced the names of Fracastor and Sigonius "although (they are) *doctissimi*", and added:

> Much the same is said of M. de Thou who wrote such a fine five-volume history in Latin and who was very learned. It is said that some Germans and some Eng-lishmen, having heard him speaking so badly at home, quaerebant Thuanum in Thuano ("sought for the de Thou in de Thou") and could hardly believe that it was he who had produced that fine history. The same is said today of M. Rigaut and M. de Saumaise.[27]

Still in the seventeenth century, Ciceronian Latin was no longer being heard in the Sorbonne: one day "Casaubon being present for a thesis . . . heard them arguing loud and clear, but in language so barbarous and so unintelli-gible to him that he could not prevent himself from saying as he left the hall: I have never heard so much Latin without understanding it".[28] The Univer-sity of Padua in the same period was no longer, according to one foreign observer, a bastion of Humanism: "Almost none of the professors with the exception of Ferrari spoke Latin without making solecisms", and Marchetti even sprinkled his Latin lectures with Italian words.[29] The Latinity displayed at the Montpellier Faculty of Medicine was no better. Locke, present at a debate there on 26 February 1676, noted in his diary: "Much French, hard Latin, little Logic and little Reason".[30] A century later nothing had changed. "The Latin country" was, in Mercier's view, "full of idiocies and solecisms"; after giving some examples, he went on: "In truth, our University professors do not know Latin any better than they know their mother tongue".[31] By the nineteenth century the Sorbonne itself resounded with appalling jargon at Latin thesis time. The Law Faculty, which had tried to maintain Latin in the competitive examinations for professorships, had had to give it up "owing to the jeers of the audience".[32] The *agrégation* in philosophy, whose oral component was in Latin, resulted in picturesque scenes like the ones noted by an examining professor in 1827. "More than one sentence," he wrote, "started in Latin and abruptly ended in French," and he cited the example of a candidate who began in a mixture of both languages: "*In hac urbe* (In this town) where I am a professor".[33]

Such mediocre oral performance brought a response. The German academic world was appalled by the poverty of spoken Latin in the eighteenth century, with lack of fluency and errors both apparent. To remedy this state of affairs two Latin societies were created at Jena (1734) and Halle (1736), whose members, many of them university professors, were supposed to speak not just Latin but pure Latin, in the case of Jena strictly Ciceronian.[34]

Another solution proposed in the seventeenth century had been a good deal more ambitious: the creation of Latin towns. The originators of these projects started from a double observation: on the one hand the weakness of Latin after a long and difficult learning process; on the other, the speed with which a child suddenly immersed in a foreign environment learns to speak its language. In 1621 Antoine de Laval suggested that the King of France "create a Latin colony for Monseigneur the Dauphin his son and for all the princes, great lords, nobles and other children of good houses": the exclusive use of Latin and the "pleasant" methods of instruction that would be adopted would guarantee rapid and perfect mastery of spoken Latin.[35] Along similar lines, but more modest, was Jean Cécile Frey's proposal for a Latin college which children would enter at the age of two; there, along with their masters and servants, they would use nothing but the Latin language in conversation and play. Thus at the age of five they would speak "more Latin, and in a more Attic fashion" than children who had spent ten painful years at school.[36] Daniel Georg Morhof believed that it would take about twenty years to establish a Latin town where even the artisans would speak Latin; to get started all that would be needed were six or seven good Latinists, who would teach Latin to poor children of both sexes; these would then learn a profession; they in their turn would then teach Latin to their apprentices, and in this way a

Latin society would take shape.[37] In the mid-eighteenth century Maupertuis, a firm believer in the universality of Latin, accepted that its "dead language" status made oral practice problematic: "One can only be sure of speaking it well," he observed, "by employing complete phrases from classical authors; departure from these immediately produces a heterogeneous jargon of whose absurdity one remains unaware only through ignorance". He considered, however, that it would be quite easy to bring the language back to life:

> All that would be necessary would be to confine all the Latin in the country to a single town and order that all preaching and all court proceedings should be conducted in Latin. I am well aware that the Latin spoken there would not be that of Augustus's court, but neither would it be the Latin the Poles speak. And the youth that would come to that town from countries all over Europe would learn more Latin in a year there than it learns in five or six years at college.[38]

During the same period La Condamine, after making the case against the colleges, sketched the idea of basic Latin instruction through usage, as for a foreign modern language. He added: "Were I to suggest founding a town where only Latin would be spoken and which would soon be populated by all the nations of Europe, some people would doubtless find the project impossible and ridiculous; and that is probably one of the best reasons I could advance for supporting it".[39] Again in the nineteenth century, soon after the Congress of Vienna, a Spanish priest living in Toulouse, Miguel Maria Olmo, proposed to the rulers of a Europe newly at peace after the Napoleonic wars that they found a Latin town to be called Roma Tullia. The inhabitants, who would initially include at least ten nationals from each country, would all speak Latin and would work, each according to his abilities and condition, towards the restoration of the language as a means of international communication.[40] Even though these utopian projects – and there were others of the same sort[41] – never looked like becoming reality, their very existence expresses – and from an early date – the strong feeling that traditional teaching methods did not work: the great majority of schoolchildren remained incapable of speaking Latin fluently and correctly even after many years of punishing effort.

2 Comprehension

In 1678 Jacques Fontaine, aged twenty, entered the Collège de Guyenne at Bordeaux to read philosophy. His memoirs recall the disarray in which he immediately found himself: "Only Latin was spoken there . . . and as in logic one chapter depends on another, I understood nothing, either of the lesson or of the explanation, and could only with extreme effort utter three words of Latin. I was like a half-deaf mute in the class."[42] This quotation gives the measure of the other aspect of the problem posed by oral Latin: compre-hension. It was not just difficult to speak Latin fluently and correctly; it was not all that easy to understand either.

This may explain the deep distress of the youthful James Melville, who longed to return home almost from the moment of his arrival at Glasgow University: "nather being weill grounded in grammer, nor com to the yeirs of naturall judgement or understanding, I was cast in sic a greiff and despear, becaus I understood nocht the regent's language that I did nothing bot bursted and grat at his lessons".[43] Long years of school Latin were no guar-antee of ease here. Vittorio Alfieri who, at school with the Jesuits in Turin, had been an excellent Latinist able to help his friends with their homework, found himself completely helpless on arriving at university. He understood none of the philosophy, "insipid in itself and moreover enveloped in Latin". The next year's physics course was no more intelligible, such was his strug-gle with the language in which it was given.[44]

So we can see why, at a time when the regulations stipulated that lectures and classes must be given in Latin, teachers were nevertheless compelled to give explanations in the vernacular. In Naples at the end of the seventeenth century, the famous law professor Domenico Aulisio would lecture *ex cathedra* in Latin, then descend from his chair and walk up and down among his stu-dents, giving further clarifications and answering questions in Neapolitan.[45] A similar practice existed at about the same time at the University of Pisa whose professors, after having "spoken" in Latin, would emerge from the *aula* into the courtyard and, leaning against a pillar, would "elucidate" in Tuscan.[46] A century later the practice had become an absolute necessity if at least some knowledge was going to reach the students. Gasparo Gozzi noted that at Padua, in the unanimous judgement of the professors, hardly a tenth of the students – perhaps thirty out of 300 – "had a middling understanding of the Latin language". How could they follow lectures in an unintelligible lan-guage? "It is true," Gozzi added, "that after such lectures, the students go to hear the explanation at a private school".[47]

So it is hardly surprising that late eighteenth-century university reformers should have vigorously denounced the custom of teaching in Latin. La Harpe, in a 1791 study plan, grumbled when he came to the philosophy course: "No more exercise books full of logic, metaphysics and morals in bad Latin: that wretched Latin, badly applied, has perpetuated in the schools the pernicious habit of talking without being understood".[48] Nor is it surprising that, for official ceremonies whose audience was not restricted to students, the vernacular started to be used even under the Ancien Régime: thus in 1706, when Jean-Pierre Crousaz, professor at the Academy of Lausanne, gave the harangue at graduation, he abandoned Latin and adopted French out of courtesy to the noble lords of the town, and more specifically because "the greater number understood it not at all".[49]

3 Pronunciation

The shoals of diversity

While the failure to understand Latin was often attributable to imperfect knowledge of the language, it could also happen that different pronunciations added to the confusion by making the words themselves unintelligible. It is appropriate to start with a text – incidentally a very well-known one – which sets out the terms of the problem clearly. It is taken from Erasmus's *De recta latini graecique sermonis pronunciatione* (first edition 1528), a work whose title states its concern with the proper pronunciation of Latin (Greek does not concern us here). As there can only be one "correct" pronunciation, the text was an attempt to introduce order into the multiplicity of pronunciations current at that time, and thus reduce the resulting confusion. To justify this attempt – in case anyone thought it needed justifying – the Dutch humanist described a comic scene witnessed by Leo, one of the heroes of his book, at the court of the Emperor Maximilian.

> L.: Let me tell you. Not very long ago, I happened to be present when the Emperor Maximilian was saluted by four orators, something that is done from time to time out of tradition, rather than from the heart. One was a Frenchman, a native of Le Mans . . . He gave a speech which had been composed, I believe, by an Italian and was not in bad Latin, but in such a strong French accent that some Italian scholars who were present thought he was speaking in French and not Latin . . . When he had finished – not without difficulty, for he had lost his thread in mid-discourse, being bothered I suppose by the laughter of those present – an orator was sought to deliver the customary improvised response. A doctor of the court was thrust forward for this task . . . He began thus: "Caesarea Maghestas pene caudet fidere fos, et horationem festram lipenter audifit, etc.,"[50] wheezing so much and with such a German accent that nobody could possibly have sounded more German even speaking the vernacular. He was received with even louder roars of laughter. Next came the orator from Denmark, a man who sounded extraordinarily like a Scotsman in his pronunciation; the response was given by a Zeelander. One would have sworn that neither one nor the other was speaking Latin.[51]

This comedy, which greatly amused the Emperor, is in no way unusual. Similar examples abound throughout the modern period. The English, Irish and Scots were often noticed for strange Latin pronunciation that rendered them incomprehensible and ridiculous. Guy Patin observed:

> These Hibernian, these Irish logicians always make me laugh with the way they pronounce Latin. I never understand anything the first time I hear it, their ous always change the meaning in my imagination. Scaliger, who was certainly a

more able man than I, had the same difficulty when he heard these kinds of
Latin spoken. After listening carefully one day to a compliment an Irishman had
addressed to him in Latin, he believed the man had been speaking Irish; and he
answered that he had understood nothing, as that language was unknown to
him.[52]

At about the same time in the mid-seventeenth century, Samuel Sorbière
complained that during a visit across the Channel he had been unable to get
any benefit from conversation with English scholars "because they are very
retiring and have little communication with foreigners; quite apart from being
unwilling to speak French, although perfectly capable of doing so, they elucidate in Latin with a certain accent and pronunciation that render it as difficult to understand as their own language".[53] Similarly, one wonders what
students at the University of Leyden towards the end of the century would
have learned from Archibald Pitcairn, a Scottish professor of medicine whose
accent when he spoke Latin made him virtually impossible to understand.[54]
From the opposite point of view, foreigners were not often well understood
in England, as Samuel Bochart discovered when staying in Oxford in 1621:
when he asked one of the masters of the university, in Latin, for permission
to attend a doctorate ceremony, he was not understood and assumed, from
his travelling clothes, to be a wandering cleric begging for his daily bread.[55]
Things had hardly changed a hundred and thirty years later when the princes
Corsini visited England, if one is to believe their travel diary: "Latin had to
be spoken, but the different way it is pronounced in England meant that they
were little understood and understood little".[56] The English themselves were
well aware of the peculiarity of their Latin pronunciation. John Evelyn in
1661 blamed the "odd pronouncing of Latine" taught at Westminster School
for the fact that "out of England no nation were able to understand or endure
it".[57] The same observation appears in correspondence to the *Gentleman's Magazine* of the late eighteenth and early nineteenth centuries:[58] it is made again
in an article in *The Times* of 13 September 1866 describing the experience of
Charles Allix Wilkinson, who had visited Hungary and Greece in 1837 as a
"travelling bachelor" of Cambridge University. In Hungary he had often
found himself in company "where all were talking Latin", but "I had the
greatest difficulty in understanding and making myself understood solely on
account of the strange pronunciation". The same had happened in Greece;
at an evening spent in the company of ten cultivated people from nine different countries, it had been decided that Latin "which all know more or less"
should serve as the common language; but it had "proved a complete failure
from the different ways of pronouncing it; and I must say," he added, "that
ours was the most extraordinary – quite different to all the others, and utterly
unintelligible".[59]

The English may have been outstanding for the peculiarity of their Latin pronunciation, but others were not far behind in giving the classical tongue a national coloration. According to Scioppius's *De orthopeia seu recta litterarum latinarum pronunciatione* it was a universal problem: thus for example the Chinese, who do not have an *r* sound, use an *l* sound instead, while the Japanese do the opposite.[60] A number of other examples could be cited from much nearer home.[61] We will quote here an anecdote involving a celebrated individual normally associated with French prose, the Duc de Saint-Simon. Travelling in Spain in 1722, he was received with the honour due to his rank by the Archbishop of Toledo and his nephews. "We spoke Latin to each other," he wrote in his *Memoirs*. "The eldest (of the nephews), although an Inquisitor, thinking that I was addressing him in another language that he did not understand, begged me to use Latin with him." Saint-Simon added: "The fact is that we, the French, pronounce Latin very differently from the Spanish, the Italians and the Germans."[62]

Another factor in modern Europe, with its distinctive dialects, was the effect of local accents on Latin pronunciation. Geoffroy Tory, in *Champ Fleury*, went through the differences discernible in the Kingdom of France letter by letter. He noted that there were

> three nations who pronounce R very badly: the Manceaux, the Bretons and the Lorrains. In Maine they add an S to an R, for if they wanted to say Pater noster or Tu es magister noster, they would pronounce it Paters nosters or Tu es magisters nosters. The Bretons pronounce only one R where two are written. The Lorrains by contrast pronounce two where there is only one.[63]

The confusion seems to have been just as bad in the Germanic world, if we are to believe Johannes Casellius; according to that pedagogue, the letter *a* alone was pronounced in at least three different ways.[64] In Scotland and northern England there prevailed a Latin pronunciation that John Caius called "Borealism" or "Scotticism":

> These people say saibai, taibai, vaita, and aita, which should actually be pronounced sibi, tibi, vita and ita. Although this sort of pronunciation is commonly disparaged by southern Englishmen . . ., its users hold fast to it – and that by obstinacy and freakishness rather than reason. Such speech is characteristic of the uncultivated and disorderly multitudes.[65]

Ignorance or limited knowledge of the language, which strongly affected pronunciation, was most apparent during Latin chanting and singing, on which the general level of education had noticeable effects. "The less erudite the community of ecclesiastics or scholars," notes Patricia Ranum in reference to the seventeenth century, "the more indistinct the consonants became, and the more frequently letters were intruded to make Latin words resemble their French equivalents".[66] The same thing happened when performers from the Opéra used to take part in major liturgical festivals at the Jesuits' church of Saint-Louis in Paris. "Latin is not a tongue with which they are acquainted; the language of the Church is not very familiar to them," noted Le Cerf de La Viéville in the early eighteenth century. "Their pronunciation is pathetic. They cut, mangle, disfigure the words in a ludicrous manner, and it is impossible to prevent oneself from laughing at the extraordinary mistakes, the droll farrago that they come up with."[67]

While the unlettered were massacring Latin pronunciation out of ignorance, mannerisms wilfully introduced by the learned caused deformations of their own, less damaging perhaps but still unhelpful to easy comprehension of the discourse. The consequences could be far-reaching in the case of scholars eminent enough to have a following: Scaliger noted of the "Dutch Flemings" that "for *sed*, they say *zed* which is Lipsius's pronunciation; all have wanted to imitate Lipsius's vices".[68] Similarly, the unaccented Latin pronunciation practised by the French in the early sixteenth century was imitated by fashion-conscious foreigners.[69] In England, a strong wish for identity and distinctness led the schools to adopt and maintain particular pronunciations, a practice that continued into the twentieth century. "You will find schools in England in which there are at least two and probably half a dozen of different pronunciations," observed one participant in the Classical Association's discussions on the subject in 1905. "Boys have to unlearn at the secondary school what they have learnt at the preparatory school . . . Neither at Oxford nor at Cambridge, perhaps not within a single college, does any uniform system prevail – not even a consistently incorrect system."[70]

These multiple pronunciations, whatever their root causes, were a source of confusion and incomprehension. In extreme cases speakers could be totally unaware that they were speaking the same language, but more usually communication would be garbled by different pronunciations of the same letter. Geoffroy Tory's *Champ Fleury* contains several examples, one of which notes that

> the letter L is badly pronounced in Latin diction in the country of Burgundy and Forez, where for the said letter L they pronounce R as I have often seen and heard said by many young scholars of those countries when they came here to the University of Paris to college where I was then teaching. Instead of saying mel, fel, animal, aldus or albus and many other similar dictions, they pronounce mer, fer, animer, ardus and arbus, which is abuse of the due and proper pronunciation, and which often causes not just confused meaning, but wrong meaning.[71]

A long and difficult march towards uniformity

It is thus not surprising that reforms of pronunciation were being proposed at a very early date; at this point we can do no better than turn to Erasmus and his *De recta latini graecique sermonis pronunciatione*. The Italian humanists had striven to end the chaos – a legacy of the Middle Ages – that prevailed in Latin spelling: they had introduced a reformed orthography based on ancient coinage and inscriptions and the teachings of classical Roman grammarians. That the Italians were not alone in addressing this issue can be seen from the writings of men like the Spaniard Antonio Nebrija, the Louvain professor Despautère or Bebel who taught at Tübingen. Moreover, both Nebrija and Bebel had called for a reform of pronunciation to accompany the new spelling. It is against the background of this movement that Erasmus's work should be seen, even though its renown and success have tended to over-shadow its forerunners.

To deal with the linguistic disorder of which the scene at Maximilian's court is a picturesque illustration, to address pronunciation that was univer-sally barbarous, Erasmus set out to rediscover the true original pronunciation which had been altered over the centuries. He took the view – and here we are reminded of his extensive travels – that there had been the least change in Rome and the most in France, with Germany and England (at that time) between the two extremes. This was a widespread impression, judging from the advice Johannes Amerbach gave his sons Bruno and Basile when they were students in Paris at the beginning of the sixteenth century:

> I forbid you absolutely to learn the pronunciation of the French and become accustomed to it, for they accentuate badly, prolonging short vowels in an ugly way and abbreviating long ones . . . Not just in Germany, but also in Italy, where the best-lettered live, such usage is thought detestable, absurd and risible, and he who speaks in such a way earns himself the reputation of a poltroon.

Erasmus did not believe, however, that Italian usage was necessarily authen-tic; just that it had changed the least. For the correct – *recta* – pronunciation he sought, he used the same sources as his predecessors, giving an important role to Quintilian. In the context of the present work, which is in no sense philological, it is hardly necessary to go through Erasmus's reform of Latin pronunciation point by point; its success in any case (in contrast to what hap-pened with Greek pronunciation) was far from universal, as the failure of attempts to introduce it in France and England plainly show.[72]

In France, where from the thirteenth century onward Latin had degener-ated in both vocabulary and syntax, Latin was pronounced like French: *u* was always pronounced *ü* and *um* in the final position was pronounced *on*, some-times as a result of absorption by a similar French word, *dictum* for example being pronounced *dicton*. Short and long vowels were ignored or interchanged (as Amerbach warned his sons) and stress was, as in French, on the last vocal-ized syllable. In the seventeenth century, the humanists tried to restore an ancient form of pronunciation in keeping with the orthographic and syntactic reforms, borrowing from Italy in the first instance and teaching the Italian pronunciation analysed by Geoffroy Tory in *Champ Fleury*. Then Erasmus's *De recta*, reprinted in Paris in the same year as its publication in Basle, inspired (rather too closely according to some critics) a text with almost the same title, *De recta latini sermonis pronunciatione*, published by Charles Estienne in 1538. Efforts to correct pronunciation were thus under way well before Ramus, who is generally regarded as the apostle of reform in France. But ingrained habit, and the difficulty the humanists had in reaching agreement on how the Ancients pronounced their words, caused the reform to lose momentum. All that it achieved was to ensure articulation of all consonants including double ones, the first consonant in a group and a consonant at the end of a word, which previously had been muted as in French; the individual pronunciation of each consonant was unchanged. Vowels retained their French pronunciation; the stress remained on the final syllable, as it had not been possible to restore the quantities of vowels in pronunciation. So the outcome of the Renaissance reform was only a compromise between the previous – late mediaeval – pronunciation and classical pronunciation, in fact a purely conventional pronunciation resulting from Italian influence, a return to classical Antiquity and meanderings due to French disagreements and indecision.[73]

In England, where Erasmus thought Latin pronunciation better than in France, the reformed pronunciation was introduced in about 1540 by two young Cambridge scholars, Thomas Smith and John Cheke. In 1542, however, a decree from the Chancellor of the University forbade the new pronunciation; the reformers resisted successfully for a while, but in 1554 a new decree from the Chancellor repeated the interdiction. After that, Latin pronunciation departed from Erasmus's reforms to follow – more and more closely – the evolution of English phonetics.[74] Although Milton was still recommending "Italian" pronunciation – with notably clear and distinct vowels – in his 1644 book *Of Education*, in a Latin grammar he produced some years later he admitted the vanity of this advice "since very few will be persuaded to pronounce Latin otherwise than their own English".[75]

The wide diversity of pronunciations and the failure to unify them led to proposals for partial or compromise solutions. Authors as different as the pedagogue Casellius, the polymath Scioppius and the Chancellor of Paris University, Rollin, compiled lists of a few simple rules intended to help avoid gross errors on the one hand and facilitate communication on the other.[76] In practice, however, nothing seems to have changed. Until (not without difficulty) Italian pronunciation was imposed in the Church, and classical or restored pronunciation in the universities, there was no universal Latin pronunciation.

One of the primary reasons, it appears from the texts cited here, involves ethnic particularities. Milton gave an imaginative explanation of this when he invited his compatriots to pronounce Latin, and its vowel system in particular, more clearly, adding: "For we Englishmen being farre northerly, doe not open our mouthes in the cold air, wide enough to grace a southern tongue; but are observ'd by all other nations to speak exceeding close and inward: so that to smatter Latin with an English mouth, is as ill a hearing as law French".[77]

Of much greater consequence was the inability of scholars to agree on how Latin should be pronounced. In sixteenth-century France the letter *u* was the subject of debates between those asserting that the Romans had pronounced it *ü* (like the French) and those who believed they had said *oo*. The humanist Peletier suggested that there might have been an intermediate sound between *ü* and *oo*, although in later work he seems to have fallen in with most of his compatriots and chosen the French *ü*. Erasmus himself leaned towards the *ü* version, believing that apart from the long *u* which ought to be pronounced *oo*, there was a shorter *u* in Latin approximating to the French *ü*. These disagreements and hesitations resulted from the impossibility of establishing the Ancients' own pronunciation with any certainty.[78] Although Ménage, in what became known as the "*Kiskis* and *Kankan* debate", peremptorily laid claim to Roman authority by asserting that Cicero and his contemporaries "used to say *ki, kae, kod* and not *qui, quae, quod*",[79] in reality things were far less certain. In one text by Charles Perrault, *Parallèle des Anciens et des Modernes*, the uncertainty seems to cause a little confusion: one of the interlocutors asserts that "It is a certainty that we do not know the way Latin ought to be pronounced", then goes on to produce various examples of differing modern and Roman pronunciations![80] Scioppius was very clear on the subject: Latin was a dead language that had started to decompose more than a thousand years earlier, and intermingled with various vernaculars so that "we cannot even suspect what its exact pronunciation was". He added that if Cicero came back to life, his utterances would be understood no better than if he spoke Arabic, while he himself would understand nothing said to him in Latin, even by the contemporary prince of Latinity Giovanni Ciampoli. Like his compatriot Johannes Casellius, Scioppius believed that modern pronunciation could be reformed and unified, but that classical Roman pronunciation could not be wholly retrieved.[81]

Any such effort was rendered still more difficult by each nation's conviction that its own pronunciation was the best, or anyway the most correct. Scioppius opened *De orthopeia* with this observation, adding that no argument or authority could shake a conviction of this sort.[82] Similar remarks appear again in 1776 in Yverdon's *Encyclopédie*, where De Felice noted in connection with Latin: "Every nation pronounces it in accordance with its own dialect and way of sounding each letter of the alphabet, and every nation imagines that its pronunciation is the best".[83] Nobody was ready to give best to anyone else.

This certainty of having the true, or at least the best, pronunciation was reinforced by educational routine, acquired mechanisms and ingrained habits: Milton, for example, eventually ceded to his compatriots' normal usage. But such usage could also be elaborated into a defensive system against all attempts to reform and unify pronunciation: that is what seems to emerge from John Caius's *De pronunciatione graecae et latinae linguae . . . libellus*, strongly hostile to Erasmus's reform. Although this reform was resolutely archaic in inspiration, and started with a determined return to the classical sources, both literary and monumental, it was denounced by Caius as a pernicious novelty upsetting to the established order, "the custom of the nation". It was in the name of tradition – conceived in this context as the product of a living usage – that the scholar battled, using extensive quotations from classical authors, against the attempt that had been made to introduce a "new pronunciation" at Cambridge. The pronunciation in question was used nowhere outside England, and even there only in one town. If people sacrificed before this novelty, if they dropped the usage accepted everywhere in England, the risk of not being understood by their compatriots would be added to the probability of not being understood by foreigners. It would be better to stay with "the old pronunciation" which "has not in the least prevented men either from speaking correctly or being understood throughout in the world". Apart from that, the usage Caius approved was influenced by a social code that avoided anything shocking or indecent. He held that the new pronunciation violated the principle of euphony, producing a disagreeable impression on listeners. "For such speech is rustic and plain, insufficiently polished, indelicate, clumsily acquired by a kind of affectation, unworthy of the mouths of the learned, violently offensive to the ears of the educated, obviously unattractive and odious to everyone, except to those who are zealous for novelty." It also offended the proprieties by making perfectly respectable words like *ascitum* (admitted) and *ascicunt* (they admit) sound rude: "For if in the first of these words you pronounce c as ch, and in the second the c as k in the new fashion, the words will be uttered with such filthiness as in my modesty I cannot explain". Erasmus's pronunciation, and humanist erudition with it, were thus condemned in the name of civilized drawing-room manners.[84] So the diversity of pronunciations persisted, and continued (whatever Caius may have thought) to detract from perfect communication. His later compatriot Samuel Johnson, who was well aware of the problem, suggested an urbane compromise solution that would respect national peculiarities while improving the comprehensibility of discourse: "He who travels, if he speaks Latin, may so soon learn the sounds which every native gives it, that he need make no provision before his journey; and if strangers visit us, it is their business to practise such conformity to our modes as they expect from us in their own countries".[85]

Throughout the Ancien Régime, then, and on into the nineteenth century, Latin pronunciation remained anything but uniform, and marked by national and even local accents, by mannerisms and by fashion. The uncertainty about authentic original pronunciation gave each nation the right to pronounce Latin in its own way. Standard usages were thus predominant. Le Cerf de La Viéville observed that the Italians were right to pronounce *fluvius* "flouvious" (i.e. more or less in the English manner) for "such was the pronunciation of the living language in which *virtu* is spoken as 'virtou' . . . They would wound ears accustomed to those sounds if they pronounced it 'flüviüs'." By the same reasoning, their pronunciation would be "shocking to French ears" since *u* is pronounced "in natural language" as it is written: just as the word in French was *vertu* and not *vertou*, it was appropriate to say *flüviüs* in France. The conclusion was obvious: "The common pronunciation should be used whenever possible, it is good when it is not invariably bad".[86] This attitude had the force of law; so in the seventeenth and eighteenth centuries Latin pronunciation – for good reasons – was nothing like that of ancient Latin, nor like French pronunciation of the period, but "a marvellous compromise between that of a dead Latin and that of an archaic French".[87]

In France and elsewhere, that is how things would have remained had not the advent of linguistics in the nineteenth century, and work by philologists and grammarians, led to the reconstruction of classical Latin pronunciation, the model being that of the cultivated classes in Rome during the first century BC. Apart from theoretical debates on the subject, the practical problem that arose after the 1870s was how to incorporate the new system in teaching. Progress was slow and resistances were many.

Attempts to introduce the "restored" pronunciation in the French *lycées* from about the last decade of the nineteenth century not only had to overcome ingrained habits, but caused divergences to appear inside the reformers' camp. Factions included those who wanted to introduce it generally and those who thought it should be restricted to the senior classes in the *lycées*, those who thought it best to allow existing teachers to continue using their own pronunciation, those who wanted to proceed gently by persuasion and those who, on the contrary, wanted the authorities to use coercion. There was controversy not only over the modalities of its application but over the very content of the restored pronunciation, specifically on the knotty question of stress or rather stresses. While classical Latin had two stresses, of pitch and emphasis, they caused difficulty to French speakers accustomed always to stress the last vocalized syllable: there was no lack of arguments between those who wanted to shelve the whole issue at the outset, those who thought it appropriate to keep only the stress of emphasis, and those who wanted to have both. The Romanists intervened to point out that the so-called classical pronunciation could not be applied, without anachronism, to mediaeval Latin, and to urge that traditional pronunciation should be used in its case; moreover, either from scientific rigour or a wish to sabotage the reform, some of them (like Edmond Farral) argued strongly for the need to indicate the pitch stress with a diacritical mark. The situation was further complicated by the fact that, between 1910 and 1930, the great majority of the French clergy gave up the French pronunciation of Latin and adopted the Roman one. The consequences were of two sorts. Some embers of the former pronunciation survived, and resistance started to take shape. In 1929, an association of "Friends of the French pronunciation of Latin" was formed in Paris, supported by the Ministry of Foreign Affairs; the ministry even formulated a diplomatic statement to the effect that "the question of the usual pronunciation of Latin throughout French territory" was "a national and political issue directly involving the public authority". An opponent of Italian pronunciation who was also one of the most ardent supporters of the "restored" pronunciation, Alcide Macé, put it more directly by saying that there was no need to "naturalize ourselves Italian".[88] So the supporters of the "scientifically reformed pronunciation", who were divided into "moderates" and "radicals", had two groups of opponents who were also mutually hostile: partisans of the Italian pronunciation (gaining ground in the churches), and those loyal to the original French pronunciation (still very much alive in the classroom).[89] Despite some progress, therefore, the reform dragged on interminably; meanwhile, Latin pronunciation could become truly appalling when schoolchildren used a mixture of all three different "styles". A grammar textbook given to sixth-grade pupils in the late 1950s contained the following: "In France there are three ways of pronouncing Latin: 1. Traditional pronunciation, strongly Gallicized. 2. The pronunciation adopted by the Church, Italianized. 3. The restored pronunciation, which is as near as possible to ancient Roman pronunciation" (the last was particularly recommended for poetry).[90] In 1960 a ministerial circular was issued ordering the "restored" pronunciation to be taught, but any practical results were overtaken by the general decline of Latin as a subject.

In England, the classical pronunciation was introduced in the universities in about 1870 without encountering much resistance, although there was no shortage of learned debates, some individuals practised both systems, and the traditional English pronunciation still had a number of supporters in the 1920s. The reform was slower to reach the schools, where it encountered particularisms and traditions of the sort mentioned above. The debates, complicated by aesthetic and moral considerations, lasted half a century, from 1870 until around 1920. The new *w* pronunciation of the Latin *v* was particularly controversial, being thought ridiculous or even "repugnant" by some scholars and defended by others, who argued that *w* was not "a coarse and wholly barbarous sound" but, on the contrary, one much favoured in English poetry; the polemic was still raging in the early 1950s, when it was asserted that the word *vigeat* lost its force and virility when pronouced *wigeat*. Before the reformed pronunciation finally prevailed, a number of compromises were proposed: teaching both pronunciations; keeping traditional pronunciation for prose and using the new system for verse; and – the most popular and widely used solution – teaching the new pronunciation in the sixth form (first grade) but keeping English pronunciation in the younger classes.[91] According to a professor of comparative philology at Cambridge, W. Sidney Allen, the new system had prevailed everywhere by the 1960s, but many errors were still being committed even by the majority of academics. The "national phobia of non-English sounds" tended to reduce Latin letters and syllables to their English equivalents; so that in the usual pronunciation of the word *agger* (slope, embankment) not a single component was even approximately correct: the *a* was pronounced erroneously (*æ*), the double consonant was pronounced as a single one, the *e* was muttered faultily in the English manner (*a*) and the *r* was totally ignored.[92] We might add that during the 1930s, the adoption of Italian pronunciation by the Catholic Church in England met resistances similar to the ones in France: although the opposition was expressed in a less absolute manner, it defended the historical legitimacy of the traditional pronunciation and vigorously refuted the Roman pronunciation's pretensions to universality.[93]

In Italy, the Italianate pronunciation survived until recent times both in the Church and in the schools, and it was not until the 1960s that the classical pronunciation variously described as "restored", "scientific" or "reformed", was genuinely debated. It had few defenders on the practical level, and there was wide agreement on retaining the traditional pronunciation in Italian schools, particularly the *scuola media*. Much was made of the remaining uncertainties over true classical pronunciation, and of problems concerning quantity and stress; but the argument most widely used emphasized the ridicule that would result from the new pronunciation of certain words, for example the name of the great Roman orator Cicero (traditionally pronounced "Chichero") which to an Italian ear sounds like bird-song when pronounced "Kikero". It was argued that Italian pronunciation derived a particular legitimacy from its unbroken tradition of speakers, from Petrarch down to Pascoli; and it was shown once again that adoption of the reform would result in two pronunciations having to be learned, the classical one for ancient texts and the Italianate one for humanist literature. The compromise generally favoured was to teach the classical pronunciation at university level, but otherwise retain the customary pronunciation, which would be used exclusively in the *scuola media*. As elsewhere, however, the problem became less acute with the decline of Latin studies. From the 1970s onward, nobody (so to speak) could be bothered with it.[94]

Being a living language, "restored" Latin did not have – probably could not have – a single standard pronunciation. Not even an institution as monolithic and absolutist as the Catholic Church could achieve that. When the Vatican Council was held in 1869, it was foreseen that given the number and origins of the prelates expected – about 700, including 120 or so English speakers – the diversity of pronunciations could well cause problems. A secretariat of twenty-three seminarists of different nationalities (thus including members accustomed to the different pronunciations) was assembled to ensure accurate transcription of the debates, directed by a priest from Turin, Virginio Marchese, who had been a stenographer in the Italian Senate. The stenography system used was "quite complicated" and was thought to have produced "mediocre results", but it did answer a real need, summed up as follows by Léon Dehon who was one of its scribes: "There were a lot of nuances in the pronunciation and during the first few days one often saw a smile breaking through the gravity of the Italian bishops and cardinals, when they heard the language of Cicero being spoken with inflections strange to their ears". The English, he specified, "were terrible with their pronunciation". They were not alone. Mgr Arrigoni, the Archbishop of Lucca, commented on a speech given by the Bishop of Nicosia: "One could understand nothing because he seemed to be speaking in his own language rather than Latin". Another Italian prelate, Mgr Tizzani, referred generally to the "variety of pronunciations" that made comprehension of what was said more difficult, and held up as examples the Bishop of Luzon and the Archbishop of Albi. In the end, though, as Dehon observed, "no matter, people understood one another", and Marchese pointed out that since the great majority of the speakers had spent time at the Gregorian University "they not only spoke Latin in the Roman fashion but on occasion spoke the Roman argot of the Piazza Mentana". Nevertheless, a letter in Latin was addressed to the Pope on 2 January 1870, asking for the plenary sessions to be preceded by specific meetings "by nation" of all the prelates speaking each language. The fact was that the difficulty some of the delegates had in dealing with delicate and specialized matters in Latin was exacerbated by problems arising from "the variety of pronunciations". Different accents had resounded in the very place where unity was supposed to reign, detracting considerably from the claimed universality of the Latin language.[95]

Closer to our own time, the "Living Latin" movement adopted the restored pronunciation to render the old language suitable for its universal vehicular role. But partisans of the Italian pronunciation continued to argue their point, and supporters of the restored pronunciation continued to colour their Latin pronunciation, wholly unintentionally, with strong national accents: close familiarity with Anglo-American phonetics was needed to understand some of the participants in this association's conferences.[96]

Only when Latin had ceased to be used as a living language was it at last possible to impose a universal pronunciation, and even then not without heated arguments and special arrangements on a local level. There was no longer any question of using the language to talk to contemporaries;[97] it was simply needed to read authors from the past. Such was the ultimate fate of an irremediably dead language that moreover, through the whole of the modern era, had hardly risen above the most mediocre level of oral practice.

Part III

What Latin Meant

Introduction

The whole cultural history of the Western world from the Renaissance to the mid-twentieth century can be inscribed under the sign of Latin. The language predominated in the schools, was heard – at least in Catholic countries – in Church, and until the eighteenth century was the main vehicle for learning in its more scholarly forms. Even when Latin declined in importance, for example in the schools during the 1950s, it still remained an important factor everywhere. That is the main finding of the first part of this work.

Although, during those five centuries, Latin was often studied intensively over many years, it was never spoken as fluently or written as easily as might have been expected. Although there were some accomplished Latinists, especially in the period leading up to the seventeenth century, the fact remains that in general, not in the Republic of Letters at its zenith, nor even in the Catholic Church, was the level of competence as high as historiography has made out. Schoolchildren, for their part, all fell far short of their masters' hopes: while it would have been naïve to expect results ever to meet expectations, the gap between target results and those achieved in practice was always a wide one. That is the finding of the second part of this book.

Not only was performance generally mediocre, but it was also claimed that Latin was useless to most of those studying it. By 1730 this had become a widespread opinion, according to the German grammarian Johannes Fredericus Noltenius, who disagreed with it and with the accompanying view that some men had risen to the highest levels without knowing Latin.[1] The next generation was not much different. La Chalotais, in his *Essai d'éducation nationale* (1763), started by noting that "of a hundred students, there are not fifty to whom Latin might be necessary", and added: "One would hardly be able to find four or five to whom it might be useful, later, to speak or write it".[2] Diderot, in the *Plan d'une université* that he drafted for Catherine II in 1775, espoused an identical point of view: people who had studied Latin for six or seven years

> become businessmen or soldiers . . . or attach themselves to court or the bar, which means that nineteen out of twenty of them go through their lives without reading a Latin author and forget what they have painfully learned . . . And then, I wonder to whom these ancient languages are of any absolute utility. Practically no one, I daresay; other than poets, orators, scholars and other classes of professional littérateurs, in other words the least necessary estates of society.[3]

While it is true that neither of these men could pass for a good friend of Latin, all they are doing here is describing contemporary reality: by the middle of the eighteenth century, with the vernaculars established almost everywhere, Latin was useful only to the minority destined for religious life and a narrow range of professions. This view was shared by Gasparo Gozzi in Italy and by a number of those debating education in America at the time. Benjamin Rush was particularly outspoken: "I see no use at the present time," he wrote in 1789, "for a knowledge of the Latin and Greek languages for a lawyer, a physician, or a divine, in the United States, except it be to facilitate the remembrance of a few technical terms which may be retained without it".[4]

Since the seventeenth century, moreover, the classics had been abundantly translated or, to quote Diderot again, "translated and retranslated a hundred times over".[5] This was true not only in Europe but in Latin America and North America too, where one contemporary called the eighteenth century "the age of translations".[6] What was the point of devoting several years to the acquisition of Latin now that these translations had made it redundant? "With the help of translations," according to Helvetius, the same knowledge could be acquired "in two or three months".[7] And that is what people did. Most of the eighteenth-century Americans who regarded ancient history as "the lamp of experience" acquired that precious knowledge from English translations.[8] The bourgeois Parisians of the nineteenth century favoured classical education and opposed the idea of "French college", but the Latin texts in their libraries were invariably vernacular editions.[9]

With knowledge of Latin losing its practical usefulness, with translations rendering it no longer necessary, reading, writing and speaking Latin gradually ceased to be primary aims. "We do not study Latin these days in order to know it. People tell you very clearly that Latin is not learned in order to know it; Latin is learned because it is a marvellous intellectual discipline; it is well understood, it is admitted in advance that it will not be known, that it has become impossible to know it," wrote Jean Guéhenno in 1959.[10] By that time there was nothing original about such an observation. As early as 1886, Anatole France answered the assertion that it was pointless to study Latin to such little effect by saying that people did not learn Latin at the *lycée* in order to know it, but in order to learn how to think.[11] The purpose of learning Latin was no longer to become competent in the language; or at least, that had become less important than the other objectives sketched by Anatole France and Jean Guéhenno. The proof of this is that it had become unusual for anyone to say that they had learned Latin simply to acquire a language making a culture and a literature accessible to them. A telling example is found in the *Classical Journal*, which in 1969 published the results of a survey among prominent Americans – starting with President Nixon – on the practical and cultural value of Latin. Nelson Rockefeller's opinion that "it will add to your cultural enjoyment by enabling you to read, in the original tongue, some of the world's great literature in both poetry and prose", may sound predictable and commonplace to Europeans over a certain age, but is in fact exceptional in the context.[12]

Thus far we have considered Latin exclusively as a language to speak, read or write, more or less equivalent to the living languages current in Europe at the time. From the foregoing observations, however, it emerges not only that the study of Latin was far from always producing linguistic competence, but that this competence had lost its practical purpose over time and had ceased, in effect, to be a main objective. The obvious question that now arises is: Latin, for what? If mastery of the language was no longer the main issue, why were its syntax and grammar still being taught at such length? What was expected of it, and how was it justified? And – setting aside the effects induced by its study – what was the role assigned to the ancient language in modern society? In short, where was the legitimacy of Latin now located in the space between its *raison d'être* and its function, its practices and its discourses, its realities and its representations? At this point, we need to adopt a different perspective to understand what – across the western world – Latin really meant.

7

Making the Man

We are therefore obliged to return to the starting point of our history, to put ourselves back *in illo tempore* – the Quattrocento – when Latin received a new lease of life. The Italian humanists centred their culture on the great writers of Antiquity, seen as the source of all learning: the direct reading of texts using a historical and critical approach was the foundation not only of instruction – the acquisition of classical Latin and Greek along with some "scientific" knowledge – but of education in the full sense of the term. As Eugenio Garin has pointed out, the objective of Guarino of Verona and his imitators was not only "to make the pupil master of a technique, but to prepare him for life, not for the exercise of this or that office – even high office – but of a single office, a single profession: the profession of man". The study of classical Latin rested on the same principles as reading ancient authors and obeyed the same requirements. While without the language the society, the people and their history were incomprehensible, a rigorous and specific study of the language was essential to anyone wishing to understand the hearts of men and the secrets of writings from the period, thus gaining a moral, human profit. This is a long way from a formal and pedantic study of the language. "You tell me that after studying Cicero so much I don't express myself like Cicero," Il Poliziano replied to a heckler. "But I'm not Cicero; and I can tell you that it's from Cicero I've learned to be myself." It is true that the study of Latin and the classical world had a special value for Italian humanists – descended as they were from the original inhabitants of the hub of the Roman empire – but it also possessed fundamental importance for all nations. It enabled people to "become aware, in the common origin of our culture, by conversing with the fathers, of a common culture", and at the same time to "recognize themselves as citizens of a single city". A cultural model was being established, hegemonic on two different levels. On one level it embraced the shaping of the whole man, aiming at specific instruction as well as education in the broad sense. On another level, basing itself on dialogue with masters recognized as archetypes for humanity, it postulated as a starting point a universal and eternal value.[1]

The model that emerges from the writings of the humanists was an ideal, the reality of things being rather different. As Anthony Grafton and Lisa Jardine have shown, most of the pupils at Guarino of Verona's school achieved a level of ability in Latin that would certainly have delighted today's Latin teachers; but this result had its cost in terms of shaping the whole man. The school day consisted of copying, learning by heart, repeating and imitating; although on occasion the master might deliver a few moral remarks, these observations were far from making "a coherent contribution to a fully articulated moral philosophy". These two authors, extending their research into the sixteenth century and outside the confines of Italy, emphasize the fact that Humanism expressed itself primarily by generating skill in the ancient languages (Latin far more often than Greek); the "preparation for life" that theoretical writings placed at the heart of the pedagogic system was much less noticeable in concrete terms. "Pragmatic Humanism" took this state of things partly into account: the moral content of education was dropped in favour of the wholly practical aim of preparing a man for his future functions, the exercise of offices and magistratures. Despite this reduction of Humanism to the Humanities, the ideal of a humanist education – belief in an intellectual and moral ideal – nevertheless survived virtually to the present day; its persistence led Grafton and Jardine to conclude that there had been a "mystification of arts education" all over the Western world.[2]

Before deciding on this point, it is appropriate to describe the workings of this model through five centuries of history, and to recall the different interpretations applied to it, the transformations it underwent and the uses that were made of it. We need to understand how a tradition was constituted and how it endured, a tradition in which Latin always occupied a central place, even when effective knowledge of the language ceased to be (as it had been in humanist education) the primary result.

1 A Constant of Western Education

While Latin was still necessary for the exercise of a number of professions (or rather: so long as these professions could not be exercised without mastery of Latin), questions about Latin hardly arose within the pedagogic system, apart from that of how to impart linguistic competence at minimum cost and with maximum success. Things changed when Latin was no longer needed in ordinary life, when it became necessary to acquire learning that did not presuppose knowledge of the old language: people then started to question the need for Latin, and this questioning elicited justifications. Significantly, this did not occur until the eighteenth century; even more significantly, it was most clearly apparent where the past had least weight: in the New World.

The schools, colleges and universities being founded in the American colonies broadly followed an English educational model, giving the leading role to classics. However, this predominance of ancient languages, in most cases Latin alone, was soon questioned under the influence of the various currents of thought – ranging from Baconian utilitarianism to Quakerism – that thrived in the free air of the American colonies. The egalitarian aspirations of new societies, and their concern with nation-building, caused the traditional curriculum – considered elitist and useless to the large majority – to be compared unfavourably with more practical and immediately useful forms of learning.

The debates between defenders of the existing system and those lobbying for the introduction of "modern" subjects became particularly embittered in the final third of the eighteenth century, partly because they strayed outside the setting of debates between specialists and used newspaper articles to mobilize a wider segment of public opinion. Opponents of Latin were able to deploy an impressive arsenal of arguments. Apart from the mediocre linguistic performance achieved, the beneficial effects Latin was supposed to have on its students were denied, sometimes with great vehemence. The modernist view was that it imparted neither instruction nor education; it made nothing accessible that could not be read in translation; it gave no help whatsoever in mastering the mother tongue, but produced an affected style and hampered literary creation; far from forming perfectly civilized gentlemen, it turned out pretentious pedants; it did not help teach people to reason, but hampered thought and stifled all natural genius and originality; it made no contribution to the Christian moral instruction of the young, but implanted impure and irreligious thoughts in their hearts; and it encouraged ideas very remote from the proper democratic, patriotic and republican sentiments needed in the new state. All of these arguments flowed from the pen of Benjamin Rush, one of the most determined opponents of classical studies, who went so far as to claim that Greek and Latin were, "with Negro slavery and spirituous liquors . . . though" (he admits) "in a less degree, unfriendly to the progress of morals, knowledge, and religion in the United States". While recognizing that the ancient languages might be necessary for some professions, he insisted that they did not serve the needs of the modern world in any way, and made the radical suggestion: "Were every Greek and Latin book (the New Testament excepted) consumed in a bonfire, the world would be the wiser and better for it". He added: "*Delenda, delenda est lingua Romana* should be the voice of the reason and liberty and humanity in every part of the world".

Supporters of the classics answered with equal vehemence, demonstrating the usefulness – the *necessity* – of the classical languages, Latin in particular.

It was essential for the exercise of some occupations, and helped people to understand technical terms used in the arts and professions. It was helpful in learning modern languages, starting with English; it developed habits of precision in the use of language and established universal principles of grammar. It disciplined the mind, exercised the memory, developed thought and judgement. It cultivated taste and provided literary models for all the forms. It constituted a lesson in elevated morality, both from the maxims contained in the texts and from the examples they described. It helped form the citizen and the politician by providing models of patriotism and rules for the conduct of the state. While this last "benefit" could be obtained by reading translations, all the others needed direct contact with the original sources.[3]

The polemics in the Old World were a good deal less overblown. When (as we have seen) criticisms of Latin became heated in the second half of the eighteenth century, the initial demand was for a reduction of classics in the school curriculum in favour of the mother tongue. Some critics, it is true, did not stop there, but questioned the formative effects of studying Latin. As early as 1726 Rollin, who was no enemy of Latin and even argued for the (limited) use of the language, recognized that its study "in a sense narrows the minds of the young by subjecting them to discomfort and constraint that inhibit free expression".[4] A much more radical line appeared with Helvetius: in 1755, referring to the "recastings" needed "in public education", he complained of the "eight to ten years" spent "in the study of a dead language which is forgotten immediately after leaving school, because it is almost never used later in life". At this point, he felt it necessary to produce and refute the arguments used by partisans of the system in force.

> They will tell you, in vain, that the reason why young people are detained so long in college is less to make them learn Latin than to make them acquire the habit of work and application. But to bend them to this habit, could they not be offered a less ungrateful, less repellent endeavour? Is no one afraid of extinguishing or blunting in them that natural curiosity which, in early youth, warms us with the desire to learn? How could this desire fail to be strengthened if, at the age when one is still undistracted by strong passions, there were substituted for the insipid study of words that of physics, of history, of mathematics, morals, poetry and so forth? The study of dead languages, they will answer, fulfils this objective in part; it subjects the young to the need to translate and explain authors; and in consequence, it adorns their minds with all the ideas contained in the best works of Antiquity. But, I will reply, is there anything more ridiculous than devoting several years to placing in the memory a few facts or a few ideas, that with the help of translations one might engrave there in two or three months?[5]

Diderot (whose plan for a university in Russia delayed teaching the rudiments of Latin until the senior class) in 1775 denounced "an educational order hallowed by use through all the centuries and in all nations" that placed the study of Greek and Latin "at the top of all schooling". The reasons traditionally advanced – that these subjects developed and exercised the memory, the only form of study suitable for a young age – he found hardly convincing: memory could be exercised just as well in other ways that were more pleasant and fruitful; moreover, he thought children perfectly capable of learning subjects that made demands on their reason. Diderot also pointed to the moral danger in which some classical authors placed the young, the peril that would result from confronting "pure and innocent eyes" with certain scenes from Plautus or Terence, certain poems by Catullus or Ovid.[6] Gosselin, writing in 1785, judged that Latin teaching as it was prac- tised – absurd exercises in prison-like colleges under the supervision of "scapegraces" and "pedants as ill-educated as those delivered into their care" – was failing utterly:

> Just look at what is called "doing the humanities"! Pretty strange humanities! You might just as well send them [children] to be guided and civilized by savages. But (people will tell you) they are associating with all the great men of Antiquity, con- versing with them daily. True enough: they are subjected to masterpieces that they understand not at all, and for which they have such distaste by the time they leave college, that they never deign to glance at them again for the rest of their lives.[7]

The other camp justified its position with the usual arguments. When reform- ers campaigned for formal teaching of French, the answer was that existing practice gave sufficient attention to French and even helped with its grammar. In 1777 the Abbé Chrétien Le Roy, an honorary professor at the La Marche College in Paris, attacking the modern teaching methods used by the Benedictines at their Sorèze boarding school, pointed out that in the class- room teachers continuously compared the two languages; the main point, he insisted, was that without a grounding in the classical languages it was impos- sible to know anything about "the basis of our own language. For can we lay claim to a radical knowledge of French, of the nature of its construction, if we do not know that of Latin and preferably Greek as well, for purposes of comparison?"[8] Abbé Proyart, spokesman of the Assembly of the French Clergy, in his *De l'éducation publique* (1758) commented on the "new speculators on education" who wanted to eliminate Latin or greatly reduce its role: "Doubtless they do not know that one learns to speak in French by reading the Latins".[9] In 1791, La Harpe emphasized that the study of Latin "obvi- ously could not be separated from a liberal education". Direct contact with classical authors – translations had been dismissed in passing as "mostly very deficient and all necessarily inferior" to the originals – gave access to an immense body of knowledge, but also served a higher purpose: "to shape in every way and from every point of view the mind, the reason, the tastes of the student youth".[10]

Thus, well before the end of the eighteenth century, people were advancing a number of arguments, both for and against Latin, that had nothing to do with the level of linguistic competence that might be acquired, but were centred on a sort of inherent moral and intellectual efficacy that Latin – or at least its study – was claimed to possess.[11] The original range of arguments hardly changed: the same reasons were still being given everywhere to justify school Latin in the middle of the twentieth century.

The objectives of school Latin, as set out by the American Classical League in 1924 after a wide survey among Latin teachers and their pupils, were still almost unchanged in 1943. They were:

> 1. Increased understanding of those elements of English that are related to Latin. 2. Increased ability to read, speak and write English, and increased efficiency in the use of the mother-tongue as an instrument of thinking itself. 3. Increased ability to learn other foreign languages. 4. Development of correct mental habits. 5. Development of an historical and cultural background. 6. Development of right attitudes toward social situations. 7. Development of literary appreciation. 8. Elementary knowledge of the simpler general principles of language structure. 9. Improvement of the literary quality of the pupil's written English.

In the early 1980s, these objectives were reformulated in the light of "contemporary challenges", being stated as follows:

> a) To enhance skills in the use of the English language. b) To build a firm foundation for the study of modern foreign languages, especially the Romance languages. c) To impart an understanding of Greco-Roman civilization and culture as a key to understanding ourselves. d) To develop a systematic acquaintance with the workings of the Latin language and an ability to handle the language, with Latin being used as an example of how a language works.[12]

Similar objectives existed in France. The Latin grammar I was given on entering sixth grade had an introduction entitled "Why learn Latin?". The answer given was:

> To learn Latin is to . . . go back to the sources of several modern languages, and in particular our own national language; to give a stronger temper to our vocabulary and our style; to enable us more fully to understand many of our own, deeply Latinized, authors. More generally, but perhaps more usefully, learning Latin, through the constant effort to compare two languages, so different despite their resemblances, trains our intelligence in a form of gymnastics that develops the qualities of observation and finesse, and consequently the scientific as well as the literary spirit. Finally, the benefit of learning Latin is moral as well as intellectual. Learning Latin is learning to know a type of humanity that embodies the

essence of civilized man, respectful of the law, eager with disciplined energy, and sensitive to the sufferings of his fellows.[13]

In Italy in the same year (1960), with a reduction in the role of Latin in the schools being officially considered, the Istituto di Studi Romani published a manifesto in defence of the old language. Rather portentously, this document reiterated:

a) The importance of studying the Latin language as a means of putting new generations in direct contact with the eternal and irreplaceable fundamental values of the classical world and Roman civilization; b) the value of Latin teaching as an excellent exercise for activating and developing the pupils' logical and intellectual capacities from an early age, as well as an instrument giving a sounder knowledge of the foundations of our conceptual patterns and means of expression; c) the suitability of a disinterested humanist training as a way of educating and developing the human personality, more necessary than ever in a time like our own, focused on technical specialization and . . . on the pursuit of material well-being.[14]

In 1980 Peter Wülfing, a professor at Cologne University, summarized the arguments still being advanced for school Latin, in Germany in particular and central and southern Europe more generally. They fell into three groups of themes: the "theme of the origins" which "signifies that being members of European society we ought to know where we come from"; the "cultural heritage theme" which "signifies that classical works of art and literature were and still are present in the works that followed Antiquity, up to the present. And that it should be edifying to see the originals"; and the "usefulness theme" which "includes eight arguments". Latin helps in learning Romance languages; it helps in understanding foreign and technical words; it is a precondition for admission to some university faculties; it helps (through comparison) with learning the mother tongue; it is a remarkable training for the mind; it is a mainstay of western culture; it represents a protected oasis in an age of materialism and technology; it is a means of civic education. Wülfing adds that some people, "recognizing that none of the advantages listed is a sufficient argument in itself, point out that no other discipline has so many advantages at once"; this is the theme of the "multivalence" or "polyvalence" of Latin. Confronted with the volume of arguments advanced to legitimize the study of Latin, he concludes that it might almost be said that "in Latin teaching, everything is important except the Latin itself".[15]

The arguments for learning Latin have hardly changed from the eighteenth century to the present day: a wide array of reasons established at the outset has been freely used ever since. The way they have been used over time and in the course of different polemics has given them additional weight and, at various moments in history, an original coloration; but they are all connected more or less directly to the humanist model formed in the fifteenth and sixteenth centuries, when a grounding in the classical tongue was seen as the special instrument of a "liberal" education. From an output as repetitive as it is immense, we will take a few examples that seem to be representative.

2 The Arsenal of Arguments

"Learning Latin . . . also, and in the first place, means learning French"

Very early on, as we have just seen, learning Latin was justified by reference to knowledge beyond the old language itself, although still in the linguistic domain. Latin supplied the etymology of the vocabulary of Romance languages and some elements imported into the Saxon languages, and helped everywhere with comprehension of technical and scientific terms. This lexicological argument has always been extremely popular, perhaps more so in public opinion than among pedagogues.[16] It was deployed widely and successfully to convince scientists, doctors in particular, and they in return have reproduced it abundantly.[17]

Linguistically, however, this etymological function is insignificant in comparison with the role Latin has had since the eighteenth century in teaching mother tongues (and not only the Romance languages). This is one of the major arguments for the old language, still thought good today. We will treat the French example as representative. After Latin had been dropped from the sixth-grade curriculum, one commentator warned that "the French speaker who is ignorant of Latin is a linguistic 'foundling'. There is peril in depending on French schooling alone to learn French."[18] In 1976, with new threats looming over the classical languages, sources in the Sorbonne insisted that "French is only properly understood with the aid of Latin".[19] Very recently, in *Le Monde* of 15/16 July 1998, an announcement by an association called Sauvegarde des Etudes Littéraires (Safeguarding Literary Studies) under the heading: "For mastery of French at college level: the right choice" began as follows: "The success of the Latin option in fifth grade, apparent since the 1997 intake, shows that many parents, many pupils, have understood that it was the best way to ensure mastery of French and favour intellectual development to the full".

It is thus hardly surprising that the "French crisis" should have been linked with the reduction of Latin studies, or that Latin should have been seen as a remedy for the decline of French. It still is today – and here documents issued by the SEL association are eloquent[20] – in much the same way as it was after the 1902 reform reducing the role of Latin in secondary education. At the time, some blamed this measure for causing the "French crisis", and insisted that Latin was a precondition for mastery of French. A Ligue de la Culture

Française (French Culture League) set up in 1911 addressed the following petition to the Minister of Public Instruction:

> Alarmed by the growing inferiority of general culture recently thrown into vivid
> relief by some excellent minds, and convinced, like them, that there is a close
> relationship between the study of classical languages and the persistence of
> French genius, we have the honour of drawing to your attention the need for a
> revision of the secondary education syllabuses established in 1902, which virtually
> abolished the study of Latin in the lycées and at the same time deplorably weak-
> ened the study of French.[21]

The reason usually given in support was the historical one based on the
Latin origin of French, but better understanding of vocabulary and familiarity with grammar were also underlined.[22] Sometimes there was a muddle over
the services that Latin and French grammar rendered each other. On page
3 of their very interesting Latin method, P. Crouzet and G. Berthet addressed
the tyro Latinist as follows: "Are you sound on French grammar to *certificat
d'études* or 7th grade level? . . . That is crucial. Without French grammar, no
progress is possible in Latin; with it, you know a little Latin already." Then,
on page 21: "the first benefit of Latin grammar is that it teaches you French
grammar", before explaining to the (surely by now somewhat baffled) child
"if only because it obliges you to know it".[23] The etymological, grammatical
and literary reasons in support of Latin as a necessary adjunct to the study
of French have been formulated a thousand times, and backed by the most
ingenious examples. Nevertheless, the primary force of this argument seems
to derive from a pedagogic practice, today forgotten but still vigorous in the
second half of the nineteenth century, under which French as a written language was not taught directly but through translations from Latin and imitation of classical authors.[24]

"General education of the mind"

Apart from any linguistic benefits, the study of Latin was considered
extremely beneficial to the development of the child's intellectual faculties,
memory as well as reason. This helps explain the grammatical emphasis in
the way the language was taught, and also the major role given to translations, an exercise which (as we have often been reminded in panegyric terms)
made demands on the capacity for both analysis and synthesis. Schoolwork
often boiled down to the mechanical absorption of Latin rules and the
patient deciphering of a short text. These laborious memorization and
decoding procedures did not result in greater fluency in reading pages of
Latin text; not surprisingly, since the objective was not so much to teach the
art of reading Latin as to impart intellectual discipline through the minute

analysis and dissection of a few lines chosen for that purpose alone. But the effects of these "mental gymnastics", to use a widespread expression, were beneficial to other subjects by way of what was called "transfer of training". A vulgate to this effect grew up in the course of the nineteenth century;[25] Latin was everywhere acknowledged to have formative value.

In France under the Empire, the literary commission responsible for syllabuses, and for applying the measures resulting from the 1802 reorganization of education, answered the detractors of dead languages by defending the benefits of Latin "versions". "When translating," the commission wrote, "one is constantly comparing, and each comparison is a judgement; this work, and for proof we have the examples of great men, seems the most apt, during youth, to impart strength, energy and measure to all the powers of the mind". This remained a *leitmotiv* of pedagogic discourse throughout the century. The *Instructions* issued following the reform of 1890 observed: "It is not a matter of producing professional Hellenists and Latinists. Greek and Latin are required only to contribute their share to the general education of the mind." To this purpose, the "theme of elegance" ceded to the "theme of precision" which "forces [pupils] to look at words and ideas through a magnifying glass" and becomes "a teacher of clarity and exactitude"; along with versions, it constituted "a summons to think explicitly and clearly".[26] In 1887, Abbé Sicard concluded a book on classical studies before the Revolution with an earnest plea in their favour: translations in particular were a first-class exercise for the child's intellectual development, making him aware of the value of effort and developing habits of orderliness, precision and clarity; in short it was more accurate to present school Latin as "a genuine graduated course in logic".[27] While the mind-forming role attributed to Latin became a leading argument during the 1880s (somewhat more clearly in France than in Germany), it had been current since the beginning of the century and continued to be invoked during the major reforms of secondary education under the Third Republic.[28]

In England, the most famous headmasters expanded warmly on the character-forming value of Latin. Thomas Arnold put it in these terms: "The study of language . . . seems to me as if it was given for the very purpose of forming the human mind in youth; and the Greek and Latin languages . . . seem the very instruments by which this is to be effected". Benjamin Kennedy, author of the famous *Latin Primer*, pointed out that the natural sciences "do not furnish a basis for education", for they were "not synthetical enough for elementary instruction"; the desired power of synthesis could only be provided by classical languages, which also inculcated "mental discipline".[29] By exercising the intellectual faculties in this way, Latin also helped develop flexibility of mind. Such a quality was valued highly by public schools in the Victorian era: at a time when it was necessary to produce civil servants and imperial administrators, the study of Latin, favouring suppleness of mind, seemed an ideal way of giving children the "adaptability" they would need in their future posts.[30]

The reasoning elsewhere was very similar. Max Bonnet, Professor of Latin at the University of Lausanne, expanded on its formative role in his inaugural address. "What is to be acquired," he explained,

> is not so much knowledge of Antiquity as the art of study itself . . . in other words a mind used to the work of thought, to methodical research, to solving scientific problems . . . And what could better fulfil this end than the study of a language different from the one they [young people] have learned by usage, but nevertheless related to it, and which therefore illuminates it and is illuminated by it in a thousand ways . . .[31]

Latin was considered such an incomparable training ground for mental gymnastics that a Brussels professor declared in 1885: "I doubt that there will ever be found, even in the distant future, a more wholesome and fortifying food, and I would say willingly of it that if it did not exist, it would have to be invented".[32]

These few quotations give some idea of how deeply rooted the belief in the formative value of Latin was. This helps explain why the criticisms that emerged from the United States in the 1920s were powerless to uproot it, although they were pretty energetic. Originating in a new educational philosophy based on pragmatism, whose moving spirit was John Dewey, they were opposed to all teaching based on discipline and memorization. Latin and its value in intellectual training were subjected to hostile scrutiny, the most formidable attack being launched by Abraham Flexner, who later became the first President of the Institute for Advanced Study at Princeton. In 1916 he published a book entitled *A Modern School* in which, in the light of new pedagogic and psychological theories, he proposed a school without Greek or Latin; he overturned all the arguments usually invoked in support of Latin, especially "the disciplinary argument" which he thought valueless in any case because

> mental discipline is not a real purpose; moreover, it would for many students constitute an argument against rather than for the study of Latin. Instead of getting orderly trained by solving difficulties in Latin composition, these pupils guess, fumble, receive surreptitious assistance or accept on faith the injunctions of teacher and grammar. The only discipline that such students get from their classical studies is a discipline in doing things as they should not be done.

The riposte was as fierce as the attack; we will return to it later.[33]

At about the same time, a much more radical attack was made on Latin as a discipline for the mind: in Soviet Russia, Latin was suppressed. The Bolsheviks not only regarded Latin as "useless" but also disapproved of its formative function, judging that it "clogged up children's minds"; moreover, it was explained, "this is done simply to stuff the skull of a man who has no need of grammar, who will forget it, and who has docilely to obey, hear and read whatever he is ordered to"; in other words, instead of awakening the intellect, Latin was turning out slaves for the bourgeoisie.[34] This reasoning was not purely circumstantial. In Czarist Russia the teaching of Latin had sometimes had aspects of disciplinary drill, especially after 1860, in reaction to the nihilist movement that had taken root among the urban youth, and which was seen – at least where the "leaders" were concerned – as the result of badly assimilated scientific notions. The Education Minister of the time, Count Tolstoy, thought classics particularly effective at protecting young minds against habits of careless and incorrect generalization. In 1871, announcing a new statute for the *gymnasium* in which classical subjects were given the leading place and natural sciences virtually eliminated, he explained that "in the study of ancient languages – and sometimes in the study of mathematics – all the knowledge imparted to the students is under constant supervision and free from error, and this inhibits the formation of independent opinions". We should add that after 1848, classics teaching in Russia became heavily dominated by grammar: the revolutions that occurred in that year in Western Europe had reminded the authorities of the republican perils that lurked in ancient texts.[35]

The Bolshevik measures merely strengthened the rest of Europe's attachment to Latin; the new transatlantic educational theories hardly dented belief in the disciplinary value of the old language. Even in the US itself, the "Classical Investigation" conducted in 1924 gave "development of correct mental habits" as one of the objectives of the study of Latin.[36] Endless variants of this argument are found everywhere: in 1937 Germany, where Latin was presented as "an instrument of precise thought and mental discipline";[37] in Italy at about the same time, it was judged a "rational language" and "particularly apt at developing judgement in adolescents";[38] in 1950s Belgium where its study had the value of "a school of thought", favouring intuition, analysis and synthesis at the same time, constituting in fact "an art of thinking" and a "school of concision";[39] in 1962, in Spain, where, in the period of "utilitarianism", humanist education and Latin with it were thought to impart "facility", "speed" and "a great spirit of reflection";[40] and again in former colonial countries, like President Senghor's Senegal where it was held that "balance", "method" and "logical vigour", all adding up to "mental order", were imparted by Latin.[41]

As this formative power over the mind has always been a constant of arguments in favour of Latin,[42] it is not surprising that it should have been much used in France immediately after the suppression of Latin in sixth grade: it was emphasized yet again that "its study constitutes, in itself, a precious discipline for the development of a rigorous and precise mind",[43] and Hippolyte

Ducos declared to the National Assembly that Latin was "not a subject for specialists. It is a discipline that prepares the ground for others".[44] Indeed the recognized formative value of Latin strengthened opposition to Edgar Faure's measure: it could only fulfil that function if learned young; delay initiation to Latin and the beneficial effect would be lost. "If the study of Latin is to bear all its fruits," explained Maurice Lacroix, a former teacher at the Lycée Henri IV,

> it must not be weakened by a late start. It is between the ages of 11 and 13 that the practice of themes and versions contributes most usefully to logic formation. The child is particularly receptive at that age . . . If the start is delayed until fourth grade, in other words the onset of puberty, the pupils will not bring the same freshness of intellect and of heart.[45]

Nowadays, although Latin has declined steeply everywhere, the argument that it has formative power has kept all its vigour. It is still being widely invoked, with unimportant variations: in France the classical languages train people in reasoning,[46] while in Germany they contribute to the *Bildung* of analytic and synthetic thought.[47] The same argument features in the opposition of some teachers to translations: although "one does not learn Latin and Greek only to know what the texts say", the benefit of a formative study of the language would be lost if the pupils worked on texts in translation.[48]

"Acquisition of character"

Latin was supposed to develop the child's intellectual faculties and teach him to think accurately and precisely, but the task of studying it gave it an additional virtue: the difficulty of learning the rudiments of Latin produced robust intelligences and sound characters. In effect, the "struggle" the child waged with Latin text – "a virile idea" – fortified and prepared him for the difficulties he would encounter later in adult life.[49] So that reducing the importance of Latin, as some were proposing in the second half of the nineteenth century, would lead, Monsignor Dupanloup warned, directly to "universal slackness", to "organized idleness" and a "weakening of character".[50]

These ideas were naturally also current in England. Sydney Smith made an impeccable statement of the effects the classical languages were supposed to possess. "They inure children to the intellectual difficulties," he wrote, "and make the life of a young student what it ought to be, a life of considerable labour." While acknowledging that this did not result solely from Latin and Greek, he added: "and, if they do nothing else, they at least ensure solid and vigorous application at a period of life which materially influences all other periods".[51] More generally, in the public schools from the Victorian period until very recently, Latin and its arduous study were regarded as an instrument for forming character.[52] The puritan ethic had some influence here; and it has been noted that in the pedagogic literature of the period, "the word 'character' appears almost as frequently in connection with Latin as it does with religion".[53] All the same, as the similar attitudes in a mainly Catholic country like France make clear, Latin possessed some virtue in its own right, which endured despite the opinions of psychological theoreticians, who emphasized the child's initial pleasure in learning the language, and the negative effects of difficulty and fear; even in the 1950s, some pedagogues on both sides of the Channel were representing this difficult language as a "means of instilling character, courage and endurance".[54]

"A supplement of soul"

In addition to developing intelligence and improving character, Latin also formed the heart; and this role grew as the sciences took an increasing share of the school curriculum. In nineteenth-century France, there was constant debate between partisans of a "classical humanism" and supporters of "scientific humanism".[55] The cases were clearly stated in 1837, during a debate in the Chamber of Deputies, by the astronomer and mathematician François Arago and the writer Alphonse de Lamartine who spoke for the two camps. A draft bill on secondary education was being discussed, and Arago expressed the opinion that ancient languages should not be taught at all in colleges, but only in higher institutions; he disputed the argument that they alone imparted "true culture of the mind and soul". "I do not claim," he said, "that Latin and Greek do not form taste . . . all I am saying is that they are not indispensable." Arago proposed replacing them with French, one other living language, and science. On the last point he had to deal with M. de Sade, who had declared to the Chamber that "scientific studies undertaken too early and too deeply pervert and narrow the mind", "desiccate the heart" and "exhaust the imagination"; apart from giving his own opinions on these allegations, Arago cited the examples of Descartes and Pascal. The next day, 24 March, Lamartine spoke. He agreed with Arago on scientific education in colleges, provided it was preceded by a "moral and literary" education. If it came to a choice, he would sacrifice science because "if all the mathematical truths were lost, the industrial world, the material world, would doubtless suffer great damage, immense loss; but if mankind lost a single one of those moral truths of which literary studies are the vehicle, it would be man himself, the whole of humanity, that would perish". He ended by denouncing any idea of "an exclusively technical, scientific and mathematical education," which he saw as "the application of eighteenth-century materialism to education".[56]

This opposition between Latin in its "humanist" function and science perceived as drying up the soul appeared again in a near-contemporary debate whose stakes were very different. It concerned the obligation of polytechnic candidates to have passed the *baccalauréat*. Until 1840 most of these, wishing to concentrate on mathematics which had a preponderant role in the examination, dropped Latin in the third grade, having by then enough of it to do the Latin translation in the examination, but not enough for the *baccalauréat*. In 1841 the Ministry of Public Instruction, using the diploma as a way of adjusting and ordering society, came out against this practice and suggested the idea of a compulsory *baccalauréat* for polytechnic candidates. Young people who failed the entrance examination would never be able to get jobs because they lacked the essential open sesame; that would be most distressing to their families, but more importantly, with a mass of dissatisfied young people out of work, a peril for the whole of society. In any case, the spokesmen added, the damage was great even for those who passed the examination. A massive intake of "theorems, solutions and formulae" had baleful psychological consequences: it produced dry and abstract minds, unable to perceive what could not be reduced to mathematical equations, and thus filled with prejudices concerning the political, religious and domestic realities of the society in which they lived. In 1842, the Minister for War made the *baccalauréat* compulsory for candidates for the examination, from 1844 onward. After that episode, debate went on for the rest of the century on whether future engineers needed to learn Latin, for the good of their general culture and in the name of an essential complementary spiritual training.[57] Very similar reasoning was used in late nineteenth-century Germany, where the dropping of Latin and Greek was presented as a national catastrophe, liable to result in the spread of "those narrow and foolhardy minds in which the premature cultivation of the sciences has perverted the intelligence and even partly stifled the moral faculties".[58]

The claims of Latin as a palliative to some of the negative effects of scientific education were advanced with renewed vigour when twentieth-century reforms at last gave the sciences the place in education that their role in society justified. With Latin stripped of its former monopoly, given a truncated role or at least subjected to strong competition ("One less Latinist means one more engineer", the slogan ran),[59] a lot of its supporters pleaded openly for reconciliation with mathematics, the old competitor now called to the purple. Not only would the study of Latin facilitate the acquisition of basic mathematics by developing certain mental faculties, it would also provide the pupil with a spiritual supplement, needed all the more urgently under the new education system. Latin was now being presented as the "conciliator between humanism and the technical".[60] The point was made in the professional press and in the National Assembly following the suppression of Latin in sixth grade: Latin and mathematics were not antagonistic in any way; on the contrary, "from their union" was born "that soundly constituted brain well prepared for the higher studies that await every *baccalauréat* holder on leaving the *lycée*".[61]

Latin was not just an antidote to the sciences (or to be more precise their pernicious effects); it gave broader protection against the dangers of the modern world, against certain ideologies. Lamartine had already – in 1837 – mentioned his fear that eighteenth-century materialism would be revived if education ever cut itself off from the humanities. When the system of "bifurcation" was inaugurated in 1852 – another stage in the decline of Latin – dire warnings were voiced that it would "usher in the inevitable and imminent triumph of material interests over moral interests".[62] This argument had a distinguished career and was being repeated with infinite variations until quite recently.

It is worth recalling that in the past, classics in general and Latin in particular had sometimes been denounced as lacking in moral values and imbued with materialist ideas. Such was the view of the liberal economists who, pleading for modern education centred on science, modern languages and economics in the 1850s, were naturally opposed to traditional schooling. One of their spokesmen, Frédéric Bastiat, argued in a book entitled *Baccalauréat et socialisme* (1850) that Latin was not only useless – having long ceased to be the key to learning – but noxious. Studying Latin led children to "impregnate, soak and saturate themselves in the sentiments and opinions of a nation of brigands and slaves, the Romans"; hardly morally uplifting. More seriously, it favoured the development of purely material interests giving as a model "a people which, hating and despising work, [had] based its entire means of livelihood on the serial pillage of all the neighbouring peoples, and on slavery". The dreadful fruits of classical schooling were none other than the "subversive doctrines which have been given the name socialism or communism", doctrines that had inspired the movements of 1848.[63]

This last, one cannot help feeling, was an unusual accusation; Latin was more commonly presented by the other side as a bulwark *against* the materialist ideologies. In the pan-Latinist campaign mounted in fascist Italy Latin appeared as, among other things, a formidable rampart against Marxism. "Latin is anti-Marxist," wrote the pedagogue Nazzareno Padellaro in 1939.

It is difficult for a man vaccinated with an ode from Horace to fall victim to the Marxist epidemic . . . the mental discipline acquired in the hard effort to master a passage from a classical author gives a man a noble intellectual dignity that prevents him from sinking to the unreasoning and ferocious passions of the mob. How can Marxism not fight a Latin which is the heir to such an immense human tradition, a promoter and defender of the highest type of human work? How can the universalizing Marxist mysticism not be inimical to a language into which have flowed, to find their expression, the universal of science, the universal of culture, the universal of thought?[64]

According to the philosopher Guido Calogero, the attribution of this role to Latin did not cease with the end of the fascist regime: when educational reforms were being discussed in the 1950s, some Latinists boosted the cause of the old language with the claim that it was a rampart against communism.[65] A similar reaction was observed in France during the protests, in 1968–69, that followed the suppression of sixth-grade Latin. Under the collective pseudonym Epistémon, a group of teachers in higher education saw the measure as a door opened to "the Marxist cultural revolution", explaining: "Marxist intellectual propaganda will be much more effective if addressed to youngsters who lack a solid intellectual training or system of references, badly-raised orphans disinherited from their intellectual patrimony, proletarians".[66] One professor of Letters went even further and saw the dropping of Latin as "a plot by unschooled and barbaric beings, for they realize that the classical languages are the ultimate rampart against the doctrines of death from the East. Really they do not want some men to retain a sure and straight judgement, but that there remain on earth only one category of men, incapable of thinking, reflecting or discussing."[67]

Of course, there was peril from the West as well. In the post-war period, Latin was seen in Italy as well as France as a protection against "Americanization", "American pseudo-civilization" or "summary Americanization", carrying with it "technomania" and "utilitarianism", the alienation of "a technological society" or even "destructive modernism". Latin worked just as well as an antidote to this other materialism, and also provided, in a world losing its spiritual references, "a supplement of soul".[68]

Under such conditions, any suppression of Latin would have fatal consequences for society as a whole. The Sorbonne professor Pierre Grimal believed that Edgar Faure's measure, by reducing the number of Latinists, would help create

> two categories of heart and mind. One, the majority, will become adept only at what we call techniques, reducing everything to calculation, lacking in any true spiritual element, wallowing in the most vulgar pleasures, in houses diabolically designed for the purpose, or (as we have seen so often already) gripped by the desire and nostalgia for a higher ideal, sick of their existence, perpetually in search of change for themselves and, worse, for the State. The other category, educated in the traditional culture, knowing how to distinguish true from false, strengthened by the experience of men in the past, will make human judgements based on the truth. Those in the first category cannot help being the slaves of things; those in the second are genuinely free, liberated from the tyranny of fortune, sociable, pleasant, rejecting all vain desire for change, without excessive attachment to their wealth, persuaded that external things are sometimes useful, but never indispensable for human happiness.

So the "villainous" measure would create "two categories of human being" unable to understand one another, and eventually it would engender "discord"; this was a serious threat to the state which, since it was no longer governed by "men who have learned what freedom is", would be exposed to extreme dangers.[69]

"Amid the greatest and finest products of Antiquity"

Behind this extreme formulation lay a widespread faith in the spiritual value attributed to Latin. It also derived from the contact that children had, through the Latin language, with the masterpieces of Antiquity. The literary commission of 1803 which, as we have seen, insisted that the study of Latin imparted valuable intellectual training, added: "see how much the imagination is enlarged by living amid the greatest and finest products of Antiquity!"[70] This aesthetic argument was widely used in England, at least until the last decades of the nineteenth century, as a justification for learning Latin, and proofs were often offered. Thus Thomas Jex-Blake, headmaster of Rugby, believed that men who had obtained good classics degrees possessed "a finish, an elegance and beauty of mind . . . possessed by no other type of man that I have ever met".[71]

In France, where the same argument seems to have been current for even longer, it took on an original coloration: Latin formed taste, and taste was the quintessential French quality. In 1853, in the commission set up after the establishment of "bifurcation", voices were raised to emphasize the importance of classical languages and literature in the formation of taste, "the ornament of our civilization, and an immense capital for our manufactures". There were repeated exhortations to "conserve for our nation that delicate instinct for taste that characterizes it in every domain; let us conserve it jealously, for it is our equivalent of England's coalfields, and the great natural resources of the United States or Russia".[72] Classical studies, Latin for the most part, and taste, came to constitute a binomial characteristic of French individuality. In 1923 Bergson, in a very favourable commentary on the Bérard reform which reintroduced Latin for all in the *lycées*, recalled that classical studies helped develop qualities of order, proportion, measure, exactitude and flexibility: all of them eminently well represented in France and shaping its reputation in all things, including the economic sphere. France excelled, in fact, in the luxury industries that needed taste and elegance. More generally, Bergson went on, our products are noted for their precision and manufacturing finish. Our workers, he admitted, have not learned Latin; but they work in a society imprinted with a Graeco-Latin stamp.[73] This binomial of Latin (with classicism behind it) and taste was used in the First World War, and even before it, as an area of contrast – both cultural and political – between France and Germany.[74] Hence the attacks led by Alfred de Tarde and Henri Massis (under the pseudonym Agathon) on Lanson's "Germanized" Sorbonne: the importation of "scientific" methods derived from German scholarship resulted in the obliteration of all contact with "the living riches of the essential masterpieces", starting with the texts in Latin of which Lanson, like Brunot, was a determined adversary. This was a grave threat to French culture, and an article entitled "Mr Lanson against the Humanities" ended with the solemn warning: "To defend Latin is also to serve our national interest against the foreigner".[75]

This aesthetic and moral argument in favour of Latin gave way to a more broadly cultural argument based on knowledge of classical civilization. Nevertheless, the conviction that some sort of spiritual education is imparted by reading Latin texts is still sometimes to be heard. Thus for Jacqueline de Romilly "these lines from another time are still carriers of primary emotion . . . Would you like to think," she writes, addressing parents directly, "that your children are not capable of feeling what so many generations before them have so manifestly felt?" Then, parrying the objection that times had changed, she went on: "That has not prevented people, generation after generation, from gaining from their contact with these texts a little more comprehension, not just of the works, but of people and life – and perhaps a little of the nobility that these great archetypes carry within them, and that we so lack".[76]

"You will feel that you are more than a man"[77]

"Learning Greek and Latin," de Romilly had written a few pages earlier, "at every stage helps with learning French; reading Latin and Greek, the end product of this learning process, serves to form the man".[78] This in fact is the fundamental point of Latin, the inspiration that underlies the intellectual and moral virtues commonly attributed to the study of Latin.

In expressing this conviction, Jacqueline de Romilly joins a long tradition of thought already solidly established by the beginning of the nineteenth century. In 1840 Victor Cousin, during his short period at the Ministry of Public Instruction, issued a series of circulars that settled the vexed issue of the humanities versus the sciences by having them taught successively. Classical studies would come first, "so aptly called humanities," as he explained, "because they form the man and because they cultivate memory, imagination, intellect and heart all at the same time". In 1873 when, in reaction to measures carried out by the minister Jules Simon, a commission (whose members included Mgr Dupanloup) pronounced in favour of classical languages as "the basis of all liberal education", the decision was justified in these terms: "The Greek and Roman civilizations are the most perfect form of development of the human mind and . . . we should not give up studying them in their own languages and receiving the highest lessons in art, morals and logic directly from so many incomparable masters".[79] In Russia, Count Tolstoy – whom we have already seen using Latin to enforce political discipline – was also a firm believer in the superior formative value of the classical tongue: "The classical education system does not in itself produce a civil servant or an officer; it produces a human being, and that is why the system is called humanist".[80] The minister's thinking was certainly influenced by the Western model: the Prussian *Gymnasium*, the French *lycée*, the British public school, all maintained classical studies in general, and Latin in particular, as a means of shaping the adult man.[81] Twentieth-century pedagogic literature has generally followed this argument when defending the classics.

With Latin serving to form the man, it necessarily formed part of a "non-vocational" secondary schooling. It was not intended to produce Latinists or to train specialists, as a number of the quotations we have used make very plain. Latin was part of a "disinterested education" and imparted "general culture". This emerges forcefully from the way it was kept distinct from sciences and living languages.

All through the nineteenth century, "modernists" who wanted to give a larger role to the sciences in the school curriculum came up against defenders of the classics. Apart from their determination not to surrender an inch of their empire – the fierce rigidity of a Latin teacher facing a rival is not something that can be concealed – these defenders were animated by a "lofty" conception of the classical languages; the sciences, they claimed, gave a lower, because merely utilitarian, form of education. In the English public schools, which gave an avowedly "non-vocational" education, classical studies were viewed as a rampart against vulgar utilitarianism; the sciences were looked down on, but an exception was made for pure sciences, especially mathematics, algebra and geometry.[82] Similar views prevailed in France where, in the late nineteenth century, advocates of "general culture" in the *lycées* thought the sciences imparted practical and inferior knowledge, valuing "quantity of information" over "quality of mind" and eventually producing "a sort of intellectual deformity": but pure sciences were excepted owing to their non-utilitarian character.[83]

This conception of secondary education as essentially non-professional resulted, during the same period, in Latin being given preferential treatment over living languages. Some individuals, accepting that learning a language subjects the pupil to "mental gymnastics", pressed for the substitution of a modern language for Latin, arguing that it would have a double benefit: the mental exercise would result in knowledge of a usable modern idiom. This is what H. Dietz, "qualified in living languages and letters", reiterated in 1886. In view of society's changing needs, he pleaded in favour of a modern secondary education in which living languages would play the formative role previously fulfilled by classical ones; the one he favoured was English, which he presented as "a sort of modern Latin". He deplored the fact that ten years were being devoted to a dead language; while recognizing that "the essential thing here is perhaps the gymnastics themselves, the gymnastics of the version", he argued that the price was too high, that "to exercise and build up strength, you do not need a de luxe trapeze" as one "made of pine can render the same services as one made of rosewood".[84] This was a very audacious suggestion at a time when modern language teaching was still undeveloped in the *lycées*, results were poor and, in the case of German for example, explanations were given by referring to Latin and Greek.[85] Needless to say, Dietz's suggestion was not adopted; the defenders of Latin thought modern languages simply unworthy of fulfilling the same pedagogic role. "Would it really be useful to replace it with modern languages, ceaselessly transformed by usage?" Abbé Sicard wrote, before going on to list the defects he felt disqualified the main modern languages: "English has no grammar; German has bizarre and convoluted construction; the Southern languages would tend to dilute and enervate our style".[86] Unsurprisingly, the inverse conviction – that Latin helped in learning the rudiments of modern languages – predominated, and for a very long time; in 1983 it could still be claimed that "a good Latinist has all the qualities necessary to become a good Germanist".[87] After 1968, faced with open competition from living languages, German in particular, defenders of Latin came up with a new argument to supplement the one based on exercising the mind. "Even admitting that it [German] has the same formative value . . . it is far from having the same cultural and civilizing value . . . and even if the linguistic and cultural heritage of German turns out to be as rich as that of Rome, it is inferior on one point at least: its universality."[88] Still in the name of the same "liberal" education, there was strong criticism in France of German humanism and its philological methods, much favoured between the wars of 1870 and 1914. The French defeat of 1871 had persuaded some eminent scholars and scientists, including Renan and Pasteur, that Prussian superiority on the battlefield had been forged in the *Gymnasium*s and universities; French recovery should therefore involve a reform of the French education system and the adoption of German practices. The Sorbonne was extensively won over to "scientific" Rhineland methods, and in the schools Latin teaching was given a strong new grammatical orientation. Enthusiasm was less than universal, however. Some commentators denounced what they saw as an arid and technical form of scholarship liable to produce "specialists" rather than *honnêtes hommes*,[89] that ignored moral teaching, that did not cultivate taste but dried it up, and that did nothing to encourage the mind to adopt a broad outlook but on the contrary narrowed it and overloaded it with a sort of pedantry of detail.[90]

Education, general culture, forming the man and Latin eventually came to be conflated into one. From that point of view the term "modern humanities" was virtually a contradiction in terms. And they were also a second-best choice. With this in mind, a form of teaching was designed for children not doing classical languages, using translations and other material to give these pupils "the essence of the classical message". Although it gave quite good results – pupils in the modern sections often knew more about ancient civilization than their "classical" contemporaries – these courses did not escape the discredit widely attached to teaching of this type.[91]

"Eternal man"

The disinterested education of which classical studies were the mainstay still drew strength from the universal and eternal value attributed to it. The study of the ancient languages carried people towards an idealized union with Antiquity; with a civilization that had attained a high level of excellence, and from which Europe had emerged. This heritage theory has been widely invoked since the nineteenth century.[92] It has sometimes been used in a very selective way; in France during the First World War, for example, the Sorbonne deployed the notion of a common Latin past, a source of high moral and civic values, to mobilize the "Latin" nations against Germany.[93] More generally, people everywhere have always insisted that this precious heritage should not only be preserved and known, but made to bear fruit. Doing away with Latin meant breaking with a tradition and cutting off an abundant source: warnings to this effect were repeated every time Latin was threatened in the nineteenth century.[94] It was often proclaimed – never perhaps more vehemently than in the aftermath of the Faure reforms – that the formative role of Latin gave access to a tradition, going back to classical Antiquity, that united the whole of Europe around a model of humanity, "eternal man". "The great benefit of classical studies," explained the group of university teachers campaigning under the name of Epistémon,

> was a certain wisdom, a certain sense of relativity, of systems of reference. It was better than schooling, an education of the mind and heart, the discovery of a past which was our past, our heritage, our civilization, our common property, and not some bizarre olden time as remote as India, China or the kingdom of the Incas . . . The dropping of Latin in 6th grade and Greek in 4th grade is the end of classics teaching, the end of the humanities, the end of a civilization, ours, the Graeco-Latin civilization.

Hence the conclusion: "To cut ourselves off from Latin is to cut ourselves off from a whole cultural past common to all Europeans". "Barbarism" loomed.[95]

Although classical studies really have declined considerably, and formidable new competitors have arrived on the scene in the form of the social sciences, the idea of the heritage of Antiquity as a focus of cultural unity is still present in the general education of children, and is being used in the promotion of the new Europe now under construction. A very concrete example is the poster entitled "Latin 2000" issued in 1993 on the initiative of Latin teachers in South Germany: it projects the European classical myth, empha-sizing the traditional link between Latin and Europe, and asserts that Latin was in the past, and will be in future, "the key to European culture". Dynam-ically in some cases, nostalgically in others, this argument has become a com-monplace of recent writings in support of the humanities.[96]

3 From Conviction to Persuasion

Thus, from the end of the eighteenth century to the present, the arguments used in support of the study of Latin hardly changed, even the few develop-ments imposed by circumstances being accepted with reluctance. Depending on the occasion, of course, one argument may sometimes have been preferred over another, and defenders of Latin had their own favourites. Very often, though, the same proofs and arguments were strung together, almost mechan-ically, into an almost complete sequence; it is true that their order is not invari-able, although usually similar to the order in which we have described them; *grosso modo*, the "utilitarian" argument – helpfulness in learning other lan-guages – came before the "disinterested" one, formation of the complete man.

The reasoning used was not, it seems, much affected by the realities of life. For example, there was an abyss between the cultural motif of discovering the world of Antiquity and the way Latin was taught in French colleges. "Not one of the writers was presented to us in the setting of his time, under the colour of his own sky, as a living being among others to whom he was speak-ing," Lavisse recalls in his *Souvenirs*. "They seemed like shadows gliding through colourless, mute surroundings . . . Greek Antiquity and Roman Antiquity became entangled before our ignorant eyes. We hardly knew who came first, the Greeks or the Romans, and there was nothing to stop us from thinking of Pericles and Cicero as contemporaries".[97] If we are to believe the teachers at *lycées*, the same diagnosis was applicable in the 1950s, when the lesson often consisted of little more than decoding a few lines of text and explaining rules of grammar. The cultural value of learning Latin was nev-ertheless still being extolled.[98]

Nor were these arguments much undermined by the reservations occa-sionally expressed by the defenders of Latin themselves. It happened some-times that these, the better to defend their cause, expressed "grave doubts" or scepticism; for example Peter Wülfing, a professor at Cologne University, showed that of the different reasons generally advanced in favour of Latin, none had "the character of necessity". But he did not conclude that classical studies should be dropped: he noted on the one hand that "comparison with other school subjects would not be so very unfavourable to us"; and on the other, after clearing away criticisms many of which came from adversaries of Latin, ended with an argument that seemed to him to be both major and "necessary": contact with Antiquity gave "access to all humanity".[99]

On close examination, finally, quite a few of the arguments turned out to be undemonstrable. In 1969, the Association for Living Latin asked a psychologist for an opinion on the assertion that "Latin constituted an especially effective mental gymnastics that accelerated the development of the child's mind and made it more capable of other achievements". One factor widely held to prove this contention was the high level of success Latinists achieved on entering the leading science schools. The expert brushed the proof aside as sophistry; there was no reason why the opposite – that their success at Latin was due to their mathematical minds – should not be equally true. Only a proper scientific study, comparing pupils of equivalent intelligence in similar conditions apart from the specific exception of Latin, would enable an opinion to be given. But quite apart from the experimental objectives – what aptitudes did Latin deploy and develop? Reason? Intuition? – the conditions under which the experiment would have to be conducted would make it difficult if not impossible to complete; no study of this sort had ever been carried out in France or anywhere else. Only too aware that his conclusions were not the ones expected, the expert pointed out that they should not be taken as a reason "to stop the pedagogue from trying and persevering".[100] Of course Latin teachers knew that already.

It may well be that demonstration or experimental verification mattered very little to them. The arguments they gave in favour of Latin and its teaching rested on the much more powerful driving force of private conviction. Moreover, as one of these teachers admitted, were not these arguments very often "rationalizations worked out *a posteriori* in support of a cause of which we were already convinced . . . but for reasons less easily expressed"?[101] So the argumentation in favour of Latin was not founded on reason and demonstration, but arose in the first place from belief, and worked better for being a coherent discourse centred on man and his formation. Endlessly repeated, the discourse became a credo that was accepted without question.[102] This can be seen plainly in the remarks made early in the twentieth century by M. Zilinsky, a professor at St Petersburg University:

What the educative value of Antiquity consists of, I do not know. But it is a fact that the classical education system has existed for a long time, that it was long ago extended to all the peoples of European culture, and that these peoples only became civilized by means of it . . . In our own time, it is still the case that the civilizing capacity of a people is all the greater if it takes classical education seriously, while those peoples that lack it play no part in the world of ideas, whatever their numerical importance and whatever their glory in the past.[103]

So one can understand why, despite the refutation sometimes brought by reality, the same arguments continued to be passed on and repeated. We have still to show that they were not just produced, but had an effect: in other words, we have to describe a persuasion. Partisans of Latin maintained three types of discourse: defence against attacks made on the discipline; advice to invite people to study it; eulogy emphasizing its superior qualities. Pleas and other forms of defence dominate written production, hardly surprisingly given the strained atmosphere – with much talk of "threats", "aggressions" and "plots" – under which they were produced; but there is no shortage of recommendations aimed at parents, nor of panegyrics on the "nobility" and "virtues" of Latin.[104] These sorts of discourse, subtended by belief in a number of recognized values associated with Latin and its study, usually took the form of assertion – sentences and paragraphs beginning with "Latin is . . ." – supported not by proofs or demonstrations, but by assurances and referrals to authorities. A few examples follow.

Invocation of the opinions of great men was a widely used technique. Prominent figures were asked to give their opinions on Latin, in the expectation that they would be favourable. This sort of strategy was first used in the United States in response to Abraham Flexner's critical broadside against the classics. The answer was as vehement as the attack. In June 1917 Andrew Fleming West, Professor of Latin at Princeton and Dean of the Graduate School, organized a conference on "classical studies in liberal education"; in his opening speech, he earnestly denounced the "modern school" proposed by Flexner, suggesting that classical studies were particularly important in the context of the moment (the entry of the United States to the European war): at a time when "the higher powers of the human soul" were more needed than usual, Latin helped form the necessary "courage", "wisdom" and "faith in freedom". The proceedings of the conference, published the same year, contained in addition to the papers that had been delivered a collection of nearly three hundred testimonies in favour of classical studies from "competent observers representing the leading interests of modern life and including many of the highest names in our land". Topping the list was the serving US President, Woodrow Wilson, and three former presidents (Taft, Roosevelt and Cleveland). Below them came notables from the worlds of politics, business, education, the Church, law, medicine, science, etc. All said they were in favour of classical education; perhaps more important was the fact that those who had not had that "privilege" themselves spoke of their regret, and the "disadvantage" they had suffered as a result.[105] Some fifty years later, the *Classical Journal* published the answers given by prominent Americans to an inquiry on the cultural and practical value of Latin. The list included many names from the A list of US politics, from President Nixon at the top to Senator Edward Kennedy, by way of the FBI Director J. Edgar Hoover, George Wallace the former Governor of Alabama, the Mayor of New York John Lindsay, followed by a number of former government ministers, senators, congressmen and senior officials.[106] The same strategy is at work, on a somewhat lower level, in the testimonies from "personalities" with which

Jacqueline de Romilly interspersed the chapters of her *Lettre aux parents*: they are variously described as coming from "leading scientists", "heads of major firms" and "men who have distinguished themselves in practical life, thereby acquiring unarguable experience".[107]

The majority of these "witnesses" were not professional Latinists; in the volume published at Princeton in 1917, classicists whose biased opinion might have weakened the case were deliberately left out. The value of the testimonies derived, in fact, from the authority associated with famous names and important functions in society (functions, moreover, for which Latin would not have been commonly seen as a necessary qualification). A decade earlier, between 1907 and 1909, on the fringes of the annual Classical Conference, three meetings were held at Ann Arbor on the value of humanist, and particularly classical, education as a preparation for law, theology and business. Jurists, churchmen and company bosses had attended to express their debt to Latin, or rather to explain how Latin and the effects of studying it had helped them in their professional lives.[108] The support of scientists was solicited, and their testimony in favour of Latin quoted, for the same purpose.[109] From all their declarations it emerged that the study of Latin, by giving an exceptional intellectual and human training, had been a first-rate preparation for the most diverse – and the highest – careers. These illustrious men not only said so, but through their eminence constituted living proof.

A similar endorsement was asked of quotations taken from Latin Antiquity; much use was made of a line from Terence (from *Heautontimorumenos*, I, 1, l. 77): "I am a man, and think nothing human foreign to me" (*Homo sum, humani nihil a me alienum puto*). Reference to this adage became especially frequent after the 1950s when, generally coupled with the words human, humanism or *humanitas*, it was used to indicate that Latin possessed human qualities in abundance. In the Latin grammar mentioned earlier, the introduction ("Why learn Latin?") ended:

> A clear brain, a clean conscience, a generous heart: such is the triple ideal presented by all the great literary geniuses of Rome; whatever they are called – Cicero, Virgil, Horace or Tacitus – all are present in this declaration by one of Terence's characters: "I am a man. Nothing human is foreign to me".[110]

Pierre Boyancé, during an interview given under the eloquent title of "Latin, a fundamental discipline", emphasized that in modern society dominated by "technical demands", people needed more than ever to have received "a culture capable of acting as a counterweight". And, he continued, "no other discipline, however excellent it may be, can possibly represent, for the awakening of human awareness, what the study of Latin represents". In support of this proposition on the character "of welcome and sympathy for all forms of human culture" possessed by Latin civilization and literature, he recalled:

"It was a Latin who said: 'Nothing human is foreign to me'. The thing to remember is that it was a Latin who said it."[111] That is how this line, which in the eighteenth century was interpreted as an expression of cosmopolitanism and human solidarity,[112] ended up in the service of classical education. It became the device of the defenders of Latin, who used it freely because it so suited their cause.[113] Even invested with a modern sense, it still drew strength from its antiquity and the Latin origin of its author; and it thus functioned as another argument based on authority, in a cause which Terence, of course, had never even imagined.

These speeches that the supporters of Latin addressed to the public at large were certainly persuasive. Indeed they were appropriated by that public, which then repeated them in somewhat simplified form. Thus, responses to the two surveys conducted in the US tend to reproduce, in mechanical fashion, the "traditional" case for Latin: apart from original biographical detail, they seem to be the expression of a perfectly internalized credo. We need look no further than four examples taken from the 1969 survey. President Nixon, after recalling that Latin had been one of his favourite subjects at high school, added: "In my opinion those courses were extremely valuable to me in the development of logical thinking and in giving me a better understanding of English grammatical construction". Latin had not been a favourite subject for John Lindsay, future mayor of New York, but he too recognized the same beneficent effects: "In retrospect it seems to me that the study of Latin gives the student a valuable familiarity with the derivational structure of the English language. Moreover, a course in Latin constitutes excellent mental exercise and cultivates scholastic discipline". Senator Kennedy, after saying what a "privilege" it had been to study Latin, went on to specify its "permanent" value:

> Our own English language has many of its roots in Latin, and because of this, one might say that Latin is, indeed, a "living language". The study of Latin also acquaints us with a fascinating and important historical era – an era which gave us much of our cultural heritage.

Nelson Rockefeller who, as we have seen, was one of the few to mention the access that Latin gave to a great literature, and the pleasure derived from it, added some other reasons for favouring the old language:

> If you study it properly it will raise the general level of your intelligence . . . Latin is the most terse and concise of all languages. If you will compare a passage in Latin with its equivalent in English, you will find we have to use more words to express what is so briefly expressed in Latin. Furthermore, the person with a knowledge of Latin has a better command of English, for much of our language stems from Latin.[114]

These same arguments were repeated always and everywhere: they are found in France in a survey conducted in 1956 among the parents of pupils at Paris *lycées*[115] as well as in the testimonies included by J. de Romilly in her "plea" on behalf of classical studies. This is not surprising when we learn that, in a survey carried out in 1969 at schools in Alsace, fifth-grade Latinists were questioned in these terms:

> Do you have the impression of having derived some benefit from studying Latin? If yes, in which of the following ways:
>
> − this subject has taught me to reflect
> − this subject has taught me to reason
> − this subject has given me better understanding of French
> − this subject has given me better knowledge of the Romans.

Their seniors in fourth grade were given a different range of answers to the same question:

> − progress in reasoning and deduction
> − enrichment of general culture
> − training in more methodical and rigorous working methods
> − training for the memory.[116]

In combination with the classical range of arguments, this constitutes a mechanism for the reproduction and perpetuation of a discourse.

Between conviction and persuasion, the discourse in support of Latin became established in a tradition that people came to regard as "sacred".[117] Hence the extremely sombre predictions as to the consequences that would result from any demotion of Latin and, *a fortiori*, from its abandonment: crisis of the mother tongue, advent of the reign of idleness, loss of moral direction, the individual cast adrift, the ruin of society, and so on. More than that, all the functions that had devolved on Latin, all the values that had been attributed to it, promised great difficulties if the day ever came when it had to be replaced. "It will not be easy to arrange the new subject or sequence of subjects in a didactic order giving equivalent results," wrote Antonio Gramsci in the *Quaderni del carcere*, after recalling the educative function fulfilled by the old language.

> One does not study Latin in order to learn the language; for a long time, as a result of a cultural and scholarly tradition . . ., Latin has been studied as an element in an ideal curriculum, an element which combines and satisfies a whole series of pedagogic and psychological requirements.

After detailing the functions thus performed by Latin, he went on: "This does not mean – it would be stupid to think so – that Latin and Greek, as such, have intrinsically thaumaturgical qualities in the educational field. It is the whole cultural tradition, which also and particularly lives outside the school, which in a given ambience produces these results".[118] We now have no choice but to examine the "cultural tradition" and "given environment" that invest Latin with these "thaumaturgical qualities".

CHAPTER 8

"Class"

When Edgar Faure removed Latin from the sixth-grade syllabus in 1968, he justified the measure in these terms: classical schooling was

> becoming less appropriate to the needs of society. On one hand . . . this type of education, made up of unchanging knowledge that secular tradition has promoted to the level of scholarly tradition, has shown itself to be broadly incapable of innovation. On the other hand, all sociological studies show that it is only accessible to those who inherit culture, in other words those from a certain family background. It cannot be disputed that it is hampering democratization.[1]

These assertions provoked an outcry. Defenders of Latin, in parliament as well as the professional journals, responded by alleging that the reform was itself "anti-democratic". Retention of sixth-grade Latin was clearly indicated by any "concern for equality"; classical schooling was not "class education" at all; examples were quoted of children from "the humblest of backgrounds" who had been given it and "succeeded brilliantly"; indeed Latin had performed a useful "social role" by enabling children from poor or foreign backgrounds to "enrich their means of expression and make it more flexible so that quite early, from fourth or fifth grade, they lose their initial disadvantage in comparison with children from different socio-cultural backgrounds". Far from being "bourgeois" in character, Latin was a "real factor for the democratization and equalization of educational opportunity"; but this might easily change as a result of the noxious measure, because the privilege of studying it would still be available to the children of the rich, who could afford private schools or individual tuition.[2] The Sorbonne professor Pierre Boyancé had already refuted the "bourgeois prejudice" attached to Latin by some people several years earlier: while admitting that in the past "the bourgeoisie (had) in effect invested a good deal in defining itself through its Latin culture", he believed that that time had passed, and there was now no "bourgeois Latin" any more than there was "bourgeois physics or maths".[3] He was quite right, of course, but the fact remains that he admitted that Latin had at one time been associated with the bourgeoisie. The same admission was implicit in a 1968 defence of Latin against the "pseudo-egalitarian" Faure measure, which emphasized the danger that classics would *once again* become a class-related subject. These arguments, freely used during the controversy, indicate that a discriminatory value was attributed to Latin: the Minister's expression "those inheriting culture" and the "egalitarian" arguments of his critics show without any ambiguity that the Latin question was no longer pedagogic so much as social. So the question that arises, a historical one, is this: how had Latin come to play this role of *discrimen*, to pass in general opinion for some sort of bourgeois "certificate of authenticity"? To answer it means entering socio-logical territory and reconstructing, from the opinions and practices of people at the time, the ways in which the sign that Latin had become worked in modern society: how it was perceived, how it was used (and sometimes manipulated), to what ends, and with what effects.[4] The French episode serves here only as the introduction to a broader examination.

1 "A Wholly Honourable Form of Learning"

When it was being "restored" during the fifteenth century, no one claimed that Latin could be used to raise anyone's social standing. True, humanist schooling was given to an elite of children to prepare them for elite functions in adult life. The – purely "literary" – education it provided developed capacities thought at that time to have practical value in professions like diplomacy, civil administration, the law or the Church.[5] However, this schooling carried risks inherent in its very teaching methods: there was a strong tendency for commentary on classical authors to be reduced to technical observations on minor points of detail, with the text disappearing completely under an avalanche of erudition. There was in fact no shortage of masters, as well as students, who would parade gratuitous learning, smugly point out errors made by Homer or Virgil and engage in violent disputes among themselves over minutiae.[6] Associated with behaviour of that sort, Latin would not have done much for anyone's social status.

Also in Italy, when court civilization was making its appearance, the same elite was given access to a different ethical and educational model: the model of the courtier. The most comprehensive manual of court manners, the "technical" education that those living and functioning in courts needed to possess, was Baldassar Castiglione's *Libro del Cortegiano* (1528). It taught that the courtier should under all circumstances display *sprezzatura*, an untranslatable word conveying something like "naturalness"; Castiglione wrote that it "hides art and shows that what one has done and said came without effort and almost without thought", while allowing the art to show "takes away all credit and results in one's being held in low esteem".

From the early sixteenth century in Italy, and then elsewhere, there was disapproval of one character notorious for "letting the art show": the pedant. This figure was ridiculed in numerous comedies, including Francesco Belo's *Il pedante* (1529), Giordano Bruno's *Il Candelaio* (1582), Gabriel Harvey's *Pedantius* (1581), and later Cyrano de Bergerac's *Le pédant joué* (1654) and Molière's *Les femmes savantes* (1673). One of the features invariably lampooned was the pedant's taste for the immoderate use of Latin, the introduction of Latin words, expressions and propositions into vernacular speech, the predilection for unusual or non-classical expressions and the frequent use of Latin constructions like the ablative absolute. This mania was coupled with a strong desire to display erudition, expressed in the first instance by the abuse of quotations (usually Latin, of course). What was ridiculed on stage was denounced in dictionaries, where the pedant was described as being "spoiled by Greek and Latin" and happy to "quote incessantly from some Greek or Latin author", to "pile on the Greek and Latin indiscriminately". Pedant and Latin ended by being confounded with each other, as in Molière's invented term for pedants like Trissotin, "gens à latin" (meaning "Latin people", but in the same sense as, for example, "beer bottles"). However, what is being mocked in this way is not Latin as such, but the degeneration of Humanist education: its reduction to mere memorizing and compilation, at the expense of a genuine moral and intellectual formation of the whole man based on reading the Ancients.[7]

This is the analysis made by Montaigne among others, in the chapter *Du pédantisme* ("On pedantry") in his *Essais*. In his opinion, however, the "reason" for this tiresome phenomenon lay in the false idea that all men are naturally equal: in fact not all natures were suitable for exercises of the mind, "mongrels and the vulgar" being "unworthy of philosophy"; but at the same time, he went on, society was so arranged that "ordinarily there is no one left to engage fully in study except people of low fortune who seek their living from it. And with such people their natures, being by family background and example of the lower sort, assimilate the fruits of knowledge falsely."[8] In keeping with this aristocratic judgement, it is noticeable that the pedant was usually described not only as triply idiotic, like Molière's Trissotin, but also as a "rustic and unpolished" creature, usually employed in subordinate tasks and without even the status of tutor or schoolmaster (from whom incidentally he gets his name). An example appears in the passage of *Histoire comique de Francion* where during his "scholastic adventures" the hero falls under the ferule of a "pedantic ass" of a form-master who delights in Latin etymologies and in weighing down his pupils with "a thousand of the most ignorant pedantic bits of rubbish imaginable". And Sorel continues on a note of social analysis: "Teachers are people who have come to the rostrum almost straight from the plough . . . For the rest, they do not know what civility is."[9]

At a time when that same "civility" was giving a growing role to French, these college pedants and their obtrusive Latin seemed the very antithesis of worldly people, of the ladies and gentlemen of the court.[10] Latin, though, was not expelled from the universe of worldly people. A glance at the *Mercure Galant* makes this apparent. The periodical was aimed at the nobility and Paris bourgeoisie, readers who were not Latinists by profession or even in some cases – women for example – by education. But this successful journal devoted quite a lot of space to Latin and Roman Antiquity: it published Latin verse as well as medallions and inscriptions in Latin, made use of Latin mythology for stylish narratives and riddles, and kept up to date on philological and antiquarian work involving the classical language, etc.[11]

At this point it is appropriate to mention a dual development that took place in France during the reign of Louis XIV, when the gentry became more lettered and the scholars more "civilized".[12] Not only did intellectuals churn out numerous writings on the correct behaviour of a "good scholar", while scolding the pedants and charlatans who had given them a bad name, but they also tried to purge their own manners of sourness and behave in a straightforward and decent fashion. They seem to have succeeded. Many of the foreign travellers who stayed in Paris during the second half of the seventeenth century saw the intellectuals they met there as embodying the ideal embraced by the Republic of Letters: the highest qualities of intellect allied to great courtesy, extreme urbanity and nobility of manners. One of them, Antonio Conti, there to complete his education, said he had also learned there that "a scholar can be a man of the world".[13] Learning, and Latin with it, thus lost what had been a certain crudity of image, and seemed less repellent to worldly people.

The worldly did not become intellectuals, but they gradually lost their traditional aversion to learning and formal education, still at that time largely based on Latin. Nobles may not have had the same respect for the humanities as magistrates, but they did recognize the need for education, if only to enable people to perform certain functions or take part in court life: the taste and judgement of future patrons of the arts had to be trained; and there had to be spectators capable of decoding the mythological references in court ballets, and of reading the Latin inscriptions at festivals. But there was no movement towards turning young aristocrats into professional *littérateurs*. An erudite approach, calling for long years of study, was not thought necessary; the favoured teaching method was based on translation – serving the pupil's French as much as his Latin – and the child was given texts on politics, history or the arts of warfare, judged most suitable to his condition. Originally this education was given at home, as noble families feared that their children might pick up bad mannerisms if thrown together at school with children of the lower classes; but this changed with the introduction of Jesuit colleges, markedly elitist in character. The sons of the nobility attended these institutions, for longer or shorter periods depending on the career envisaged for them (army or Church), and supplemented by appropriate extra tuition. These children thus studied Latin at greater or lesser length in institutions specifically intended to educate men of the world.[14] The same outlook can be discerned in the education given to princes. In the many treatises written at the beginning of the seventeenth century, the importance attributed to Latin is proportional to its utility: it was the language used by the nations of Europe for official communication with each other; apart from that, it could help the prince to "penetrate even to the understanding of good and evil", and above all it taught him (as Héroard points out) the ways in which the Ancients waged war; but he was expected to avoid getting bogged down in subtleties and to be content with an "overall understanding".[15] So the education given to nobles and even princes did not reject Latin; Latin was included, but stripped of everything that might encourage pedantry. Although even in the late eighteenth century there were still nobles who thought that "a lord doesn't need to be a doctor", they sent their offspring to college nevertheless.[16]

Once fully accepted as part of the education of society's elites, Latin became a "noble" subject. It no longer mattered if the teaching given in the colleges was obsessed with minutiae. Latin had become the emblem of liberal education, and its growing uselessness – for it figured less and less in most pupils' future professional lives – helped confirm it in that symbolic role. Here was another example of Castiglione's dictum that the art should not be allowed to show. Hence all the eulogies we have seen of a classical education not intended to produce Latinists. Hence too the disdain shown in France and perhaps even more in England for the German philological approach that turned pupils into specialists.[17]

Furthermore, although the social elites had to learn Latin, nobody expected them to know it. This attitude is perfectly expressed in the dialogue between two characters in George Eliot's *The Mill on the Floss*, the youth Tom Tulliver and his cleverer and more advanced schoolmate Philip Wakem.

> "I can't think why anybody should learn Latin," said Tom. "It's no good."
>
> "It's part of the education of a gentleman," said Philip. "All gentlemen learn the same things."
>
> "What! Do you think Sir John Crake, the master of the harriers, knows Latin?" asked Tom, who had often thought he should like to resemble Sir John Crake.
>
> "He learned it as a boy, of course," said Philip. "But I daresay he's forgotten it."[18]

So what counted was not so much knowing Latin as having learned it. As Raoul Frary wrote in 1885, among the "good bourgeoisie . . . you have to

know Latin, or rather you have to have spent a number of years in establishments where it is taught". He went on to state in the clearest possible
fashion that once the *baccalauréat* had been obtained, once the test that brought
a Latin-rich secondary education to a close had been passed, it is "permitted
to forget all the fine knowledge whose acquisition you have just proved".[19]
The same idea can be discerned a few years later in Edmond Goblot's famous
book *La barrière et le niveau* (1925) in which it was shown that in practice, Latin
distinguished between those who do not know it and those who, without
knowing it, have learned it at some time.[20]

Latin thus abandoned erudite and pedantic tendencies that would have
been fatal to it in good society. In the process its status had changed: it was
no longer a "purely useful" or even utilitarian subject needed for a few rather
unglamorous professions. To the elite which sent its children to endure a
heavy dose of Latin it had become "a purely honourable form of learning"
which, it went without saying, served no purpose and of which nothing would
ever be made. In that respect alone, it "imparted class": it defined the gentleman in England and the bourgeois in France, by ostentatiously expressing
membership of a class that could "waste" money, time and energy on learning something that, in professional terms, had limited practical utility. With
these observations, much indebted to Thorstein Veblen's analysis of classical
studies in the leisure class,[21] we are now in a position to examine the actual
modes and procedures of "class definition" associated with Latin.

2 The Elect

The humanist school had been an elite phenomenon, and the teaching of
Latin (to which it could be reduced) remained so, if only through the fact that
such teaching lasted a long time, and therefore excluded in advance the great
mass of children (especially in the countryside) who, for obvious economic
reasons, stayed at school only long enough to acquire basic literacy. It is
noticeable, moreover, that as time passed those establishments that offered the
most advanced schooling – for example the fully functioning colleges in
France – tended to become more elitist: they started leaving basic instruction
in reading and writing to the small schools, so that the distinction between
elementary school and learning Latin was accentuated. "Big college" – secondary school – had its own social profile: stripped of the lowest, most
elementary classes, its intake was sharply skewed in favour of the upper and
more prosperous classes of the locality – of course the cost of boarding counted
here – which were over-represented, in the eighteenth century representing
two thirds to four fifths of pupils; of the children who came from the same
town, the day boys, their social origin largely determined the length of their
education. Thus in a typical sixth-grade intake, half of the artisans' sons would
have left by third grade, while children of officers and the nobility nearly all

stayed at school until Rhetoric. In other words secondary schooling, which included prolonged study of Latin, was largely an elite phenomenon.[22] Latin retained this character in the nineteenth-century *lycée*, and the appearance of "modern" methods and subjects may even have strengthened it. More of this later.

The English public schools, one of the enduring bastions of Latin, recruited their pupils from the classes that could afford their fees and boarding costs. The Latin that occupied so much of their effort was one of the ways in which these establishments maintained their elite status. Some schools were required, under the terms of their foundation, to educate a few local boys free or for reduced fees; by eliminating their elementary classes, the schools ensured that only boys who had been privately tutored, or attended a paying preparatory school, had sufficient basic Latin to meet their entry requirements.[23]

In the middle years of the twentieth century Latin could still be used to assess social disparities. In France in 1956, the children of members of the liberal professions constituted 12.6 per cent of pupils doing classics, but only 4.1 per cent of pupils on the modern side; the children of peasants and manual workers, twice as numerous in the school population, supplied only 13.2 per cent of classicists, but 26.1 per cent of those taking modern subjects.[24] In the faculties of letters, "where the influence of social origin is most clearly marked", Pierre Bourdieu and Jean-Claude Passeron noted that in 1961–62 "the proportion of students who have done Latin at secondary school varies from 41 per cent for sons of workers and peasants to 83 per cent for sons of senior managers and members of the liberal professions", adding: "which is sufficient to show *a fortiori* (in the case of arts students) the relationship that exists between social origins and classical studies".[25] A survey carried out in the same year at the Besançon Academy showed that the proportion of Latinists varied with the size of the town and the composition of the population. While the average proportion of childen doing Latin in sixth grade was 50 to 55 per cent at the academy, it rose to 63 per cent at the Lycée Victor-Hugo and 72 per cent at the Lycée Pasteur in Besançon, but fell to 27 per cent at the Pontarlier *lycée*. There was also a persistent inequality between girls and boys: thus at Belfort there were 73 per cent of Latinists at the boys' *lycée*, but only 44 per cent at the girls' establishment. The social disparity was also found among girls, with 27 per cent of manual workers' daughters and 28 per cent of white-collar workers' daughters doing Latin, against 46 per cent of daughters of managers and professionals; at the girls' *lycée* in Besançon, where the proportion of Latinists was higher overall, the social differences were of the same order, with 48, 53 and 71 per cent respectively.[26]

In view of these figures, which would be still more eloquent if related to the percentages of these different socio-professional categories in the French population, one is forced to the conclusion that Edgar Faure was not altogether wrong when he referred to classically educated children as "those who inherit culture". But while these figures, and the sociological surveys mentioned by the minister, expressed the real weight of Latinists in the educational world, they did not give any idea of the logic of inheritance that had made Latin – for some – a patrimony.

Originally, perhaps, there had been nothing more solid than "a prejudice in favour of old customs and habits", one which, to borrow Benjamin Franklin's analysis, had continued to exist after the circumstances that made the practices useful had vanished. There had, after all, been a time when learning was contained entirely in books written in Latin, and only educated men – men who knew Latin – could get access to it. Although that time was long gone, children were still being taught Latin, which had stopped being useful and become a sign that now denoted membership of the social elite. To give his observation clarity and force, Franklin used as an example something universally recognized as an external sign in the society of his time: the hat. The contemporary fashion for curled and powdered wigs, and the availability of umbrellas, had now made wearing a hat, useful in the seventeenth century, both difficult and pointless. For all that, the view that the hat was an element of correct dress still prevailed, so much so that a man of fashion was not regarded as properly dressed if he did not have "something of the sort" about him, carried under his arm. He added that there was a multitude of polished individuals in the courts and capitals of Europe who had never (nor their fathers before them) worn a hat in any other way than as a *chapeau bras* (arm-hat), although carrying a hat in this way did not seem in any way useful and was attended not only by expense but constant inconvenience. The same considerations applied to Latin, as arduous to learn as it was useless in practical life, but nevertheless indispensable to the elite; Franklin called Greek and Latin the "*chapeau bras* of modern learning".[27] Tradition and social sign would thus be brought together. In the next century, Raoul Frary resorted to the same sartorial imagery to convey the social function attached to Latin: "The truth is that one learns Latin to be a man of the world, to enter polite and cultivated society. Polite society has its requirements. Just as one has to wear black clothes even in summer, and an awkward hat in all seasons, so one has to know Latin."[28]

Latin and membership of the dominant classes in society could come to mean one and the same thing, eloquently expressed in the remark made by Zagloba, the hero of the Polish writer Sienkiewicz's novel *Trilogja*: "I am a gentleman, *loquor latine*". It was a reality extending far outside the Polish nobility, whose strong attachment to Latin has already been mentioned.[29]

Although in seventeenth- and eighteenth-century England some thought a gentleman could be "very knowing, though he has not a word of Latin",[30] the opposite view generally prevailed. Locke was particularly emphatic on this point, writing that "Latin I look upon as absolutely necessary to a gentleman".[31] A century later the English aristocracy, which at one time had despised the classics, had changed its view: education was what made a gentleman, and what education meant, according to Walpole, was that "every gentleman must understand Greek and Latin".[32] An education without Latin had become unimaginable, as Lord Chesterfield explained to his son: "Classical knowledge is absolutely necessary for everybody, because everybody has agreed to think and to call it so". Of course everybody did not really mean everybody. The classics were the regalia and the label of an elite, something that was said repeatedly until at least the 1960s.[33] Two quotations are enough. In an article published in *The Times* in 1866, Robert Lowe said that the study of Latin was "an indispensable part of the education of a gentleman".[34] In 1938 Louis MacNiece, in reference to the education provided at Marlborough (a public school), mentioned "the privilege . . . of learning a language that is incontrovertibly dead" in connection with "the classical student [who] is bred to the purple" rather than "the boy on the Modern side".[35]

In France the term "gentleman" had fallen out of use after the Revolution, and during the nineteenth century there was a certain pressure, even among the bourgeoisie, for an education better adapted to the needs of modern society; but that same bourgeoisie, especially its richest sector, continued to send its children for classical education which would give them, in Matthew Arnold's expression, "social cachet".[36] Latin and the elite went together. Some of the remarks made at the time are revealing: Albert Duruy wrote of "Latin, that aristocrat"; Marcelin Berthelot attacked "this current opinion according to which a young man who has not done his humanities does not belong to the elite of his generation"; and in the Chamber, Mgr Dupanloup made the famous assertion: "The ruling classes will always remain the ruling classes . . . because they know Latin".[37]

Latin thus indicated membership of the dominant group. "Did you spend your youth with sons of the good bourgeoisie?" Frary wrote. "Were you subjected to the same exercises, the same ordeals, as the bulk of the people whose equal you claim to be? Then the door is open to you."[38] *A contrario*, the absence of this qualification merited exclusion. "A man who does not smile intelligently on hearing a quotation from Homer or Virgil is a condemned man," noted Emile Zola. "He is not one of us, he has not worn the seat of his trousers shiny over ten years on the benches of a college; he knows neither Greek nor Latin, and that suffices to classify him among the poor devils."[39] These few lines contain an admirable sociological analysis that we can round off with an equally pithy text from Paul Valéry, who noted in his *Cahiers* of the education he was given in the France of 1945: "we only develop that which (according to the conventions) identifies a class and that which enables us to move and navigate within a restricted circle – as *passwords*, for Greek and Latin are no more than *passwords*. There's no question of actually knowing them."[40]

"Class", "classify", "one of us", "circle", "passwords": all notions that can be seen clearly at work in one of the practices – often, in fact, the only practice – that indicated a person had learned the classical tongue: the decoration of discourse with Latin quotations. Samuel Johnson thought classical quotations the "parole" of "cultivated men" everywhere.[41] In nineteenth-century England the characteristic possessed a particular defining force, since the pronunciation of Latin – and indeed of English – audibly proclaimed the speaker's social status.[42] Quoting Latin more or less knowledgeably and correctly was a mark of distinction, the visible symbol of belonging to the world of cultivated people. Hence, for example, the smug pride with which Johannes Cristoph Händler, a Nuremberg tailor who had frequented Latin School (for a while), introduced the classical quotations in his autobiography with the phrase "as we lettered people say . . .".[43] On the other hand a serious error in a quotation could be fatal, and blank incomprehension, as Zola pointed out, more or less guaranteed exclusion.[44] All of this led to the appearance of books like the *Flore latine des dames et des gens du monde* ("Latin pocket-book for ladies and men of the world"), published in 1861 and reprinted at least six times before 1914: at a time when French prose was studded with Latin quotations, the *Flore* was sold to those who had not been "initiated into the mysteries of the language of Cicero", or who had forgotten it, as a "handy and discreet phrasebook" that they could consult without any fear of being misled or, more importantly, humiliated.[45] All of this helps explain why Andrew Amos in 1846 advised boys destined for business careers to try to obtain some supplementary classical education. It would give them the confidence and polish of gentlemen in worldly society, and above all would save them from the embarrassment of being seen to be ignorant of Latin by failing to understand some tag.[46]

With Latin and elite social status thus closely connected, groups whose membership of the elite was under threat loudly proclaimed their attachment to the classics as a means of maintaining rank. The position of the "impoverished gentry" in Victorian England is a case in point. When the types of secondary education suitable for children of different social origins were under consideration during the 1860s, there was much discussion of expanding the teaching of sciences and modern languages. The "upper classes" – the aristocracy, "gentry" both rich and poor, the liberal professions and the clergy – were quite favourably disposed to this, but only on condition that it did not affect their own children: it was hoped that they would stay with the classics. This conservative attitude was particularly marked among the impoverished gentry, for reasons that the School Inquiry Commission stated with exemplary clarity:

> They would no doubt, in most instances, be glad to secure something more than classics and mathematics. But they value these highly for their own sake, and

perhaps even more for the value at present assigned to them in English society. They have nothing to look to but education to keep their sons on high social level. And they would not wish to have what might be more readily converted into money, if in any degree it tended to let their children sink in the social scale.[47]

The same logic lies behind the powerful social prejudice in favour of the old language that until very recently caused the French elite to enrol its children for classics more or less automatically, and to perceive a switch to the non-Latin side "as a disgrace".[48] The expression *descendre en moderne* – "going down to modern" – was used to describe what happened to a child whose results in classics were mediocre enough to get him moved to the modern side. The implication that a loss of status was involved is crystal clear.[49]

As an instrument of discrimination in itself, Latin was naturally used as a battle-standard by those whose profession it was; it was a symbol of "aristocratic" status within the teaching profession. At Eton, where in the second half of the nineteenth century twenty-six masters out of thirty-one taught classics, their numerical superiority was accompanied by superior social and professional status. A little later at Oundle, a school later to become renowned for its science teaching, the classics master enjoyed a privileged position: "He teaches classics, but he teaches much more than classics: from him the boys get their inspiration and ideals".[50] It is hardly surprising that the decline of Latin in English secondary education during the 1970s should have been seen by the Latin teachers themselves as an attack on their social status. According to a survey conducted in Swansea, in Wales, most of these teachers came originally from the working and lower middle classes, and their profession had involved a social promotion based on their competence in Latin; so the change in the status of Latin as a subject – from *the* academic subject to a simple option – caused a certain demoralization in their ranks.[51] In France, the 1968 measure was seen as a blow not only to the discipline but to its teachers; a defensive response to this may help explain a demand that was made for Latin teachers to be given the status of *professeur principal*. Its promoters added: "The French teacher cannot be anyone but him, and the teachers of modern languages cannot have any effectiveness without him".[52] In Switzerland, the "Latin affair" that erupted in Lausanne in 1954 shows the leading place the Latin teacher occupied and the dignity he wanted to maintain. The plan had been formed to set up a "common trunk" consisting of the first two years of secondary school without Latin: there was widespread and multiple resistance (not least from senior teachers who would have felt insulted if asked to teach those years). For there was an established tradition, "probably originating in the Reformation", when in the first secondary schools, the principal [master] taught Latin and the noble disciplines to selected older pupils, the second master had responsibility for the middle age and ability levels, and the third master for unselected new boys and beginners to whom he would teach the rudiments [of Latin] along with the disciplines thought to be less noble.

Around Latin, that prestigious subject intended for an elite of pupils – an elite we may consider as much social as intellectual – schoolmasters had built up their own system of dignities over several centuries. It is not hard to understand their hostility to a reform that, aside from its pedagogic content, rode roughshod over this tradition and threatened to demote them socially.[53]

3 The Excluded

Another reason why Latin and its teaching became an elite phenomenon was that it was withheld from those who sought access to it without belonging to the dominant classes. The reasons put forward for this refusal stemmed from the conservative vision of a society in which everyone would play the role appropriate to their station. The view was that it was pointless to make Latin available to people who by definition had no need of it whatsoever and finally, in fact, no right to it. That would be to throw doubt on the traditional arrangements, with a consequently increased risk of upsetting a valuable balance, overturning the established order or at least ruffling the harmonious progress of events.

These reasons were clearly stated everywhere in eighteenth-century Europe. At a time when everyone was supposed to be "raised according to his station, and with a view to the functions he will have to fulfil in society", as Cardinal de Bernis put it in his *Mémoires*,[54] Latin was not of the slightest use to the son of a peasant or artisan whose life would be spent behind a plough or bent over a counter or workbench, while for a merchant's son mathematics would serve better than Latin verse. In fact learning Latin was not just useless to the children of the lower classes, it might even be harmful, and not just to them but to the whole social fabric. For with Latin these children might also absorb ambitions above their station, which they would not be able to satisfy; so there was a serious risk that these men in adult life might become embittered enough to embrace extreme opinions or even rebel. Such views were widespread at the time; and while rulers, reformers and educationalists might agree on the provision of basic education for the people, they shared these reservations on an extended education, still necessarily based on Latin.

Spanish reformers thought Latin dangerous for the mass of the population because liable to encourage chimerical aspirations to unattainable professions. Eventually it would lead to a general weakening of the nation, even to rebellions; in the short term it would cause economic problems by diverting manpower away from agriculture and the mechanical arts. In 1747 Ferdinand VI set a limit to the number of Latin schools, ratifying an ordinance to the same effect by Philip IV. Even in the previous century Latin had been seen in Spain – by the *arbitristas* – as responsible for the country's decadence: it took young people away from agriculture, the artisanate and commerce, and installed them in ecclesiastical or administrative careers, seen as unproductive in economic terms. The whole social balance was affected, the very existence of the nation. Fernandez de Navarette wrote in 1621 that the 4,000 Latin schools – far too many – had their share of blame for the decline in the power of the kingdom: while an uneducated soldier would hurl himself into the fray, one lightly brushed with Latin would ponder and allow victory to escape. Military defeat thus taught that the roles each person is called to fulfil in society could not be changed with impunity.[55]

The Prussian Cameralists were of the opinion that education ought to be *standesmässig*, or compatible with the subject's role in the social organization, the occupation to which he is destined by birth. For small peasants, learning to read and write was all that was necessary; any more would incite these children to leave for the towns, to swell an academic proletariat of plebeians who had been rendered inept at all manual labour but who still lacked the means to accede to official posts or the liberal professions. Rulers came up with various measures to deal with this; in Austria Charles VI, and then Maria Theresa, tried to restrict access to the *Gymnasien* for the sons of artisans and peasants; in 1766, an edict of the Empress declared that "not all children should be admitted to Latin schools, but only those of exceptional talent whose parents are sufficiently propertied to support them". In Silesia, the agents of Frederick II reasoned in the same way: the education of young peasants should answer the economic imperative of tilling the land and the (equally urgent) concern with social discipline. Latin was condemned on both counts. It was noted that it "only stimulates a desire to enter the priesthood, thereby destroying their natural inclination to practice the occupation of their fathers"; so in 1763 the teaching of Latin was forbidden in the rural schools of Silesia. The measure was motivated at least in part by the conviction that Latin made peasants arrogant and disobedient; the minister in charge of Silesia was explicit on this point: "Various Landräte have assured me that the most good-for-nothing, stubborn peasants in their districts are precisely those who have studied Latin". This opinion was endorsed by the Archbishop of Breslau who had observed that "Those peasants who have learned Latin . . . are in all respects the most disobedient".[56]

Similar views prevailed in France. The people should certainly be educated, but the instruction should be elementary: reading, writing and basic arithmetic, along with some sort of moral tuition. A good example of this outlook is found in the passage on his early education in Rétif de la

Bretonne's *Monsieur Nicolas*. Two of his classmates at the time were children who "were not supposed to learn the Latin language: their parents were protected by some rich Jansenists who were paying for the children's education, but who did not want them to rise above the condition of artisans".[57] It was for this reason that people deplored the "mania" of the humble for making their children learn Latin. In his *Tableau de Paris*, Louis Sebastien Mercier made a point of pouring scorn on the ambition of "the lowly townsman who cannot read" to make his son into "a Latinist". Long years of college turned the child into "an idler who disdains all manual work"; incapable, later, of getting a place as bookkeeper or cleric, he ended up at home living at his father's expense, for ever. "The Latinist," Mercier went on, "no longer knows how to use his hands, it is too late to take up a trade, and anyway this doctor who knows four lines of Cicero would not stoop to it". Hence the earnest appeal to the government to close the colleges from which came "a deluge of loafers and idlers"; they constituted a veritable "gangrene" that was corroding the lower middle class, in fact a "plague" on the whole of society. The Benedictine Gourdin went even further; in a work with the blunt and explicit title "On physical and moral education considered in relation to the place children occupy or should occupy in the order of society" (1780), he wrote:

> It is only too clearly shown by grim experience that the man of the people who is put to Latin, and always with the intention of making a priest of him, if for lack of talent, application or similar he does not achieve the goal, becomes a tiresome and often dangerous burden on the State.[58]

The thinking in Italy was no different. In the competitions held by the Modena Academy in 1772 and 1774 to arrive at a teaching system for the less prosperous classes, all the competitors agreed that the children of the lower classes should be given instruction appropriate to their condition; with this in view, they were all resolutely opposed to Latin education for the sons of peasants and artisans, for it would not train them for a trade or occupation but merely turn them into unhappy creatures useless to themselves and to society.[59] Concrete financial measures were taken to curb any ambitions in this direction. In Maria Theresa's Lombardy, or rather in some of its provinces, primary schools had been founded to prepare pupils for the higher schools; a certain amount of Latin was therefore taught in them. These schools were hardly attended by working-class children; although they were theoretically free, the Latin masters could charge a monthly fee of 20 to 25 sous (equivalent to a franc or slightly more) for each pupil.[60] And while the secondary colleges were free in Piedmont at the end of the Ancien Régime, not all of the primary schools were free or anything like it, and the *settima* had to be paid for: the Latin class was thus used deliberately as a filter to ensure that children thought unsuitable for further education would not get access to it.[61]

There was little change in the next century. The children of the lower classes would receive an education, but one that was proportionate to their condition and future activities. Latin was therefore useless to them, and efforts were made to limit their access to it. In Piedmont under the first Restoration, Galeani Napione suggested that the number of Latin masters be reduced, and that they should no longer be paid by the communities; he saw this as "the most effective expedient for preventing those destined for the mechanical arts and agriculture from embarking, purely through the vanity of their parents, on the study of the sciences".[62]

In France, the education system was reorganized in the imperial period to establish two streams corresponding to the two classes of which society was now composed: bourgeoisie and people. "Segregation" was based on Latin and the payment of a special tax. The instruction issued on 13 August 1810 specified: "All pupils admitted to an establishment where Latin is taught will be subject to the charge". As André Chervel commented on this measure, "Latin was thus pressed into service to maintain the social order". This state of affairs was an enduring one,[63] clearly visible in many nineteenth-century debates on education. Under the July monarchy, for example, while there was virtual agreement that sons of the bourgeoisie should not leave school immediately after finishing the primary stage, there were differences over whether secondary education should be the same for everyone. It was often pointed out that the existing classical system was not without drawbacks for the middle and small bourgeoisie, since it imparted knowledge unlikely to be needed on those levels and, perhaps more seriously, trained people to be rootless and socially mobile. This point was much in Victor Cousin's mind when he suggested an intermediate school between primary school and college. Children should receive a "suitable education", but college had "serious disadvantages" for some of them. "In general," he wrote, "those young people who do not feel destined for an elevated career, do their studies negligently"; the resulting weak accomplishments, which were never going to be needed, would be quickly forgotten. And apart from that,

> often too these young people contract friendships and tastes at college that make it difficult or even impossible for them to follow the lowly occupations of their fathers: whence a race of restless men, dissatisfied with their lot, with others and with themselves, the enemies of a social order in which they do not feel at all at home, ready to plunge with some learning, a greater or lesser degree of ability and an unbounded ambition into all the byways of servility and revolt.[64]

The same views were expressed by Guizot in 1833 during his defence in the Chamber of proposals for a "higher degree of primary instruction":

A very numerous part of the nation, which although lacking the advantages of fortune is not exposed to any severe difficulty, is entirely lacking in the intellectual and moral learning and culture appropriate to its position . . . So considerable a proportion of our compatriots ought to be put in the way of arriving at a certain level of intellectual development without being obliged to resort to secondary education . . . which is so expensive and at the same time so perilous. For every few happy talents that [such] education drags usefully out of their primary state, how many mediocrities pick up tastes from it that are incompatible with the modest condition to which they will have to return.[65]

Ministerial pronouncements on "social mobility" seem to find an apologia in Jules Vallès's novels *L'enfant* and *Le bachelier*. For the petit-bourgeois family of his character Jacques Vintgras, Latin functions as a means of going up in the world; but the young Jacques fails his *baccalauréat*, goes to Paris and discovers that the study that has cost him such effort is not going to save him from poverty. That is why *Le bachelier* bears the embittered dedication "To those fed on Greek and Latin who have died of starvation, I dedicate this book".[66] The same suggestion that teaching people Latin would give them ideas above their station was made at the very end of the century to the Ribot commission on educational reform: representatives of the conservative tendency, among them the philosopher Alfred Fouillée, alleged that giving classical education to children of humble background would not prepare them for the occupations they would have to follow but, on the contrary, make them incapable of fulfilling those functions. This would lead eventually to profound "demoralization".[67] From a much more democratic viewpoint, critics in the 1950s deplored the dubious consequences that a prolonged, because compulsory, schooling in classical establishments might have on "country children" who really had no business there. "The poor victims endure Cicero, philosophy and algebra with resignation; or indeed become discouraged on finding themselves not up to the work required. Who can tell what inferiority complexes might not be created in this way?"[68]

Motives of the same conservative order had ensured that Mexican Indians in the sixteenth century were denied any education beyond simple reading and writing; there too it was feared that they, like the working classes in Europe, might try to emerge from their subordinate condition. Although the Dominican missions to New Spain were always hostile to establishing colleges and teaching Latin to the natives, the Austin friars took a very different view, founding a college in Mexico City in 1537, open to Spaniards and Indians alike, where a professor taught in Latin. The objective was to train a native elite from which a local clergy could be recruited. The college, which enjoyed royal favour, was successful for a time, visitors marvelling at the spectacle of Indians spouting "Latin as elegantly as Cicero". But the establishment was soon in trouble, succumbing notably to the hostility of its many opponents.

One of these, the *escribano* Jeronimo Lopez, complained in 1545 that the Indians had become insolent and were refusing to be treated as slaves, attributing this rebellious conduct to the teaching of Latin.[69]

Where Latin was concerned, women were treated in much the same way as the working classes and South American Indians. In their case, however, the reasons given were sometimes moral. "Woman who speaks Latin never comes to a good end", warned a widespread proverb of the early eighteenth century. The reasoning was that ancient languages contained obscenities that no one would dare to utter in a living language; so ignorance of Latin did not just preserve women's innocence, it protected them from licentious thoughts and blameworthy disorder. However, the argument hardly stood up; people pointed out that there were translations and bilingual editions of the "bad" Latin authors; the living languages had produced plenty of free-spoken books that were just as dangerous; indeed the only way to make this logic succeed would be to forbid women the alphabet. *A contrario*, people gave examples of superior virtue in women known to have outstanding knowledge of Latin, and cited admirable examples of wisdom displayed by ladies in Roman Antiquity.[70]

The truth is that the reasons why women were refused access to Latin were to do with their position in society and the functions they were expected to fulfil in it. This was perfectly explained by Charles Rollin in the *Supplement* to his celebrated *Traité de la manière d'enseigner et d'étudier les belles-lettres* ("Treatise on how to teach and study literature"). He began by sweeping aside the objection that girls lacked the ability for extended education, and more specifically the ability to learn Latin: a number of examples, starting with that of Mme Dacier, made it perfectly clear that "gender, in itself, makes no difference to the mind". The issue was of a different kind. The world, Rollin recalled, "is certainly not ruled by chance . . . There is a Providence that orders the conditions and assigns his duties to each individual." While men were destined for occupations that required knowledge of Greek and Latin, "the keys to all the sciences", this was not the case for women. Their "vocation" was different. "They are not meant in any way", Rollin went on, "to educate peoples, to govern States, to make war, to administer justice, to plead causes or practise medicine. Their share is shut inside the home, and is restricted to functions that are no less useful, but less laborious." Admittedly some women had excelled in the profession of arms, in government or the study of science; but they were only exceptions confirming the "general rule", a rule all the more absolute in that "this division of functions between men and women [was] founded in nature, since it [was] the same at all times and in all countries". The inevitable conclusion was that "study of the Latin language, generally speaking, does not suit members of that sex". Rollin allowed only two exceptions in the cases of women whose "condition" had taken them out of the domestic universe: nuns, "angels on earth", who would have to recite or sing the offices in Latin; and "Christian virgins and widows living in the world, but separated from it in heart and mind, having wholly renounced its dangerous pleasures". In both cases some knowledge of Latin – usually in practice a light smattering – was possible, even recommended, for it would enable them to understand the psalms they were reciting and thus to recite them "with greater attention and fervour". Thus, in the name of a division of roles decided by Providence and endorsed by nature, Latin was an instrument for men, and *ipso facto* denied women, "imprisoned" as they were both in domestic space and in the use of the vernacular.[71] Once again, Latin and the knowledge that went with it, by arousing unheard-of ambitions, might have distracted women from their duties and led to bad consequences for their families, and in the long term for society as a whole. But first and foremost they were unnatural to women; as Hester Chapone explained in her *Letters on the Improvement of the Mind Addressed to a Young Lady* (1773), women should avoid Latin and other "abstruse" learning because of the "danger of pedantry and prescription in a woman . . . of her exchanging the graces of imagination for the severity and preciseness of a scholar".[72] Even *The Lady's Magazine*, an English publication that generally favoured reform of women's education, said in the same year that it would not want society to be "filled with doctors in skirts" who would "regale" people with Latin and Greek.[73] There was no lack of authors who thought this situation advantageous to women. "Excused" from the lengthy apprenticeship in Greek and Latin, they had the time to cultivate their own language in different ways, to read novels and poems, to acquire the art of civilized conversation from their mothers. In this respect, concluded the author of the *Essay in Defence of the Female Sex* (1697), boys of seventeen or eighteen were hardly the equals of girls aged nine or ten.[74]

This might just possibly have been some consolation for their enduring educational disadvantage. Throughout the Ancien Régime, the education girls were given at school was centred on "the same three poles: religion tinged with morality, the rudiments of the three Rs and the use of needle and thread". It was very unusual for a young girl to receive proper instruction in Latin, and the Ursuline practice of teaching reading on Latin texts was the absolute opposite of a modern technique.[75] Things only changed very slowly. For most of the nineteenth century, girls' schooling was without Latin, and mainly concerned with preparing the pupil for her future domestic functions. In Germany, where the elementary education of girls was widespread and the literacy rate high, the next stage of education was inaccessible to the great majority of the female population: proposals to give the same education to children of both sexes were met with strident claims that that would cast doubt on "the foundations of the natural, and therefore inalienable, difference that the inequality (of the sexes) is".[76] Under such conditions, as James C. Albisetti has rightly noted, the issue of Latin for girls did not even arise; it was also pointed out that the logical capacities developed by studying Latin "were not really feminine", that girls' minds could "be better exercised on German grammar", that French would serve in their case to fulfil some of the formative aspects that Latin had for boys.[77] This absence of Latin from the girls' curriculum was particularly apparent in English co-educational schools; at the Fleet Street Senior School in Hampstead in 1851, for example, the two and a quarter hours a week that boys spent on Latin were devoted to history and (English) grammar by girls.[78]

During the nineteenth century, however, Latin was gradually introduced into girls' education: timidly, as an option; or in schools for an elite; or in institutions aiming to offer complementary instruction without preparing pupils for a profession.[79] But there was a lot of opposition before Latin came to be offered as generally to girls as it was to boys. Doubt was no longer being cast on the ability of girls to learn Latin, but, as in the past, the arguments were based on the division of roles in society described by Rollin.

In France, the secondary education for girls established in 1880 was not intended, anyway by most of those who voted for the Camille Sée law, for "the fulfilment of women, but for the stability and harmony of the household"; the objective was to avoid the development of "intellectual divorce" between educated men and their ignorant wives. So there was no question of preparing young girls for a profession, still less of making them into scholars. The result was an education "of upper primary level and spirit"; Latin would have been incongruous.[80] Later some elements of Latin were introduced; here again, there was no intention to develop the girl intellectually, but rather to prepare her for her traditional role as a mother. It was to this end that Henri Marion in 1882 suggested to the Conseil Supérieur de l'Instruction Publique that girls do an hour of Latin a week in their last two years at the *lycée*. "It seemed to me," he wrote in his report, "that future housewives and mothers would be happy later on to find themselves able to supervise their sons' first steps in the subject".[81] This was not a new argument. It had been used in 1838 by a Latin professor who had worked out a method for teaching the rudiments of that language "by women in particular". After showing that it was useful – even necessary – for women to have a "complete education", he underlined the advantage to them, to their children and to the whole of society of their knowing Latin: under present circumstances, the young boy could not get any help with his homework from his mother: he would have to seek the precious aid elsewhere, outside the house, with all the tiresome consequences that would entail. After hinting at an apocalyptic situation, the pedagogue went on: "In our day, a woman's knowlege of Latin should not be seen as a luxury ornament, a vanity: it is on the contrary . . . the rigorous accompaniment of motherhood".[82] Latin should only be introduced with caution, however, as events in the United States showed: in 1895, in a prize-giving speech at the Niort *lycée*, the rector of the Poitiers academy reminded his audience that the aim of *lycées* was to prepare women for their family duties, and went on to warn girls against the American model shaped by Bryn Mawr and Wellesley: too much science, and especially too much Latin and Greek, would put women off "family life" and "commonplace household concerns" for ever; worse still, it would lead to a reversal of basic social roles, as shown by a "detail" that the rector reported with deep distaste: these women left it "to the men, when the family went out for a walk, to carry the children in their arms".[83] So Latin, which ought to have enabled women to accomplish fully their role as mothers, could end by denaturing them and upsetting the fundamental balance of society. In 1897 the optional Latin courses were suppressed,[84] and not until 1924 was Latin offered in girls' *lycées* on the same basis as for boys.[85]

Not without success, for less than thirty years later Pierre Boyancé was able to mention an "enormous increase" in the study of Latin "in female education", with the result that there were "more women than men students" at the Sorbonne. He went on: "In France, the accession of women to cultural equality has taken the symbolic form of their accession to Latin".[86] One of his colleagues, Robert Flacelière, drew very different conclusions from this majority female presence – two to three women for every male student – in the audience for Latin courses in higher education: far from interpreting it as an advance for women, he saw it as representing a decline in the status of the discipline. Latin was a training only for teaching, which was very badly paid; so it could hardly be considered a fitting occupation for a "head of family"; it was hardly sufficient to provide "a married woman with pin money, or a *spinster* with a bare living".[87] So in becoming feminized, Latin lost its prestige.[88] Progressively, while remaining an instrument of discrimination, it had ceased to be a sign of distinction; under the flag of Latin, the old division of society endured; but the leading role was now returning to people who did not know it, or (to be more precise) made little of it.[89]

All of this makes it fairly apparent that "Latin was not socially neutral"; it is also clear that it could function as a "barrier", to quote part of the title of Edmond Goblot's celebrated work *La barrière et le niveau*.[90] It could be seen working very concretely in the early eighteenth-century classroom organization described by Jean-Baptiste de La Salle: those learning to write sitting on either side of wide tables, those reading but not writing sitting on simple benches in another part of the room, and desks in "the most honourable part . . . for those who are learning Latin or going to learn it". In addition the rich were separated from the poor, "persons of quality not being very happy for their children to be put with the poor who are usually very verminous and filthy in their clothing as well as their speech". If we recall that the children of low-income families seldom continued their schooling beyond the rudiments sometimes of reading alone, it is not difficult to see that the little Latinists seated in "the most honourable part" of the classroom would generally have been children "of quality".[91]

Similarly, Latin helped to trace frontiers in the professional world, eliminating confusions and establishing hierarchies between linked professions. At the end of the Ancien Régime in France, for example, medical statutes emphasized Latin as a distinction between doctors and other health professionals. Pharmacists made much of their knowledge of Latin to ensure that they would not be confused with grocers; when the pharmacists of Angers listed their grievances in 1789, one of their demands was that doctors be compelled to write their prescriptions in Latin.[92] During the reorganization of higher education under the Empire, it was stipulated that two of the five examinations taken by aspiring doctors must be in Latin; those taken by mere health officers were all in French.[93] Latin also marked the distinctions between different bodies of engineers, surveyors and so on. Polytechnicians who, as we have seen, during the rest of the nineteenth century tended increasingly to have the *baccalauréat* (in other words, to have learned Latin), differed in that respect not only from pupils at the technical schools, who came from a more modest class background, but from their great rivals at the Ecole centrale, more than 60 per cent of whom had done no Latin even on the eve of the First World War.[94] It seems unlikely that Latin had any practical usefulness to these professions, not even for access to "original sources" or to the etymology that medical men could use. Its role was really to indicate social status. This emerges with particular clarity from the response of German civil engineers to proposals that their professional association be opened to graduates of non-classical secondary schools: they were afraid the standing of their profession would decline if Latin were abandoned as a precondition.[95]

Exclusion and discrimination boosted the prestige attached to Latin and the fascination it possessed for those who did not have access to it. In Vallès's novel *L'enfant*, the hero's mother forbids her son to associate with the children of a cobbler. The cobbler and his wife, far from being offended by this woman's petit-bourgeois views, are "all abashed with the honour being done their kids, by the implication that they were the companions that Jacques, who was learning Latin, liked best".[96] The "excluded" could come to internalize the distinction between the classes operated by Latin, and adopt for their own the conservative views of the authorities and the elites. This emerges from the late eighteenth-century account by Samuel Bamford in his autobiography, one of the most moving texts I have ever read. A clever child, top of his class, he had been invited by the master to move up to the next class, the Latin class. But he had to accede to the different wishes of his father, a weaver, who "did not wish me to go into the latin class at present, but desired that I might remain in the class to which I then belonged". At the time it had been a "sore humiliation" when his classmates "passed over to the latin side, whilst I remained in a class lower than theirs, and consequently stood in a situation inferior to that of those I had been in the habit of leading". But that was as nothing compared to the much more serious consequences the paternal decision brought to the rest of his life: if he had crossed "the threshold of classics", university and its different careers would have been open to him. But, he went on,

> my father had more humble views, founded on serious and conscientious reasons I have no doubt. He said latin should be learned by such only as were intended to become doctors, or lawyers, or parsons; and as I should never be any of these, the time spent learning it, would only be thrown away. A knowledge of English grammar, he said, was worth more than Greek or latin to an Englishman; and he wondered why, in the name of Goodness, English grammar was not taught at this English grammar school.[97]

Even in the 1960s, when the social prejudice in favour of Latin was still strong, there were still families of workers and peasants who thought in these terms and refused to let their children, even very gifted children, stay on the classical side for fear of "giving them ideas above their station".[98]

The opposite attitude was far more usual. It will be recalled that under the Ancien Régime the petty bourgeoisie, farmers and artisans were keen to make their children learn Latin, either out of vanity or a wish for social advancement. The point is that in these circles the idea that there could be no education without Latin became entrenched very early; Locke had noted the anxiety of shopkeepers and farmers to send their children to Latin schools even though they had neither the intention nor the means to make scholars of them.

> If you ask them, why they do this? they think it as strange a question, as if you should ask them why they go to church? Custom serves for reason, and has, for those that take it for reason, so consecrated this method, that it is almost religiously observed by them; and they stick to it, as if their children had scarce an orthodox education, unless they learned Lilly's grammar.[99]

This text from 1693 enables us to measure the strength and endurance of a secular prejudice that was still vigorous in the late twentieth century. Indeed, given its early date, one wonders whether the conviction of the lower classes might not have predated that of the social elites; or at least played an important role in a complex process, with the earnest wish to imitate on one level strengthening the will to remain different on the other.

For whatever reasons, Latin appeared to be a means of rising above one's condition, moving up in society. The hero of Thomas Hardy's novel *Jude the Obscure* saw Latin as the almost "magic" instrument that would enable him to escape rural life and enter the dreamed-of world of Oxford colleges, raised still higher by the difficult and solitary study of the language under very unfavourable circumstances.[100] This quest for social advancement through

Latin was expressed, if anything, even more concretely in the United States, when working-class children entered secondary education en masse between 1890 and the first years of the twentieth century. Classical and traditional subjects were chosen by large and increasing numbers: 35 per cent in 1889–90, 50 per cent by 1905. The more educators tried to adapt the curriculum to these children's needs, the more insistently the pupils opted for traditional subjects; for them, or for a lot of them, secondary education meant Latin, not metalwork or sewing. Educationalists quickly realized that there was a potential danger here of children being given unrealistic aspirations. They tried to manoeuvre children away from the choice of classics by edging them towards "practical" subjects better adapted to their "likely or obvious destinies", and by trying to limit Latin to those with the means – financial in the first instance – to continue their education after secondary school.[101] So Latin finally became something that resulted from social advancement, a sort of trophy. Certainly some such process was at work in 1960s France: "It cannot be denied," we read in the *Encyclopédie pratique de l'éducation*,

> that a powerful social prejudice continues to weigh in favour of Latin: it has been said that Latin studies amounted to a sort of "certificate of bourgeoisness": when a family has risen in the social scale, it enshrines this success by putting its children in the classical section; the father who has not done Latin is proud to see his son being the first in the family to learn how to decline rosa.[102]

When Edgar Faure suppressed sixth-grade Latin in 1968, some called him a "Bolshie"[103] (Latin, remember, had been banned from the Soviet education programmes put in place in the 1920s). But the minister's detractors were not moved by any such historical concern. What the term meant in this case was that Faure had done something iconoclastic, breaking a tradition. And this tradition was surely even stronger than they realized. Since at least the seventeenth century, Latin had functioned as a mode of social discrimination; it had served to classify individuals, to reproduce and shore up the structure of society. In the hands of social elites, it had not been a pure scholarly accomplishment at all, but it had represented an inheritance and acted as a title in support of their position. This background enables us to measure the scale of the minister's action: dropping Latin in sixth grade, far from being a simple pedagogic decision, was a revolutionary act abolishing a resource – real as well as symbolic – that had belonged to the social and intellectual elites. It is ironic that the measure seemed to be obeying the watchword heard everywhere during the events of May in that same year: "Change society".

CHAPTER 9

The Power to Say and to Conceal

The Latin autobiography produced by Pedro Gonzalez in 1582 might have been written as an epilogue to the last two chapters. Gonzalez had originally been a "savage". Born in the Canary Islands – at that time hardly distinguished from the Americas, so that the inhabitants of the Canaries, perceived in a confused manner as Indians, were regarded as an inferior type of human – he also looked more like a beast than a man, being covered in fur. This rare peculiarity earned him a place in a book by Ulisse Aldrovandi, *Monstrorum historia*. It seems reasonable to suppose that it was his double status as a natural curiosity that led to his being given, at the age of ten, to King Henri II of France (as his son was later to Cardinal Farnese). At the French court, however, the savage had been civilized and dressed in European clothing; in his image in Aldrovandi's work he is dressed as a seventeenth-century noble, complete with ruff. Much more than that, he had been educated; by his own admission he had "given up his savage customs and learned the liberal arts and Latin". Just as his new clothes marked his adopted membership of European civilization, so the Latin in which his *vita* was written expressed a different acculturation, that of a savage establishing himself as a man. Latin, as we have seen, had no thaumaturgical virtue in its own right. It was society that attributed to Latin, and the education that went with it, the power to "make the man" and to impart "class". The former savage had understood this perfectly, and his new status had been proclaimed in Latin; no matter that the text was short and the prose hardly Ciceronian.[1]

Thus Pedro, with his Latin autobiography, was proudly demonstrating his competence and – to borrow a sociological type of analysis – proclaiming his possession of a "sign of wealth" to which the society of the time attached value.[2] Not much is known about the way he turned this sign to profit, but historical situations we will examine in this chapter will demonstrate the relations of authority, inevitably asymmetric, that used to exist between those who knew Latin and those who did not. The power to say possessed by the first group had as a counterpart the silence of the second, necessarily reduced to belief and obedience and displaying at best some awareness of their condition. But in the act of saying, this Latin also concealed, for the content of the discourse was unintelligible to those who did not know the old language. What is immediately apparent is the presence of a power to dominate, manipulate and oppress with a view to producing a certain range of effects on others. But other examples will enable us to assess the far more complex game that involved Latin when social codes forbade the discussion of certain things in certain circumstances in front of certain people. When it was necessary to say them nonetheless, Latin could be used to express in detail those realities that upbringing and decency prevented people from saying, let alone writing, in everyday language. In this practice of euphemization, derived from self-censorship (and thus once again from power), Latin, while still referring back to a hierarchical order, was resorting not to force and constraint but to protection. For those who knew it, it was a way of speaking while fully observing the social niceties, without offending – indeed while shielding – any third parties who might be present.

1 Domination

Because it was unknown to most people, because it was the accoutrement of a small minority, because that elite exercised authority, Latin had a prestige that was perceived in terms of power: a combination of its quasi-institutional weight with the mysterious meaning it possessed in the imaginations of those who did not know it. A celebrated literary text – Manzoni's *I promessi sposi* – will serve as our starting point. In this novel, Latin is the language of those who represent power to a weaver like the book's hero Renzo: the Lord Chancellor of Milan, aristocrats, priests and scholars. It is the cultural vehicle of people who "rule the world", and who "nail down" on paper the words uttered by "poor devils", with a view to making use of them later when the occasion arises. These masters of writing also use "another trick . . . when they want to entangle a poor boy who hasn't studied much and they can see he's beginning to catch on, abracadabra! they throw a few Latin words into what they're saying to confuse his brain and make him lose the thread". Renzo himself had been defeated by Don Abbondio, who had wielded the mystificatory power of "*Latinorum*" to persuade him of the hindrances to his marriage. Taught by experience, Renzo discerned alongside "a sincere Latin, sacrosanct as that of the mass", something rather different: "a rascally Latin, outside the church, that sets about you treacherously". Hence the threat he perceived in the "Latin" words – *siés baraòs trapolorum* – that he attributed to Ferrer, the Lord Chancellor of Milan: in this mishmash of Spanish and Italian, in which the only Latin was the ending *-orum*, the only intelligible word was *trapolorum*, a Latinized form of the Italian word *trappole*, meaning traps. So even Ferrer, "a friend of the poor", who had "kept the price of bread down", revealed by using a "Latin" phrase the formidable character of a man of power. More than that, the Latin employed to confuse poor devils already worked in its own right, through its "mysterious meaning" alone, as an unarguable instrument of authority. In chapter VIII, when Renzo, his fiancée Lucia and her mother Agnese have taken refuge at the monastery of Pescarenico, the sacristan Brother Fazio is offended by the presence of the two women, and expresses his objections to Fr Cristoforo, the superior. The latter ends by saying

> "Omnia munda mundi" . . . turning suddenly to Brother Fazio without remem-
> bering that he did not know Latin. But this forgetfulness itself produced its effect:
> if the priest had started to argue, giving reasons, Brother Fazio would not have
> failed to come up with contrary reasons; and heaven alone knows when and how
> the debate would have ended. But when he heard these words, heavy with mys-
> terious meaning, pronounced in such a resolute tone, it seemed to him that they
> must contain within them the answer to all his doubts. He calmed down and
> said: "After all, you know more about it than I do".[3]

Thus Latin, to quote Manzoni, "produced its effect". While Fr Cristoforo had used the Latin expression unthinkingly, in the habitual manner of a priest used to handling Latin, others used the classical tongue calculatedly, for conscious reasons. One of the most celebrated English journals of the eighteenth century, the *Spectator*, carried an epigraph, usually in Latin, at the top of each issue. The practice had nothing to do with learned taste for quotations or a craze for Antiquity, but resulted from its editor Addison's clear awareness of the power of an "unknown" language over those who did not know it; the fascination exercised by the Latin quotation would win the reader's favourable attention: "The natural love to Latin, which is so prevalent in our common People, makes me think that my Speculations fare never the worse among them for that little Scrap that appears at the Head of them".[4]

The prestige associated with Latin gave credit to people with knowledge of it; by the same token, it placed them "above others", as the Florentine artisan Giambattista Gelli noted in his *Capricci*.[5] Hence the anxiety of these "experts" to protect their monopoly by refusing to express themselves in the vernacular. Ambroise Paré, whose *Oeuvres* (1575) were written in French, complained at the same time about those "who want to cabalize the arts and lock them under the laws of some specific language".[6] At the beginning of the eighteenth century, Father Gaichès, in a speech given at the Soissons Academy, attacked the self-interested attitude of "adorers of venerable antiquity" in these terms:

> Hardly able to bear that a vulgar tongue understood by the ignorant should
> diminish the standing of those respectable and mysterious languages with which

they bedeck themselves, they have joined in opposition to it with those who, since they make a profession of teaching them, have an even more lively interest in maintaining their use.[7]

People who possessed knowledge of Latin did not just try to monopolize a competence which, for them, expressed prestige and authority; they also used that knowledge as a basis for dominating others or, as Renzo put it, to "confuse poor devils". Neither the expression nor the grievance is of recent date. During the trial of Campanella – in the 1590s – a prosecution witness reported that the monk "wanted to burn all Latin books, because that was to confuse people who did not understand things".[8] The best that those "confused" in this way could hope for was a lucid awareness of their condition. "I am of this opinion," protested the subsequently celebrated miller Menocchio, "that the act of speaking Latin is a betrayal of the poor, because in court proceedings poor men do not know what is being said and are misled and, if they want to say four words, they need to have a lawyer".[9]

A power system

These few general observations give some idea of the unequal relations established under the sign of Latin, in practice a whole range of mechanisms hinged on prestige, authority and manipulation eliciting reactions of admiration, submissiveness and resignation. Latin was thus written into the apparatuses of power, shoring them up and sometimes even organizing them. Some concrete examples are needed to show how this worked.

The medical world supplies an admirable anthology on this point. It seemed a good idea to start with Molière, two of whose most celebrated comedies – *Le malade imaginaire* and *Le médecin malgré lui* – satirize the power that doctors, by their dress and theatrical posturing, in the absence of reliable science, used to wield over the common run of mortals. Latin, or a sort of Latinizing jargon, was what made doctors like Sganarelle, once he had become "a doctor despite himself": in reality this character is a woodcutter, whose medicine he has learned by working for "a famous doctor" for six years, and his Latin from the "rudiments" he had been taught as a child. When at the patient's bedside, however, dressed in a doctor's robe and "the most pointed of hats", and muttering Latin phrases that include Church Latin and a few mangled rules of grammar, he is not just taken for a doctor by those present – the patient's father, a rich but ignorant bourgeois, and his two equally ignorant servants – but greatly admired. "Ah! What haven't I studied!", "He's a deep one, and no mistake!", "Aye, it's all so proper, I can't understand a word of it," they exclaim one after another.[10] While medicine, as satirized by Molière, tended to bog down in verbiage – the final scene of *Le malade imaginaire*, a burlesque degree ceremony conducted in the doggiest

of Latin, being a good example – those Latin words, devoid of genuine
science, worked on the patients like charms. Among the English playwrights
who, like Molière, highlighted the use of hollow, pompous Latin by doctors
to gain ascendancy over patients (an ascendancy that translated into heavy,
ringing bullion) was William Bullein: the character Medicus in his *Dialogue
Against the Fever Pestilence* (1564) uses Latin more fluently than his native language to abuse rich patients and extract money from them.[11]

Leaving the theatre, we can sometimes find this mystificatory use of Latin
referred to by those who knew most about it: the doctors themselves. Latin
could be used as a way of ensuring their power over others, an instrument of
trickery serving their advantage. "The wiser and more perspicacious doctors,"
wrote Antonio Vallisneri in a dissertation given in 1722,

> recognize the weakness of their art, the small understanding they have of the true
> and incontestable internal reasons for illnesses . . . that is why they strive through
> artifices to cover all that up and hide it behind Greek, Arabic, Latin and barbar-
> ian words, being unable to tolerate it when any sincere doctor writes in the
> vulgar tongue, for fear that the art if understood by all will lose its credit, and
> they their gains.[12]

Mystification or not, though, Latin still worked: difficult to understand, medicine appeared more effective when practised by "Latinizers", as Montaigne
seems to have noticed: "We do not accept medicine that we understand any
more readily than herbs we gather ourselves".[13]

Indeed, the alliance of Latin and medicine had a long career in the context
of power relations. Even doctors known to favour the vernacular used Latin
occasionally to proclaim their quality clearly. Antonio Vallisneri, who
denounced the misleading use of Latin, still wrote down his consultations in
Latin: in these "official" records the classical tongue, part of the doctor's recognized prestige, lent added authority to his opinion.[14] The same purpose can
be discerned in William Buchan's – very limited – use of Latin in *Domestic
Medicine* (1769). This very successful book, which had nineteen editions in its
author's lifetime, was one of a number of original works and translations
aimed at the health education of the population; by listing the precepts of
hygiene and giving commonsense medical advice, their authors hoped to help
ordinary people to maintain their health and stay out of the noxious hands
of charlatans. Buchan wrote his book in English, but on the reverse of the
title page he placed Latin quotations from Cicero and Celsus, two medallions
that, by certifying its technical competence, invited readers to have every confidence in the text although it was in the vulgar tongue.[15] So, even among
doctors who wanted to popularize medicine, Latin retained some of its
authority; by means of a simple quotation the asymmetry of the relationship
was again reaffirmed.

Relations between the doctor and his patient were made still more unequal by the development of medical science, as the progress of medicine expanded its technical vocabulary and caused increasing recourse to Latin. This emerges very plainly from the record of the Bristol Infirmary, a hospital for the poor founded in 1737. At first based on the patients' own accounts and using their terms, in the last third of the eighteenth century the doctors' notes were based entirely on a physical diagnosis made by the practitioner. The reports had ceased to be written in everyday language and made increasing use of technical terms borrowed, in this case, from a nosology established by the Edinburgh professor William Cullen. At the same time Latin was substituted for the vernacular: while in the late 1770s seven out of ten diagnoses were given in English, by the end of the century the proportion had been more than reversed, with nearly eighty per cent delivered in Latin. So the patient no longer had any say in his own case, being reduced to a clinical problem discussed in a language that was doubly unintelligible: technical Latin. Under the sign of Latin the doctor and his patient drew further apart, something quite apparent to both parties. The physician Thomas Beddoes noted in 1804 that instead of consulting the hospital doctors, poor patients chose to discuss their cases with their neighbours "because they speak to the sick in their own language".[16] Eventually the distance between the two parties seems to have become so great that the relationship was unworkable: the patient would have felt drawn to other, more intelligible authorities, the very ones the doctors wanted to keep him away from: officious but ignorant lay advisers, or (worse still) charlatans.

These last, while being altogether more accessible than real doctors, were every bit as conscious of the power conferred by Latin; and in order to deck themselves in doctor's prestige, to assert their right to offer treatments and cures, to solicit people's confidence, they made great use of the classical tongue, not least when naming patent nostrums like *Elixir magnum stomachum, Pilulae in omnes morbos, Pilulae radiis solis extractae, Gremelli pulmonates, Panchimagogum febrifugum,* some of the more fanciful drugs available in England in the early modern era, along with numerous more commonplace products like *Elixir vitae, Aurum potabile* and *Aqua coelestis.*[17] They delighted in studding their discourse with Latin words and decorating their leaflets and prospectuses with Latin quotations, like the Breton quack who in 1786 distributed a flyer bearing the slogan *Nolite confidere verbis, sed factis* ("Trust not in words, but in deeds")![18] While charlatans were generally keen to decorate their discourse with Latin or Latinizing jargon, the oculist John (Chevalier) Taylor offers the rarer example of one constructing English sentences according to Latin syntax: "Of the eye on the marvels will I speak", he began on one occasion, having assured his audience that he would speak "in the true Ciceronian, prodigiously difficult and never attempted in our language before". Such was the craze for Latinizing that quacks often disparaged each other's "Latinity", accusing one another of spelling mistakes and syntactical howlers.[19] It was a good way of undermining a rival's reputation, since this reputation was partly based on Latin which proclaimed competence and had its predicted effect on non-professionals. The eighteenth-century physician Daniel Langhans, in his book published in French (1786) as *Art de se traiter et de se guérir soi-même*, warned that quacks "from time to time let fall some word of bad Latin" to persuade "the simple" that the speaker is a learned man "expert in his art".[20] The same dodge was used by the quacks who practised in the Piazza Navona in Rome in the 1680s:

> I have seen some of them [wrote a French visitor] arrive laden with several volumes in Latin and Greek, and justify what they charged that ignorant populace with a lot of passages that they did not understand themselves and in which there was no rhyme or reason, but which nevertheless made such an impression on their audience that people deserted the other practitioners who now seemed next to these doctors of the public square no better than mountebanks, jugglers and quacks.[21]

The power that accrued to those possessing some knowledge – even a very limited one – of the old language can also be seen at work in the legal world, in the relations between magistrates and accused, between notaries and lawyers and their clients. If we are to believe the artisan Giambattista Gelli, the notaries and lawyers of sixteenth-century Florence were pretty mediocre Latinists. They nevertheless wrote their notes and documents in the classical tongue, the instrument – all the more real for being manifest in economic terms – of their dominance over the ignorant populace. "And the reason why human laws are not stated," Gelli complained,

> is also because of the dishonesty of the many doctors and advocates who want to sell us the most ordinary things; and to be better able to do it, they have found this fine trick that contracts cannot be written in the vulgar tongue, but only in that wonderful Latin that they themselves have difficulty in understanding and others understand not at all.[22]

The Florentine artisan's complaint was echoed in the next century, in the juridical summary published in 1673 by Giovanni Battista De Luca under the eloquent title *Il Dottor volgare*. De Luca who, before becoming a cardinal of the Catholic Church, was one of the most celebrated lawyers in the Italian peninsula, had collected all the jurisprudence related to civil, canon, feudal and municipal law in nine quarto volumes, and published it not in Latin but Italian. As if to justify this, at the beginning of the first volume he placed a ten-page reflection on whether it was appropriate to deal with juridical matters in the vulgar tongue; he laid out the reasons for the maintenance of Latin, then those for the adoption of the vernacular, before coming down in favour of the language ordinary mortals could understand. In discussing the issue, he described Latin as a formidable instrument for exerting power over "idiot" – meaning "ignorant" – persons: the old language delivered them, bound so to speak hand and foot, to the arbitrary acts of lawyers and the courts. Latin was already "full of ambiguities" in itself, which meant that documents written in that language were all sources of further legal proceedings; lawyers made use of this prerogative for their own exclusive profit. The move into the vernacular was essential: in this way "will be largely avoided," De Luca wrote, "the abuses and tricks of these lawyers – rightly known as street barkers and babblers – who oppress the uneducated people who come to them for help, or give them bad advice for their own advantage, causing them to launch and maintain unjustified legal proceedings by persuading them that black is white". At the same time there would be an end to the fraudulent court practices in which judges "by prolonging the proceedings, made themselves masters not only of the matter under litigation but of the will and even the liberty of the litigants".[23]

Gelli's attack on the mystificatory use of Latin was extended to the language spoken in the Church. In chapter 2 we heard the protests that aspiring sixteenth-century reformers made against a Latin unintelligible to the mass of the faithful and, for that reason, an instrument that helped clerics to dominate their flocks. We will not return here to the liturgical decisions taken at the Council of Trent, except to recall that their adoption of Latin sanctioned a hierarchical conception of society, with bearers of knowledge on one side and passive recipients of instruction on the other.[24] We would emphasize, on the other hand, the distance that Latin also introduced within the Protestant world, too widely regarded as being uniformly vernacular. In fact the pastors, as a result of the extended classical, and particularly Latin, education they had received, were beings just as remote from the mass of the faithful as Catholic priests, perhaps even more so. Bruce Tolley, in a study of Würtemberg, and Bernard Vogler (the Rhine), have both emphasized the split that arose after the Reformation, under the sign of Latin, between a clergy that was cultivated and populations that were not; the same conclusions on "a segregation between the clerical order and the illiterate masses" hold good for the Lutheran Germany of the eighteenth century.[25] It would be interesting to know how this prestige in which pastors were supposedly swathed would have worked on their parishioners. There is certainly an anecdote that shows how Latin sometimes played a part in a power strategy in the Protestant world. It concerns two rival preachers in a small provincial village in early eighteenth-century England, each trying to attract the bigger congregation. One of them, very learned and well versed in patrology, kept making Latin quotations in front of "illiterate hearers, who it seems found themselves so edified by it, that they flocked in greater numbers to this man than to his rival". The other preacher, seeing the decline of his congregation and learning the reason, decided "to give his parish a little Latin"; but knowing no patrology and lacking scholarly texts, he used Lily's grammar to sprinkle his sermons with random extracts from the rules of syntax, followed by explanations of his own.[26]

The frontier between those who knew Latin and those who did not was of enduring importance in the scientific world. This general remark finds an original illustration in the split that appeared, in botany, between specialists and amateurs after the reform carried out by Linnaeus. This reform, as we have seen, represented a considerable advance for professional naturalists in a discipline that had been threatened with collapse; but at the same time, owing to its Latin nomenclature, it helped to keep amateurs, women in particular, out of the study of plants, or anyway made it more difficult for them. In addition, there was "the dead language obstacle": as Elizabeth Kent noted of Latin in the 1820s, "that language, not being generally studied by ladies, still has power to scare them from an attempt, of which it leads them to overrate the difficulties".[27]

In the wider framework of unequal relations, Latin was deliberately used as a means of manipulation or coercion. In the William Bullein comedy quoted above, Latin is used as an instrument of power not only by the doctor over the patient, but by the husband over the wife; thus Civis, when saying something he does not want Uxor to understand, does so in Latin and refuses to translate it into English.[28] Sometimes Latin could be used in such a way as to bulldoze all resistance, to hijack the consent of others: a story by the Canadian humorist Stephen Leacock, *The Arrested Philanthropy of Mr. Tomlinson*, is partly based on this procedure. Boomer, President of Plutoria University (perhaps based on McGill where Leacock taught political science), and another professor use Latin to persuade the rich farmer Tomlinson to make a charitable endowment. When the patron-to-be hesitates they "douse him with Latin", coming at him from all angles with Latin quotes to soften him up. They are merely using their standard strategy for businessmen, knowing from experience

> that nothing pleases them so much as the quiet, firm assumption that they know Latin . . . So it was that Dr. Boomer would greet a business acquaintance with a roaring salutation of "Terque quaterque beatus" ("Thrice and four times blessed") or stand wringing his hand off to the tune of "Oh et presidium et dulce decus meum" ("O thou, my support and sweet glory"). That got them every time.[29]

Tyranny of the Latin inscription

The examples examined above show that Latin played an instrumental role in the relations of authority that exist between individuals. The same "hierarchizing" function can be discerned in the political order. This emerges forcefully from the "quarrel of the inscriptions" in Louis XIV's France, when a debate arose over whether to inscribe public monuments in Latin or French. Academic studies of the subject have concentrated on purely linguistic and literary aspects of the debate,[30] while many of the arguments advanced by the participants at the time can only be fully and correctly understood against a wider context. It then becomes apparent that the "quarrel of the inscriptions" is not just a moment in French literary history, but the scene of a much wider confrontation between two different conceptions of the political and social order, as it were two different visions of the world. Let us recall at the outset that the inscriptions placed on public monuments are not innocent "patterns of letters" whose function is purely ornamental, but "state writings" conveying and referring to messages reflecting the play of power.[31] In this context, the linguistic choice has just as much importance as the content, character and disposition of the text, on which historiography has tended to concentrate. In the famous "quarrel", then, language was the very issue at stake; and it was a political issue.

The first skirmishes took place in 1669, and the problem might have remained theoretical had not the erection of a triumphal arch at the Porte Saint-Antoine in 1670 demanded a prompt concrete answer to the question of whether the inscriptions to commemorate the achievements of Louis XIV were going to be in Latin or French. For more than ten years the supporters of the two languages were locked in battle, arguing the case endlessly in front of the Académie Française, lobbying for the support of lords, ministers, Colbert, the King himself. Eventually, in fact, the royal will brought hostilities to end by favouring French. In the course of the quarrel, the two parties issued a large number of writings containing arguments in support of their positions. Both sides reasoned using a common stock of arguments based on what were held to be the right qualities for a language: adequacy, stability, universality. But these arguments were interpreted differently according to the background conception of the prince and the subject.

The pro-Latin position emerges excellently from a harangue that its champion, the Jesuit Lucas, delivered – in Latin – at the Clermont college on 25 November 1676. After giving the background to the controversy, he stated his intention to plead for Latin. He began by refuting the "patriotic" argument that Latin, as a foreign language, would only be favoured by bad Frenchmen with little love for their country. For one thing, Latin was not foreign to France, having "lived" there for a very long time; and even more importantly, in the present order of things, what mattered was not language but sentiment: love of country did not imply that one had to write in French, but that one should choose the most suitable language for the purpose. And that purpose was to ensure eternal and universal existence for the glory of the king inscribed on a monument. In Lucas's view only the Latin language, owing to its secular stability and wide diffusion, could guarantee that.

The Latin language, moreover, was perfectly suited to the monument on which the inscription was going to be placed. Just as the triumphal arch commemorating the king's exploits was built with materials thought indestructible so that it would endure as long as possible, perhaps eternally, so the inscription which was "to the stone what the soul is to the body" ought to be written in a language offering the same guarantees of endurance. French could not satisfy these high requirements, as was shown by inscriptions in the vulgar tongue placed on people's gravestones in the past, which now appeared unintelligible and ridiculous. Latin on the other hand, a constant and immutable language, would proclaim the King's glory for ever with the greatest dignity and the most perfect clarity. It would also proclaim it everywhere. Latin was not, so to speak, a language "domestic and private, but common to varied and diverse peoples, and known by them"; it would thus ensure that the prince's renown would not stop at the frontiers of one state, but would resound across the entire universe. To write the inscription in French, on the other hand, would be to imprison the prince's glory within narrow contemptible bounds, to reduce an illustrious monarch to "an obscure family man" shut inside the narrow walls of his dwelling.

Such was the essence of the prince's eternal and universal renown that it would be degraded and besmirched by being put in the vernacular, and thus rendered accessible to a low populace (*vilis popellus*), an ignorant people of "shopkeepers", "porters" and "women" (*tabernarii, bajulii* and *mulierculae*). Glory shone from the prince as from a sun; thence it was communicated first to the learned, to those who "know more than others" and who became in their turn its exact interpreters for the people, for all peoples. So the inscription would be in Latin, and "scholars" would then provide an explanation; this last would be in the vernacular, in all the vernaculars of the world. This mediation would not just guarantee exactness in comprehension of the message, it would also help to raise the glory of the prince still higher in the eyes of a people (*plebs*) which, according to Lucas, was the more inclined to love and admire that which it did not know directly and could not understand for itself.

The Jesuit then drew a parallel with what had been standard practice in the Catholic Church since the Council of Trent: the sacred text, he recalled, should not be accessible to all without distinction, but only to educated men, priests, who would then explain it to the majority. He was thus associating *ipso facto* the supporters of French for inscriptions with those other "innovators" who had introduced the vernacular into religious observance, not without dire consequences. For Lucas, mediation of knowledge where things of extreme importance were concerned was a guarantee of respect for authority and cohesion of the community.

At this point the priest returned to the classical arguments for Latin. He listed its titles: language of the Roman Empire, language of the Catholic

Church, language of learning; he ran through the qualities usually attributed to it: brevity, concision, forcefulness. Finally, while noting that the spread of French was progressing, he concluded that the universality of Latin was superior because written into its very nature: a language without a country and yet nowhere foreign, a language therefore especially apt for proclaiming far and wide the King's renown.

While Fr Lucas did list at the end of his tract the literary and linguistic qualities making Latin a particularly suitable language for inscriptions, these had nothing to do with the real reasons for his choice. This seems to have been ordered by the primary wish to serve the universal and eternal glory of the King, subtended by an authoritarian and strongly hierarchized conception of society in which the monarch appears in relation to the subject in the guise of a God on earth. In the context of this vision of reality, the problem of comprehension of inscriptions by the populace did not arise. Indeed it is the very mystery of the text that gives it its sense, eliciting a response of admiration further intensified by the commentary contributed by an elite of scholars.[32]

We will spend less time on the arguments put forward by the French camp, who for their part emphasized, apart from the qualities of richness, precision, concision and stability the language now possessed, the immediate intelligibility that inscriptions should have. A classical language, by definition only comprehensible to a minority, was ruled out for that reason, and supporters of Latin were taxed with being bad Frenchmen. The case for vernacular inscriptions thus became a national cause, with the interests of the prince and the interests of the language becoming identified and reinforcing each other: French being the language of the King. From that time on, the use of French – increasingly often described as the "national language" in texts of the period – acquired a political dimension, the more so as the triumphal arch on which the inscription was to be placed was a public monument, "the work . . . of all France". So the reading of an inscription, intelligible to all, listing the prince's exploits would increase the respect of the subjects for their sovereign and, on a wider scale, unite them into one nation around his person, represented in the monument.[33] This is a long way from the absolutist vision that emerges from the Jesuit Lucas's harangue, of a personal power from above imposing itself on subjects reduced to silent, unseeing, passive obedience. French, in whose favour the King eventually decided, brought with it a somewhat different conception of monarchy, in which the prince's authority was backed by the voluntary co-operation of the subjects in the task of constructing a "modern state".

Although the "quarrel of the inscriptions" ended in a victory for the supporters of French, the immediate results did not amount to much, as the triumphal arch in question was not completed. In the years that followed, there was a return to Latin for inscriptions on monuments and statues, in Paris as well as the provinces: habit, existing models and standard practice all played a part here.[34] But the arguments produced by supporters of the vernacular were not forgotten. They can be seen appearing several times in the following century, although the context now was not so much the French language, its intrinsic qualities and its contribution to the glory of the prince and of France, but the subjects and their "civic" education. When the issue had been raised again in the 1770s, Louis Sebastien Mercier suggested "planting the town" with "selected" inscriptions in French that would "form a lesson in morals and engrave on the minds of the people short maxims for everyday use";[35] the same idea of a "course of instruction" for the use of the people can be found in the *Dissertation on the question of whether inscriptions should be written in Latin or in French* that President Rolland published in 1784. These proposals for a pedagogy through inscription are about as remote as they could possibly be from the instrument of order and authority that inscription represented for the Jesuit Lucas.

The French Revolution inevitably revived the question. Under the Convention, the Committee of Public Instruction was charged with drawing up a report on the idiom to be adopted for inscriptions on public monuments. It was written by the Abbé Grégoire. He started by recalling the previous century's debates on the subject and observed that this issue, still unresolved, ought now to be settled "under the empire of liberty". Two extremes were to be avoided: on one hand "the unjust scorn directed against languages that once had the accent of liberty, and knowledge of which will always smooth the path of science and engineering" – here the Revolution's debt to classical Antiquity was being acknowledged – and on the other, "the ridiculous prejudice that always places foreigners and the Ancients above nationals and moderns, admiring only that which is done at a distance of 2,000 years or 2,000 leagues". Next Grégoire defined the limits of Latin: it was incapable of expressing modern realities and was unintelligible to the immense majority ("ninety-nine hundredths of the nation are ignorant of Latin"); considered as part of the historical process, it had not generally favoured the progress of learning or reason. All of this argued for the vernacular, especially as a public monument could be defined as "the abridged dramatization of a great event"; as such it should be fully intelligible to all. And Grégoire, that ardent advocate of the French language, listed all the arguments in its favour. The result was the decree of 22 Nivôse year 2 (11 January 1794) whose first article stipulates: "The inscriptions on all public monuments will henceforth be in the French language".[36]

Latin had not yet thrown in the towel, however. Under the Empire, Latin inscriptions were placed on the Hôtel de Ville in Paris to mark Napoleon's coronation; classically inspired, they were published in a collection entitled *Fastes. Fasti* ("Annals. Fasti"), a prime justification of Latin following the Roman model, for the advancement of a regime that used the classical reference. It was recalled that the purpose of "annals" was to "transmit to posterity through lasting inscriptions the concise account of a nation's principal deeds": so they were not addressed to the current population, but to a future and higher memory. They would have to be, because "the inscription is generally above the vulgar intelligence, the causes no doubt lying both in the laws of its style and in our frequent practice of supplementing facts with allusions". That being the case, the linguistic question was no longer posed in terms of immediate and universal intelligibility. What was important was to use a language suited by its qualities of brevity, concision, simplicity and precision for lapidary purposes. Latin had these qualities, and also possessed the advantage of prestigious models and the virtue of a long tradition. Hence the choice of language for the twenty-five Latin inscriptions that decorated the imperial banqueting room.[37]

The debate was relaunched yet again under the Restoration with the erection of a statue of Henri IV on the Pont-Neuf, or more exactly the placement of a Latin inscription on its pedestal. Its critics reiterated all the classical reasons in favour of French, "its great beauties", its precision, its concision; they added the argument of the profound identification of the language with the nation; but most of all they denounced the use of Latin as an absurdity: there were not in Paris "above five hundred persons capable of reading Latin inscriptions". Worse than that, this inscription in Latin seemed to run counter to the paternalist conception of the monarchy that the restored Bourbons were trying to promote, around the very person of Henri IV.

> It seems an insult to the Parisians to present them with an inscription they cannot understand and that appears not to have been written with them in mind. Oh! Good Henri, you who so liked to converse with the subjects you regarded as your children, what would you say about this language being offered, about you, to those Frenchmen who have watched with such pleasure as your statue rose among them?

A paternal monarchy, a king who was a family man, needed an inscription in the vulgar tongue: the same equation that the Jesuit Lucas had drawn in an earlier time, but from the opposite point of view.[38]

2 Protection

Hitherto, Latin has been considered as the expression of a power exerting dominance over others; written into a strongly hierarchical set of relations, bolstering the prestige of those who know it and commanding the trust and respect of those who do not; functioning, consequently, as an instrument of authority, sometimes even of coercion or manipulation, and embodying a power all the more absolute and formidable for being unintelligible. These remarks will not seem surprising, reflecting as they do a conception of power, emphasized by recent historiography, based on force, exclusion and interdiction. But to leave it at that, to consider only the hostile, brutal and violent face of power, is to ignore the fact that it also represents protection of the weak by the strong, the duty of those who hold authority to exercise it for the good of others. This too was a role that Latin played: while remaining the property of the dominant, it could be deliberately used by them not to subject and reduce, but to preserve and protect.

In the first instance, of course, to protect those who did not know it. Medicine offers classical examples of the use of Latin to dissimulate disagreeable or frightening realities. To spare the sensibilities of patients, physicians have often preferred the opacity of Latin terms to the brutal transparency of the vernacular: hence for example the use of *lues* instead of syphilis, *hepar* when mentioning the liver and, in English-speaking countries, *cor* instead of heart.[39] As well as protecting the other, Latin could be used for protecting oneself from the other. It was sometimes used in this way in private diaries to discourage unauthorised snooping; Cardinal Newman kept one of his diaries in Latin so "that servants and scouts might not read".[40] Finally, Latin in this same function could protect by giving a person using it at a critical moment a measure of distance from a difficult reality. On 27 February 1661, the Rev. Newcome noted in Latin in his diary the account of a quarrel he had had with an insolent servant; later, when his anger had abated, he related the same incident in English, but in more measured terms than he would have used earlier.[41] *A fortiori*, the same reasoning inhabits the expression "gone *ad exitum*" used by German hospital doctors to note the death of their patients;[42] the doubly indirect form of discourse – using both metaphor and another language – seems to be a way of talking about death while ignoring it, of keeping an all-too-everyday reality at a safe distance.

Needless to say this euphemizing function of Latin was much exploited in the sexual domain, for designating things that the conventions prevented from being said or written, even in contexts that were in no way pornographic, obscene or even erotic. Although this use as a "language of forbidden things"[43] amounted in reality to a form of censorship (and thus to yet another exercise of power), its purpose in this case was to spare people's modesty (starting, perhaps, with that of the author using it).

Medicine offers a fine range of examples, starting in earnest when the vernacularization process was becoming significant in the second half of the seventeenth century. There are however significant earlier examples: in 1578, for example, Laurent Joubert, Professor of Medicine at Montpellier, published a book dedicated to Marguerite, Queen of Navarre, entitled *Les erreurs populaires au fait de la médecine et du régime de santé* ("Common errors in medical and health care practice"), a work that despite its title was principally concerned with obstetrics. This earned it the violent disapproval of many doctors, who reproached their colleague for dedicating to a "most virtuous and generous princess" a work containing "what is called gross matter". This, they pointed out, "would have been better in Latin than French", because (among other reasons) "these things do not sound as bad in a foreign language as in the vulgar tongue, and because women and girls, whose modesty is most offended by them, would not then have known about it".[44] The Florentine anatomist Coltellini had suffered the same criticism on the publication of his *Instituzioni dell'anatomia del corpo umano* (1651): he was accused of obscenity for dealing with anatomy in Italian instead of using Latin to describe the human body, or anyway certain of its parts, thus imperilling women's modesty.[45]

In England, largely for social reasons, so-called "popular" medicine started to appear after the puritan revolution, based partly on original writings but principally on translations of Latin works; their authors and translators were obliged to explain why they had abandoned Latin and used "low" English terms to describe the sexual organs and reproductive functions. They protested their honest intent, insisted that they were not publishing obscenities and strove to reassure readers, especially women, that their "modesty" was not under threat.[46]

The same declarations of intent are to be found in medical works published throughout the eighteenth century; authors continued to resort to Latin. The book on venereal diseases published in 1736 by Jean Astruc, the King's physician and a professor at the Collège Royal, was in Latin; its author was well aware that it would not be accessible to surgeons, who did not know Latin; but higher reasons had prevailed, concerning "decency" and the problem of using French to discuss certain "shameful" diseases and parts of the body. In support of his position Astruc quoted one of the pillars of the medical world, Celsus, who had written on the subject of illnesses affecting the private parts: "The correct terms for discussing these matters are more bearable in Greek and are more commonly understood by custom . . . while in Latin they appear obscene and shock modest persons". Latin is thus justified by analogy, being as it were the Greek of the modern era.[47] The famous treatise on onanism by the Swiss doctor Simon André Tissot supplies an example every bit as eloquent. This work, which first appeared in Latin under the title *Tentamen de morbis ex manusturpratione* (1758), had an extraordinary success, at least partly because of the new conception it embodied: replacement of theological interpretation (masturbation as sin) with pathological interpretation (masturbation as disorder). New editions, reprints and translations were many, the first French version being published in 1760 by Tissot himself as *L'Onanisme ou dissertation physique sur les maladies produites par la masturbation* ("Onanism or a physical dissertation on the disorders caused by masturbation"). In the preface Tissot referred to "the difficulty of executing this enterprise in a living language"; more specifically, "What made this work much more arduous than it would have been if I had written in Latin, was the embarrassment of conveying images for which the terms and expressions have been declared indecent by custom". In the name of "utility", however, he had vanquished his reticence and written entirely in French, at the same time adding some corrections and new revisions: thus on page 229, he added the "clinical" case of a girl who was "subject to pollutions" even when kneeling at the feet of her repellent and decrepit confessor. In 1764 there appeared under the Lausanne address a so-called third edition, in fact a Paris impression. In certain copies, pages 225–9 consist of an insert in which the passage concerning the above-mentioned girl was in Latin. Censorship had compelled the printer to withdraw the already printed text and recompose the offending passage; to fit exactly into the edition the original page had had to be stretched to four: the extra space had been filled with new details of the wretched girl and her sinister illness, as well as other examples along the same lines. Censorship in this case had shot itself in the foot, for the reader's eye is naturally and inevitably drawn to this passage in Latin, which is also printed on different paper. It is true, however, that not everyone could read Latin. In later editions the passage in question was sometimes deleted (as in the 1770 impression) and sometimes left in Latin, as in the *Oeuvres complètes* of 1809.

The same reasons that had driven doctors into Latin were advanced in the context of university academic reforms in favour of maintaining Latin. In Enlightenment Spain, for example, the reformers who lobbied for the use of Castilian in the universities made exceptions of medicine, anatomy and surgery: in these subjects Latin was to be retained, as Fr Sarmiento explicitly stated, "for reasons of modesty".[48]

This use of Latin lasted longest in the writings of the doctors and psychiatrists who worked on sexual pathology in the latter half of the nineteenth century. In 1857 the French doctor Ambroise Tardieu, later to become Dean of the Faculty of Medicine in Paris, had published by Baillière (a house specializing exclusively in medical texts) a book entitled *Etude médico-légal sur les attentats aux moeurs* ("Medico-legal study of moral outrages") dealing with outrages to public modesty: rape, pederasty, sodomy, etc. In the introduction, he justified his use of French as a professional duty.

> The nature of the subject confronts us with details designed to arouse every
> feeling of decency and modesty, but I have not thought it appropriate to recoil
> from them. No physical or moral misery, no running sore, however putrid it may
> be, should daunt one who has devoted himself to the science of humanity; and
> the sacred ministry of medicine, which obliges him to see all and know all, also
> enables him to say all. I have not even felt it necessary, except on one point, to
> resort to the veil of the Latin tongue.

In fact Tardieu moved into Latin when discussing "certain varieties of pederast", explaining that "I would quail before these unspeakable details were it not possible for me to hide them behind a short Latin periphrasis".[49] The sacred ministry of medicine had its limits. This "short periphrasis", in fact a good half-page of text, was quoted wholesale a few years later by the Viennese psychiatrist Richard von Krafft-Ebing in his *Psychopathia sexualis* (1886), the first work that attempted a systematic description of the whole range of what were then called sexual perversions or disorders. Krafft-Ebing not only quoted Tardieu but, in several passages in the chapter entitled *"Conträre Sexualempfindung"*, himself moved from German into Latin for what he called "obvious reasons".[50]

A consistent feature of these examples is the insistence with which doctors dealing with matters of anatomy, obstetrics or sexual disorder indicated the honesty of their intentions. Evidently they were not unaware of the uses to which these texts were put, as sexual instruction manuals or pornographic material. In 1639 Johannes Heinrich Meibom, Professor of Medicine at Helmstedt University, published in Latin a work entitled *De flagrorum in re venerea usu*, in which he examined and described in strictly medical terms the incapacity of some men and some women to have sexual relations without being whipped. In 1670 Meibon's son at first opposed a reprint, publicly expressing a fear that it might arouse libertine tendencies in some individuals, before giving way and consoling himself with the thought that the edition would be in "a language familiar only to scholars". The more openly pornographic character of the 1718 English edition makes it clear that the anxieties of Meibon *fils* were not unfounded.[51]

One of the excuses given by doctors for the descriptions they gave of anatomical and sexual realities was that the same things could be found in writings on moral theology. It is true that in these cases they were in Latin, and long remained so. An interesting case in point is a work from the frontier between medicine and theology, the *Abrégé de l'embryologie sacrée ou du Traité du devoir des prêtres, des médecins et autres, sur le salut éternel des enfants qui sont dans le ventre de leur mère* ("Abridged sacred embryology or Treatise on the duty of priests, doctors and others concerning the eternal salvation of children who are in their mothers' wombs"), a work posing in medical and theological terms the problem of the "spiritual conservation"of infants who are stillborn, buried with mothers who have died or who have died at birth. Published in Paris in 1762, it was an abridged translation of a folio work in Latin by an Italian prelate. The French translator, Abbé Dinouart, confessed the difficulty he had had and the expedients – cuts and Latin – that he had been compelled to use.

> I have not translated at all in some of the more delicate places; I thought it more decent to leave them in the author's own language. I would even like to have left the whole abridged version in Latin, because that would have left me free to give it greater scope and develop many more interesting issues . . . I have thus been

obliged to omit a large part of this work's useful content in the anatomical and surgical areas, and not to translate many of the issues and details connected with them. The French language would not always have allowed me to to deal with all these different objects as they are treated by the author; that is what decided me to leave a number of things in Latin.

An example of these difficulties is the chapter on "different opinions as to the time of animation", including reference to the Wolff theory "in which the spermatic worms are neither human beings nor the principle of their generation"; Dinouart made no attempt to translate the original text, here particularly long and detailed, explaining: "We will spare ourselves the task of following it, because this discussion contains things that can only be said decently in Latin".[52]

Writings in moral theology intended only for clerics stayed in Latin for a very long time, not surprisingly in view of the use the Catholic Church made of the language. More interestingly, from our point of view, is the finding that when – in the nineteenth century – a timid vernacularization started to take place, it still happened that writings in the vernacular would break into Latin at certain moments. *Théologie morale à l'usage des curés et des confesseurs* ("Moral theology for parish priests and confessors"), by Mgr Gousset, Archbishop of Reims and later a Cardinal, is a telling example. Although written in French, this very successful book – seventeen editions between 1844 and 1877 – contains very long passages in Latin: in volume I, everything concerning sins against the sixth commandment; in volume II, dealing with the sacrament of marriage, all the explanations of "nullifying impediments", impotence in particular, and those covering conjugal duties and consummation of marriage. From this point of view things had hardly advanced by the 1920s, as can easily be seen from the contemporary reference work the *Dictionnaire de théologie catholique*. The author of the chapter on the "duties of the married couple" starts by warning the reader that "the subject is delicate"; he switches to Latin when it is time to spell out "the duties of the couple from the viewpoint of perpetuating the race", and in particular "on the licit in the conjugal act from the viewpoint of the circumstances in which it occurs", explaining: "and our use of Latin here needs no explanation". The article on "lust", eighteen columns of it, deals exclusively in Latin with the sins in this area, both *juxta* and *contra naturam*. The article on "impotence" is interesting in another way: the ten columns of detailed description it contains is not just in Latin, but breaks with general practice elsewhere in the *Dictionnaire* by being printed in Roman characters rather than the italics normally used for Latin, as if to avoid drawing the attention of casual readers to the material.[53] The liturgical reform that followed Vatican II posed moral problems to some with its introduction of the vernacular. Certain verses of the Song of Songs, in all the transparency of the vernacular, seemed to have a potential for distracting the faithful from strictly religious thought. Problems even arose in the Missal itself: the mass for the Third Sunday in Lent lost (for moral reasons) the epistle concerning the chaste Susannah, appearing as a figure of glorified innocence in contrast with the gospel of the woman taken in adultery, the pardoned sinner. No matter that the reading was now lopsided: it had seemed too daunting to read aloud, in the vernacular, the passage that starts with Daniel xiii, 8. One traditionalist commented: "The truth of the matter is that with Latin, these problems did not arise".[54]

The use of Latin to veil certain realities was not limited to the obvious traditional domains of medicine and theology. It is to be found, in fact, in writings on the widest possible range of subjects and in all registers. In eighteenth-century England, it was used in private diaries to record embarrassing illnesses and medical details.[55] Historical narratives sometimes switch into Latin: the Chevalier de Solignac, for example, in his *Histoire générale de Pologne*, lists in Latin (to avoid "offending the delicacy of [his] readers") the sexual tortures and humiliations that could be inflicted on fornicators and adulterers in the tenth century.[56] Edward Gibbon used Latin in *The Decline and Fall of the Roman Empire* when describing sexual matters, for example the "vices" of the Empress Theodora; when some critics accused him of publishing indecent material, his defence included the argument that "My English text is chaste, and all licentious passages are left in the obscurity of a learned language".[57] Similar examples can be found in literature, even in authors not normally seen as prudish. Brantôme, in *Dames galantes* ("Fast ladies"), deserted French when describing the amatory positions depicted by Aretino: after repeating descriptions given by casuists, he continued in Latin on his own account.[58] Rétif de la Bretonne made the same decision in *Monsieur Nicolas* for the description of early sexual emotions, writing: "to express this . . . I will use a learned language", then switching from French to Latin and back in the body of the text, and sometimes relegating to Latin footnotes what he could not explain in the text.[59]

This brief summary cannot conclude without a mention of school. The school world, which consumed such terrifying quantities of Latin between the sixteenth and twentieth centuries, also assigned formative and moral roles to it. That led to the suppression of texts that might shock young boys (or rather give them bad thoughts). For one reason or another, however, there were some texts that, although undeniably risky, could not be wholly ignored. While the so-called "classic" selections of extracts were the most usual solution, it also happened that Latin texts were partly rewritten. These bowdlerized rewritings were still being produced late in the nineteenth century; the 1887 English edition of Terence, "carefully expurgated for use in Schools", is a case in point. In the play entitled *Phormio*, the pimp Dorio is no longer presented as a *leno* but as a *mercator* (merchant), and no reason is given for his having so many young women in his charge. Certain lines have to be rewritten, if only to replace the word *leno*, with a resulting cascade of knock-on alterations to maintain the laws of Latin prosody and metre. Still at school, Latin could even be used in translations of Greek literature for passages thought scabrous, obscene or indecent. Thus Nicolas Artaud, in his 1841 French translation of an Aristophanes play, *The Acharneans*, was reduced to adding to line 1220 – "As for me, I want to go to bed; I've had enough, I need relief" – the note: "The crudity of the terms . . . cannot be rendered in French", before continuing in wholly uninhibited Latin: "*Tentigine rumpor, et in tenebris futuere gestio*".[60]

Classical publishing remained very timid into the late 20th century, even in publications not intended for school use. The 1963 Loeb version of the *Greek Anthology*, for example, gave the Latin, not English, versions of several of the poems in *Satirical Epigrams* and Straton's *Musa puerilis*, sometimes for the whole poem, sometimes just for one or two lines.[61] What can be done with classical texts can also be done with writings from other cultures. The German edition of the *Erzählungen aus den Tausendundein Nächten* ("Tales from the Thousand and One Nights"), published in 1953 by Insel contains a short passage in Latin preceded by the explanation: "The nine lines that follow are so obscene that they cannot be rendered in German".[62] Even more recently, in 1976, a German–Uighur bilingual collection of ethnographic documents on eastern Turkestan carried passages on sexual ailments and zoophiliac practices in Latin translation.[63]

These examples indicate that this use of Latin, in wholly respectable contexts, was a widespread and enduring phenomenon. Perhaps this is the moment to wonder why. In the case of France, the explanations we shall be examining were formulated during the seventeenth century, more precisely in its second half. After that there was hardly any attempt at justification, as if the practice, once fully internalized by the people of the time, no longer needed to be excused.

In many of the texts quoted, Latin was used for the benefit of "modest" persons, almost invariably women whose "modesty" had to be protected. If certain things were written in a language they did not understand, then their blushes would be spared. It will be recalled that women only gained access to Latin at a relatively recent date: in the seventeenth century women who knew it were very rare. The few who did – and the same names are always cited – tended to hide the fact "like a crime",[64] being perfectly well aware of the moral suspicion it might bring down on them. Latin in effect was considered a path to perdition for women. Brantôme pointed to the peril there was in allowing women to study Latin and read (for example) Ovid's *Metamorphoses*. Of course "lascivious fables" and "lubricious suggestions" could be found in French, Spanish and Italian authors; but these would be read privately, under circumstances very different from the study of Latin which would be conducted by a tutor, invariably a man; they were also, inevitably at that time, individual lessons held in "theire privie chambers and offices, all among theire fripperies". To these potential dangers of the studious *tête-à-tête* were added of course those presented by the texts themselves. On reaching some passage freer than normal the master would either quickly turn the page, thus arousing a curiosity which would end by being victorious, or he would offer a paraphrase at the outset, something more pernicious in practice than a literal translation. Brantôme indicated the sinister effects that resulted and the perdition that lay in wait for "student girls".[65] The same view of reality is found a century later in the work of an anonymous author, this time a supporter of the right of women to education. Starting from the objection that knowledge was morally dangerous to women, he went on: "The study of languages is usually claimed to be ill-omened, in particular that of the Latin language, following the proverb that a woman who speaks Latin will come to a bad end". The author refuted this "truth" by citing examples of ladies of great virtue who were nevertheless learned, before going on to wonder what lay behind it: "Perhaps I will be told that in these learned languages we find obscenities no one would dare write down in a living language, and that this teaches girls things we would rather keep hidden from them".[66]

At the same time, Latin was presented in the examples cited as the "language of scholars", in other words the language of a – male – cultural elite. The question that arises here is therefore the following: if the message is the same, in what respect does it lose its shocking character when the recipient is a man who knows Latin? The educational practice of the time here makes itself heard: while for women Latin was a dependable route to perdition, for men its study had the opposite, beneficent effect: in their case Latin was thought to function as a sort of strengthener, training and forming the judgement, protecting not only against error but against impulsiveness, against any first impression going beyond the established letter. Some such thinking was already current by the end of the seventeenth century, so that Pierre Bayle, in a tract in defence of his *Dictionnaire*, could examine the argument that "those who know Latin are better fortified than other men against the malign influence of filthy objects".[67]

While Latin was used to spare the innocence of modest persons, the linguistic evolution that was taking place at the same time also conferred on Latin another specialized function: the enunciation of "forbidden things". The apologetics of the French language, as it developed from around 1650, here played a fundamental role. These lines from Boileau's *Art poétique* (1674) constitute a central text that summarizes this process:

Le latin dans les mots brave l'honnêteté;
Mais le lecteur français veut être respecté;
Du moindre sens impur la liberté l'outrage,
Si la pudeur des mots n'en adoucit l'image.

(Latin defies decency in words;
But the French reader wants to be treated with respect;
Freedom with the slightest impure meaning offends him,
Unless the modesty of the words softens its impact.)

Boileau, along with the other main apologists for the French language in the second half of the seventeenth century – Vaugelas, Boursault, Desmarets de Saint-Sorlin, Fr Bouhours, etc. – claimed for French the privilege of modesty, chastity and decency. As a result Latin, in competition with which French was being promoted as a language of literature, was automatically identified as excessively "free" or even obscene.[68]

With Latin coming increasingly to represent everything that departed from "seemliness", linguistic theorists soon came up with their own explanation, their own confirmation. The logicians of Port-Royal made a series of observations on the meaning of words, including this one which seemed to them of fundamental importance: "a word, apart from the main idea regarded as the proper meaning of that word, stimulates several other ideas that may be called subsidiary, which are not taken into account although the mind registers their impression". They then raised the question of "unseemly" words, whether they were so because they expressed "unseemly" things; here too, everything depended on the subsidiary meanings attached to them, so that words and expressions that were not in themselves originally "unseemly" had managed to become so.[69] Pierre Bayle used a similar argument in 1685 when composing an answer to the *Histoire du calvinisme* written by a Jesuit called Maimbourg. On the subject of the insults exchanged by authors, Bayle argued that "excessive heat is less blameworthy in Latin than in the vulgar tongue". Insults spoken in Latin gave less offence than the same ones in French. He went on:

> Our language has become so delicate that the doctors themselves when giving anatomical lectures in French express a hundred things in Latin although only men are present. The terms they borrow from the language of the scholars mean the same things as the French words they dare not use and nevertheless they are less shocking than the French words.

Then he recalled the passage from the Port-Royal *Logique* cited above, and drew the following conclusion:

> it would be reasonable to think that of two men saying the same thing, one in French, the other in Latin, the second is more modest than the first, because although he awakens the idea of the object signified by the French words whose use he is avoiding, he does not awaken the ideas of effrontery and lack of respect that are attached to these words in French.

So although "the conventions that the nation's delicacy and seemliness have brought into use in the present century" prevented certain terms from being used in French, the same things could be said in Latin "without any suggestion that the new civility is being flouted. No new ideas are attached to that language; worldly urbanity has not made its expressions seem harsher and cruder than they used to be."[70] By using Latin, then, an author makes it clear that he is not out to shock or subvert his reader, while the reader for his part will not see the author as an insolent and unseemly being, but a man perfectly conversant with the social rules of his time; a tacitly neutralized code has been employed to this effect.

Many of the texts quoted explain the use of Latin in terms of "decency". When Rétif de la Bretonne switched to Latin in *Monsieur Nicolas* to descibe his first sexual feelings, he said he was using "a learned language that men will be forced to translate decently to women".[71] This decency was closely connected to a feeling known successively as shame, modesty or chasteness, a complex feeling that in one of its guises, the one that most concerns us here, boils down to the embarrassment felt in connection with matters of a sexual nature.[72] The French philosopher Michel Foucault showed that on sexual questions, contrary to the predominant "repressive hypothesis" on the behaviour of Western society in the modern era, what was really taking place was a "discursive explosion", an intense "discursive fermentation" or even a "generalized discursive erethism", all in contexts that were entirely respectable, tolerated, authorized. The Catholic Church, with its casuistry and auricular confession; the law; then medicine, pedagogy, even economics, all produced their own discourses on sex, amounting to what can almost be called a *scientia sexualis*. Foucault added: "Rather than the uniform concern to conceal sex, rather than a general prudishness, what really marks our last three centuries is the variety of apparatuses for talking about it". At this point, still following Foucault, it is important to distinguish between language and discourse. There may well have been a phenomenon of "discursive explosion", but it still had to coexist with a "police of statements and formulations", a "restrictive economy on language". Here we converge with Latin once more. When everything needed to be said, and much already had been said, but when certain words were forbidden, certain expressions censored, Latin provided a solution: the use that the great contributors to the *scientia sexualis* made of it will be recalled. Once a certain limit had been reached – "I would recoil before these unspeakable details", Tardieu wrote – Latin made it possible to pursue the discourse, to say things, but also to make the discourse on sex morally acceptable, and technically useful, to the society of the time.[73] And Latin, as a "language of learning", automatically placed the message couched in it in a scholarly context, stripping the language of every expressive and conative function, or rather transcending them in a purely metalinguistic function: Latin then became no more than a code, a means for transmitting certain technical data.

Latin thus served to bring discourse into line with the predominant social and moral code. It made it possible to say things that had to be said – it is not always practical to leave blanks or proceed by allusion – but that the prevailing norms would not allow to be stated in everyday language. It thus protected those whom the society of the time, for reasons of its own, regarded as minors who needed to be protected against certain realities: women and, as schoolbook publishing shows, schoolboys. For those who employed it, of course, it was wholly neutralized, entirely disinfected. At least, they meant it to be, and said it was.

3 Seduction

For the risk existed, in fact, that Latin might stray outside its designated role, that its intended function might be subverted. We have seen the young form the habit of pouncing on any passage in Latin, so eager were they to see what it was thought fit to hide from them.[74] More than that, because of this use that was made of it, Latin came *ipso facto* to be regarded as referring to the "forbidden things"; to be identified with them. This is what Flaubert was referring to when he noted in his *Dictionnaire des idées reçues* in the entry under "Latin": "Distrust quotations in Latin: they always hide something dubious".[75] The medium had become the message. While metalinguistic uses persisted, Latin was going to be used "poetically" in literary texts to denote distance from the norm and produce a formal effect of meaning. To hide now became to make explicit, seductively so. Three examples will show what I mean.

The first comes from what had been a European pornographic best-seller of the seventeenth and eighteenth centuries, *Académie des dames* ("Ladies' academy"). Allegedly written by a woman in Spanish and translated into Latin by "one of the great philologists of the day", in reality composed in Latin by a Grenoble lawyer, Nicolas Chorier, this work first appeared in 1658–60 and then went through numerous Latin editions as well as being translated into various vernaculars. In 1881 – one would have thought its vein might have run out after 200 years – the publisher Isidore Lisieux put out a so-called "mixed Franco-Latin" edition in four volumes. The text alternated French and Latin, the latter language used of course for the ruder passages of varying length, from a phrase to a paragraph or more. Here the veil of Latin no longer hid anything. Of great grammatical simplicity, it was extremely easy to understand and further clarified by the French passages before and after; a "glossary of more difficult Latin words" removed any remaining ambiguities. So Latin had come to function as an added suggestive element in itself, further accentuated by the fact that the characters in this work who discuss at length such a free range of subjects are women: women who all know how to use Latin, to good effect.[76]

The second example is taken from a French author of the late nineteenth century, Joséphin Péladan, the very man who called Latin the "language of the forbidden things". Péladan, who belonged to a so-called decadent group of writers, used Latin in several of his works to symbolize both decadence of language and decadence of morals. In one of them, *Vice suprême* (1884), at a series of "casuistical Tuesdays", a character reads out to an audience consisting mainly of ecclesiastics and pretty women extracts from a work of moral theology, more specifically from the chapter on lust. When there is something that cannot be said in the vernacular the reading switches to Latin, Latin of a particular sort:

> He read the Latin from the margin and the princess started to laugh to arouse people's curiosity.
> "You are fortunate indeed to know Latin."
> "I want to learn it. It is the language of forbidden things."

Latin has thus become both the language of the forbidden and the instrument of a double transgression, linguistic and moral, of which the woman demands her share.[77]

In the third example Latin is deliberately presented and used as producing in itself an effect of erotic type. It is a poem by Baudelaire entitled *Franciscae meae laudes*, in praise of a supposedly learned mistress. Below this poem, Baudelaire placed a note justifying his use of Latin which had been decadent rather than classical. The decadent period was associated by the poet with the "sensuality pole" of love, as opposed to its other pole, "mysticity". He went on: "In that marvellous language, solecism and barbarism seem to me the tribute of carelessness exacted by a passion forgetful of everything and contemptuous of rules". Latin in this poem serves less to veil licentious allusions – here in fact of small consequence – than to express through the flustered incorrectness of the language a form of love that broke through the moral norms of the society of the time.[78]

Evolution of the moral code and with it, increasingly wide and blurred "dividing lines", have greatly reduced the scale of the use of Latin we have been discussing. The "authorized" discourse hardly resorts to Latin any longer; in literature, rare are the writers who switch to Latin, even very briefly for a title or a word or so, generally from the "official" erotic lexicon.[79] A growing ignorance of Latin and the loosening of moral attitudes have both had their effects here. When the British film director Derek Jarman was making his film *Sebastiane*, whose script is in Latin – part of the decadent thematic central to Jarman's *oeuvre* – he was forced by the incompetence of some actors in Latin to abridge their lines.[80] It really is all over, what the Goncourts coarsely called "going to bed with Latin books",[81] the fruitful commerce that Western civilization maintained with the classical tongue for centuries. Latin no longer says anything, or hides anything.

CHAPTER 10

Yearning for the Universal

A story by Jorge Luis Borges, *The Congress*, recounts the meeting of fifteen men in Buenos Aires at the beginning of the twentieth century to "create a world Congress representing all men of all nations". The question immediately arises of "what language the delegates would use". Two of the founders are sent abroad on a fact-finding trip. One of them, the narrator, goes to London where he spends time in the British Museum "in quest of a language that would be worthy of the world Congress"; there, while considering various possibilities for a universal language – including Esperanto, Volapük and "John Wilkins's analytical language" – he is brought to consider "the arguments for and against the resurrection of Latin, nostalgia for which has dogged our footsteps for centuries".[1] The fact is that in real life and on many occasions Latin has been put forward as a solution to the problem of communication between all the peoples of the earth, to cut through the Babel of the modern world. There were proposals to bring it back into use, and it was used as a source for the construction of auxiliary international languages. Behind these various efforts and projects lay a belief in some of the values associated with Latin, whose common denominator was the universality attributed to that language.

1 Claims to Universality

Latin had history on its side. Over the centuries it had acquired real claims to universality by being the language of three great powers, political, religious and intellectual, which had ruled over immense territories: the Roman Empire, the Church, the Republic of Letters. It could justly be presented as "the common interpreter of the most cultivated nations".[2] Much was made of this tradition which conferred on the classical tongue something signally lacking from ever-changing modern vernaculars: a "privilege of perpetuity".[3]

That alone, however, was far from sufficient to make it a universal language, and even on these points Latin had its opponents. In seventeenth-century England, for example, it was denounced by fanatical puritans as the language of Rome, the Catholic Church, "the Beast".[4] At the same time the world of scholarship, anxious to possess a universal language that would also be clear, regular, precise and concise, in keeping with the new learning, expressed reservations on the intellectual qualities of Latin. Comenius took the view that, quite apart from being difficult to learn, the language had several defects: the large number of its different cases, the irregularity of its declensions, conjugations and syntax, its weakness in composite words, and its frequent ambiguity. Similar criticisms are made by John Wilkins in his *Essay Towards a Real Character and a Philosophical Language* (1668), and more generally by fabricators of philosophical languages in the late seventeenth and early eighteenth centuries. These proposed a variety of solutions to a single problem: how to establish a rational, perfectly logical language for written and oral communication between all men, starting with scholars. Latin of course lacked this rational, logical character, and was widely criticized for it. Most scholars did not believe it could perform the role of international language; Leibniz for example thought that Latin – and a rectified and regularized Latin at that – could at best serve as a temporary stopgap between living languages and the philosophical language he dreamed of inventing.[5]

Latin nevertheless had real advantages, starting with the universality of its origin as the language of the Roman Empire. At the beginning of the modern era this aspect was much emphasized, especially in Italy where fragmentation and political divisions, internal and foreign wars, had led some to look backwards, seeking consolation in nostalgic memories of past grandeur. The language was by now the sole remnant of universal domination. To Lorenzo Valla (1407–57), the true grandeur of Rome and its heritage was not political but cultural. "We have lost Rome," he wrote in the preface to his *Elegantiae*,

> we have lost political dominance and power – albeit less through our own fault than the fault of the times – yet nevertheless, by virtue of this even more splendid power, we reign still over a large part of the world. Ours is Italy, ours is France, ours is Spain, along with Germany, Pannonia, Dalmatia, Illyria and many other nations. In fact, the Roman empire is where the language of Rome reigns.[6]

With mastery of the old language came the conviction of being eye to eye with the universe. This was an argument in Latin's favour and against the vernacular throughout the sixteenth century. In a lecture entitled *De latinae linguae usu retinendo*, given at Venice University in 1556, Carlo Sigonio sounded a little like Valla: "There is virtually no remnant of that former freedom, that ancient lustre, that past dignity that was once Italy's," he declared, "except the very honourable possession of this language, which once gave orders to the entire world"; he therefore invited his young listeners to cultivate the Latin language, so as not to leave all the glory for foreigners, and to enrol themselves in continuity with Rome in its greatness, when its empire stretched to the limits of the world.[7]

This universal value attributed to Latin explains why it appears to be a way of attaching a specific community to a larger group. When the first republic was being set up in Poland, Latin – which marked the "frontier" with the Byzantine world – was considered a factor of common identity between the various Slavic and non-Slavic peoples thus brought together in one state; at the same time it expressed the link with the West, with a form of civilization then considered of universal reach. This conviction was still alive in the 1950s, when a formula more than a century old was still current in Warsaw: "Europe ends where Latin ends".[8] Much the same was true in Czarist Russia which, we should remember, had no Latin tradition, the introduction of that language being a wholly imported phenomenon. The importance it came to have in the nineteenth-century *Gymnasium* curriculum has been interpreted as having a "denationalizing" effect, distracting the child from the concrete problems of his own country; this seems irrefutable given the instrumental use that was then made of Latin. But its promoters, from Peter the Great to Count Tolstoy, also wanted to bring Russia into the Republic of Letters, to attach it to the wider civilized world by adopting the classic ideal.[9]

The inherent universalism of Latin came to be interpreted as a *de facto* neutrality: a language belonging to all could not be seen as the possession of any one nation; it created no hierarchy between those who used it, and offended no sensibilities. It is not surprising that this projection of a fundamentally egalitarian mode should have earned it a lot of votes, initially in diplomatic circles. In 1653 the Swedish Chancellor Axel Oxenstierna spoke to the English Ambassador Bulstrode Whitelocke in

> clear, fluent and expressive Latin, and although he knew French he would not speak it, saying he did not understand why that nation should be honoured more than the others by foreigners being made to use its language. He thought Latin was richer, more valid and more appropriate, because the Romans had ruled a very large part of the world and Latin was no longer exclusive to any nation.[10]

Early in the nineteenth century, when French reigned supreme in diplomacy, protests were heard in England against a practice held to be "an admission of inferiority", and some suggested a return to Latin: "If it were restored . . . in diplomatic writings and negotiations, one instrument of dominion would be removed; and the several nations of Europe would meet in the cabinet on more equal terms".[11] In the twentieth century, petitions were sent to the League of Nations urging the adoption of an auxiliary international language; "some American groups" suggested the resurrection of Latin, emphasizing the advantage of its neutrality.[12]

The universal character attributed to Latin owes a great deal to its having existed before other languages. Rather than looking at the Latin origins of several West European languages, let us examine the normative role Latin has had in linguistic research on modern idioms. A classical exemplarism predominated until the middle of the eighteenth century; Latin remained the language of reference in any attempt to rationalize the linguistic domain, other languages being judged by their degree of concordance with it. The description of Latin was extended and used as a model for grammar in general, and carried authority in the elaboration of grammars for other languages. Thus, according to Georges Gusdorf,

> the first French grammars are constructed along two convergent lines. The first of these is found in Latin teaching methods: in order to be better understood by the pupil, the master translates wholly or in part either explanatory text, or examples, or paradigms, or all of them; the structure of the Latin language, and the analyses that describe it, offer, so to speak, a double or image of French. The second line is outside, but hinged on Latin; it seeks to identify common denominators in the Latin and French cultures to assert the worth of our young idiom.[13]

What may seem more surprising is that this normative role attributed to Latin could be applied just as thoroughly to a non-Romance language like English. Ben Jonson compiled an English grammar on the Latin model in 1623; in 1624, John Hewes published an English grammar whose title summarizes the effort that had been made to impose order on English by making it conform with Latin: *A Perfect Survey of the English Tongue Taken According to the Use and Analogies of the Latine*. Attempts to reduce English to rules like the ones in Lily's Latin grammar were by no means rare, and Latin was also a model for the crazed reformers who wanted to recreate English with tonal suffixes and improve it with explicit grammatical gender (some even dreamed of establishing the Latin gerundive). While most of those ideas stayed in the realms of utopia, the notion that Latin "guides our language" became a basic element of grammatical teaching in English. One consequence was the attempt by some authors of textbooks to introduce formal designations of case, which English lacks. Lindley Murray, the author of the *Grammar of the English Language* (1795) that most influenced teaching in England and the United States for at least a century, in commonsense fashion criticized other grammars for making too many distinctions, and dismissed the idea that English had "as many cases as Latin". He nevertheless listed six Latin cases in the singular and plural along with their English equivalents: "nominative: a Lord, Lords; genitive: Lord's, of a Lord, of Lords; dative: to a Lord, to Lords; accusative: a Lord, Lords; vocative: o Lord, o Lords; ablative: by a

Lord, by Lords".[14] The extraordinary authority with which Latin drove grammarians to seek, and find, systems of declension to impose on languages that
did not have them, lasted for a considerable time longer. Early in the twentieth century the Danish linguist Otto Jesperson, denouncing the Latin
"straitjacket" in which grammatical analysis imprisoned modern idioms, lam-
basted a Birmingham University professor of classical literature who had
written an English grammar which listed five cases for nouns: "nom. rat, voc.
o rat, acc. rat, gen. rat's, dat. rat, and in the plural: rats, o rats, rats, rats' and
rats".[15]

As well as being used for many years as a grammatical model, Latin was
also a vast reservoir of words on which people could draw at need. We have
already seen that the sciences resorted to it on a large scale; everyday and
literary language benefited too. To limit ourselves to one example, the neol-
ogizers in eighteenth-century France were all "convinced, even rabid Latinizers". Rétif de la Bretonne reminded his "fellow citizens in general that, the
French tongue being a dialect of Latin, all words can be borrowed from it;
and that all that are taken from it, whether directly or by analogy, are clear,
and above all French". Louis Sébastien Mercier, who was vocally opposed to
Latin "for all", nevertheless in his book *Néologie* gave the classical tongue as
the source of a number of words used (and in some cases created) by him:
agreux (*agrosus*), ascendre (*ascendere*), attédier (*ad taedium*), calcable (*calcare*),
cathédrant (*ex cathedra*), etc.[16]

More generally, Latin seemed to represent an indispensable "switchboard"
even to a man like Diderot, who favoured a sharp reduction of its role in education. In 1741–42 he had translated Temple Stanyan's *History of Greece* from
English. For this job, which was well paid and good for his literary reputation, he used a knowledge of English apparently acquired mainly through his
own efforts and by using an English–Latin dictionary. So he suggests, in any
case, in the "encyclopédie" entry, in the famous work of that name:

> nothing is a worse idea for a Frenchman who knows Latin than to learn English
> using an English–French dictionary instead of an English–Latin one. Whether
> the English–French dictionary has been compiled or corrected in accordance
> with an unvarying and common measure, or even based on an extensive and
> regular use of either language, we do not know; for each word we have to rely
> on good faith and the enlightenment provided by our guide or interpreter; when
> making use of a Greek or Latin dictionary, on the other hand, we are illumi-
> nated, satisfied, reassured by what we learn; we assemble our own vocabulary in
> the only way – if there can be said to be one – that is almost equal to having
> direct commerce with the foreign nation whose idiom is being studied. For the
> rest, I am speaking from my own experience: this method has served me very
> well; I regard it as a sure way of acquiring in a short time very accurate notions
> of correctness and force.

No matter from our point of view that translations based on this method were "not exempt from offences against language", as the *Journal des savants* reported in its description. What counts here is the character of "unvarying and common measure" attributed to Latin in relation to modern languages.[17] Diderot again thought of giving this role as a reliable intermediary to Latin in 1767, when he was working on a project for a Russian encyclopaedia to be composed in French by him and translated into Russian by "others". "When I have finished," he announced, "I will go to St Petersburg in person to confer with my Seventy" (in this case the members of the Russian academy of science). "By means of Latin, which will serve as common go-between, we will give the translation all the conformity possible with the original."[18]

Latin's claim to be recognized as a common standard was made more convincing by its claim to be eternal. Such was Ferdinand Brunétière's view when he wrote, on the characters of languages: "There are languages that sing, there are others that draw or paint. Latin engraves, and what it engraves is ineradicable. One might say that something that is not universal or eternal cannot be Latin".[19] Quite apart from its history, its use on innumerable inscriptions had made it the language of marble and bronze, a tongue as imperishable as the materials on which it was graven. We know that partisans of Latin for inscriptions in the modern era used this argument in support of their position. It was again used in Italy during the fascist period, when the exaltation of "Romanness" led to restoration of the epigraphic tradition: Latin inscriptions, which had inscribed in the stone and marble of ancient monuments and churches "the will to dominion, to power and everlastingness" of emperors and popes, was expected to become "an essential element in the Regime's works".[20]

This specialized use of Latin as the language of inscriptions stayed in force for so long in the Western world that it ended by giving the old language a sort of inner strength. Guido Bacelli, who was Minister of Public Instruction in various Italian governments, made a speech to the Senate in 1894 celebrating, along with the Latin language and the virtues of the Romans, "the plastic strength [*scultoria*] with which this great people spoke".[21] It may be that this is also one of the reasons why authors chose to give their writings, especially shorter pieces, and poems above all – I am thinking here of Victor Hugo in particular – titles in Latin. This lapidary quality, the *brevitas* of Latin and its unchangeability, may be what made it a way of saying the essential and at the same time inscribing it for ever.[22] What is offered here as an interpretation carried for the so-called Decadent writers the force of profound conviction. Thus, to one of the Romans in Jean Richepin's *Contes de la décadence romaine*, a writer worthy of the name had to use "a choice Latin, with words as clear and hard as diamonds, with full and sonorous phrases, able to stand up by themselves heavy as bronze plaques", and should write "a sonorous Latin solid as a stele . . . of this unique jewel enchased by me in the bronze of an indestructible prose". The desire to imitate the lapidary form and thus give the literary work longevity and universality underlies José Maria de Hérédia's *Epigraphic Sonnets*: in this sequence of poems evolved out of Latin epigraphs and printed in Roman capitals, "the page becomes," as Marie-France David points out, "a votive marble carved by their hand", and has the durability and solidity of marble conferred on it.[23]

So Latin, by its historical qualifications and record, was not just a universal language – and here its role in the aptly-named Catholic Church should be borne in mind[24] – but also became, through the uses that were made of it, a language with a vocation to state the universal.

2 Latin as "Universal Language and Language of Convention"

In modern Europe, during the rise of the vernaculars, Latin seemed to be the only solution. We have already seen that a number of works originally in the vernacular were translated into Latin to give them a proper circulation, to ensure their wider diffusion.[25] Certainly the multiplication of vernaculars started to pose problems to scholars at a very early date. Marin Mersenne complained in a letter written in 1640 that "neither God nor science is linked to any language in particular, and all of them, in effect, are capable of expressing anything; but the trouble is we need to know all of them, to share in the labours of those writing in the ones we do not understand." He hoped at least for the creation of

> some kind of excellent academy composed of 15 or 20 men of substance and learning from each nation, and this in each several kingdom that they might have responsibility for translating into the common tongue of Christian Europe, which is Latin, those works they judged worthy of that language, so that all could have their say.[26]

A century later, d'Alembert, in the "Discours préliminaire" to the *Encyclopédie*, started from the same observation and expressed a similar hope. After noting, with approval, the growing practice of writing in the vernacular, he also noted the "inconvenience" that resulted from each country writing in its own language,

> So that . . . by the end of the eighteenth century, a philosopher who wants to know all about the work of his predecessors will have to burden his memory with seven or eight different languages; and after using up the most precious years of his life learning them, he will die before starting to learn anything. The use of Latin, whose absurdity has been exposed in matters of taste, can be of much value only in works of philosophy, all of whose merit lies in their clarity and

precision, and which need no more than a universal language of convention. It is thus to be hoped that this practice will be re-established. But there are no grounds for optimism.[27]

In this he was mistaken.

In fact the intellectual world produced many pleas, and even some plans, for a revival of Latin. These efforts reached a peak around the end of the nineteenth century and the beginning of the twentieth, when the Babel of modernity looked like posing a threat to learning itself. In 1800, scientific works had been published in Europe in ten (or so) different languages; a century on, scholarship was having to contend with twenty. The problem appeared most acutely in a new setting for intellectual sociability that had made its appearance in the middle decades of the century and rapidly spread and multiplied: international conferences. The weakness of scientists in foreign languages, and the increase in the number of nations taking part in these gatherings – from two or three in the early 1880s to six or seven by 1914 – hampered true discussion, reducing sessions to straightforward reading of papers which some of the audience could hardly follow. The linguistic obstacle became increasingly important as the rapid fragmentation and specialization of disciplines made international meetings into an essential forum in the quest for true scientific synthesis. Hence the need for a language to serve as a vehicle for international exchanges; Leibniz's and Wilkins's idea of a constructed philosophic language was long gone, and what was needed now was a conventional instrument that would lend itself to the communication of scholarship in general, and its newer forms in particular. Among the solutions envisaged was the adoption of a national language, perhaps the one spoken by the largest number of Europeans, or perhaps one that had the right to serve as auxiliary language for historical, political, cultural or linguistic reasons. In the turn-of-the-century context of strong national tensions, the rival claims of French or English on one side and German on the other were a more or less insuperable obstacle to the adoption of a national language.[28]

All of this largely explains why there were still calls for a return to Latin. The rapid success and equally rapid decline of the artificial language Volapük here weighed in Latin's favour: there really was a possibility that an international language might be adopted, and the elegance of Latin, its literature and tradition, gave it superior claims in the view of its supporters. One of the earliest of these ardent advocates was the Italian Minister of Public Instruction, Guido Baccelli, who proposed several times that Latin should become the language of international conferences; in his capacity as a professor of medicine, incidentally, Bacelli had practised what he preached, addressing the Paris International Medical Congress of 1867 in Latin.[29] But the most interesting and imposing attempt was the proposal by an Englishman, George Henderson, to set up a *Societas Internationalis Latinitatis Modernae*. It had the

support of eminent scholars and scientists, including in France Egger, Col-
lignon, Havet, Salomon, Reinach, Maurice Prou, Alcide Macé, and also the
economist Paul Leroy-Beaulieu, a professor of the Collège de France, who
affirmed in 1888: "It is not as a literate person that I write, but as an economist. I believe that Latin is one of the strengths in reserve for the civilization
of the future; for, on mature consideration, I prefer Latin to Volapük." Differences quickly arose, however, between the purist bearers of classical Latin
and supporters of a utilitarian mediaeval Latin that would be adapted to
modern needs and realities; in 1901, ten years after his project had been
launched, Henderson gave up, convinced that there was no chance of Latin
being adopted as an international language, even by scholars.[30] Others persisted, however, for example Professor Hermann Alexander Diels, a member
of the Berlin Academy of Science: an illustrious philologist, he was a tireless
promoter of widespread Latin teaching on the double basis that every cultivated German should know it and that it was "a neutral means of communication". He gave his backing to the establishment in 1900 of popular Latin
courses in Berlin, for adults wishing rapidly to acquire enough of a smattering to read a few lines of Latin. In 1912 he was still convinced that Latin could
make an international language, although he now admitted that it might need
to be simplified a little.[31] Over the same few years, Latin had been trying hard
to make a place for itself in international meetings, hopes to that effect being
expressed at the second and third International Congresses of the Historical
Sciences (Paris, 1900; Rome, 1903).[32] The first congress of the Società Elleno-
Latina, held in Rome in 1903, discussed the question of Latin as "a language
for international use", and heard the proposal that an "international Latin
college" be established in Rome; all the familiar arguments in favour of Latin
were aired, and there was much emphasis on its fulfilling "the condition of
being an idiom that is *neutral* in today's struggle between the national languages".[33] This same neutrality was the best point in Latin's favour in 1919
when the International Research Council in Brussels discussed the problem
of an international auxiliary language; given the deficiencies of the artificial
languages and the "jealousies" that the choice of English would surely arouse,
the old language possessed undeniable advantages: it had peerless historical
and literary qualifications, and triggered no national prejudices.[34] The same
argument was used in Italy a few years later to impose Latin as "a language
for international exchanges" (this time, however, in a strongly nationalist
context). Under the Fascist regime, various bodies proposed that Latin be
used for international conferences on a level of parity with the five major
modern languages. Some went even further: in a letter to the prime minister
dated 26 April 1933, the Circolo di Cultura fra i Ragioneri dell'Urbe
expressed full support for the proposal made at the third national Congress
of Roman Studies that Latin be used to facilitate international exchanges;
after recalling in grandiloquent style the universal and eternal qualities of

Latin, the letter pointed out that this most "learned" of languages would also be handy for "spreading the fascist spirit" abroad.[35]

But while its supporters insisted that Latin was especially qualified to be the international auxiliary language the intellectual world so urgently needed, others pointed out that it was difficult to learn and had irregular constructions, lacunae and ambiguities. It was also argued again and again that any linguistic option involving Latin would have awkward consequences. The purist solution of strictly classical Latin would hamper the full expression of modern realities, especially in scientific areas, except by means of intricately roundabout periphrases tiresome to decipher; a modern, simplifying option would risk evolving a Latin that had nothing in common with the classical version, and that in the final analysis would hardly differ from an *a posteriori* artificial language formed on a Latin base. As a result there would eventually be two languages instead of one: fixed classical Latin and evolving neo-Latin, unless the latter chased out the former like debased currency. In any case, the aim being pursued – communication between men – would surely not be achieved.[36]

These objections, and a revealing paucity of practical achievements – a handful of more or less ephemeral periodicals, a few articles in learned journals like *Anthropos* and a number of speeches at conferences[37] – did not prevent Latin from being promoted as a language of communication yet again during the 1950s. The association for "living Latin", which lobbied in this direction, held the old language to be the only solution to "the Babel of modernity". In a 1952 article the movement's kingpin, Rector Capelle, pointed to the "contrast" between "the power of technical means of communication and the weakness of the apparatus available to men for understanding their foreign-language counterparts". He underlined the poor showing in practice of artificial languages like Esperanto, and the difficulty he thought any modern language would have in securing the role: "that would mean, in effect, that one of the nations had managed to dominate the others and impose its own law on the rest of the world". He therefore proposed a return to Latin, not because of its literary qualities but for practical reasons. It would not only provide a solution to the disarray of the world of learning, but also be a means of strengthening scientific sociability in particular and human solidarity in general. The article ended with a declaration of faith in Latin as "an instrument marvellously adapted to the commerce of things and ideas, and therefore a powerful factor of progress, fraternity and peace".[38] Having recruited to his cause many members of the teaching profession, led by the grammarian Jean Bayet and other university professors, Capelle held the first of the movement's international conferences at Avignon in 1956. The great majority of participants at these meetings, at least among those giving papers, were teachers of Latin or humanities; very few were the "scientists and technicians" that Capelle, himself a scientist by training, had aimed to attract in the first place. At the first congress there was agreement on four points intended to "create permanent means to bring Latin to life", to make it a "utilitarian" or "practical" language: a simplified grammar; a standardized pronunciation (the "restored" version); modern teaching methods; and principles for the formation of neologisms. At the end of the congress, the participants were invited to "enter into relations with scientific colleagues to involve them in the development of Latin as an international scientific language"; and it was recommended: "Firstly – That in scientific collections of international interest (critical editions of ancient texts, classical lexicons, etc.) Latin be used instead of national languages; Secondly – That in scientific journals, articles of international interest be written in or accompanied by a summary in Latin."[39]

The same concern with practicalities lay at the heart of the second congress, which took place at Lyon in 1959 on the theme of "Latin: means of connection". Rector Capelle was clear on the goal being pursued: "it is just not enough for Latin to be used to bring extra distinction to the elegance of a culture," he said, adding (probably to the distaste of some of his audience) "something that the practice of other languages and disciplines could doubtless also develop"; and he insisted on the "active role in the oral and written transmission of thought between men" that "living Latin" would be expected to fulfil. The hopes and recommendations expressed at Avignon were reiterated; in addition, Unesco and other international organizations were asked to press international periodicals and conferences to make a place for Latin, at least in summaries, and the hope was expressed that Unesco would publish short Latin résumés of scientific works. Lastly, the establishment of a Latin periodical was approved, to be called *Vita latina* and serve as a link between all the supporters of "living Latin".[40] Like the first, this congress comprised an overwhelming majority of teachers of Latin or humanities; but among the more noteworthy testimonies published in the collected papers was one from a M. Gain, director of a research institute for oils and oil sources. This expressed full adherence to the cause of "living Latin", ran through its qualifications for use, including its "neutrality", and held it up as the only solution "that will enable us to understand one another and above all to understand the Asiatics whose scientific role is increasing daily".[41]

Further Congresses of Living Latin were held at Strasbourg in 1963, Avignon in 1969 and Pau in 1976. By that time the initial enthusiasm had declined considerably. The dropping of Latin in sixth grade had altered the conditions; in any case practical achievements had been few, and although interest had been international, it had hardly existed outside the circle of academics teaching classics, so that the conferences, or anyway their papers, were hardly more than professional seminars. The dream that had once been nurtured of "living Latin" as a remedy to the modern Babel had ended by fading away ingloriously. All that remains of the career as an international auxiliary language once postulated for Latin is one last faint trace: appeals for the institutions of the European Community to make room for Latin alongside the modern languages in which they publish their documents.[42] So far these requests have been without effect.

3 A Basis for Artificial International Languages

Although Latin could not be restored to the role of "universal language and language of convention", to use d'Alembert's expression, it nevertheless served as a reference (or, to be more precise, a source) for the many international artificial languages planned and formed between 1880 and 1914. Most of these – there were 116 all told – were so-called *a posteriori* languages, based on the grammatical structures and semantic roots of existing languages, often drawing on Latin itself, either exclusively or in part.[43] Although these projects were especially numerous in the period between 1880 and 1914, the wave of invention persisted: fifteen new *a posteriori* languages based exclusively on Latin were proposed between the end of the First World War and 1948, including Simplified Latin (Neuchâtel, 1925), Latino Viventi (Turin, 1925), Latinesco (Birkenhead, 1925), Neo-Latinus (Buenos Aires, 1939), Latini (Albany, NY, 1941), Universal Latein (Vienna, 1947) and Europa Latin (Amsterdam, 1948).[44]

The inventors of these languages borrowed widely from Latin, and they explained why. In 1887, the German philologist von Grimm saw Latin as the most appropriate language to serve as a guide in forming fundamental roots, having the triple advantage of being a dead language, of being closely related to all the Indo-European language groups, and being already known – to the educated at least – in all nations. Others shared this point of view. Eugen O. Lauda, the originator of Kosmos (Berlin, 1888), gave the same reasons for his wide borrowings from Latin for its vocabulary, adding that "cultivated people who have studied Latin will know the universal language in advance". A. Volk and R. Fuchs, the creators of Weltsprache (Berlin, 1905), used Latin vocabulary as a base "because not only is it known to all cultivated people, it is also the foundation of the Romance languages".[45]

These *a posteriori* systems all use Latin and are consequently not without similarities. They all start with the principle of international lexicological elements, the differences residing in the way this principle is applied; either they start with Latin and add neologisms taken from non-Romance modern languages or, starting from the principle of internationality, they give a preponderant role to Latin elements.[46] It is not surprising that the inventors of these languages should have chosen, in naming them, to underline the Latin element or the universal element, which boil down to the same thing. To give a few examples, we could mention Nov Latin (Turin, 1890), Universalia (Stuttgart, 1893), Latino Sine Flessione (1903), Lingua Internacional (Warsaw,

1905) and Novilatin (Leipzig, 1907).[47] Another result is that the names are sometimes very similar indeed, and one has to be careful not to confuse Latinesce (London, 1901) with the Latinesco cited above, Latino Sine Flexione (1903) with Latin Sin Flexion (1929), Novilatiin (Leipzig, 1895) with Novilatin (Leipzig, 1907), or Neo-Latin (Hungary, 1920) with Neo-Latina (Holland, 1920), Neolatine (Bologna, 1922), Neolatino (Sweden, 1927) and Neo-latinus (Buenos Aires, 1939).

Behind the diversity of solutions adopted, all of these languages obey the same principle: simplification. Moreover, a number of them start from critiques of some earlier attempt, aiming to improve on it and make it easier to learn and use. A few words of Neolatinus illustrate this ambition: *Lingua neolatina est fachilissima, nam constat verbis latinis et modernis et insuper ábeat solum duas declinasionas, unam pro verbis másculis et álteram pro verbis femineis* ("Neolatinus is very easy, for it includes Latin and modern words and moreover has only two declensions, one for masculine words and the other for feminine words").[48] Despite the efforts of their fabricators, however, none of these languages, intended to be morphologically and syntactically simpler than natural languages (encumbered as these are with rules, irregularities and ambiguities) ever progressed beyond the status of projects; so far as we know, the "very easy" Neolatinus was never spoken. There is much to amuse in the bizarre ingenuity of some of these languages, not to mention the linguistic delirium of the inventors themselves; but there is something striking, too – moving even – in their impassioned quest for an ideal language that would facilitate exchanges. However, what these (usually rather strange) constructions really reveal is a linguistic imagination in which, between hope and chimera, Latin through its universal dimension provided a guarantee for the future: people from all over the world were going to understand one another in perfect transparency, and the curse of Babel would be lifted at last.

We now need to return to Borges's story. We left the narrator working in the British Museum; and his quest for a universal language had been fruitless. The chairman of the World Congress declared, in effect, that the Congress had "started with the first moment of the world's existence and will still continue after we have become dust. It is not based anywhere".[49] In other words, the World Congress – meaning the whole of humanity – is and will always be multilingual. An optimistic interpretation of this fable leaves the possibility that, despite the diversity of languages, there might be real communication between men. This is close to "the possibility of companionship in a continent multilingual by vocation" mentioned by Umberto Eco in the conclusion of his study on the quest for a perfect language.

> The problem of European culture in the future certainly does not reside in the triumph of total polyglotism . . . but in a community of individuals capable of grasping the spirit, the scent, the atmosphere of a different language. A polyglots'

Europe is not a Europe of persons who speak a lot of languages, but at best of persons who can communicate by speaking their own languages and understanding other people's, persons who, although they cannot speak other languages fluently and may have difficulty understanding them, do understand the "genius", the cultural universe, conveyed by anyone who is speaking the language of his ancestors and his tradition.[50]

At this point, with the question of a universal language no longer relevant, Latin would no longer have any use or purpose, and no one would even miss it.

Conclusion

When Edgar Faure ended sixth-grade Latin in 1968, the Secretary of State for Education commented: "We are in the process of initiating what amounts to a genuine demystification".[1] One cannot help recalling the conclusion drawn by Anthony Grafton and Lisa Jardine, in their study of humanist schooling, on the survival of the classical pedagogic ideal into the twentieth century: that there had been a "mystification of liberal education".[2] From this point of view, the decline of Latin in secondary schools and its consequent erasure in the Western world should be welcomed as a salutary and authentic liberation. Here we think, not without compassion, of the generations of children who struggled and groaned under the weight of a Latin too bulky for their young shoulders, while their masters added insult to injury by viewing their generally mediocre output in terms of profit and loss: "We should not worry unduly about the immense waste apparent in the record of classical teaching," wrote Pierre Grimal, a Sorbonne professor, in 1959; "the waste is negligible, so long as a single seed has taken root".[3] The suppression of compulsory Latin did put an end to much pointless suffering and fruitless effort; one cannot say, however, that it put an end to a fraud as well.

Because really, after what we have learned from this study, to talk about mystification would be abuse of language. There was never, in the pedagogic world, any considered wish to mystify, to pull the wool over anyone's eyes or deform reality; but on the contrary a sincere belief – widely shared outside the academic universe – in the powers of Latin, and in a number of values that were attributed to it everywhere. So an illusion, perhaps, but not a fraudulent trick, and still less the void suggested by H.G. Wells when he compared teachers of humanities to people endlessly fiddling with the keys to an empty room.[4] Throughout this study, what we have found has been not a void but its opposite, something filled to bursting. The preceding pages show in some detail the multiplicity of uses to which Latin has been put by different societies at different times: training and educating children, praying to God, carrying learning, "classifying" men, saying the unsayable, communicating with the universe. Not only did Latin have multiple uses, but the things that were said about it were as numerous as they were different, even contradictory: this astonishing plasticity made it lend itself to everything, made it apt for saying anything, legitimizing anything. Of course the uses and the things said did not always work perfectly, but well enough on the whole to sustain belief: so they bolstered each other mutually, and in their synergy took root, enduring through their presence in the institutions of major importance in people's lives: in all countries, school, and in Catholic countries, the Church.

These remarks expose what is exaggerated in giving English the title of "the Latin of the twenty-first century". While it is true that this language today performs an important role in international exchanges – and there is no reason to suppose that this role will not become larger still in future – for those who use it in this way it is reduced to a simple vehicle of instrumental thought, an auxiliary working language. As a consequence of this eminently practical function, English does not carry for those using it – with the exception of course of those whose language it is – a corpus of cultural references; and a major difference of course is that English lacks a symbolic capital common to the whole of Europe, a capital composed not only of texts, both sacred and profane, but also of shared values, beliefs and experiences.[5]

It seems appropriate at this point to examine the disappearance of Latin which, it is not without interest to note, occurred everywhere in the Western world during the 1960s. Purely linguistic reasons can be dismissed at once. By that time, vernaculars had everywhere sealed the fate of the old language centuries earlier, and (except in ecclesiastical circles) the use of Latin, whether written or spoken, was already extremely limited. It cannot be denied that the measures taken by the tutelary institutions – the Church and the education system – were severe, even mortal blows. But it is worth remembering that Latin was already in decline and that these brutal measures, painful though they may have been, accompanied an evolving situation. One could say, in fact, that Latin died of exhaustion; but certainly not exhaustion of the language itself which had been dead since at least the eighteenth century. On that end, historians and neo-Latin literature specialists are in agreement, although their explanations are markedly divergent. In the historians' view, "the decline of Latin was due not to those opposed to the classical heritage, but to its own promoters, the humanists, whose insistence on the classical norm ended by turning Latin into a dead language". The vitality of Latin – mediaeval Latin – had been irremediably broken by the humanist restoration, and neo-Latin, "a reconstitution by committee", had subsequently lived an artificial, specious existence; its death was in some sense written into its very renewal. Neo-Latin specialists support an opposite point of view, hinged on fifteenth- and sixteenth-century works and writings of literary type: the decline and death of Latin had nothing to do with the humanists; indeed they had given it new life, or at least prolonged its existence, until its reduction to the school and university world eventually proved fatal.[6] No matter from our point of view. The exhaustion of which Latin died in the 1960s was not exhaustion of the language. Latin disappeared because it no longer meant anything to the contemporary world. All that it had once embodied – a certain idea of humanity, a form of discrimination, a system of power, a universal outlook, with an underlying conception of society, its order, its standards – no longer carried meaning, or was being said differently, and the hegemonic cultural model to which it referred was now victoriously rivalled.

Under these conditions it is clear that Latin will no longer be playing – that it cannot play – the role it once played. It is not unreasonable, though, at the end of this inquiry, to consider its future. So far as the present situation is concerned, there are various possibilities, starting with the break from and rejection of "an apparatus of obsolete old rubbish" so radically expressed by Alain Bosquet in the aftermath of May 1968 with his rousing cry of "Down with Latin!" In the "atomic age", he wrote, there were other priorities; when you had to be of your own time, there was no longer a place for Latin; a symbol of the past, glorious and sick, it had no obvious function in a society of the living and had found itself naturally cast in the role of a "monument to the dead". Bosquet went on: "We should incline our heads in passing to our monuments to the dead, but not make a religion of them".[7] Without irony, that is probably the most widespread current attitude: Latin these days is something glimpsed in the antique-shop window, arousing respectful indifference rather than passion, with perhaps a few well-polished "campaign stories" from the veterans who once "did it". At the other end of the spectrum is the full restoration currently on display in St Petersburg. A humanist *Gymnasium* was founded in the Czars' former capital in 1989: it gives children a schooling heavily dominated by Latin, with two sections for written and spoken Latin. This institution – exceptional in many ways – was not only a pedagogic project, but expressed a desire to attach Russia to the Western world through Latin and classical culture, an echo in a sense of the measures taken by Peter the Great and Count Tolstoy.[8] Outside the academic world Latin has become, for those who still use it, a reservoir of words and sounds. When Peter Greenaway uses a Latin text as a pictorial decoration,[9] when Jean-Luc Godard has Latin verses chanted in his "self-portrait",[10] when the Compagnie Générale des Eaux rebaptizes itself Vivendi,[11] these borrowings from a world which has become foreign – if not yet exotic – seem to express a wish to make meaning out of the very strangeness of the words. So Latin would seem to be functioning in the same way as the eighteenth-century fashion for beautifully-drawn Chinese characters as wall decoration in aristocratic houses: their actual meaning – sometimes they had none – was of little importance, so that those seeing them could read into them whatever they liked. Thus, the chief executive of the former Compagnie Générale des Eaux explained the choice of the Latin name Vivendi – in itself a pure verbal form, to be precise the genitive of the gerundive – as follows: "It's a warm name, full of life and movement, that resembles our services."

Since the reduction of Latin to a decorative motif is obviously deeply unsatisfactory, and abandoning the study of Latin altogether would be as excessive, in my opinion, as a total restoration along St Petersburg lines, I would suggest a fourth possibility that also represents a radical change from the traditional pedagogic approach: Latin as a language and its study as a speciality. Latin is long dead and buried, and that makes everything much simpler. We do not have the problem that faced the men of the eighteenth century, who dithered over the method for teaching a language that was "neither living, nor dead".[12] Nevertheless, the study of this language – this dead language – should not reproduce the work of anatomy carried out on a corpse[13] that Latin teaching used to be until the 1960s, still less the superficial smattering imparted today in the context of optional Latin. At this point we can do no better than embrace the opinion given in a classics text used by Italian universities: "Latin will be saved not by making many study it badly, but by making a few study it well. In other words, the study of Latin should be reserved for professionals of humanist literary culture." The necessarily prolonged training of these future specialists would be based systematically on "texts drawn from all Latinity, but also with discrimination from the Middle Ages and the humanist period".[14] Providing the means to read Latin fluently: that is what the primary objective of Latin teaching should be. Not so much to read the classics – which, as Diderot remarked, have been translated and retranslated a hundred times – as to have access to those wellsprings of our own culture, the Fathers of the Church and the *Corpus juris*, along with the colossal mass of documents, both manuscript and printed, that contains much of the record of our ancestors' lives and thought through the Middle Ages and into the modern era. One can only hope that Latin will finally become a speciality in the full sense of the word. That is its best chance, and our best hope, if we want the words Europe and memory to have real meaning in the cultural order.

Select Bibliography

Only works on Latin are listed here. Sources and works which were only partially or indirectly relevant have been left out, although some of these provided a lot of information. Similarly, the works of general history and social, religious and cultural history which were consulted and used are not listed. These can be found through the index, as can the methodological works used in the analysis of documents.

General Works on Latin in the Modern Period

This bibliography focuses mainly on literary aspects but also gives general information:

Ijsewijn, Jozef, *Companion to Neo-Latin Literature.* part I: *History and Diffusion of Neo-Latin Literature* (second entirely rewritten edition), Leuven University Press, 1990 (a second volume is in preparation).

The proceedings of the congresses of the International Association of Neo-Latin Studies concentrate mainly on literary works and on the period from the Age of Humanism to the seventeenth century; they contain some articles on the teaching of Latin and the history of knowledge:

Ijsewijn, J. and Kessler, E. (eds), *Acta conventus neo-latini lovaniensis. Proceedings of the First International Congress of Neo-Latin Studies, Louvain 23–28 August 1971*, Munich, Wilhelm Fink Verlag, 1973.

Tuynman, P., Kuiper, G.C. and Kessler, E. (eds), *Acta conventus neo-latini amstelodamensis. Proceedings of the Second International Congress of Neo-Latin Studies. Amsterdam, 19–24 August 1973*, Munich, Wilhelm Fink Verlag, 1979.

Margolin, Jean-Claude (ed.), *Acta conventus neo-latini turonensis. Tours, 6–10 septembre 1976. 3e Congrès international d'études néo-latines*, Paris, Vrin, 1980.

Schoeck, Richard J. (ed.), *Acta conventus neo-latini bononiensis. Proceedings of the Fourth International Congress of Neo-Latin Studies. Bologna 26 August to 1 September 1979*, Binghamton, Medieval and Renaissance Texts and Studies, 1985.

McFarlane, I.D. (ed.), *Acta conventus neo-latini sanctandreani. Proceedings of the Fifth International Congress of Neo-Latin Studies, St Andrews 24 August to 1 September 1982, Binghamton, Medieval and Renaissance Texts and Studies, 1986.

Revard, Stella P., Rädle, Fidel and Di Cesare, Mario A. (eds), *Acta conventus neo-latini guelpherbytani. Proceedings of the Sixth International Congress of Neo-Latin Studies. Wolfenbüttel 12 August to 16 August 1985*, Binghamton, Medieval and Renaissance Texts and Studies, 1988.

Dalzell, Alexander, Fantazzi, Charles and Schoeck, Richard J. (eds), *Acta conventus neo-latini torontonensis. Proceedings of the Seventh International Congress of Neo Latin Studies. Toronto, 8 August to 13 August 1988*, Binghamton, Medieval and Renaissance Texts and Studies, 1991.

Rhoda Schnur *et al.*, *Acta conventus neo-latini hafniensis. Proceedings of the Eighth International Congress of Neo-Latin Studies (1991)*, Binghamton, Medieval and Renaissance Texts and Studies, 1994.

For a general overview

Burke, Peter, "*Heu domine, adsunt Turcae*", in *Lingua, società e storia*, Bari, Laterza, 1990, pp. 33–104.

For a single country or period

Axer, Jerzy, "Latin in Poland and East-Central Europe: Continuity and Discontinuity", *European Review*, 2 (1994), pp. 305–9.

Béranger, Jean, "Latin et langues vernaculaires dans la Hongrie du XVIIe siècle", *Revue Historique*, CCXLII (1969), pp. 5–28.

Binns, James W., *Intellectual Culture in Elizabethan and Jacobean England: The Latin Writings of the Age*, Leeds, Francis Cairns, 1990.

Brunot, Ferdinand, *Histoire de la langue française des origines à nos jours*, vol. II: *Le XVIe siècle*; vol. III: *La formation de la langue classique 1600–1660*; vol. V: *Le français en France et hors de France au XVIIe siècle*; vol. VII: *La propagation du français en France jusqu'à la fin de l'Ancien Régime*; vol. IX: *La Révolution et l'Empire*, Paris, Librairie Armand Colin, 1966–7 (new edition). (Although the subject of this work is French it is by far the best study on Latin in France from the sixteenth to nineteenth centuries.)

Cian, Vittorio, "Contro il volgare", in *Studi letterari e linguistici dedicati a Pio Rajna*, Florence, Ariani, 1911, pp. 251–97.

Feo, Michele, "Tradizione latina", in Alberto Asor Rosa (ed.), *Letteratura italiana*, vol. V, *Le questioni*, Turin, Einaudi, 1986, pp. 311–78.

Cesbron, George and Richer, Laurence (eds), *La réception du latin du XIXe siècle à nos jours. Actes du colloque d'Angers des 23 et 24 septembre 1994*, Angers, Presses de l'Université, 1996.

Reinhold, Meyer, *Classica Americana. The Greek and Roman Heritage in the United States*, Detroit, Wayne State University, 1984.

The Teaching of Latin

A large number of publications on education between the sixteenth and twentieth centuries naturally devote some space to Latin. Only those particularly or primarily on Latin and its study and teaching are listed below.

General and comparative studies

Bierlaine, Franz, "Colloqui di scuola e educazione infantile nel XVI secolo", in Egle Becchi and Dominique Julia (eds), *Storia dell'infanzia*. I. *Dall'Antichità al Seicento*, Bari, Laterza, 1996, pp. 204–30. (French translation: *Histoire de l'enfance en Occident*. I. *De l'Antiquité au XVIIe siècle*, Paris, Seuil, 1998.)

Bierlaine, Franz, "Le jeu à l'école et au collège', in Philippe Ariès and Jean-Claude Margolin, *Les jeux à la Renaissance*, Paris, Vrin, 1982, pp. 489–97.

Garin, Eugenio, *L'educazione in Europa. 1400/1600. Problemi e programmi*, Bari, Laterza, 1976. (French translation: *L'éducation de l'homme moderne. La pédagogie de la Renaissance*, Paris, Hachette, 1995.)

Grafton, Anthony and Jardine, Lisa, *From Humanism to Humanities: Education and Liberal Arts in Fifteenth- and Sixteenth-Century Europe*, London, Duckworth, 1986.

Jacob, Maurice, "Étude comparative des systèmes universitaires et place des études classiques au XIXe siècle en Allemagne, en Belgique et en France", in M. Bollack, H. Wismann and Theodor Lindken (eds), *Philologie und Hermeneutik im 19. Jahrhundert*, Göttingen, Vandenbroek & Ruprecht, 1983, pp. 108–40.

Wülfing, Peter, "L'enseignement des langues anciennes en Europe", *L'Athénée*, 69 (March–April 1980), pp. 22–6.

France

Bellot-Antony, Michel and Hadjadj, Dany, "La querelle de l'enseignement des langues dans l'*Encyclopédie*', in *Eclectisme et cohérence des Lumières. Mélanges offerts à Jean Ehrard*, Paris, Nizet, 1992, pp. 35–53.

Chervel, André, *Les auteurs français, latins et grecs au programme de l'enseignement secondaire de 1800 à nos jours*, Paris, INRP, Publications de la Sorbonne, 1986.

Choppin, Alain, *Les manuels scolaires en France de 1789 à nos jours*, vol. 3: *Les manuels de latin*, Paris, INRP, Publications de la Sorbonne, 1988.

Colombat, Bernard, "La description du latin à l'épreuve de la montée des vernaculaires", in Sylvain Auroux (ed.), *Histoire des idées linguistiques*, vol. 2: *Le développement de la grammaire occidentale*, Liège, Mardage, 1992, pp. 509–21.

Colombat, Bernard, "Les grammaires latines en France", *Dix-huitième siècle*, 27 (1995), pp. 25–41.

Compère, Marie-Madeleine and Pralon-Julia, Dolorès, *Performances scolaires de collégiens sous l'Ancien Régime. Étude de six séries d'exercices latins rédigés au collège Louis-le-Grand vers 1720*, Paris, Institut National de la Recherche Pédagogique, Publications de la Sorbonne, 1992.

Falcucci, Clément, *L'humanisme dans l'enseignement secondaire en France au XIXe siècle*, Toulouse, Privat; Paris, Didier, 1939.

Gascard, Carole, "L'enseignement du latin au XVIIe siècle à travers les textes théoriques et les grammaires", diploma thesis, Paris, 1994, manuscript.

Hummel, Pascale, *Humanités normalienne: L'enseignement classique et l'érudition philologique dans l'École normale supérieure du XIXe siècle*, Paris, Les Belles Lettres, 1995.

Institut National de Recherche et de Documentation Pédagogique, "Controverses autour du latin: eléments bibliographiques", Paris, 1974, manuscript.

Julia, Dominique, "Livres de classe et usages pédagogiques", in Henri-Jean Martin and Roger Chartier (eds), *Histoire de l'édition française*, vol. II: *Le livre triomphant, 1660–1830*, Paris, Promodis, 1984, pp. 468–97.

Sicard, Augustin, *Les études classiques avant la Révolution*, Paris, Librairie Académique Didier, Perrin & Cie, 1887.

Other countries

L'affaire du latin. Réquisitoires et plaidoiries, Lausanne, F. Rouge et Cie, 1954.

Borle, Jean-Pierre, *Le latin à l'Académie de Lausanne du XVIe au XXe siècle*, Lausanne University, 1987.

Campbell, F., "Latin and the Elite Tradition in Education", in P. W. Musgrave (ed.), *Sociology, History and Education. A Reader*, London, Methuen & Co., 1970, pp. 249–64.

Clarke, M.L., *Classical Education in Britain, 1500–1900*, Cambridge University Press, 1959.

Druet, François-Xavier, "Cinquante ans de 'disparition' des langues anciennes dans l'enseignement secondaire", *Les études classiques*, LII (1984), pp. 291–9.

Fedeli, Paolo, "Studio e uso del latino nella scuola fascista", in *Matrici culturali del fascismo*, Bari, SIE, 1977, pp. 209–24.

Kagan, Richard L., "Il latino nella Castiglia del XVII e del XVIII secolo", *Rivista storica italiano*, LXXXV (1973), pp. 297–320.

Murru, Furio and Pessolano Filos, Giuseppe, *Alla riscoperta della didattica del latino in Italia nel Settecento e nell'Ottocento*, Rome, Edizioni Nuova Rivista Pedagogica, 1980.

Raicich, Marino, "Itinerari della scuola classica dell'Ottocento", in Simonetta Soldani and Gabriele Turi (eds), *Fare gli Italiani. Scuola e cultura nell'Italia contemporanea*, vol. I: *La nascita dello Stato nazionale*, Bologna, Il Mulino, 1993, pp. 131–70.

Stray, Christopher, *Classics Transformed: Schools, Universities and Society in England, 1830–1960*, Oxford University Press, 1998.

Stray, Christopher, *Grinders and Grammars: A Victorian Controversy*, Reading, The Text Book Colloquium, 1995.

Church Latin

Borella, Pietro, "La lingua volgare nella liturgia", *Ambrosianum*, XLIV (1968), pp. 71–94, 137–68, 237–66.

Coletti, Vittorio, *L'éloquence de la chaire: victoires et défaites du latin entre Moyen Âge et Renaissance*, Paris, Éditions du Cerf, 1987 (first published Casale Monferrato, 1983).

Schmidt, Hermann A.P., *La constitution de la sainte liturgie: texte, genèse, commentaire, documents*, Brussels, Éditions Lumen Vitae, 1966.

Schmidt, Hermann A.P., *Liturgie et langue vulgaire: le problème de la langue liturgique chez les premiers réformateurs et au concile de Trente*, translated from the Dutch, Rome, apud Aedes Universitatis Gregorianae, 1950.

Latin, Language of Learning

Basile, Bruno, "Uso e diffusione del latino", in Lia Formigari (ed.), *Teorie e pratiche linguistiche nell'Italia del Settecento*, Bologna, Il Mulino, 1984, pp. 333–46.

Benner, Margareta and Tengström, Emin, *On the Interpretation of Learned Neo-latin: An Explorative Study Based on Some Texts from Sweden (1611–1716)*, Göteborg, Acta Universitatis Gothoburgensis, 1977.

Burke, Peter, "Translations into Latin in Early Modern Europe", in R. Avesani (ed.), *Il latino nell'età moderna*, Rome, Bulzoni, forthcoming.

Chartier, Roger and Corsi, Pietro (eds), *Sciences et langues en Europe*, Paris, École des Hautes Études en Sciences Sociales (1996). Chapters include: Ann Blair, "La persistance du latin comme langue de science à la fin de la Renaissance"; Isabelle Pantin, "Latin et langues vernaculaires dans la littérature scientifique européenne au début de l'époque moderne (1550–1635)"; Jeanne Peiffer, "La création d'une langue mathématique allemande par Albrecht Dürer. Les raisons de sa non-réception"; Anne Rasmussen, "A la recherche d'une langue internationale de la science 1880–1914".

Grant, W. Leonard, "European Vernacular Works in Latin Translation", *Studies in the Renaissance*, I (1954), pp. 120–56.

Stearn, William T., *Botanical Latin: History, Grammar, Syntax, Terminology and Vocabulary*, London, Nelson, 1966.

Latin Pronunciation

Allen, W. Sidney, "Some Observations on the Pronunciation of Latin", *Didaskalos*, 1 (1963), pp. 45–63.

Beaulieux, Charles, "Essai sur l'histoire de la prononciation du latin en France", *Revue des Études Latines*, V (1927), pp. 68–82.

Bonioli, Maria, *La pronuncia del latino nelle scuole dall'Antichità al Rinascimento*, Turin, Giappichelli, 1962.

Brittain, Frederick, *Latin in Church: Episodes in the History of its Pronunciation, Particularly in England*, Cambridge University Press, 1934.

Couillaut, Camille, *La réforme de la prononciation latine*, Paris, Bloud et Cie, 1910.

Damas, Pierre, *La prononciation française du latin depuis le XVIe siècle*, Paris, Les Belles Lettres, 1934.

Macé, Alcide, "La prononciation du latin dans l'Eglise catholique", *Revue des cours et conférences*, 21 (1912–13), pp. 62–6.

Marouzeau, Jules, *La prononciation du latin (histoire, théorie, pratique)*, Paris, Les Belles Lettres, 1955 (fourth edition).

"La pronuncia del latino nelle scuole", *MAIA*, 18 (1966), pp. 254–62, 19 (1967), pp. 255–78.

Ranum, Patricia, *Méthode de la pronciation dite vulgaire ou à la française: petite méthode à l'usage des chanteurs et des récitants d'après le manuscrit de Dom Jacques Le Clerc*, Arles, Actes Sud, 1991.

Renaudet, Augustin, "Erasme et la prononciation des langues antiques", *Bibliothèque d'Humanisme et Renaissance*, 18 (1956), pp. 190–6.

Latin as a Universal Language

Couturat, Louis and Léau, Léopold, *Histoire de la langue universelle*, Paris, Hachette, 1903–07.

Eco, Umberto, *La ricerca della lingua perfetta nella cultura europea*, Bari, Laterza, 1993 (French translation: *La recherche de la langue parfaite dans la culture européenne*, Paris, Seuil, 1997).

Ijsewijn, Jozef and Sacré, Dirk, "The Ultimate Efforts to Save Latin as the Means of International Communication", *History of European Ideas*, 16 (January 1993), pp. 51–66.

Knowlson, James, *Universal Language Schemes in England and in France, 1600–1800*, University of Toronto Press, 1975.

Notes

Introduction

1 Jean-François Domenget, "La langue de l'exil: Montherlant et le latin", in Georges Cesbron and Laurence Richer (eds), *La réception du latin du XIXe siècle à nos jours. Actes du colloque d'Angers des 23 et 24 septembre 1994*, Angers, Presses de l'Université, 1996, pp. 311–19 (p. 311).

2 James W. Binns's book *Intellectual Culture in Elizabethan and Jacobean England: The Latin Writings of the Age* (Leeds, Francis Cairns, 1990) represents, even for the period covered – 1530–1640 – a notable exception. It is a pity however that to support his conviction that "The history of Western civilization is in fact written in Latin" the author should have followed an exclusively enumerative and descriptive course.

3 For convenience I refer to my book co-written with Hans Bots, *La république des lettres*, Paris, Belin-De Boeck, 1997.

4 Peter Burke's panoramic article *"Heu domine, adsunt Turcae"*, in *Lingua, società e storia*, Bari, Laterza, 1990, pp. 33–104, contains more description than analysis.

5 Jozef Ijsewijn's *Companion to Neo-Latin Literature* is the best illustration of the current vitality of neo-Latin studies: published in 1977, it was republished, with the first three chapters amended, in 1990, and a second volume is in preparation. For the most recent period, see Jacques Chomarat's account in "Les études néo-latines en France (et un peu hors de France), 1983–1993", in *Nouvelle revue du seizième siècle*, 12 (1994), pp. 91–107.

6 For an example of this, see issue 27 (1995) of *Dix-huitième siècle* devoted to Antiquity.

7 Henri-Jean Martin, *Livre, pouvoirs et société à Paris au XVIIe siècle (1598–1701)*, Geneva, Droz, 1969, p. 607.

8 With one exception: Marie Madeleine Compère and Dolorès Pralon-Julia, *Performances scolaires de collégiens sous l'Ancien Régime. Étude de six séries d'exercices latins rédigés au collège Louis-Le-Grand vers 1720*, Paris, Institut National de la Recherche Pédagogique, Publications de la Sorbonne, 1992.

9 I am in full agreement with the viewpoint of Anthony Grafton and Lisa Jardine (*From Humanism to the Humanities: Education and the Liberal Arts in Fifteenth- and Sixteenth-Century Europe*, London, Duckworth, 1986, p. xii).

10 In this context, casting doubt on Latin really amounted, as Jean Travers noted, to "taking on the drama of a civilization" (Introduction to issue 11 [1947] of *Maison-Dieu*, devoted to "liturgical languages and translations").

1 "Latin Country": School

1 Quoted by Ferdinand Brunot, *Histoire de la langue française des origines à nos jours*, vol. VII: *La propagation du français en France jusqu'à la fin de l'Ancien Régime*, Paris, Librairie Armand Colin, 1967, p. 126. Abbé Halma gives a similar view, 1791 (Dominique Julia, *Les trois couleurs du tableau noir: la Révolution*, Paris, Belin, 1981, p. 250).

2 Augustin Sicard, *Les études classiques avant la Révolution*, Paris, Librairie Académique Didier, Perrin & Cie, 1887, pp. 50–51; Ferdinand Brunot, *Histoire de la langue française des origines à nos jours*, vol. V: *Le français en France et hors de France au XVIIe siècle*, Paris, Librairie Armand Colin, 1966, pp. 32–43; François Lebrun, Marc Venard, Jean Quéniart, *Histoire générale de l'enseignement et de l'éducation en France*, vol. II: *De Gutenberg aux Lumières*, Paris, Nouvelle Librairie Française, 1981, pp. 294 and 438; Dominique Julia, "Livres de classe et usage pédagogiques", in Henri-Jean Martin and Roger Chartier (eds), *Histoire de l'édition française*, vol II: *Le livre triomphant, 1660–1830*, Paris, Promodis, 1984, pp. 468–73; Carole Gascard, "L'enseignement du latin au XVIIe siècle à travers les textes théoriques et les grammaires", diploma thesis, Paris, 1994, manuscript, pp. 34–6 (p. 36).

3 A. Sicard, *Les études classiques*, p. 47.

4 The statutes of the Faculty of Arts in Paris (1598) stipulated that "when in college, none of the students are to speak in the vulgar tongue, but the Latin tongue should be a familiar usage to them" (Georges Gusdorf, *Les sciences humaines et la conscience occidentale*, VI: *L'avènement des sciences humaines au siècle des Lumières*, Paris, Payot, 1973, p. 132). Again, in 1667, according to the Jesuit Pomey, form-masters ought to press on their disciples "the gentle but indispensable necessity always to speak Latin, not only in class and among themselves but at home and everywhere else and with all persons who are not ignorant of that tongue" (D. Julia, "Livres de classe", p. 487).

5 Marie-Madeleine Compère and Dolorès Pralon-Julia, *Performances scolaires de col-légiens sous l'Ancien Régime. Étude de six séries d'exercices latins rédigés au collège Louis-Le-Grand vers 1720*, Paris, Institut National de la Recherche Pédagogique, Publications de la Sorbonne, 1992, pp. 160, 241, 246.

6 A. Sicard, *Les études classiques*, pp. 48–9.

7 On colleges under the Ancien Régime and "secondary" education, see generally *Encyclopédie pratique de l'éducation en France*, published under the patronage and with the help of the Institut Pédagogique National, Paris, IPN and SEDE, 1960, pp. 627–9; F. Lebrun, M. Venard, J. Quéniart, *Histoire générale de l'enseignement*, pp. 315–73 and 501–47; A. Sicard, *Les études classiques*; G. Gusdorf, *Les sciences humaines*, VI, pp. 129–37; Lawrence Brockliss, *French Higher Education in the Seventeenth and Eighteenth Centuries: A Cultural History*, Oxford, Clarendon Press, 1987; Marie-Madeleine Compère, "Collèges", in *Dictionnaire de l'Ancien Régime: royaume de France, XVIe–XVIIIe siècle*, published under the direction of Lucien Bély, Paris, PUF, 1996, pp. 278–82; M.-M. Compère and D. Pralon-Julia, *Performances scolaires*; C. Gascard, "L'enseignement du latin".

8 Ferdinand Brunot, *Histoire de la langue française des origines à nos jours*, vol. III: *La*

formation de la langue classique 1600–1660, Paris, Librairie Armand Colin, 1966, pp. 717–18.

9 Translator's note: The numbering of classes in the modern French *lycée* is the reverse of the system used in British and American schools. Twelve-year-olds arriving at the *lycée* enter the class of *sixième*, which I have rendered as sixth grade (equivalent to British Year 7 or US seventh grade) and graduate from the top class, which I have called first grade, the equivalent of the British sixth form/US twelfth grade. So French "fifth grade" is the equivalent of US eighth grade, fourth grade the equivalent of US ninth grade and so on. Secondary education in France, as elsewhere, lasts from the age of twelve to the age of eighteen, although some children leave at sixteen or seventeen.

10 F. Lebrun, M. Venard, J. Quéniart, *Histoire générale de l'enseignement*, p. 514; Agnès Cornevin, "La *Ratio studiorum* du père Houbigant, témoignage de l'enseignement oratorien des humanités", in Jean Ehrard (ed.), *Le collège de Riom et l'enseignement oratorien en France au XVIIIe siècle*, Paris, CNRS Editions; Oxford, Voltaire Foundation, 1993, pp. 133–9; Michel Bellot-Antony and Dany Hadjaj, "L'enseignement des langues à Riom et à Effiat", in *ibid.*, pp. 191–225; Peter France, "La rhétorique chez les Oratoriens au XVIIIe siècle", in *ibid.*, pp. 239–49.

11 Anacharsis Combes, *Histoire de l'école de Sorèze*, Toulouse, L. Jougla, 1847, pp. 7–31.

12 Joël Fouilleron and Anne Blanchard, "Réforme et éducation, positions et propositions", in *La réforme et l'éducation*, Toulouse, Privat, 1972, pp. 181–90.

13 Quotation from D. Julia, "Livres de classe", p. 485.

14 F. Brunot, *Histoire de la langue française*, vol. VII, pp. 100–105; D. Julia, "Livres de classe", pp. 485–8; André Chervel, "L'enseignement des langues dans les collèges de l'Oratoire", in J. Ehrard (ed.), *Le collège de Riom*, p. 232; L. Brockliss, *French Higher Education*, p. 192.

15 F. Brunot, *Histoire de la langue française*, vol. VII, pp. 90–101.

16 Apart from the general works listed in note 7, see Michel Bellot-Antony and Dany Hadjaj, "La querelle de l'enseignement des langues dans l'*Encyclopédie*", in *Eclectisme et cohérence des Lumières. Mélanges offerts à Jean Ehrard*, Paris, Nizet, 1992, pp. 35–53.

17 Bernard Magne, *Crise de la littérature française sous Louis XIV: humanisme et nationalisme*, Lille III, 1976, pp. 390–91.

18 F. Brunot, *Histoire de la langue française*, vol. V, pp. 58–9; vol. VII, pp. 110–13.

19 Ferdinand Brunot, *Histoire de la langue française des origines à nos jours*, vol. IX: *La Révolution et l'Empire*, Paris, Librairie Armand Colin, 1967, p. 109.

20 *Ibid.*, pp. 110–27 and 268–75 (p. 112); Bronislaw Baczko, *Une éducation pour la démocratie: textes et projets de l'époque révolutionnaire*, Paris, Éditions Garnier, 1982; D. Julia, *Les trois couleurs*, ch. VII.

21 F. Brunot, *Histoire de la langue française*, vol. IX, pp. 423–75.

22 Jules Simon, *Premières années*, Paris, Flammarion, n.d., p. 83.

23 Quotation from Jean Palacio, "Parler latin en français: ou l'écolier limousin à la fin du XIXe siècle", in Georges Cesbron and Laurence Richer (eds), *La réception du latin du XIXe siècle à nos jours: actes du colloque d'Angers des 23 et 24 septembre 1994*, Angers, Presses de l'Université, 1996, p. 247.

24 Victor Hugo, *Les contemplations*, in Jean Martin (ed.) *Oeuvres complètes: édition chronologique*, Paris, Club Français du Livre, 1971, vol. IX, book. 1, p. 74.

25 F. Brunot, *Histoire de la langue française*, vol. V, p. 39 (footnote).

26 J. de Palacio, *Parler latin*, p. 247.

27 Apart from a brief reversion to French from 26 March to 8 September 1829. Clément Falcucci, *L'humanisme dans l'enseignement secondaire en France au XIXe siècle*, Toulouse, Privat; Paris, Didier, 1939, pp. 140, 150, 153.

28 Antoine Prost, *Histoire de l'enseignement en France, 1800–1967*, Paris, Armand Colin, 1968, pp. 53–61, 245–51; Françoise Mayeur, *Histoire générale de l'enseignement et de l'éducation en France*, vol. III: *De la Révolution à l'école républicaine*, Paris, Nouvelle Librairie de France, 1981, pp. 499 ff.; André Chervel, *Les auteurs français, latins et grecs au programme de l'enseignement secondaire de 1800 à nos jours*, Paris, INRP, Publications de la Sorbonne, 1986, p. 4.

29 F. Mayeur, *Histoire générale*, p. 511; A. Prost, *Histoire de l'enseignement*, p. 251.

30 *Encyclopédie pratique de l'éducation*, pp. 629–30; A. Prost, *Histoire de l'enseignement*, p. 254.

31 Pascale Hummel, *Humanités normaliennes: l'enseignement classique et l'érudition philologique dans l'École normale supérieur du XIXe siècle*, Paris, Les Belles Lettres, 1995, ch. 1.

32 Bruno Neveu, "L'Église et l'Université de France: les facultés de théologie catholique des académies (1808–1885)", doctoral thesis, Paris, 1993, manuscript.

33 Alain Choppin, *Les manuels scolaires en France de 1789 à nos jours*, vol. 3: *Les manuels de latin*, Paris, INRP, Publications de la Sorbonne, 1988, pp. 18–19.

34 A cartoon that appears in Louis Reybaud, *Jérôme Paturot à la recherche d'une position sociale*, Paris, J.-P. Dubochet, Le Chevalier et Cie, 1846, pp. 422–3. I am greatly indebted to Michèle Sacquin for drawing this document to my attention.

35 Gustave Flaubert, *Madame Bovary*, Paris, Gallimard, 1972, p. 24; Maxime Du Camp, *Souvenirs Littéraires*, Preface by Daniel Oster, Paris, Aubier, 1994, p. 116 (Du Camp also mentions Flaubert's impositions); V. Hugo, *Les contemplations*, p. 86.

36 Anatole France, *La vie en fleur*, in *Oeuvres complètes*, Paris, Calmann-Lévy, 1932, vol. XXII, ch. 6, "La bifurcation" (p. 354).

37 On nineteenth-century educational reforms in France, see F. Mayeur, *Histoire générale*, pp. 499–514; A. Prost, *Histoire de l'enseignement*, pp. 55–60, 245–57; R.D. Anderson, *Education in France, 1848–1870*, Oxford, Clarendon Press, 1975, p. 38 ff.; and especially on the "Latin question", C. Falcucci, *L'humanisme dans l'enseignement secondaire*.

38 Corinne Saminadayar, "Du latin comme langue naturelle de l'écriture", in *La réception du latin*, pp. 161–8.

39 P. Hummel, *Humanités normaliennes*, pp. 34, 37.

40 A. Prost, *Histoire de l'enseignement*, pp. 252–65 and 416–21 (p. 260); *Education, société et politique: une histoire de l'enseignement en France, de 1945 à nos jours*, Paris, Seuil, 1992, pp. 76–81 (p. 78).

41 Jean Guéhenno, "La querelle des humanités", in *La table ronde* (March 1959) p. 18; "La querelle du latin", in *ibid.*, pp. 28–9.

42 *Encyclopédie pratique de l'éducation*, pp. 632, 636–7, 639–40.

43 Translator's note: *Agrégation*, literally "admittance", is the system that in France appoints teachers by competitive public examination.

44 A good bibliography of these writings has been assembled by the Institut National de Recherche et de Documentation Pédagogiques, entitled "Controverses autour du latin: éléments bibliographiques", Paris, 1974, manuscript. The article by E. de Saint-Denis appeared in the *Bulletin de l'Association Guillaume-Budé* (June 1954), pp. 21–36.

45 A. Prost, *Education*, pp. 148 and 166 (footnote 3); text of the edict in *Bulletin officiel de l'Education nationale*, 39 (1968), pp. 2939–40.

46 On 8 October 1968 in the National Assembly, while presenting the law on the orientation of higher education, and on 18 October during a speech to the general conference of Unesco.

47 Fernand Robert, "Chronique de la lutte pour nos études", in *Bulletin de l'Association Guillaume-Budé* (1976), 3, p. 245.

48 For one example among many, that of the academy of Montpellier, see Raymond Cuby (Inspecteur Pédagogique Régional), "L'enseignement des langues anciennes dans les *lycées*", in *L'information littéraire*, 36, no. 2 (March/April 1984), p. 78.

49 *Bulletin de l'Association Guillaume-Budé* (1992), 3, p. 229.

50 S.E.L., *Colloque sur l'avenir des humanités*, May 1995, manuscript, p. 3.

51 A. Choppin, *Les manuels*, p. 18.

52 At least, according to the brochure *Recherches. Ressources. Structures. Guide 1996–1997*, published by that body in 1996.

53 S.E.L., *Comptes rendus* of general assemblies held on 10 February 1996 and 22 February 1997, manuscript.

54 G. Gusdorf, *Les sciences humaines*, VI, p. 129.

55 M.L. Clarke, *Classical Education in Britain, 1500–1900*, Cambridge University Press, 1959, ch. 1.

56 Paul F. Grendler, "The Teaching of Latin in Sixteenth-Century Venetian Schools", in Richard J. Schoeck (ed.), *Acta conventus neo-latini bononiensis: Proceedings of the Fourth International Congress of Neo-Latin Studies, Bologna 26 August to 1 September 1979*, Binghamton, Medieval and Renaissance Texts and Studies, 1985, pp. 258–76.

57 Franz Bierlaine, "Colloqui di scuola e educazione infantile nel XVI secolo", in Egle Becchi and Dominique Julia (eds), *Storia dell'infanzia*, I: *dall'Antichità al Seicento*, Bari, Laterza, 1996 (*Histoire de l'enfance en Occident*, I: *de l'Antiquité au XVIe siècle*, Paris, Seuil, 1998), pp. 204–30; Franz Bierlaine, "Le jeu à l'école et au collège", in Philippe Ariès and Jean-Claude Margolin (eds), *Les jeux à la Renaissance*, Paris, Vrin, 1982, pp. 489–97.

58 Jean-Luc Le Cam, "La politique scolaire d'Auguste le Jeune de Brunswick-Wolfenbüttel et l'inspecteur Cristoph Schrader, 1635–1660/1680", doctoral thesis, University of Paris IV, 1992, manuscript, pp. 277–82 (p. 281). I quote from the manuscript which the author was kind enough to make available; this thesis was published in 1996 by the Herzog August Bibliothek at Wolfenbüttel under the title *Politique, contrôle et réalité scolaire en Allemagne au sortir de la guerre de Trente Ans*.

59 *Ibid.*, *passim* (p. 634); Kristian Jensen, "The Latin Grammar of Philipp Melanchthon", in Stella P. Revard, Fidel Rädle, Mario A. Di Cesare (eds), *Acta conventus neo-latini guelpherbytani: Proceedings of the Sixth International Congress of Neo-Latin Studies, Wolfenbüttel 12 August to 16 August 1985*, Binghamton, Medieval and Renaissance Texts and Studies, 1988, pp. 513–19.

60 Miriam Usher Chrisman, *Lay Culture, Learned Culture: Books and Social Change in Strasbourg, 1480–1599*, Yale University Press, 1982, pp. 192–201; Pierre Schang and Georges Livet (eds), *Histoire du Gymnase Sturm, berceau de l'Université de Strasbourg, 1538–1988*, Strasbourg, Oberlin, 1988, p. 245.

61 Jean-Pierre Borle, *Le latin à l'Académie de Lausanne du XVIe au XXe siècle*, Lausanne University, 1987, chs 1 and 4 (p. 47).

62 Marijke Spies, "Amsterdam School-Orations from the Second Half of the 17th Century", in *Lias*, 22 (1995), pp. 99–118.

63 Max J. Okenfuss, "The Jesuit Origins of Petrine Education", in J.G. Garrard (ed.), *The Eighteenth Century in Russia*, Oxford, Clarendon Press, 1973, pp. 106–30.

64 Meyer Reinhold, *Classica Americana: The Greek and Roman Heritage in the United States*, Detroit, Wayne State University, 1984, pp. 25–8.

65 M.L. Clarke, *Classical Education*, p. 35. Also see Rosemary O'Day, *Education and Society, 1500–1800: The Social Foundations of Education in Early Modern Britain*, London, New York, Longman, 1982, p. 69.

66 Vittorio Alfieri, *Vita scritta de esso*, vol. I, edited by Luigi Fasso, Asti, Casa d'Alfieri, 1951, p. 31.

67 Quoted from a letter by his mother Lady Waldegrave to Thomas Walpole the younger, dated Navestock, 4 July 1792 (*Horace Walpole's Correspondence*, vol. 30: *Horace Walpole's Correspondence with the Walpole Family*. Edited by W.S. Lewis and Joseph W. Reed Jnr., with the assistance of Edwine M. Martz, New Haven, Yale University Press, 1973, p. 284).

68 Roberto Ballerini, "Alla ricerca di un nuovo metodo: il corso grammaticale nel secolo dei Lumi", in Gian Paolo Brizzi (ed.), *Il catechismo e la grammatica*, vol. I: *istruzione e controllo sociale nell'area emiliana e romagnola nel Settecento*, Bologna, Il Mulino, 1985, p. 232.

69 M.L. Clarke, *Classical Education*, p. 47.

70 J.-P. Borle, *Le latin*, p. 54.

71 Anthony J. La Vopa, *Grace, Talent and Merit: Poor Students, Clerical Careers and Professional Ideology in Eighteenth-Century Germany*, Cambridge University Press, 1983, pp. 63 and 81. Quotation from Karl Philipp Moritz, *Anton Reiser* (translated by Georges Pauline), Paris, Fayard, 1986, p. 134.

72 Gian Paolo Brizzi, *La formazione della classe dirigente nel Sei-Settecento*, I: *Sminaria nobilium nell'Italia centro-settentrionale*, Bologna, Il Mulino, 1976, pp. 225–6.

73 R. Ballerini, "Alla ricerca", pp. 236–75; Anna Maria Bernardinis, "Una riforma di due secoli fa (G. Gozzi e il problema del latino)", in *Rassegna di pedagogia*, 23 (1965), pp. 307–68.

74 M. Reinhold, *Classica Americana*, chs 2 and 4 (p. 63).

75 Ambrose Jobert, *La commission d'éducation nationale en Pologne (1773–1794)*, Paris, Les Belles Lettres, 1941.

76 Marina Roggero, *Insegnar lettere: ricerche di storia dell'istruzione in età moderna*, Piacenza, Edizioni dell'Orso, 1992, pp. 137–203.

77 Peter Burke, *Lingua, società e storia*, Bari, Laterza, 1990, p. 45; G. Gusdorf, *Les sciences humaines*, VI, p. 130.

78 Juan Gutiérrez Cuadrado, "La sustitución del latín por el romance en la universidad española del siglo XVIII", in *Universidades españolas y americanas: epoca colonial*, Valencia, Generalitat Valenciana, 1987, p. 239; Margarita Terremocha Hernández, *Ser estudiante en el siglo XVIII: la universidad vallisoletana de la Ilustración*, Valladolid, Junta de Castilla y León, 1991, pp. 27, 93, 95.

79 Antonio Favaro, *Galileo Galilei e lo studio di Padova*, Padova, Editrice Antenore, 1966, vol. I, pp. 137, 217; Antonio Vallisneri, *Epistolario*, vol. I, *1679–1700*, edited by Dario Generali, Milan, Franco Angeli, 1991, p. 524 (a letter in which Vallisneri complains of having to speak Latin for eight months of the year); on Beccaria, see V. Alfieri, *Vita*, book I, p. 44.

80 Sven Lunderström "Latin", in *Uppsala University 500 Years, 6: Faculty of Arts at Uppsala University; 2: Linguistics and Philology*, Uppsala, Almqvist & Wiskell, 1976, pp. 47–62; Rolf Westman, "Observations on Neo-Latin Scholarship in Finland",

in J. Ijsewijn and E. Kessler (eds), *Acta conventus neo-latini lovaniensis, Proceedings of the First International Congress of Neo-Latin Studies, Louvain 23–28 August 1971*, Munich, Wilhelm Fink Verlag, 1973, p. 718.

81 M.L. Clarke, *Classical Education*, pp. 66–7; Martha Ornstein, *The Role of Scientific Societies in the Seventeenth Century*, University of Chicago Press, 1928, pp. 237–8; Charles Edward Mallet, *A History of the University of Oxford*, vol. II: *The Sixteenth and Seventeenth Centuries*, New York, Barnes & Noble; London, Methuen & Co, 1968, pp. 9, 44, 179, 201, 240. See (for Cambridge) John Twigg, *A History of Queens' College, Cambridge, 1448–1986*, Woodbridge, The Boydell Press, 1987, p. 217.

82 Edward G. Bill, *Education at Christ Church Oxford, 1660–1800*, Oxford, Clarendon Press, 1988, p. 250.

83 Franco Venturi, *Settecento riformatori: da Muratori a Beccaria*, Turin, Einaudi, 1969, pp. 526–31, 562–4.

84 M. Torremocha Hernández, *Ser estudiante*, pp. 95–7.

85 J.-P. Borle, *Le latin*, pp. 57–8, 63.

86 P. Burke, *Lingua*, p. 46; Lazzaro Spallanzani, *Edizione nazionale delle opere, parte seconda: lezioni; Scritti letterari*, edited by Pericle di Pietro, Modena, Mucchi Editore, 1994.

87 P. Burke, *Lingua*, pp. 46–7 (contains further examples involving inaugural lectures and official speeches).

88 John A. Armstrong, *The European Administrative Elite*, Princeton University Press, 1973, pp. 134 ff.

89 *Ibid.*, pp. 135–9; Maurice Jacob, "Etude comparative des systèmes universitaires et place des études classiques au XIXe siècle en Allemagne, en Belgique et en France", in M. Bollack, H. Wisman and Theodor Lindken (eds), *Philologie und Hermeneutik im 19. Jahrhundert*, Göttingen, Vendenbroeck & Ruprecht, 1983, p. 113; Rosalind M. O. Pritchard, *The End of Elitism? The Democratization of the West German University System*, New York, Oxford, Munich, Berg, 1990, pp. 148–50; Suzanne L. Marchand, *Down from Olympus: Archaeology and Philhellenism in Germany, 1750–1970*, Princeton University Press, 1996, pp. 117, 136–7; Jörg Biehl, "Le temps scolaire en Allemagne: les grands traits de son développement (XVIe–XIXe siècle)", in Marie-Madeleine Compère (ed.), *Histoire du temps scolaire en Europe*, Paris, INRP, Editions Economica, 1997, p. 36.

90 Marino Raicich, "Itinerari della scuola classica dell'Ottocento", in Simonetta Soldani and Gabriele Turi (eds), *Fare gli Italiani: scuola e cultura nell'Italia contemporanea*, I: *La nascita dello Stato nazionale*, Bologna, Il Mulino, 1993, pp. 131–70; Dario Ragazzini, "Le temps scolaire en Italie: entre la proclamation de l'Unité et l'affirmation des différences régionales", in *Histoire du temps scolaire*, p. 167.

91 M.L. Clarke, *Classical Education*, chs VI and VII; Rupert M. Wilkinson, *The Prefects: British Leadership and the Public School Tradition. A Comparative Study in the Making of the Rulers*, Oxford University Press, 1964, pp. 65–9; F. Campbell, "Latin and the Elite Tradition in Education", in P.W. Musgrave (ed.), *Sociology, History and Education: A Reader*, London, Methuen & Co, 1970, pp. 249–50; Anne Digby and Peter Searby, *Children, School and Society in Nineteenth-Century England*, London, Macmillan Press, 1981; and from among Christopher Stray's many articles, while awaiting publication of his book on Latin teaching in England, "The Smell of Latin Grammar: Contrary Imaginings in English Classrooms", in the *Bulletin of the John Rylands University Library of Manchester*, 76, 3 (1994), pp. 209–12.

92 Alexander Vucinich, *Science in Russian Culture: A History to 1860*, Stanford University Press, 1963, pp. 218–56; *Science in Russian Culture, 1861–1917*, Stanford University

Press, 1970, pp. 40–61; Patrick L. Alston, *Education and the State in Tsarist Russia*, Stanford University Press, 1969, pp. 66–86; Alain Besançon, *Education et société en Russie dans le second tiers du XIXe siècle*, Paris, La Haye, Mouton, 1974, pp. 15–27; James C. McClelland, *Aristocrats and Academics: Education, Culture and Society in Tsarist Russia*, University of Chicago Press, 1979, pp. 11–27.

93   M. Reinhold, *Classica Americana*, pp. 79–80; for attacks on the classics curriculum and its defence, see also Lawrence W. Levine, *The Opening of the American Mind: Canons, Culture and History*, Boston, Beacon Press, 1996, pp. 37–9.

94   August Strindberg, *Le fils de la servante*, in *Oeuvres autobiographiques*, vol. I, edited and introduced by Gustav Bjurström, Paris, Mercure de France, 1990, p. 83.

95   Wladimir Berelowitch, *La soviétisation de l'école russe, 1917–1931*, Lausanne, L'âge d'homme, 1990, pp. 38–9; Paolo Fedeli, "Studio e uso del latino nella scuola fascista", in *Matrici culturali del fascismo*, Bari, SIE, 1977, pp. 209–24; Michel Ostenc, *L'éducation en Italie pendant le fascisme*, Paris, Publications de la Sorbonne, 1980, pp. 338–9; Guido Calogero, "Il panlatinismo" (1955), in *Scuola sotto inchiesta*, Turin, Einaudi, 1965, pp. 35–45.

96   M. Reinhold, *Classica Americana*, pp. 343–4 (postface by George A. Kennedy); Harry N. Rivlin (ed.), *Encyclopaedia of Modern Education*, Port Washington, NY, Kennikat Press, 1943, p. 443; Lee C. Deighton (ed.), *The Encyclopaedia of Education*, New York, The Macmillan Company and The Free Press, 1971, vol. V, p. 344; John van Sickle, "Informatica e studi classici: Didattica e ricerca tra mito e mezzo", in Biagio Amata (ed.), *Culture e lingue classiche: convegno di aggiornamento e di didattica, Roma, 1–2 novembre 1985*, Rome, LAS, 1986, p. 65.

97   Birger Berth, "Renseignements sur l'étude du latin en Suède", in *Caesarodunum*, 3 (1969) p. 95; Anton van Hoof, "L'enseignement des langues anciennes aux Pays-Bas: Les études classiques dans une société bourgeoise", in *Bulletin d'information de la Fédération des professeurs de grec et de latin*, 91 (1994), p. 7 (warm thanks to Hans Bots for drawing this document to our attention); François-Xavier Druet, "Cinquante ans de 'disparition' des langues anciennes dans l'enseignement secondaire", in *Les études classiques*, LII (1984), p. 296. For other examples, see the section of *Caesarodunum* cited above and more generally, Peter Wülfing, "L'enseignement des langues anciennes en Europe", in *L'Athénée*, 69 (March–April 1980), p. 17.

98   M. Reinhold, *Classica Americana*, pp. 341–2 (Postface by George A. Kennedy); E. Triffou, "L'état des humanités classiques en Amérique deu Nord", *Caesarodunum*, 4 (1963), pp. 139–45; the figures are taken from *MLA Newsletter*, 28, 4 (winter 1996), pp. 1–2.

99   Cambridge dropped the requirement of Latin for all entrants in 1960–61; Oxford dropped it for scientists in 1960 and for all other entrants in 1978 (acknowledgements to James Raven for this information). In the more conservative public schools Latin continued in a strong position for some time: there were still 37 classics masters at Eton in 1965, but – and this is the major difference with the past – there were now 19 science masters, 13 teaching mathematics and another 19 teaching other languages including English (F. Campbell, "Latin", p. 251).

100 Jean-Maurice Nivat, "L'enseignement du Latin en France et en Allemagne", in *Repères: revue pour l'expansion des recherches éducatives et sociales*, 7 (July–September 1965), pp. 64–70. Thanks to Professors Rütten and Zimmermann for information provided.

101 René Freneaux, "Rosa la rose", in *Caesarodunum*, 3 (1969), pp. 101–5 (the introduction of *rosa* is due to Burnouf who thought there were more inconveniences

than advantages in using the same paradigm, *musa*, for Latin and Greek); Karl-Heinz Stubenrauch and Volker Zimmermann, *Kursus der Medizinischen Terminologie (Grammatik, Termini, Übungen)*, Göttingen, Georg-August-Universität, 1995, p. 3; Institut für Theorie und Geshichte der Medizin der Universität Münster, *Kursus der Medizinischen Terminologie*, Tecklenburg, Burgverlag, 1987, p. 16.

102 J.-M. Nivat, "L'enseignement", pp. 64–74.

103 Paul Monceaux and René Pichon, "L'enseignement du grec et du latin à l'étranger", in *Revue universitaire*, 10 (1901), pp. 252–6 (pp. 254 and 256).

104 Matthew Arnold, *Schools and Universities on the Continent*, edited by R.H. Super, Ann Arbor, University of Michigan Press, 1964, pp. 111–14, 240–42, 278–9.

105 René Hoven, "Programmes d'écoles latines dans les Pays-Bas et la principalité de Liège au XVIe siècle", in P. Tuynman, G.C. Kuiper and E. Kessler (eds), *Acta conventus neo-latini amstelodamensis: Proceedings of the Second International Congress of Neo-Latin Studies, Amsterdam, 19–24 August 1973*, Munich, Wilhelm Fink Verlag, 1979, pp. 546–59.

106 J.-L. Le Cam, "La politique scolaire", pp. 288–9, 693–4.

107 L. Brockliss, *French Higher Education*, pp. 136–9.

108 D. Julia, "Livres de classe", p. 483.

109 M. Reinhold, *Classica Americana*, p. 26.

110 *Encyclopédie pratique de l'education*, p. 632. An impression of "minor authors" was conveyed by the use of "selected pieces of prose and poetry" (from fourth to first grade) and a "choice of moral pages and thoughts" (final year); Paul Martin, "Le latin dans l'enseignement secondaire: rien ne va plus", in *Caesarodunum*, 3 (1969), p. 29.

111 Marc Genester, "Danger d'une double faillite en 4me", in *Cahiers pédagogiques*, 12 (12 October 1956), p. 50.

112 See, for example, L. Nadjo, "Le latin aux Etats-Unis", in *Caesarodunum*, 3 (1969), p. 70; J.-M. Nivat, "L'enseignement du latin", p. 72. But some works or authors might receive special attention in particular countries, like Tacitus's *Germania* in Germany.

113 D. Julia, "Livres de classe", p. 483.

114 René Hoven, "L'utilisation internationale des livres scolaires aux XVIe et XVIIe siècles, in *Gutenberg-Jahrbuch*, 1973, pp. 298–300; and more specifically, on M. Cordier's *Colloquia*, J.-P. Borle, *Le latin*, ch. 2; on Despautère's grammar, C. Gascard, "L'enseignement du latin" part III; on Melanchthon's grammar, K. Jensen, "The Latin Grammar", pp. 513–19.

115 Carlos Sommervogel, *Bibliothèque de la Compagnie de Jésus: nouvelle édition*, Brussels, O. Stephens; Paris, A. Picard, 1890–1900, see under Aler, Paul and Chastillon.

116 A. Jobert, *La commission d'éducation*, pp. 76–7.

117 Jozef Ijsewijn, *Companion to Neo-Latin Literature*, part I: *History and Diffusion of Neo-Latin Literature*, Leuwen University Press, 1990, pp. 119 and 321.

118 P. Wülfing, "L'enseignement", p. 27.

119 Information obtained at the launch of this CD-ROM during the "Journées de la Science" (University of Paris VII, 12 October 1996).

120 L. Brockliss, *French Higher Education*, p. 138; A. Chervel, *Les auteurs*, pp. 13–15.

121 M.L. Clarke, *Classical Education*, pp. 8 and 41; Marie-José Desmet-Goethals, "La littérature neo-latine ouest-flamande", in *Acta conventus neo-latini lovaniensis*, pp. 199–206; P.F. Grendler, "The Teaching of Latin", p. 263.

122 F. Bierlaine, "Le jeu", pp. 489–97 (p. 494).

123 L. Brockliss, *French Higher Education*, pp. 142, 150–51; M.L. Clarke, *Classical*

Education, pp. 167–8, 171–2; M. Reinhold, *Classica Americana*, pp. 25–7; R.D. Anderson, *Education in France*, p. 27; J.A. Armstrong, *The European Administrative Elite*, pp. 142–3.

124 M.L. Clarke, *Classical Education*, pp. 11 and 43.

125 M. Reinhold, *Classica Americana*, pp. 117, 129–30; Bernard Vincent, *Thomas Paine ou la religion de la liberté: biographie*, Paris, Aubier, 1987, p. 21.

126 A.J. La Vopa, *Grace*, p. 65. In the other schools of the Lutheran world the classical *corpus* was retained.

127 Claude Foucart, "Louis Veuillot et la querelle de l'abbé Gaume", in *La réception du latin*, pp. 211–18. In 1850 the liberal economist Frédéric Bastiat published a book called *Baccalauréat et socialisme* in which, among other things, he made analogous criticisms of Latin and ancient literature: what moral good was to be expected of a society that had slavery, conquest and pillage as institutions?

128 L. Brockliss, *French Higher Education*, pp. 142–3.

129 See for example the grammar I myself used in sixth grade: Lucien Sausy and Robert France, *Grammaire latine abrégée: 6e édition revue et augmentée*, Paris, Librairie Fernand Lanore, n.d.

130 Quotation from R.M. Wilkinson, *The Prefects*, p. 66; similar examples from Paul Valéry (*Tel quel*, in *Oeuvres*, vol. II, Paris, Gallimard, Pléiade, 1960, p. 696) and Marcel Pagnol (*Le temps des amours: souvenirs d'enfance*, Paris, Editions de Fallois, 1988, pp. 105 and 107).

131 Walter McDonald, *Reminiscences of a Maynooth Professor*, London, Jonathan Cape, 1925, p. 24.

132 In Czarist Russia where the German *Gymnasium* model was predominant, the teaching of Latin was often reduced to grammar alone for political reasons (J.C. McClelland, *Aristocrats*, p. 12; A. Vucinich, *Science in Russian Culture, 1861–1917*, p. 60); M. Raicich, "Itinerari", p. 156; P. Hummel, *Humanités normaliennes*, notes to ch. VI: "La querelle des lettrés et des érudits et le modèle allemand".

133 We owe this expression to Robert Schilling, "La situation des langues classiques dans l'enseignement français", in *Didaskalos* 1 (1963), p. 40. On the hyper-grammatical character of French secondary teaching see, among others, "La réforme de l'enseignement secondaire" (1900), p. 17; the results of a survey published in *L'Education Nationale*, 10 (15 December 1954), pp. 256–7, 264–8; Jacques Villette, "Du latin, langue inutile en soi", in *L'Education Nationale*, 12 (10 May 1956), p. 9; P. Martin, *Le latin*, pp. 27–8.

134 Jean Cousin, "Les responsables", *L'Education Nationale*, 10 (15 December 1954), p. 256, which is notably critical of the complexity of grammar textbooks intended for secondary education.

135 See generally the texts of colloquies held by the "Latin vivant" association, and (among others) for the United States, *The Encyclopaedia of Education*, under "Latin, teaching of"; for Britain, the programme called "A New Latin for a New Situation", developed by the Joint Association of Classical Teachers at the beginning of the 1960s.

2 The "Latin Stronghold": the Church

1 Ferdinand Brunot, *Histoire de la langue française des origines a nos jours*, vol. VII: *La propagation du français en France jusqu'à la fin de l'Ancien Régime*, Paris, Librairie Armand Colin, 1967, p. 67.

2 On liturgical Latin, see Domenico Sartore and Achille M. Triacca (eds), *Diction-naire encyclopédique de la liturgie*, vol. I, Brussels, Brépols, 1992, under "Langue/langue liturgique", pp. 616–17; A Vacant, E. Mangenot, E. Amann (eds), *Diction-naire de théologie catholique*, vol. VIII–2, Paris, Letouzé, 1903–50, under "Langues liturgiques", cols 2580–82; Vittorio Coletti, *L'éloquence de la chaire: victoires et défaites du latin entre Moyen Age et Renaissance*, Paris, Editions du Cerf, 1987 (first published Casale Monferrato, 1983), ch. II (p. 21). On the end of Latin linguistic unity, see Joseph Herman, *Le latin vulgaire*, Paris, PUF, 1970, ch. VIII, 1: "A quelle époque a-t-on cessé de parler latin?". On the contrast between *litterati* and *illitterati*, see Michael Richter, "A Sociolinguistic Approach to the Latin Middle Ages", in Derek Barker (ed.), *The Materials, Sources and Methods of Ecclesiastical History*, Oxford, Blackwell, 1975, pp. 69–82.

3 G.G. Coulton, *Europe's Apprenticeship: A Survey of Mediaeval Latin with Examples*, Thomas Nelson and Sons, 1940, chs 1–3; V. Coletti, *L'éloquence*, p. 27.

4 *Dictionnaire de théologie catholique*, vol. VIII–2, under "Langues liturgiques", cols 2583–4; V. Coletti, *L'éloquence*, pp. 26–7.

5 V. Coletti, *L'éloquence*, chs 3 (p. 29) and 4.

6 *Ibid.*, p. 27; *Dictionnaire encyclopédique de la liturgie*, vol. I, under "France (La liturgie en)", pp. 470–72.

7 Robert Ricard, *La "conquête spirituelle du Mexique": essai sur l'apostolat et les méthodes missionnaires des ordres mendiants en Nouvelle Espagne de 1523–24 à 1572*, Paris, Institut d'Ethnologie, 1933, especially chs II, IV and VII; Shirley Brice Heath, *La politica de lenguaje en México: de la colonia a la nación*, Mexico, Instituto nacional indigenista, 1972, p. 21 ff.; Ignacio Osorio-Romero, "La enseñanza del latín a los Indios", in Alexander Dalzell, Charles Fantazzi, Richard J. Schoeck (eds), *Acta conventus neo-latini torontonensis: Proceedings of the Seventh International Congress of Neo-Latin Studies, Toronto, 8 August to 13 August 1988*, Binghamton, Mediaeval and Renaissance Texts and Studies, 1991, pp. 863–4.

8 Hermann A.P. Schmidt, *Liturgie et langue vulgaire: le problème de la langue liturgique chez les premiers réformateurs et au Concile de Trente*, part 1, translated from Dutch, Rome, apud Aedes Universitatis Gregorianae, 1950; Peter Burke, "*Heu domine, adsunt turcae*", in *Lingua, società e storia*, Bari, Laterza, 1990, p. 38; P. Burke, "Latin Language", in Hans J. Hillerbrand (ed.), *The Oxford Encyclopaedia of the Reformation*, Oxford University Press, 1996, p. 400; V. Coletti, *L'éloquence*, pp. 187–90; *Diction-naire encyclopédique de la liturgie*, vol. I, under "France (La liturgie en)", pp. 472–3, 481.

9 V. Coletti, *L'éloquence*, ch. IX (*Libellus* quotation: p. 176; Bruccioli: pp. 184–5; Catharin: p. 196); *Dictionnaire de théologie catholique*, vol. VIII–2, under "Langues liturgiques", cols 2584–5; Ferdinand Brunot, *Histoire de la langue française des origines a nos jours*, vol. II: *Le XVIe. siècle*, Paris, Librairie Armand Colin, 1967, pp. 14–23 (p. 15).

10 Jean-Pierre Massaut, *Josse Clichtove, l'humanisme et la réforme du clergé*, vol. II, Paris, Les Belles Lettres, 1968, p. 243.

11 V. Coletti, *L'éloquence*, ch. VIII; Armando L. De Gaetano, *Giambattista Gelli and the Florentine Academy: The Rebellion against Latin*, Florence, Olschki, 1976.

12 V. Coletti, *L'éloquence*, pp. 200–217; H.A.P. Schmidt, *Liturgie*, pp. 81–95.

13 V. Coletti, *L'éloquence*, ch. X; and in particular H.A.P. Schmidt, *Liturgie*, part II. The quotation from the decree of 17 September 1562 is drawn from *Les conciles oecuméniques*, vol. II–2, *Les décrets: Trente à Vatican II*, original text established by

G. Alberigo, J.A. Dossetti, P.-P. Joannou, C. Leonardi and P. Prodi, with the collaboration of H. Jedin. French edition under the supervision of A. Duval, B. Lauret, H. Legrand, J. Moingt and B. Sesboüé, Paris, Editions du Cerf, 1994, pp. 1495, 1497.

14 On this point see – apart from the work by V. Colletti already cited – Adriano Prosperi, "Intellettuali e Chiesa all'inizio dell'età moderna", in *Storia d'Italia, annali, 4: Intellettuali e potere*, Turin, Einaudi, 1981, pp. 202 ff.

15 F. Brunot, *Histoire de la langue française*, vol. II, pp. 23–5 (p. 24).

16 Henri-Jean Martin, *Livre, pouvoirs et société à Paris au XVIIe siècle (1598–1701)*, Geneva, Droz, 1969, pp. 102–4, 609–11.

17 Nicolas Le Maire, *Le sanctuaire fermé aux profanes ou le Bible défendue au vulgaire*, Paris, Sébastien et Gabriel Cramoisy, 1651 (quotations: unnumbered preface, part titles, pp. 190, 467, 468, 470).

18 On these translations, see H.-J. Martin, *Livre, pouvoirs et société*, pp. 611–13 and 776–8; Ferdinand Brunot, *Histoire de la langue française des origines à nos jours*, vol. V: *Le français en France et hors de France au XVIIe siècle*, Paris, Librairie Armand Colin, 1966, pp. 25–30.

19 I am indebted here to François Bontinck's comprehensively documented book *La lutte autour de la liturgie chinoise aux XVIIe et XVIIIe siècles*, Louvain, Paris, Nauwelaerts, 1962.

20 *Ibid.*, p. 518.

21 *Ibid.*, p. 466.

22 *Ibid.*, p. 137.

23 *Ibid.*, pp. 103, 137, 288.

24 *Ibid.*, pp. 400–401.

25 *Ibid.*, p. 88.

26 *Ibid.*, pp. 33–4.

27 *Ibid.*, p. 537. ("Opinion" by Fr Orazi, 1737).

28 For example, *ibid.*, p. 87.

29 *Dictionnaire encyclopédique de la liturgie*, vol. I, under "France (La liturgie en)", pp. 479–80. Translations were provided for the faithful, generally in a separate column alongside the Latin text; in many cases the canon of the mass was accompanied by a paraphrase rather than a translation or sometimes prayers for private devotions.

30 M. Montalant-Bougleux, *J.-B. Santeul ou la poésie latine sous Louis XIV*, Paris, Dentu, 1855, pp. 36–7; Ann Moss, "The Counter-Reformation Latin Hymns", in I.D. McFarlane (ed.), *Acta conventus neo-latini sanctandreani: Proceedings of the Fifth International Congress of Neo-Latin Studies, St Andrews 24 August to 1 September 1982*, Binghamton, Mediaeval Texts and Studies, 1986, pp. 375–6.

31 *Dictionnaire encyclopédique de la liturgie*, vol. I, under "France (La liturgie en)", p. 479.

32 *Dictionnaire de théologie catholique*, vol. VIII–2, under "Langues liturgiques", col. 2586; René Taveneaux, *Le jansénisme en Lorraine, 1640–1789*, Paris, Vrin, 1960, p. 501.

33 F. Brunot, *Histoire de la langue française*, p. 67.

34 Ludovico Antonio Muratori, *Opere*, vol. I, ed. Giorgio Falco and Fiorenzo Forti, Milan, Naples, Riccardo Ricciardi, 1964, pp. 929, 931–4.

35 *Atti e decreti del Concilio diocesano di Pistoia dell'anno 1786, vol. I, ristampa dell'edizione Bracali*, index edited by Pietro Stella, Florence, Olschki, 1986, pp. 50, 66, 131, 206.

36 Olivier Rousseau, *Histoire du mouvement liturgique: esquisse historique depuis le début du XIXe siècle jusqu'au pontificat de Pie X*, Paris, Cerf, 1945, pp. 70, 73–5.

37 Ferdinand Brunot, *Histoire de la langue française des origines jusqu'a nos jours*, vol. IX: *La Révolution et l'Empire*, part I, *Le français, langue nationale*, Paris, Librairie Armand Colin, 1967, pp. 128–33; Michel de Certeau, Dominique Julia, Jacques Revel, *Une politique de la langue. La Révolution française et les patois: l'enquête de Grégoire*, Paris, Gallimard, 1975, pp. 206–8.

38 F. Brunot, *Histoire de la langue française*, vol. IX, part I, pp. 374–405 (pp. 376–7, 383, 387); *Dictionnaire encyclopédique de la liturgie*, vol. I, under "France (La liturgie en)", p. 480; Edmond Préclin, *Les jansénistes du XVIIIe siècle et la constitution civile du clergé: le développement du richérisme. Sa propagation dans le bas clergé, 1713–1791*, Paris, Librairie Universitaire J. Gamber, 1928, pp. 513–14.

39 Dominique Julia, "L'éducation des ecclésiastiques aux XVIIe et XVIIIe siècles", in *Problèmes d'histoire de l'éducation: actes des séminaires organisés par l'Ecole française de Rome et l'université de Rome-La Sapienza (janvier–mai 1985)*, Rome, Ecole française de Rome, 1988, pp. 141–205 (pp. 171, 177); Charles Berthelot du Resnay, *Les prêtres séculiers en Haute-Bretagne*, Rennes, Presses de l'Université de Rennes 2, 1984 (p. 135), who points out that in this region the training of most clerics was done by colleges, not seminaries.

40 Stendhal, *Le rouge et le noir*, in *Romans et nouvelles*, Paris, Pleiade, 1963, pp. 378–81 (p. 379).

41 Francis Trochu, *Le curé d'Ars: Saint Jean-Marie-Baptiste Vianney (1786–1859) d'après toutes les pièces du procès du cononisation et de nombreuses documents inédits*, Paris, Librairie Catholique Emmánuel Vitte, 1935, pp. 46–9, 86–102 (pp. 97–8).

42 Philippe Boutry, "'Vertus d'état' et clergé intellectuel: la crise du modèle 'sulpicien' dans la formation des prêtres au XIXe siècle", in *Problèmes d'histoire de l'éducation*, pp. 207–28; Christian Dumoulin, *Un séminaire français au XIXe siècle: le recrutement, la formation, la vie des clercs à Bourges*, Paris, unpublished, 1971 (pp. 68, 223); Michel Launay, *Le bon prêtre: le clergé rural au XIXe siècle*, Paris, Aubier, 1986 (p. 27).

43 Bruno Neveu, "L'Eglise et l'Université de France: les facultés de théologie catholique des académies (1808–1885)", doctoral thesis, Paris, 1993, manuscript, pp. 284–5 (similar quotations: pp. 295, 310), 339.

44 John Talbot Smith, *The Training of a Priest: An Essay on Clerical Education with a Reply to the Critics*, New York, Longman, Green & Co., 1908 (first edition 1896), pp. 258–65.

45 Walter McDonald, *Reminiscences of a Maynooth Professor*, London, Jonathan Cape, 1925, pp. 183–7.

46 *Leonis XIII Pontificis Maximi Acta*, XIX (1899), Rome, ex typographia vaticana, 1900, pp. 164–6.

47 Pius XI, *Epistola apostolica de seminariis et de studiis clericorum*, 1 August 1922, in *Acta Apostolicae Sedis*, XIV (1922), pp. 452–4.

48 Pius XI, *Epistola apostolica ad summos moderatores ordinum regularium aliarumque sodalitatum religosorum variorum*, 19 March 1924, in *Acta Apostolicae Sedis*, XVI (1924), pp. 141–2.

49 Pius XI, *Motu proprio de peculiari litterarum latinarum schola in Atheneo Gregoriano constituenda*, 20 October 1924, in *Acta Apostolicae Sedis*, XLIII (1951), p. 737.

50 Pius XII, *Allocutio ad docentes ex ordine Fratrum Carmelitarum Discalceatorum*, 23 September 1951, in *Acta Apostolicae Sedis*, XLIII (1951), p. 737.

51 Joseph Rogé, *Le simple prêtre, sa formation, son expérience*, Paris, Casterman, 1965, p. 123.

52 Chateaubriand, *Génie du christianisme et defense du Génie du christianisme*, vol. II, Paris, Garnier, 1926, pp. 95–6.

53 Joseph de Maistre, *Du Pape*, Paris, Charpentier, 1841 (first edition 1819), pp. 133–40.

54 Prosper Guéranger, *Institutions liturgiques*, vol. III, Paris, Julien Lanier et Cie, 1851, pp. 52–159. On Dom Guéranger, see *Dictionnaire Encyclopédique de la liturgie*, vol. I, pp. 487–8.

55 H.A.P. Schmidt, *Liturgie*, pp. 14–21.

56 Gaetano Moroni, *Dizionario di erudizione storico-ecclesiastica*, Venice, Tipografia Emiliana, 1846, vol. XXXVII, p. 246, vol. XXXVIII, pp. 249–53.

57 From a dispatch sent by the French Ambassador in Rome, 31 July 1858 (quotation from B. Neveu, "L'Eglise et l'Université de France", pp. 320–21).

58 *Dictionnaire de théologie catholique*, vol. VIII–2, under "Langues liturgiques", cols. 2580–91.

59 *Ibid.*, vol. VIII–2, cols. 2587–8.

60 Aimé-Georges Martimort, "Les leçons d'un enquête", in *La Maison-Dieu*, 11 (1947), pp. 84–130 (p. 106).

61 *Dictionnaire encyclopédique de la liturgie*, vol. I, under "France (la liturgie en)", pp. 487–94.

62 Jean Travers, "Introduction", in *La Maison-Dieu*, 11 (1947), pp. 7–14 (pp. 8–10).

63 Felix Messerschmid, "La langue liturgique en pays germaniques", in *ibid.*, pp. 76–83 (pp. 82–3).

64 Gérard Cholvy and Yves-Marie Hilaire, *Histoire réligieuse de la France contemporaine*, 3: *1930–1988*, Toulouse, Privat, 1988, pp. 265, 272–4.

65 Anne-Marie Malingrey, *Initiation au latin de la messe*, Paris, Editions de l'Ecole, 1951 (p. 7).

66 André Ville, *Le latin liturgique aux enfants chrétiens de 7 à 11 ans. Première année: réponses à une messe dialoguée (Edition abrégée)*, Paris, privately published by the author, 1963.

67 A.-G. Martimort, "Les leçons", pp. 121–4.

68 We will refer mainly to Herrmann Schmidt, *La constitution de la sainte liturgie: texte, genèse, commentaire, documents*, Brussels, Editions Lumen Vitae, 1966; Pietro Borella, "La lingua volgare nella liturgia", in *Ambrosianum*, XLIV (1968), pp. 71–94, 137–68, 237–66; Annibale Bugnini, *La riforma liturgica (1948–1975)*, Rome, CLV-Edizioni Liturgiche, 1983.

69 H. Schmidt, *La constitution*, p. 238.

70 *Ibid.*, pp. 88–9.

71 Quotations are from a French translation published in 1975.

72 H. Schmidt, *La constitution*, p. 235; the two authors, and more particularly the two passages, quoted by the future Paul VI had been cited by reformers in the past in support of their case for the vernacular; hence the accusations levelled at him by traditionalists (see note 78 for the pamphlet by Abbé Georges of Nantes).

73 *La liturgie: constitution "Sacrosanctum Concilium"*, Paris, Mame, 1965, p. 82.

74 *Dictionnaire encyclopédique de la liturgie*, vol. I, under "Langue/langage liturgique", p. 618.

75 G. Cholvy and Y.-M. Hilaire, *Histoire réligieuse*, pp. 274–5; René Rémond, "Un chapitre inachevé", in Jacques Le Goff and René Rémond (eds), *Histoire de la France réligieuse*, vol. IV, Paris, Seuil, 1992, pp. 415–23; and a case study, Yves Lambert, *Dieu change en Bretagne: la réligion à Limerzel de 1900 à nos jours*, Paris, Cerf, 1985, pp. 241–54.

76 On the specific subject of language there was no shortage of books: examples include Bernadette Lécureux, *Le latin, langue de l'Eglise*, Paris, Spes, 1964; Aimon-Marie Roguet, *Pourquoi le canon de la messe en français*, Paris, Cerf, 1967; or the work that presents both positions from top to bottom: Abbé Georges Michonneau, *Pour la liturgie d'apres Concile*; Edith Delamare, *Contre la liturgie d'après Concile*, Nancy, Berger-Levrault, 1977.

77 See for example Georges Cerbelaud-Salagnac, "Lingua latina et Ecclesia catholica", in *Quatrième congrès international pour le latin vivant, Avignon, du 1er au 3 avril 1969*, Avignon, Aubanel, 1970, pp. 184–6; Jean Recurt, *Langues latine et vernaculaire dans l'Eglise, textes et documents*, Paris, unpublished, 1971. More generally on traditionalist and integralist currents in the Church of France, see Bernard Gouley, *Les catholiques français aujourd'hui: survol d'un peuple*, Paris, Fayard, 1977, pp. 189 ff.

78 Abbé Georges de Nantes, *Liber accusationis in Paulum sextum*, Saint-Paul-lès-Vaudes, La Contre-Réforme Catholique, 1973, p. 59. See also the supplement to no. 20 of *La Contre-Réforme Catholique* (January 1978) in which the new *ordo missae* is denounced for being inspired by "criteria dangerously opposed to Tradition".

79 Quotations from B. Gouley, *Les catholiques*, p. 197.

80 Yves Congar, *La crise dans l'Eglise et Mgr. Lefebvre*, Paris, Cerf, 1977 (p. 30).

81 Quotation from Bernadette Lécureux, *Le latin*, p. 18. This work contains exposés of all the arguments advanced in defence of Latin as the language of the Church: unchanging language, sacred language, universal language, traditional language.

82 Preface (p. 12) to Tito Casini's book *La tunique déchirée*, Paris, Nouvelles Editions Latines, which develops these arguments.

83 M.A. Fitzsimons, "England", in M.A. Fitzsimons (ed.), *The Catholic Church Today: Western Europe*, University of Notre-Dame, 1969, pp. 335–6. For an example of opposition to the Vatican II liturgical reform, see Evelyn Waugh's article "The Same Again, Please", in *The Spectator* (23 November 1962), and his correspondence with Cardinal Heenan (Scott M.P. Reid (ed.), *A Bitter Trial: Evelyn Waugh and John Carmel Cardinal Heenan on the Liturgical Changes*, Southampton, The Saint Austin Press, 1996).

84 Quotation from T. Casini, *La tunique déchirée*, pp. 60–61.

85 On Latin as the *publicus sermo* of the Holy See, see Carlo Egger, "Latino: lingua ancora attuale?", in Biagio Amata (ed.), *Cultura e lingue classiche: convegno di aggionamento e di didattica, Roma, 1–2 novembre 1985*, Rome, LAS, 1986, pp. 134–7; for the documents quoted, see *Acta Apostolicae Sedis*, respectively LXXX (28 June 1988), p. 863, and LXXXIV (7 January 1992), p. 252.

86 Paul VI, *Litterae apostolicae motu proprio datae "Studia latinitatis"*, 22 February 1964, in *Acta Apostolicae Sedis*, LVI (1964), pp. 225–31.

87 From an interview published in the Baltimore *Sun*, 26 February 1996, p. 2A.

88 H. Eyraud, "La question du latin", in *La quinzaine universitaire*, 684 (1 October 1969), p. 74; J. Revel, "L'étude des langues anciennes est-elle toujours indispensable?", in *ibid.*, 702 (20 October 1970), pp. 207–8; Pierre Grimal's remarks were made during the fourth "Latin vivant" conference and are quoted from an account of the occasion by Claude Houbeau. "Le latin vivant", in *Otia: Association des classiques de l'université de Liège*, 17, 1–2 (December 1969), p. 35; and see, along similar lines, Jozef Ijsewijn, *Companion to Neo-Latin Literature*, part I: *History and Diffusion of Neo-Latin Literature*, Leuwen University Press, 1990, p. 43.

89 John Twigg, *The University of Cambridge and the English Revolution, 1625–1688*, Cambridge University Press, 1990, p. 81.

90 R. Taveneaux, *Le jansénisme*, p. 501.

91 P. Burke, "Latin Language", p. 400.

92 Jean-Pierre Borle, *Le latin à l'Académie de Lausanne du XVIe au XXe siècle*, Lausanne University, 1987, pp. 31–5.

93 Claire Gantet, "La religion et ses mots: La Bible latine de Zurich (1543) entre la tradition et l'innovation", in *Zwingliana*, XXIII (1996), p. 144.

94 Bruce Tolley, *Pastors and Parishioners in Württemberg During the Late Reformation, 1581–1621*, Stanford University Press, 1995, ch. 2.

95 Bernard Vogler, *Le clergé protestant rhénan au siècle de la Réforme (1555–1619)*, Paris, Editions Orphys, 1976, pp. 227–9, 284–5.

96 J.-P. Borle, *Le latin*; "Académies", in Pierre Grisel (ed.), *Encyclopédie du protestantisme*, Paris, Cerf; Geneva, Labor et Fides, 1995.

97 André Encrevé, *Protestants français au milieu du XIXme siècle: les réformes de 1848 à 1870*, Geneva, Labor et Fides, 1986, pp. 978–80.

98 Birger Berth, "Renseignements sur l'étude du latin en Suède", in *Caesarodunum*, 3 1969, p. 96.

3 Latin Scholarship

1 *Encyclopédie ou Dictionnaire raisonné des sciences, des arts et des métiers, par une société de gens de lettres*, vol. IX, Paris, Briasson et autres, 1765, under "Langue", p. 265.

2 Anton Maria Salvini, "Sopra la lingua latina", in *Discorsi accademici . . . sopra alcuni dubbi proposti nell'Accademia degli Apatisti*, Florence, Giuseppe Manni, 1965, p. 241; Silvia Scotti Morgagni, "Latino e italiano nel primo settecento: Note in margine a una lettera inedita di A. Vallisnieri a L.A. Muratori", in *Rendiconti dell'Istituto Lombardo: Classe di Lettere e Scienze morali e storiche*, 110 (1976), p. 156.

3 Hans Bots and Françoise Waquet, *La République des Lettres*, Paris, Belin-De-Boeck, 1997, p. 146.

4 Bordeaux, 18/28 August 1656 (Thomas Hobbes, *The Correspondence*, edited by Noël Malcolm, Oxford, Clarendon Press, 1994, p. 302).

5 Charles E. Raven, *John Ray, Naturalist: His Life and Works*, Cambridge University Press, 1986, p. 30.

6 Françoise Waquet, "Les éditions de correspondances savantes et les idéaux de la République des Lettres", in *XVIIe siècle*, 45 (1993), p. 302.

7 Paris, 29 July 1654 (Blaise Pascal, *Oeuvres complètes*, II: edited and annotated by Jean Mesnard, Paris, Desclée de Brouwer, 1970, p. 1140).

8 Henri-Jean Martin, "Classements et conjonctures", dans *Histoire de l'édition française*, vol. I: *Le livre conquérant. Du Moyen Age au milieu du XVIIe siècle*, edited by R. Chartier and H.-J. Martin, Paris, Promodis, 1982, pp. 445–9; "Une croissance scolaire", in *ibid.*, vol. II: *Le livre triomphant, 1660–1830*, Paris, Promodis, 1984, pp. 95, 101. These indications are confirmed by tabulations carried out on the archives of the Bibliothèque Nationale (Emmanuel Le Roy Ladurie, "Histoire de la civilisation moderne", in *Annuaire du Collège de France, 1996–1997: résumé des cours et travaux*, 97 (1998), pp. 903–14).

9 Marco Santoro, *Storia del libro italiano: libro e società in Italia dal Quattrocento al Novecento*, Milan, Editrice Bibliografica, 1994, pp. 174–6, 180–81, 183.

10 Reinhard Wittmann, "Die deutsche Buchproduktion", in S. Cavaciocchi (ed.), *Produzione e commercio della carta e del libro, secc. XIII–XVIII: atti della "Ventitreesima Settimana di Studi", 15–20 Aprile 1991*, Florence, Le Monnier, 1992, p. 527.

11 James W. Binns, *Intellectual Culture in Elizabethan and Jacobean England: The Latin Writings of the Age*, Leeds, Francis Cairns, 1990 (pp. 1–2).

12 On this point, see my article "Les réimpressions des éditions patristiques françaises en Italie au XVIIIe siècle", in *Les Pères de l'Eglise au XVIIe siècle: actes du colloque de Lyon 2–5 octobre 1991*, Paris, IRHT, Cerf, 1993, pp. 481–91.

13 Howard Stone, "The French Language in Renaissance Medicine", in *Bibliothèque d'Humanisme et Renaissance*, XV (1953), pp. 321–2.

14 Henri-Jean Martin, *Livre, pouvoirs et société à Paris au XVIIe siècle (1598–1701)*, Geneva, Droz, 1969; Henri-Jean Martin and Odile Martin, "Le monde des éditeurs", in *Histoire de l'édition française*, vol. III: *Le temps des éditeurs: du Romantisme à la Belle Epoque*, Paris, Promodis, 1985, p. 187; Jean-Dominique Mellot, "Dynamisme provincial et centralisme parisien: l'édition rouennaise et ses marchés (vers 1600–vers 1730)". doctoral thesis, University of Paris I, 1992, pp. 162–3, 336, 632; "Clés pour un essor provincial: le petit siècle d'or de l'édition rouennaise (vers 1600–vers 1730)", in *Annales de Normandie*, 45 (1995), p. 272; Alain Choppin, *Les manuels scolaires en France de 1789 à nos jours*, vol 3: *Les manuels de latin*, Paris, INRP, Publications de la Sorbonne, 1988, pp. 18, 22.

15 J.W. Binns, *Intellectual Culture*; Harry Carter, *A History of the Oxford University Press*, vol. I: *To the Year 1780*, Oxford, Clarendon Press, appendix.

16 Bruno Lagarrigue, *Un temple de la culture européenne (1728–1753): l'histoire externe de la Bibliothèque des ouvrages des savants de l'Europe*, Nijmegen, unpublished, 1993, p. 202.

17 Georges Bonnant, "La libraire genevoise dans les Provinces-Unis et les Pays-Bas méridionaux jusqu'à la fin du XVIIIe siècle", in *Genava* (special issue), XXXI (1983), p. 71.

18 H. Carter, *A History*, p. 186. For a similar remark by John Ray at the end of the seventeenth century, C.E. Raven, *John Ray*, p. 31.

19 Luigi Balsamo, *Bibliography: History of a Tradition*, Berkeley, B.M. Rosenthal, 1990, p. 100; Joachim Kirchner, *Die Grundlagen des deutschen Zeitschriftenwesens mit einer Gesamtbibliographie der deutschen Zeitschriften bis zum Jahre 1790*, Leipzig, Karl W. Hiersemann, 1931; David A. Kronick, *A History of Scientific and Technical Periodicals: The Origins and Development of the Scientific and Technical Press, 1665–1790*, Metuchen, The Scarecrow Press, 1976, pp. 78–9, 81–2, 84–6, 132, 188.

20 A similar point has been raised concerning the mediaeval period by André Vernet, "Les traductions latines d'oeuvres en langues vernaculaires au Moyen Age", in *Traductions et traducteurs au Moyen Age: colloque international du CNRS, 26–28 mai 1986*, Paris, Editions du CNRS, 1989, pp. 225–41.

21 W. Leonard Grant, "European Vernacular Works in Latin Translation", in *Studies in the Renaissance*, I (1954), pp. 120–56 (p. 155); Peter Burke, "Translations into Latin in Early Modern Europe", to be published in R. Avesani (ed.), *Il latino nell'età moderna*, Rome, Bulzoni. I am most grateful to Peter Burke for making this article available in manuscript.

22 Georges Bonnant, "La librairie genevoise en Grande-Bretagne jusqu'à la fin du XVIIIe siècle", in *Genava* (special issue), XXXVIII (1990), p. 134; Bernhard Fabian, *The English Book in 18th-Century Germany*, London, The British Library, 1992, ch. II: "Modes of Transmission".

23 On this point, see pp. 126–7.

24 Francis Bacon, *Works*, vol. X: *The Letters and the Life*, London, Longmans, Reader and Dyer, 1868, p. 302.

25 Johannes Swammerdam, *Historia insectorum generalis . . . ex belgica latinam fecit*

Henricus Christianus Henninius . . . Editio nova. Lugduni Batavorum, apud Johannem van Abkoude, 1733, advice to reader unnumbered (original edition 1669; 1st Latin edition 1685).

26 F. Bacon, *Works*, vol. XIV, p. 434.

27 L. Balsamo, *Bibliography*, p. 99; B. Fabian, *The English Book*, p. 49.

28 René Descartes, *Oeuvres publiés par Charles Adam et Paul Tannery*, VI: *Discours de la méthode & Essais*, Paris, Vrin, 1982, pp. v–vi.

29 B. Fabian, *The English Book*, p. 48.

30 W. Leonard Grant, "Vernacular Works", p. 144.

31 Elfrieda T. Dubois, "La polémique autour des 'Lettres provinciales': quelques réflexions concernant l'utilisation respective du latin et du français", in Jean-Claude Margolin (ed.), *Acta conventus neo-latini turonensis, Tours, 6–10 septembre 1976: 3e. Congrès international d'études neo-latines*, vol. I, Paris, Vrin, 1980, pp. 609–20 (p. 617).

32 For diffusion in Sweden, see Marco Beretta, *The Starry Messenger and the Polar Star: Scientific Relations Between Italy and Sweden from 1500 to 1800. Catalogue of an Exhibition Held at the Naturhistoriska Riksmuseet Stockholm*, Florence, Giunti, 1995, p. 80.

33 B. Fabian, *The English Book*, pp. 51–2; W. Leonard Grant, "Vernacular Works", pp. 146–7.

34 Derek Gjertsen, *The Newton Handbook*, London, New York, Routledge & Kegan Paul, 1986, p. 531.

35 Michele Feo, "Tradizione latina", in Alberto Asor Rosa (ed), *Letteratura italiana*, vol.V, *Le questioni*, Turin, Einaudi, 1986, p. 370.

36 These publications have not attracted much attention from literary historians, so all we can do here is list a few examples (the titles ruthlessly shortened) noted at random in the course of research: B. de Montfaucon, *L'Antiquité expliquée*, Paris, 1719–24 (Latin–French); *Les monuments de la monarchie française*, Paris, 1729–33 (Latin–French); (J. Negelein), *Thesaurus numismatum modernorum*, Nuremberg, 1711 (Latin–German); A.J.G. Batsch, *Elenchus fungorum*, Halle, 1783 (Latin–German); *Analyses florum e diversis plantarum generibus*, Nuremberg, 1790 (Latin–German); J. Commelin, *Horti medici amstelodamensis*, Amsterdam, 1697 (Latin–Dutch); G.W. Knorr, *Thesaurus rei herbariae hortensisque universalis*, Nuremberg, 1750 (Latin–German); M.S. Merian, *Dissertation sur la génération et la transformation des insectes du Surinam*, The Hague, 1726 (Latin–French); A.J. Rösel von Rosenhorf, *Die natürlische Historie der Frösche heisigen Landes*, Nuremberg, 1758 (Latin–German); J. Swammerdam, *Biblia naturae, sive historia insectorum*, Leiden, 1737 (Latin–Dutch); W. Hunter, *Anatomia uteri humani gravidi*, Birmingham, 1774 (Latin–English); W. Smellie, *Sammlung anatomischer Tafeln*, Nuremberg, 1756 (Latin–German); F. de Stampaert and A. de Brenner, *Prodromus, seu preambulare lumen reserati portentosae magnificentiae theatri* (imperial collection of paintings and sculptures) Vienna, 1735 (Latin–German).

37 For examples, see the titles of German periodicals listed by J. Kirschner (*Die Grundlagen*) which lists no fewer than sixteen so composed even in a relatively late period (1741–70).

38 Karl Philipp Moritz, *Anton Reiser*, Tr. Georges Pauline, Paris, Fayard, 1986, p. 125.

39 Ferdinand Brunot, *Histoire de la langue française des origines à nos jours*, vol. V: *Le français en France et hors de France au XVIIe siècle*, Paris, Librairie Armand Colin, 1966, pp. 21–4.

40 Peter Burke, *Lingua, società e storia*, Bari, Laterza, 1990, pp. 42–3; Jozef Ijsewijn,

Companion to Neo-Latin Literature, part I: *History and Diffusion of Neo-Latin Literature*, Leuven University Press, 1990, pp. 66–7, 279.

41 See p. 25.

42 Geoffrey Keynes, *The Life of William Harvey*, Oxford, Clarendon Press, 1978, pp. 84–5.

43 D. Gjertsen, *The Newton Handbook*, pp. 295, 409; John. R. Harrison, *The Library of Isaac Newton*, Cambridge University Press, 1978, pp. 15–21, 74.

44 Christiaan Huygens, *Oeuvres complètes*, vol. XXII, Amsterdam, Swets & Zeitlinger, 1977, pp. 788–811; Jonathan Swift, *The Prose Writings*, edited by Herbert Davis, vol. XIV, Oxford, Blackwell, 1968, pp. xiii, 16–35.

45 *Prima Scaligerana, nusquam antehac edita, cum praefatione T. Fabri, quibus adjuncta et altera Scaligerana quam antea emendatiora, cum notis cujusdam V.D. anonymi. Gronigae, apud Petrum Smithaeum*, 1669.

46 Georges Gusdorf, *Les sciences humaines et la pensée occidentale*, III: *La révolution galiléenne*, vol. II, Paris, Payot, 1969, p. 304.

47 Bruno Basile, "Uso e diffusione del latino", in Lia Formigari (ed.), *Teorie e pratiche linguistiche nell'Italia del Settecento*, Bologna, Il Mulino, 1984, p. 338.

48 Adrien Baillet, *La vie de Monsieur Des-Cartes*, vol. II, Hildesheim, New York, Georg Olms Verlag, 1972 (original edition Paris, 1691), pp. 471 and 107.

49 Maria Luisa Altieri Biagi, "Lingua del scienza fra Seicento e Settecento", in *Lettere italiane* 28 (1976), pp. 445–50.

50 Jeanne Peiffer, "La création d'une langue mathématique allemande par Albrecht Dürer: Les raisons de sa non-réception", in Roger Chartier and Pietro Corsi (eds), *Sciences et langues en Europe*, Paris, Ecole des Hautes Etudes en Sciences Sociales, 1996, pp. 79–93.

51 Ann Blair, "La persistance du latin comme langue de science à la fin de la Renaissance", in *ibid.*, pp. 33–9.

52 Gary Marker, *Publishing, Printing and the Origins of Intellectual Life in Russia, 1700–1800*, Princeton University Press, 1985, pp. 46–7.

53 Iiro Kajanto, "The Position of Latin in Eighteenth-Century Finland", in P. Tuynman, G.C. Kuyper and E. Kessler (eds), *Acta conventus neo-latini amstelodamensis, Proceedings of the Second International Congress of Neo-Latin Studies, Amsterdam, 19–24 August 1973*, Munich, Wilhelm Fink Verlag, 1979, pp. 601–6.

54 Charles Webster, *The Great Instauration: Science, Medicine and Reform, 1612–1660*, London, Duckworth, 1975, pp. 266–7, 272. See, for the preceding period, observations along the same lines by Ann Blair ("La persistance du latin", pp. 24–33), Isabelle Pantin ("Latin et langues vernaculaires dans la littérature scientifique européenne au début de l'époque moderne (1550–1635)", in *Sciences et langues*, pp. 43–58) and especially Ferdinand Brunot (*Histoire de la langue française des origines à nos jours*, vol. II: *Le XVIe siècle*, Paris, Librairie Armand Colin, 1967, book I, chs V–VII).

55 André Stegmann, "La littérature politique européenne en latin (1580–1640)", in *Acta conventus neo-latini turonensis*, vol. II, pp. 1019–38.

56 Guy Thuillier, *La première école d'administration: l'académie politique de Louis XIV*, Geneva, Droz, 1996, pp. 175–6.

57 Piero Fiorelli, "La lingua giuridica dal De Luca al Buonaparte", in *Teorie e pratiche linguistiche*, pp. 129–30; similar observations can be found in B. Basile, "Uso e diffusione del latino", pp. 338–9.

58 Antonio Pertile, *Storia del diritto italiano, dalla caduta dall'Impero romano alla codificazione*, vol. VI, part I, *Storia della procedura*, Turin, Unione Tipografico-Editrice, 1900, p. 269.

59 Antonia McLean, *Humanism and the Rise of Science in Tudor England*, London, Heinemann, 1972, pp. 229–31.

60 A. Blair, "La persistence du latin", p. 37.

61 Karl J. Fink, *Goethe's History of Science*, Cambridge University Press, 1991, p. 71.

62 Ferdinand Brunot, *Histoire de la langue française des origines à nos jours*, vol. VI: *Le XVIIIe siècle*, part I, fascicule II, Paris, Librairie Armand Colin, 1966, pp. 603–4.

63 Innocento Mazzini, *Introduzione alla terminologia medica: decodificazione di composti e derivati di origine greca e latina*, Bologna, Pàtron Editore, 1989, pp. 22–7; Carmelo Scavuzzo, "I latinismi del lessico italiano", in Luca Serianni and Pietro Trifone (eds), *Storia della lingua italiana*, II: *Il scritto e parlato*, Turin, Einaudi, 1984, p. 485.

64 John H. Dirckx, *The Language of Medicine: Its Evolution, Structure and Dynamics*, New York, Praeger, 1983, ch. 3: "Our Classical Heritage" and pp. 152–66 for examples of unorthodox Latin words and expressions.

65 Claude Longeon, "L'usage du latin et des langues vernaculaires dans les ouvrages de botanique du XVIe siècle", in *Acta conventus neo-latini turonensis*, vol. I, pp. 751–66.

66 Maurice P. Crosland, *Historical Studies in the Language of Chemistry*, London, Heinemann, 1962, pp. 139–43; F. Brunot, *Histoire de la langue française*, vol. VI, pp. 613–16; William T. Stearn, *Botanical Latin: History, Grammar, Syntax, Terminology and Vocabulary*, London, Nelson, 1966 (p. 6).

67 M.P. Crosland, *Historical Studies in the Language of Chemistry*, pp. 115–87, 264–76.

68 *Le Monde*, 4 November 1997, p. 29.

69 P. Burke, *Lingua*, p. 61; Eric A. Blackall, *The Emergence of German as a Literary Language, 1700–1715*, Cambridge University Press, 1959, p. 13.

70 M.L. Altieri Biagi, "Lingua della scienza", p. 61; E. A. Blackall, *The Emergence of German*, p. 13.

71 P. Burke, *Lingua*, p. 48.

72 John A. Armstrong, *The European Administrative Elite*, Princeton University Press, 1973, pp. 130–31.

73 The same observation is to be found in Istvan Györgytoth (ed.), *Relationes missionarum de Hungaria et Transilvania (1627–1707)*, ed., Rome, Budapest, Római Magyar Akad, 1994, pp. 151, 230–31.

74 Jean Béranger, "Latin et langues vernaculaires dans la Hongrie du XVIIe siècle", in *Revue historique*, CCXLII (1969), pp. 5–28; Bernard Michel, *Nations et nationalismes en Europe centrale, XIXe–Xxe siècle*, Paris, Aubier, 1995, pp. 31–3; more specifically on Joseph II, Derek Beales, *Joseph II: In the Shadow of Maria Theresa, 1741–1780*, Cambridge University Press, 1987, pp. 46, 47, 64, 361–2.

75 R.W. Seton Watson, *The Southern Slav Question and the Habsburg Monarchy*, London, Constable & Co, 1911, pp. 25–9; Robert A. Kann, *The Multinational Empire: Nationalism and National Reforms in the Habsburg Monarchy, 1848–1918*, vol. I: *Empire and Nationalities*, New York, Columbia University Press, 1950, pp. 238–41.

76 Jocelyne G. Russel, *Diplomats at Work: Three Renaissance Studies*, Wolboro Falls, Alan Sutton, 1992, p. 7.

77 F. Brunot, *Histoire de la langue française*, vol. V, pp. 383–429; Lucien Bély, *Espions et ambassadeurs au temps de Louis XIV*, Paris, Fayard, 1990, pp. 450–54.

78 F. Brunot, *Histoire de la langue française*, vol. VIII: *Le français hors de France*, part II, *L'universalité en Europe*, Paris, Librairie Armand Colin, 1967, pp. 799–835 (pp. 815 and 821).

79 Ragnhild Marie Hatton, *Charles XII of Sweden*, London, Weidenfeld and Nicolson,

1968, pp. 47–8, 180; P. Burke, *Lingua*, p. 49 (for examples from the sixteenth and early seventeenth centuries).

80 *Ibid.*, p. 49 (for sixteenth- and seventeenth-century examples).

81 William Riley Parker, *Milton: A Biography*, Oxford, Clarendon Press, 1969, pp. 352–3, 400–401 (activity as an interpreter), p. 967.

82 F. Brunot, *Histoire de la langue française*, vol. V, p. 393.

83 *Ibid.*, pp. 418–19; L. Bély, *Espions*, p. 454.

84 Before the famous Villers-Cotterêts ordinance (1539) which imposed the use of French for acts of the jurisdictions of the kingdom, measures had been taken ordering use of the vernacular language for administrative and juridical purposes (Peter Rickard, *La langue française au seizième siècle: étude suivie de textes*, Cambridge University Press, 1968, pp. 22–3; Danielle Trudeau, "L'ordonnance de Villers-Cotterêts et la langue française: histoire ou interprétation", in *Bibliothèque d'Humanisme et Renaissance*, XLV (1983), pp. 461–72).

85 F. Brunot, *Histoire de la langue française*, vol. V (p. 390).

86 G. Thuillier, *La première école*, pp. 80 and 175.

87 Harold Nicolson, *Diplomacy*, Oxford University Press, 1950, ch. X: "Diplomatic language".

4 A Familiar World

1 Armando Petrucci, *Jeux de lettres: formes et usages de l'inscription en Italie, 11e–20e siècles*, Paris, Editions de l'Ecole des Hautes Études en Sciences Sociales, 1993 (original edition Turin, 1980).

2 Bernard Cousin, *Le miracle et le quotidien: les ex-voto provençaux, images d'une société*, Aix-en-Provence, Sociétés, Mentalités, Cultures, 1983, p. 262.

3 See the attack on this "habit" by Abbé Grégoire, *Rapport sur les inscriptions des monuments publics, séance du 22 nivôse, l'an II*, Paris, de l'Imprimerie Nationale, n.d. (1794), p. 10.

4 Carmelo Scavuzzo, "I latinismi del lessico italiano", in Luca Serianni and Pietro Trifone (eds), *Storia della lingua italiana: il scritto e parlato*, Turin, Einaudi, 1984, pp. 486–7.

5 On the general problem of Latin and the vernacular in the Catholic Church and its theological aspects, see ch. 2.

6 On this point, see F. Waquet's article "Au 'pays de belles paroles'. Premières recherches sur la voix en Italie au XVIe et XVIIe siècles", in *Rhetorica*, XI (1993), pp. 258–9. Textbooks on rhetoric intended for the clergy insisted on *pronunciatio* and consequently the need for voice training; the examples they give show the inadequacies and the negative effects produced by a badly controlled, grating or inaudible voice.

7 "It is not true that when the people unites its voice with those of ministers of the Church, it absolutely does not know what it is saying; it knows at least in a confused way the meaning of the prayers it is saying and that suffices to feed its faith and its piety" (Gaetano Moroni, *Dizionario di erudizione storico-ecclesiastica*, vol. XXXVIII, Venice, Tipografia Emiliana, 1846, p. 252).

8 See pp. 231–3.

9 François Lebrun, Marc Venard and Jean Quéniart, *Histoire générale de l'enseignement en France*, vol. II: *De Gutenberg aux Lumières*, Paris, Nouvelle Librairie de France, 1981, pp. 101, 119–20.

10 Benoît Neiss, "Marie Noël: Une imprégnation latine par la liturgie", in Georges Cesbron and Laurence Richer (eds), *La réception du latin du XIXe siècle à nos jours: actes du colloque d'Angers des 23 et 24 septembre 1994*, Angers, Presses de l'Université, 1996, pp. 385–91 (pp. 385, 386, 388, 389).

11 Eamonn Duffy, *The Stripping of the Altars: Traditional Religion in England, c.1400–c.1580*, New Haven, Yale University Press, 1992, ch. 6 (p. 221).

12 Michele Feo, "Tradizione latina", in Alberto Asor Rosa (ed.), *Letteratura italiana*, vol. V, *Le questioni*, Turin, Einaudi, 1986, pp. 366–7.

13 Idelfonso Nieri, "Parole e modi del parlare lucchese derivati della Bibbia e dal rito ecclesiastico", in *Atti della reale Accademia lucchese di scienze, lettere ed arti*, XXXII (1904), pp. 518–20.

14 Pierre Jakez Hélias, *Le cheval d'orgueil: mémoires d'un Breton du pays bigouden*, Paris, Plon, 1975, pp. 132–3.

15 Vittorio Coletti, *L'éloquence de la chaire: victoires et défaites du latin entre Moyen Age et Renaissance*, Paris, Editions du Cerf, 1987 (first published Casale Monferrato, 1983), pp. 27, 220–22.

16 Nicolas Le Maire, *Le sanctuaire fermé aux profanes ou la Bible défendue au vulgaire*, Paris, Sébastien et Gabriel Cramoisy, 1651, preface, no page number.

17 "This Latin, which reigns from one end of mass to the other, for us is 'Sunday Breton', the one that is never heard during the week or from any mouths except those of priests. Even the teachers, who speak French with such ease, do not use it" (P.J. Hélias, *Le cheval d'orgeuil*, pp. 132–3).

18 Aimé-Georges Martimort, "Les leçons d'un enquête", in *La Maison-Dieu*, 11 (1947), pp. 88–9.

19 See, on this point, Stanley J. Tambiah, "Il potere magico delle parole", in *Rituali e cultura*, Bologna, Il Mulino, 1995 (original edition Harvard University Press, 1985), pp. 41 ff.

20 Gianfranco Venturi, "Langue/langage liturgique", in Domenico Sartore and Achille M. Triacca (eds), *Dictionnaire encyclopédique de la liturgie*, vol. I, French adaptation edited by Henri Delhougne, Brussels, Brépols, 1992, pp. 615–16.

21 E. Duffy, *The Stripping of the Altars*, pp. 213–19.

22 Keith Thomas, *Religion and the Decline of Magic: Studies in Popular Beliefs in Sixteenth and Seventeenth Century England*, London, Weidenfeld and Nicolson, 1971, esp. pp. 51–77 and, for examples, pp. 178–85, 215, 232.

23 This expression is borrowed from René Rémond, "Un chapitre inachevé", in J. Le Goff and R. Rémond (eds), *Histoire de la France religieuse*, vol. 4, Paris, Seuil, 1992, p. 415.

24 Aimon-Marie Roguet, *Pourqui le canon de la messe en français*, Paris, Cerf, 1977, p. 73.

25 Yves Congar, *La crise dans l'Eglise et Mgr Lefebvre*, Paris, Cerf, 1977, p. 73.

26 Abbé Georges Michonneau, *Pour la liturgie d'áprès Concile*, Nancy, Berger-Levrault, 1977, pp. 70–72.

27 A.-G. Martimort, "Les leçons", pp. 122–3.

28 On this point, see Pierre Bourdieu's analysis in *Ce que parler veut dire: l'économie des échanges linguistiques*, Paris, Fayard, 1982, pp. 111–19.

29 Georges Brassens, *Poèmes et chansons*, Paris, Seuil, 1993, p. 404.

30 Chateaubriand, *Génie du christianisme et Defense du Génie du christianisme*, Paris, Garnier, 1926, p. 96.

31 Yves Lambert, *Dieu change en Bretagne: la religion à Limerzel de 1900 à nos jours*, Paris, Cerf, 1985, p. 254.

32 Mary McCarthy, *Memoirs of a Catholic Girlhood*, London, Heinemann, 1957, p. xxxi.

33 See pp. 132–51.

34 Cartoon reproduced by Christopher Stray in "The Smell of Latin Grammar: Contrary Imaginings in English Classrooms", *Bulletin of the John Rylands University Library of Manchester*, 76 (1994), p. 218.

35 On this matter, see the fundamental articles by Christopher Stray, "*Quia nominor leo*: vers une sociologie historique du manuel", in *Histoire de l'éducation*, 58 (1993), pp. 71–102; "The Smell of Latin Grammar",

36 See pp. 138–45.

37 On the prince's Latin education, see Raghnild Marie Hatton, *Charles XII of Sweden*, London, Weidenfeld and Nicolson, 1968, p. 47; on his games, see Karl Gustafson Klingspor, *Charles the Twelfth King of Sweden*, translated from the manuscript by John A. Gade, Boston and New York, Houghton Mifflin Company, 1916, p. 23.

38 Jean-Jacques Rousseau, *Les Confessions*, Paris, Garnier-Flammarion, 1964, p. 275.

39 C. Stray, *Quia nominor leo*, p. 99.

40 Jacques Brel, *Oeuvre intégrale*, Paris, Robert Laffont, 1982, p. 222.

41 C. Stray, "The Smell of Latin Grammar", p. 215.

42 Walter Gottschalk, *Französischer Schülersprache*, Heidelberg, Karl Winter, 1931, pp. 19, 56, 70.

43 Ernest Lavisse, *Souvenirs*, Paris, Calmann-Lévy, 1912, pp. 143, 168–9.

44 Albert Léonard, "La formation au latin dans le souvenir de Vallès (*L'enfant*) et de Stendhal (*Vie de Henri Brulard*)", in *La réception*, p. 149.

45 Etienne Wolf, "Locutions et citations latines chez Alphonse Allais", in *Bulletins de l'Association Guillaume-Budé*, 4 (December 1991), pp. 401–13 (pp. 409–10). Teachers used to play on the same conceit. One of mine at the *lycée*, if I may include a personal anecdote, used to exclaim when confronted with an exasperating piece of ignorance by a pupil: "Quousque tandem!" The class would always fall about laughing.

46 Jules Romains, *Les copains*, Paris, Gallimard, 1958 (first edition 1913), pp. 93–8.

47 Claude Simon, *Histoire*, Paris, Editions de Minuit, 1967, pp. 123–9; Dominique Duquesne, "Latin et Nouveau Roman", in *La réception*, p. 314.

48 Translator's note: this practice and its variants were still current in the 1950s, as was Kennedy's *Primer*.

49 C. Stray, "The Smell of Latin Grammar", p. 216. Shortbread is a sweet grainy biscuit.

50 Jean-François Domenguet, "La langue de l'exil: Montherlant et le latin", in *La réception*, p. 314.

51 Anatole France, *La vie en fleur*, in *Oeuvres complètes*, vol. XXII, Paris, Calmann-Lévy, 1932, p. 360. Similarly, see Marcel Pagnol, *Le temps des secrets: souvenirs d'enfance*, Paris, Editions de Fallois, 1988, p. 252.

52 Paul Verlaine, *Mes prisons*, in *Oeuvres en prose complètes*, edited, collected and annotated by Jacques Borel, Paris, Gallimard, Pleiade, 1972, pp. 322–3.

53 See, generally, Jean-Claude Boulogne, *Histoire de la pudeur*, Paris, Olivier Orban, 1986.

54 C. Simon, *Histoire*, pp. 123–9; D. Duquesne, "Latin et Nouveau Roman", p. 326.

55 Chateaubriand, *Mémoires d'outre-tombe*, vol. I, Paris, Pléiade, 1951, pp. 56–7.

56 The conclusions of Kenneth J. Dover's analysis in reference to Greek texts ("Expurgation of Greek Literature", in William den Boer (ed.), *Les études classiques aux XIXe et XXe siècles: leur place dans l'histoire des idées*, Geneva, Fondation Hardt,

1980, pp. 55-82, followed by a discussion, pp. 83-9) are valid, without the slightest doubt, for Latin school editions; see also pp. 36-7 and 249-50.

57 *Ibid.*, pp. 84-5.

58 *Ibid.*, p. 85.

59 C. Simon, *Histoire*, pp. 108, 110; D. Duquesne, "Latin et Nouveau Roman", p. 324.

60 J. Brel, *Oeuvre intégrale*, pp. 222-3.

61 C. Stray, "*Quia nominor leo*", p. 96.

62 M. McCarthy, *Memoirs*, p. 130.

63 Notable examples are *Histoire* and *Bataille de Pharsale* by Claude Simon, and Danielle Sallenave's *Paysage de ruines avec personnages*; more generally, see D. Duquesne, "Latin et Nouveau Roman".

Part II Standards and Ability: Introduction

1 Joseph de Maistre, *Du Pape*, Paris, Charpentier, 1841 (first edition 1819), p. 137.

2 Jozef Ijsewijn, whose overview of the subject, accompanied by an impressive bibliography, appeared in 1977 as the *Companion to Neo-Latin Literature*, published the first volume of a greatly augmented new version in 1990 (*Companion to Neo-Latin Literature*, Part I: *History and Diffusion of Neo-Latin Literature* (second edition), Leuwen University Press); see p. vii for selection criteria adopted. A second volume is under preparation. James W. Binns, in *Intellectual Culture in Elizabethan and Jacobean England: The Latin Writings of the Age* (Leeds, Francis Cairns, 1990), limited to one country and a timespan of one century, has more than 700 densely-packed pages, more than proving the vitality of neo-Latin literature and underlining the importance of the Latin dimension in the English Renaissance (see, on this point, the survey by Anthony Grafton in the *TLS*, 8 March 1991, pp. 3-4).

3 J. Ijsewijn, *Companion*, p. 44.

4 See, notably, Manara Valgimigli's introduction to the *Carmina*, Milan, Mondadori, 1951; Alfonso Traina, *Il latino del Pascoli: saggio sul bilinguismo poetico*, Florence, Le Monnier, 1971.

5 For an example see Emin Tengström, *A Latin Funeral Oration from Early 18th Century Sweden: An Interpretative Study*, Göteborg, Acta Universitatis Gothenburgensis, 1983.

6 Ferdinand Brunot, *Histoire de la langue française des origines aà nos jours*, vol. V, *Le français en France et hors de France au XVIIe. siècle*, Paris, Librairie Armand Colin, 1966, pp. 1-9 (pp. 7, 8); vol. VII: *La propagation du français en France jusqu'à la fin de l'Ancien Régime*, Paris, Librairie Armand Colin, 1967, pp. 7-11; Bernard Beugnot, "Débats autour du latin dans la France classique", in P. Tuynman, G.C. Kuiper and E. Kessler (eds), *Acta conventus neo-latini amstelodamensis: Proceedings of the Second International Congress of Neo-Latin Studies, Amsterdam 19-24 August 1973*, Munich, Wilhelm Fink Verlag, 1979, pp. 93-106; Abbé Vissac, *De la poésie latine en France au siècle de Louis XIV*, Paris, Aug. Durand, 1862; M. Montalant-Bougleux, *J.-B. Santeul ou la poésie latine sous Louis XIV*, Paris, Dentu, 1855; C.-A. Fusil, *L'Anti-Lucrèce du cardinal de Polignac: contribution à l'étude de la pensée philosophique et scientifique dans le premier tiers du XVIIIe. Siècle*, Paris, Editions Scientifica, 1918; Dirk Sacré, "La poésie neo-latine en France au XIXe. Siècle", in Georges Cesbron and Laurence Richer (eds), *La réception du latin du XIXe. siècle à nos jours: actes du colloque d'Angers des 23 et 24 septembre 1994*, Angers, Presses de l'Université, 1996, pp. 67-77.

7 For England, see Leicester Bradner, *Musae anglicanae: A History of Anglo-Latin Poetry, 1500-1925*, New York, Modern Language Association of America, 1940; for

didactic poetry, James R. Naiden, "Newton Demands the Latin Muse", in *Symposium*, 6 (1952), pp. 111–20.

8 Veljko Gortan, "Les derniers latinistes croates de Dubrovnik (Raguse)", in J. Ijsewijn and E. Kessler (eds), *Acta conventus neo-latini lovaniensis: Proceedings of the First International Congress of Neo-Latin Studies, Louvain, 23–28 August 1971*, Munich, Wilhelm Fink Verlag, 1973, pp. 261–74.

9 For an example of this sort of neo-Latin poetry placing a high value on technical perfection, see G. Tournay and T. Sacré (eds), *Pegasus devocatus: studia in honoris C. Arii Nuri sive Harry C. Schnur*, Leuven University Press, 1992.

10 See Manuel Briceño Jáuregui, "La poesia en latín in Iberoamerica", in *Acta conventus neo-latini amstelodamensis*, pp. 153–6.

11 F. Brunot, *Histoire de la langue française*, vol. V, p. 8.

5 Written Latin

1 Quotation from Corinne Saminadayar, "Du latin comme langue naturelle de l'écriture", in Georges Cesbron and Laurence Richer (eds), *La réception du latin du XIXe. siècle à nos jours: actes du colloque d'Angers des 23 et 24 septembre 1994*, Angers, Presses de l'Université, 1996, p. 161.

2 James W. Binns, *Intellectual Culture in Elizabethan and Jacobean England: The Latin Writing of the Age*, Leeds, Francis Cairns, 1990, esp. pp. 297–306.

3 Margareta Benner and Emin Tengström, *On the Interpretation of Learned Neo-Latin: An Explorative Study Based on Some Texts from Sweden (1611–1716)*, Göteborg, Acta Universitatis Gothoburgensis, 1977.

4 Gilles Ménage, *Menagiana*, Amsterdam, 1762 (original edition 1693), p. 184.

5 Adrien Baillet, *La vie de Monsieur Des-Cartes*, vol. II, Hildesheim, New York, Georg Olms Verlag, 1972 (original edition Paris, 1691), pp. 471–2.

6 Ludovicus Montaltus (Blaise Pascal), *Litterae provinciales, de morali et politica Jesuitarum disciplina. A Wilhelmo Wendrockio Salisborgensi theologo, e gallica in latinam linguam translatae et theologicis notis illustratae, quibus tum Jesuitarum adversus Montaltum criminationes repelluntur, tum praecipua theologiae moralis capita a novorum casuistarum corruptelis vindicantur. Coloniae, apud Nicolaum* Schouten, 1658, unnumbered preface; Elfrieda T. Dubois, "La polémique autour des *Lettres provinciales*: quelques réflexions concernant l'utilisation respective du latin et du français", in Jean-Claude Margolin (ed.), *Acta conventus neo-latini turonensis, Tours, 6–10 septembre 1976: 3rd International Congress of Neo-Latin Studies*, vol. I, Paris, Vrin, 1980, pp. 609–20. See also, on publications of this sort, pp. 84–7; for brief remarks on language and style, W. Leonard Grant, "European Vernacular Works in Latin Translation", in *Studies in the Renaissance*, I (1954), pp. 155–6.

7 See also the remarks made by J.W. Binns, *Intellectual Culture*, p. 268.

8 *Encyclopédie ou Dictionnaire raisonné des connaissances humaines*, arranged by M. de Felice, *Supplement: vol. IV*, Yverdon, 1776, under "Latinité".

9 [Voltaire], *Le tombeau de la Sorbonne*, 1752, p. 26.

10 Maria Luisa Altieri Biagi, "Lingua della scienza fra Seicento e Settecento", in *Lettere italiane*, XXVIII (1976), p. 447.

11 Lamindo Pritanio (Ludovico Antonio Muratori), *A' generosi letterati d'Italia* (2 April 1703), in *Raccolta delle opere minori*, vol. I, Naples, G. Ponzelli, 1757, p. 13.

12 Lazzaro Spallanzani, *Edizione nazionale delle opere, parte prima: carteggi*, vol. IV, edited by Pericle di Pietro, Modena, Mucchi, 1985, p. 245 (letter dated 20 July 1770).

13 Id., *Edizione nazionale delle opere, parte seconda: lezioni, scritti letterari*, vol. II, edited by Pericle di Pietro, Modena, Mucchi, 1994, p. 288.

14 Sergio Bertelli, *Erudizione e storia in Ludovico Antonio Muratori*, Naples, Istituto Italiano per gli Studi Storici, 1960, p. 348.

15 Claude Longeon, "L'usage du latin et des langues vernaculaires dans les ouvrages de botanique du XVIe. siècle", in *Acta conventus neo-latini turonensis*, vol. I, p. 761; William T. Stearn, *Botanical Latin: History, Grammar, Syntax, Terminology and Vocabulary*, London, Nelson, 1966, pp. vii–viii, 10–11, 46.

16 Brigitte du Plessis, "Les thèses de patristique en latin de 1870 à 1906", in *La réception du latin*, pp. 307–10 (p. 309).

17 Louis Couturat and Léopold Léau, *Histoire de la langue universelle*, Paris, Hachette, 1903–07, p. 529.

18 See pp. 76–7; Paul VI, *Litterae apostolicae motu proprio datae "Studia latinitatis"*, in *Acta Apostolicae Sedis*, LVI (1964), p. 229.

19 George E. Ganss, *Saint Ignatius' Idea of a Jesuit University: A Study in the History of Catholic Education*, Milwaukee, Marquette University Press, 1954, pp. 240–44 (p. 241).

20 Paul Claudel, *Oeuvres complètes*, vol. III, *Extrême-Orient*, Paris, Gallimard, 1952, p. 354.

21 Generally, see ch. 1; Giosuè Carducci, *Ricordi autobiografici: saggi e frammenti*, in *Edizione nazionale delle opere, vol.trentesimo*, Bologna, Zanichelli, 1940, p. 6; John Stuart Mill, *Autobiography*, edited by John Jacob Coss, New York, Columbia University Press, 1924, pp. 6–7.

22 Marie-Madeleine Compère and Dolorès Pralon-Julia, *Performances scolaires de collégiens sous l'Ancien Régime: étude de six séries d'exercices latins rédigés au collège Louis-le-Grand vers 1720*, Paris, Institut National de la Recherche Pédagogique, Publications de la Sorbonne, 1992.

23 M.L. Clarke, *Classical Education in Britain 1500–1900*, Cambridge University Press, 1959, pp. 58–9 and 89–92; Leicester Bradner, *Musae Anglicanae: A History of Anglo-Latin Poetry, 1500–1925*, New York, Modern Language Association of America, 1940.

24 Jules Mouquet, *Charles Baudelaire: vers latins*, Paris, Mercure de France, 1933; Jacques Landrin, "Sainte-Beuve et le latin", in *La réception du latin*, p. 35; Arthur Rimbaud, *Oeuvres complètes*, edited by Louis Forestier, Paris, Robert Laffont, 1992, pp. ii–iii, 1–27, 429–35; Alain Chantreau, "Stendhal latiniste", in *La réception du latin*, p. 109; Albert Léonard, "La formation au latin dans le souvenir de Vallès (*L'enfant*) et de Stendhal (*Vie de Henry Brulard*)", in *ibid.*, p. 147.

25 Clément Falcucci, *L'humanisme dans l'enseignement secondaire en France au XIXe. siècle*, Toulouse, Privat; Paris, Didier, 1939, pp. 310–12; Jules Simon, *Premières années*, Paris, Flammarion, n.d., p. 84.

26 Giovanni Pascoli, *Il latino nelle scuole: un esercizio di prosodia e metrica*, in *Prose I: pensieri di varia umanità*, Milan, Mondadori, 1971 (original edition 1946), pp. 610–27 (p. 617). This exercise was presented by Pascoli as emblematic of his teaching style.

27 "Agrégation de lettres: Concours de 1903, Rapport du président du jury (Maurice Croiset)", in *Revue universitaire*, 12, 2 (1903), pp. 369–86; "Agrégation de lettres: Concours de 1903, Rapport du président du jury (Maurice Croiset)", in *ibid.*, 14, 2 (1905), pp. 277–89 (pp. 285–6).

28 Simone Deleani, "Les niveaux en latin dans les collèges et les *lycées*: tests, commentaires et conclusions", in *Bulletin de l'Association régionale (Académie de Besançon) des professeures de langues anciennes*, 6 (February 1977), pp. 3–7.

29 Gerald Hugh Tyrwhitt-Wilson, Lord Berners, *First Childhood*, London, Constable & Co., 1934, p. 105.

30 Ernest Lavisse, *Souvenirs*, Paris, Calmann-Lévy, 1912, p. 17.

31 Miguel de Unamuno, *Recuerdos de niñez y mocedad*, in *Obras completas*, VIII: *Autobiografía y recuerdos personales*, Madrid, Escelicer, 1966, p. 133.

32 Paul Martin, "Pour gagner au latin et au grec les défenseurs qu'ils méritent", in *L'éducation nationale*, 10 (15 December 1954), p. 331; Colette Mercier-Nast, "L'enseignement vivant du latin, son rôle dans l'affirmation de la personnalité de l'adolescent", in *Quatrième congrès international pour le latin vivant: Avignon du 1er. au 3 avril 1969*, Avignon, Aubanel, 1970, p. 88.

33 Chateaubriand, *Les mémoires d'outre-tombe*, vol. I, Paris, Gallimard, Pléiade, 1951, p. 48.

34 M.L. Clarke, *Classical Education*, pp. 58–9.

35 Valery Larbaud, "Devoirs de vacances", in *Enfantines*, Paris, Gallimard, 1950, pp. 198–9. I am indebted to Marie-Odile Germain for drawing this text to my attention.

36 Jean Cécile Frey, *Via ad divas scientias artesque, linguarum notitiam, sermones extemporaneos, nova et expeditissima*, Jenae, apud Petrum Brösselin; Arnstadiae, typis Meurerianis, 1674, pp. 7–8; John Milton, *Of Education* (1644), in *Complete Prose Works*, vol. II: *1643–1648*, Yale University Press, pp. 370–71.

37 Carole Gascard, "L'enseignement du latin au XVIIe. siècle à travers les textes théoriques et les grammaires", diploma thesis, Paris, 1994, manuscript, part I, p. 206.

38 See also Ferdinand Brunot, *Histoire de la langue française des origines à nos jours*, vol. VII: *La propagation du français en France jusqu'à la fin de l'Ancien Régime*, Paris, Librairie Armand Colin, 1967, pp. 90, 130; (La Condamine), *Lettre critique sur l'Education*, Paris, Prault, 1751, p. 11; Louis Sébastien Mercier, *Tableau de Paris*, vol. I, edited by Jean-Claude Bonnet, Paris, Mercure de France, 1994, p. 206.

39 Helvetius, *De l'esprit*, Verviers, Editions Gérard et Co., 1973, p. 493.

40 Ferdinand Brunot, *Histoire de la langue française des origines à nos jours*, vol. IX: *La Révolution et l'Empire*, Paris, Librairie Armand Colin, 1967, pp. 112–18 (p. 113).

41 C. Gascard, "L'enseignement", part I, p. 76.

42 Michel Bellot-Antony and Dany Hadjaj, "La querelle de l'enseignement des langues dans l'*Encyclopédie*", in *Eclectisme et cohérence des Lumières, Mélanges offerts à Jean Ehrard*, Paris, Nizet, 1992, p. 37.

43 F. Brunot, *Histoire de la langue française*, vol. VII, p. 126.

44 L.S. Mercier, *Tableau de Paris*, vol. I, p. 206.

45 Dominique Julia, *Les trois couleurs du tableau noir: la Révolution*, Paris, Belin, 1981, p. 251.

46 Pascale Hummel, *Humanités normaliennes: l'enseignement classique et l'érudition philologique dans l'Ecole normale superieure du XIXe. siècle*, Paris, Les Belles Lettres, 1995, pp. 120 and 125 (for the period 1831–33), p. 186 (more generally).

47 Antoine Augustin Cournot, *Des institutions d'instruction publique en France*, Paris, Hachette, 1864, p. 46.

48 C. Falcucci, *L'humanisme*, p. 323.

49 "La réforme de l'enseignement secondaire", in *Revue universitaire*, 9 (1900), p. 15.

50 René Lavaud, "Une petite réforme pédagogique: l'enseignement de la syntaxe latine et la question du mot à mot", in *Revue universitaire*, 13 (1904), p. 93.

51 Henri Bornecque, "Comment rendre nos élèves plus forts en latin", in *Revue universitaire*, 13 (1904), pp. 205 and 207.

52 A. Lortholary, "Pour le latin plus facile", in *Revue des études latines*, V (1907), p. 191.

53 M. Brun-Laloire, "En quoi le latin est irremplaçable", in *L'éducation nationale*, 10 (15 December 1954), p. 242.

54 See respectively *L'éducation nationale*, 10 (15 December 1954), and *Revue de la Franco-Ancienne*, 122 (July 1957), pp. 130–38.

55 See for example *Encyclopédie pratique de l'éducation en France, publiée sous le patronage et avec le concours de l'Institut pédagogique national*, Paris, IPN et SEDE, 1960, pp. 633–7; Etiemble, "Contre le latin", in *Le Figaro littéraire*, 14–20 October 1968, p. 16; A. Revel, "Vers la désuétude des langues anciennes", in *La quinzaine universitaire*, 742 (5 June 1973), p. 725; S. Deleani, "Les niveaux", pp. 8–11; Paul Jal, "Rapport moral", in *Bulletin de l'Association Guillaume-Budé*, 3 (October 1992), p. 229.

56 Paul Martin, "Le latin dans l'enseignement secondaire. Rien ne va plus", in *Caesarodunum*, 3 (1969), p. 27.

57 Paul Valéry, *Cahiers: Edition établie*, vol. II, edited and annotated by Judith Robinson, Paris, Gallimard, Pléiade, 1974, pp. 1576 and 1582.

58 M.-M. Compère and D. Pralon-Julia, *Performances*, p. 234; see, similarly, on pp. 232, 241 and 247, the papers of boys called Champvremont, Labarre and Noël. The authors' suggested translation of the text in question (p. 201) provides a key to Coulombier's version and reveals the scale of his errors. "As Horatius's sister was mourning the death of one of the Curiatii, the heart of that fierce young man was inflamed on seeing her in tears in the very midst of his victory and of such great popular rejoicing. Then he drew his sword and stabbed the young girl with it. This crime seemed horrible to the senators and the people. Horatius was already being led to execution when his father embraced him, indicated the remains of the Curiatii and said: 'The man you have just seen in triumph, can you see him chained amid tortures? Will the lictor dare bind the hands that once took up arms to give the Empire to the Roman people?' The people was so moved by these words that it pardoned Horatius."

59 Claude Simon, *La bataille de Pharsale*, Paris, Editions de Minuit, 1969, pp. 51–3; see similarly pp. 17–18, 43, 81–3, 220–21.

60 On constant and "servile" use of the dictionary as a permanent "interloper" between pupil and text for translation, see A. Lortholary, "Pour le latin", p. 194; survey published in *L'éducation nationale*, 10 (15 December 1954), esp. pp. 238, 240 and 317; *Encyclopédie pratique*, pp. 633 and 638. This is a commonplace of pedagogic literature which generally argues for suppression or restricted use of the dictionary and the acquisition of vocabulary. Similarly, for Italy, see Guido Calogero, "Il panlatinismo", in *Scuola sotto inchiesa: nuova edizione accresciuta*, Turin, Einaudi, 1965, pp. 40–41, 43; Raffaele Simone, "L'auspicabile riscoperto del mondo classico", in *Lettere dell'Italia*, X, 40 (October–December 1995), p. 64.

61 S. Deleani, "Les niveaux", pp. 8–9.

62 J. Milton, *Of Education*, pp. 370–71.

63 Daniel Georg Morhof, *Polyhistor Lubecae*, vol. I, P. Böckmann, 1708 (original edition 1688), p. 458.

64 Furio Murru and Giuseppe Pessolano Filos, *Alla riscoperta della didattica del latino in Italia nel Settecento e nell'Ottocento*, Rome, Edizioni Nuova Rivista Pedagogica, 1980, p. 18. The same observation is made by Antonio Vallisneri (Silvia Scotti Morgagni, "Latino e italiano nel primo Settecento: note in margine a une lettera

inedita di A. Vallisneri a L.A. Muratori", in *Rendiconti dell'Istituto Lombardo: classe di lettere e scienze morali e storiche*, 110 (1976), p. 160.

65 Meyer Reinhold, *Classica Americana: The Greek and Roman Heritage in the United States*, Detroit, Wayne State University Press, 1984, pp. 176, 180.

66 Anne Digby and Peter Searby, *Children, School and Society in Nineteenth-Century England*, London, Macmillan Press, 1981, p. 38.

67 Matthew Davenport Hill, *Public Education: Plans for the Government and Liberal Education of Boys, in Large Numbers, as Practised at Hazelwood School* (second edition), London, C. Knight, 1825, pp. 220–21.

68 Christopher Stray, *Grinders and Grammars: A Victorian Controversy*, Reading, The Text Book Colloquium, 1995, p. 37.

69 M. Reinhold, *Classica Americana*, p. 180.

70 *Value of the Classics: Conference on Classical Studies in Liberal Education*, Princeton University Press, 1917, p. 10; M. Reinhold, *Classica Americana*, p. 339.

71 G.E. Ganss, *Saint Ignatius' Idea of a Jesuit University*, p. 224.

72 J. Rémy, "Une association monstrueuse", in *L'Athénée*, 45, 4 (October–November 1956), p. 448.

73 G. Calogero, "Il panlatinismo", p. 35.

74 R. Simone, "L'auspicabile riscoperta", p. 63.

75 See the "relazione" of the rapporteur of this commission, Giovanni Pascoli, in his *Prose*, pp. 591–604.

76 *La réforme de l'éducation secondaire*, p. 15.

77 Jules Marouzeau, "La crise des études classiques en France", in *Neue Jahrbücher für das klassische Altertum Geschichte und deutche Literatur und für Pädagogik*, 32 (1913), p. 201.

78 Paul Crouzet, *Nouvelle méthode latine et exercices illustrés (classes de 6e. et 5e.)*, Toulouse, Privat; Paris, Didier, 1951, p. xviii.

79 Pierre Chambon, "Esquisse d'une méthode mieux adaptée aux conditions actuelles", in *L'éducation nationale*, 10 (15 December 1954), p. 312.

80 *Encyclopédie pratique de l'éducation*, p. 636.

81 *La réforme de l'éducation secondaire*, p. 15.

82 M. Brun-Laloire, "En quoi le latin est irremplaçable", p. 242.

83 See pp. 10–11 and 15–16. These changes to the exercises were accompanied by changes to text books.

84 Jean-Jacques Rousseau, *Les confessions*, edited by J. Voisin, Paris, Garnier-Flammarion, 1964, p. 275.

85 Like Charles Darwin, although as a schoolboy at Shrewsbury he had been good at Latin (*The Autobiography*, edited by Nora Barlow, London, Collins, 1958, pp. 27 and 58).

86 Heinrich Heine, *Memoirs from his Works, Letters and Conversation*, vol. I, edited by Gustav Karpeles, English translation by Gilbert Connan, New York, John Lane Company, 1910, p. 12.

87 Goethe, *Memoirs*, translated by Jacques Porchat, Paris, Hachette, 1862, p. 26.

88 Marmontel, *Mémoires*, annotated edition by John Renwich, Clermont-Ferrand, G. de Bussac, 1972, p. 5.

89 M. de Unamuno, *Recuerdos*, pp. 133, 135.

90 See also, for examples, Hector Berlioz, *Mémoires*, ed. Pierre Citron, Paris, Garnier-Flammarion, 1969, p. 44; Edgar Quinet, *Histoire de mes idées: autobiographie*, Paris, Flammarion, 1972, p. 151; Louis Forestier, "Rimbaud et le latin", in *La réception du latin*, p. 30.

91 A. Léonard, "La formation", p. 150.

92 Quoted from Randolph S. Churchill, *Winston S. Churchill*, vol. I: *Youth, 1874–1900*, London, Heinemann, 1966, p. 47.

93 Edward Gibbon, *Memoirs of my Life, Illustrated from his Letters, with Occasional Notes and Narrative by John Lord Sheffield*, edited by A.O.J. Cockshut and Stephen Constantine, Keele University Press, 1994, p. 69.

94 Rupert Wilkinson, *The Prefects: British Leadership and the Public School Tradition. A Comparative Study in the Making of Rulers*, Oxford University Press, 1964, p. 65.

95 Dominique Duquesne, "Latin et nouveau roman", in *La réception du latin*, p. 326.

96 Stendhal, *Vie de Henri Brulard*, in *Oeuvres intimes*, Paris, Gallimard, Pléiade, 1966, p. 112.

97 Vittorio Alfieri, *Vita scritta da esso*, vol. I, edited by Luigi Fassò, Asti, Casa d'Alfieri, 1951, p. 38.

98 Thomas Hughes, *Tom Brown's Schooldays*, Oxford University Press, 1989 (original edition 1857), p. 262

99 A. Léonard, "La formation", p. 149.

100 T. Hughes, *Tom Brown's Schooldays*, pp. 260–61; M.L. Clarke, *Classical Education*, p. 59.

101 Walter McDonald, *Reminiscences of a Maynooth Professor*, London, Jonathan Cape, 1925, p. 25.

102 Marcel Pagnol, *Le temps des amours: souvenirs d'enfance*, Paris, Editions de Fallois, 1988, p. 107.

103 V. Alfieri, *Vita scritta di esso*, p. 31.

104 E. Lavisse, *Souvenirs*, p. 205; Otto Jespersen, *A Linguist's Life: An English Translation*, edited by Arne Juul, Hans F. Nielsen, Jørgen Erik Nielsen, Odense University Press, 1995, p. 16. Masters reciprocally deplored the apathy of their pupils: see, for example, the transcription of a harangue to this effect in Geoffrey Keynes's memoirs (*The Gates of Memory*, Oxford, Clarendon Press, 1981, pp. 38–9).

105 James Boswell, *Life of Johnson*, vol. I, edited by George Birkbeck Hill, revised and enlarged by L.F. Powell, Oxford, Clarendon Press, pp. 43–4.

106 E. Gibbon, *Memoirs*, pp. 69–70.

107 August Strindberg, *Le fils de la servante*, in *Oeuvres autobiographiques*, vol. I, edited by Carl Gustaf Bjurström, Paris, Mercure de France, 1990, p. 61.

108 Maxime Du Camp, *Souvenirs littéraires*, Paris, Aubier, 1994, p. 116; similar thoughts from Flaubert (*ibid.*, pp. 116–7) and Remy de Gourmont (L. Forestier, "Rimbaud", p. 30).

109 George Eliot, *The Mill on the Floss*, ed. Gordon S. Haight, Oxford, Clarendon Press, 1980, p. 24.

110 Augustin Sicard, *Les études classiques avant la Révolution*, Paris, Librairie Académique Didier, Perrin et Cie, 1887, p. 94.

111 A. Léonard, "La formation", p. 149.

112 A. Strindberg, *Le fils de la servante*, vol. I, pp. 89–90.

113 L. Forestier, "Rimbaud", pp. 29–30.

114 Apart from the phenomenon of entirely sterile teaching, resumed voluntarily in adulthood. For a good example of this, see E. Quinet, *Histoire de mes idées*, p. 151: "So long as classics were being taught me, they appeared to be a form of servitude; I obstinately withheld my mind and my memory. As soon as they ceased to be compulsory, I became very keen on them; I set out to give myself the education and instruction I had refused from my masters."

115 Sebastiano Timpanaro, *Classicismo e Illuminismo nell'Ottocento italiano*, Pisa, Nistri Lischi, 1965, p. 55; Anthony Trollope, *Autobiography*, French translation by Guillaume Villeneuve, Paris, Aubier, 1994, pp. 27–8; M. Du Camp, *Souvenirs littéraires*, pp. 116–17 (Flaubert's reaction), 159–60 (Du Camp himself); other examples in Albert Léonard, "Aspects de la didactique du latin au XIXe. siècle en France et échos de sa réception par les élèves", in *International Journal of the Classical Traditions*, 3 (1997), pp. 319–52.

116 P. Valèry, *Cahiers*, vol. II, p. 1556.

117 C. Gascard, "L'enseignement", part 1, p. 202 and, for other seventeenth-century examples, pp. 50–51, 63, 77, 88, 168–9, 173, 191–2, etc.

118 Quotation from D. Julia, *Les trois couleurs*, p. 251; see similarly p. 252; other examples in F. Brunot, *Histoire de la langue française*, vol. VII, pp. 10, 91, 125–7 (La Condamine), *Lettre*, p. 31.

119 M. Davenport Hill, *Public Education*, pp. 220 ff.; see also M.L. Clarke, *Classical Education*, pp. 58–9.

120 P. Paillet, "La crise du latin", in *Enfances*, 5 (November–December 1954), pp. 542–3; survey in *L'éducation nationale*, 10 (15 December 1954) and in particular Jean Cousin's article "Les responsables", pp. 255–9; *Encyclopédie pratique*, p. 635; P. Martin, "Le latin".

121 For example, Christoph August Heumann, *Poecile sive Epistolae miscellaneae ad literatissimos aevi nostri viros*, Halae, ex officina Rengeriana, 1722, vol. I, book I, p. 100; or Diderot quoted by Jean-François La Harpe, *Lycée ou Cours de littérature ancienne et moderne, dernière partie: philosophie du dix-huitième siècle*, vol. XVI, part 1, Paris, Agasse, year XII, p. 154; also La Harpe himself, *ibid.*, part 2, pp. 386–7: "It could only be with a view to getting rid of children whom nobody knows what to do with at home that people send them at the age of five or six to lisp grammatical terms and Latin words." In the middle of the twentieth century, poor results caused some to form the opinion that starting Latin should be delayed until fourth grade (survey in *l'Education nationale*, 10 (15 December 1954), p. 306.

122 See, for example, J.-F. La Harpe, *Lycée*, vol XVI, part 2, pp. 591–2.

123 Antoine de Laval, *Desseins de professions nobles et publiques*, Paris, Claude Cramoisy, 1621, fol. 348; Justus Christophorus Böhmer, *Oratio II de latinarum litterarum atque eloquentiae studiis negligenter hodie cultis*, in *Orationes tres*, Helmestedii, typis Georg. Wolfgangi Hammii, 1715, no page numbers; C.A. Heumann, *Poecile*, pp. 100–101; etc. For examples of pedantic teaching, restricting ourselves to the Ancien Régime: Charles Sorel, *Histoire comique de Francion*, in *Romanciers du XVIIe. siècle*, ed. Antoine Adam, Paris, Gallimard, Pléiade, 1958, pp. 182–3; Johannes Noltenius, *Lexicon linguae latinae antibarbarorum: praemittitur ejusdem oratio de hodierno linguae latinae cultu negligentiori*, Helmstatii, impensis Christiani Frider, Weygandi, 1730, pp. 11–12; the "college" entry of the *Encyclopédie*; L.S. Mercier, *Tableau de Paris*, vol. I, pp. 206–7, 288–9, 404–5.

124 For examples, see criticisms of Latin verse (Abbé Vissac, *De la poésie latine en France au siècle de Louis XIV*, Paris, Aug. Durand, 1862, pp. 21–2, 24; C. Stray, *Grinders*, pp. 32–3, 37), Latin tragedies ("College" entry in the *Encyclopédie*), verse translation exercises (S. Timpanaro, *Classicismo*, p. 54), the way text is explained (Jean Capelle, "Le latin ou Babel", in *L'éducation nationale*, 23 October 1952, p. 8), the choice of texts that are too difficult or boring for children (J. Capelle, "Le latin"; J. Cousin, "Les responsables", pp. 257–8; R. Simone, "L'inauspicabile", p. 64); and so on.

125 See the long footnote on pp. 370–71 of J. Milton, *Of Education*, which includes

other examples from the sixteenth century and the first half of the seventeenth century.

126 Quotation from C. Gascard, "L'enseignement", part I, p. 88.

127 Quoted from an account of a book by Facciolati in *Mémoires de Trévoux*, October 1730, pp. 1789–90.

128 Quotation from J.-F. La Harpe, *Lycée*, vol XVI, part 1, p. 154; see also M. Bellot-Anthony and D. Hadjaj, "La querelle", pp. 35–9.

129 F. Murru and G. Pessolano Filos, *Alla riscoperta*, pp. 11–63 (pp. 56, 63).

130 M. Davenport Hill, *Public Education*, pp. 258–63 (pp. 258, 262).

131 See statements by Riccardo Avallone and Barthélemy Taladoire to the *Troisième congrès international pour le latin vivant*, pp. 65, 129; P. Martin, "Le latin", p. 28.

132 See notably, for the sixteenth century, Rosemary O'Day, *Education and Society, 1500–1800: The Social Foundations of Education in Early Modern Britain*, London, New York, Longman, 1982, pp. 66–7; for the seventeenth century, as an example, Scioppius's *Grammatica philosophica* (1688) described by its author as *honesta, jucunda* (because restricted to the essential rules with very few exceptions); and more generally, C. Gascard, "L'enseignement", parts IV and V; for the eighteenth century, Bernard Colombat, "Les grammaires latines en France", in *Dix-huitième siècle*, 27 (1995), pp. 25–41; for the nineteenth and twentieth centuries, Alain Choppin, *Les manuels scolaires en France de 1789 à nos jours*, vol. 3: *Les manuels de latin*, Paris, INRP, Publications de La Sorbonne, 1988.

133 For seventeenth- and eighteenth-century France, see C. Gascard, "L'enseignement"; Dominique Julia, "Livres de classe et usages pédagogiques", in Henri-Jean Martin and Roger Chartier (eds), *Histoire de l'édition française*, vol. II, *Le livre triomphant 1660–1830*, Paris, Promodis, 1984, pp. 473–97.

134 *Encyclopédie de l'éducation*, vol. I, p. 639.

135 Quotation from C. Gascard, "L'enseignement", part I, pp. 86–7.

136 Kristian Jensen, "The Latin Grammar of Philipp Melanchthon", in Stella P. Revard, Fidel Rädle, Mario A. Di Cesare (eds), *Acta conventus neo-latini guelferbytani: Proceedings of the Sixth International Congress of Neo-Latin Studies, Wolfenbüttel 12 August to 16 August 1985*, Binghamton, Mediaeval and Renaissance Texts and Studies, 1988, pp. 513–18.

137 C. Gascard, "L'enseignement", part I, pp. 190–99 (p. 199); A. Léonard, *Aspects*, p. 313. Remember Rousseau's reaction to the Port-Royal grammar: "These Ostrogothic verses made me sick to my heart and could not get into my ear. I was lost in these crowds of rules, and every time I learned a new one, I forgot all that had gone before" (*Les confessions*, p. 275).

138 On Kennedy's *Primer*, see C. Stray, "Paradigms of Social Order: the Politics of Latin Grammar in 19th-Century England", in *Henry Sweet Society Newsletter*, 13 (November 1989), pp. 13–23; *Grinders*, pp. 75 and 24.

139 J. Cousin, "Les responsables", p. 256.

140 John Locke, *Of Education*, in *Works*, vol. X, Scientia Verlag Aalen, 1963 (reprint of edition published in London, 1823), pp. 152–60 (p. 155). See similarly, D.G. Morhof, *Polyhistor*, pp. 455–80. That diagnosis lay behind schemes for learning Latin by oral practice, the "living Latin" movement and the idea of Latin towns (see pp. 157–8).

141 A. Sicard, *Les études classiques*, ch. 5; D. Julia, "Livres de classe", pp. 486–7; B. Colombat, "Les grammaires latines"; M. Bellot-Anthony and D. Hadjaj, "La querelle", pp. 41–3.

142 P. Chambon, "Esquisse d'une méthode", pp. 312–30.

143 See records of the *Premier congrès international du latin vivant, Avignon, 3–6 septembre 1956*, Avignon, Edouard Aubanel, 1956; P. Crahay-Ciselet, "Congrès international pour le latin vivant", in *L'Athénée*, 45 (November–December 1956), p. 33.

144 On a pedagogic experiment along these lines in Belgium between 1953 and 1955, see J. Rémy, "Une association monstrueuse", pp. 50–52.

145 P. Campbell, "Latin and the Elite Tradition in Education", in P.W. Musgrave (ed.), *Sociology, History and Education: A Reader*, London, Methuen & Co, 1970, p. 264. This emerges especially from some of the ways the CD-ROM *Perseus* is used in French schools; moreover, the Latin teacher no longer wishes to be an arts teacher but a humanities teacher (see pp. 35 and 40).

146 For a seventeenth-century example, see Gabriel de Foigny, *L'usage du jeu royal de la langue latine avec la facilité et l'élégance des langues latine et française comprises en XCI leçons, le tout expliqué avec tant de clarté qu'on pourra se perfectionner en l'une et l'autre langue en six ou sept mois*, Lyon, Vve de Benoît Coral, 1674; for the 1950s, *Encyclopédie pratique de l'éducation*, pp. 638–9.

147 C. Gascard, "L'enseignement", part I, p. 94; "collège" entry in the *Encyclopédie*.

148 Anthony Grafton and Lisa Jardine, *From Humanism to Humanities: Education and Liberal Arts in Fifteenth- and Sixteenth-Century England*, London, Duckworth, 1986, pp. 15, 20, 87.

6 Oral Latin

1 Quoted by James Knowlson, *Universal Language Schemes in England and France, 1660–1800*, University of Toronto Press, 1975, pp. 7–8.

2 Pronunciation alone seems to have aroused some interest (see below).

3 See chapters 1, 2 and 3.

4 Piet Steenbakkers, "Accent-Marks in Neo-Latin", in Rhoda Schnut *et al.* (eds), *Acta conventus neolatini hafnensis. Proceedings of the Eighth International Congress of Neo-Latin Studies, Copenhagen, 12 August to 17 August 1991*, Binghamton, Mediaeval and Renaissance Texts and Studies, 1994, pp. 925–34.

5 Quoted by Jean-François La Harpe, *Lycée ou Cours de littérature ancienne et moderne. Dernière partie: philosophie du dix-huitième siècle.* Paris, Agasse, an XIII, vol. XVI, part 1, p. 160.

6 John XXIII, *Veterum Sapienta. Du développement de l'étude du latin. Constitution apostolique du 22 février 1962.* Paris, Editions de la Nouvelle Aurore, 1975, pp. 8, 13.

7 Carlo Egger, *Quomodo lingua litteraeque latinae in Pontificio Instituto Altioris Latinitatis traduntur*, in *Quatrième congrès international pour le latin vivant. Avignon, du 1er au 3 avril 1969.* Avignon, Aubanel, 1970, pp. 52–3.

8 Primo Levi, *La tregua*. Turin, Einaudi, 1963, p. 55. Acknowledgements are due to Mario Infelise for drawing this text to my attention.

9 *Notes and Queries*, 5th series, vol. VIII, p. 132.

10 Letter from Descartes to Isaac Beeckmann, 17 October 1630 (*Journal kept by Isaac Beeckmann from 1604 to 1634, published and with introduction and notes by Cornelis de Waard.* vol. 4, The Hague, Martinus Nijhoff, 1953, p. 202).

11 *Relazioni degli ambasciatori veneti al Senato, a cura di Eugenio Alberi*, 1st series, vol. III, Florence, Tipografia all'Insegna di Clio, 1853, p. 256.

12 Goethe, *Mémoires*, translated by Jacques Porchat, Paris, Hachette, 1862, pp. 208, 411.

13 President des Brosses, *Lettres d'Italie.* vol. I, edited by Frédéric d'Agay, Paris, Mercure de France, 1986, p. 99.

14 Byron, *Letters and Journals,* vol. I, edited by Leslie A. Marchand, London, John Murray, 1973, p. 215.

15 Horace Walpole, *Correspondence,* vol. II: *Horace Walpole's correspondence with the Rev. William Cole,* edited by W.S. Lewis and A. Dayle Wallace, New Haven, Yale University Press, 1937, p. 313.

16 See p. 61.

17 Stanislas Breton, *De Rome à Paris: itinéraire philosophique,* Paris, Desclée de Brouwer, 1992, pp. 57–8.

18 Léon Dehon, *Diario del Concilio Vaticano I, a cura di Vincenzo Carbone,* Rome, Tipografica Poliglotta Vaticana, 1962, pp. 43–4 etc.

19 Maurilio Guasco, "Una giornata di Vaticano II", in *Le deuxième concile du Vatican (1959–1965). Actes du colloque Rome, 28–30 mai 1986.* Ecole française de Rome, 1989, pp. 447–8, 461.

20 "Ferdinando I de Medici", in *Dizionario biografico degli Italiani.*

21 Ferdinand Brunot, *Histoire de la langue française des origines à nos jours,* vol. VII, *La propagation du français en France jusqu'à la fin de l'Ancien Régime,* Paris, Librairie Armand Colin, 1967, p. 131.

22 Quoted by Clément Falcucci, *L'humanisme dans l'enseignement secondaire en France au XIXe siècle,* Toulouse, Privat; Paris, Didier, 1939, p. 47.

23 Denis Diderot, *Plan d'une université,* in *Oeuvres,* vol. III, *Politique,* edited by Laurent Versini, Paris, Robert Laffont, 1995, p. 450.

24 Carole Gascard, "L'enseignement du latin au XVIIe siècle à travers les textes théoriques et les grammaires", diploma thesis, manuscript, Paris, 1994, part I, p. 202.

25 M.L. Clarke, *Classical Education in Britain 1500–1900,* Cambridge University Press, 1959, p. 14.

26 Ambroise Jobert, *La Commission d'éducation nationale en Pologne (1773–1794),* Paris, Les Belles Lettres, 1941, p. 308.

27 *Naudeana et Patiniana ou singularitez remarquables prises des converstions de Mess. Naudé et Patin,* Paris, Florentin et Pierre Delaulnes, 1701, p. 38 (concerning *Patiniana*).

28 *Menagiana ou les bons mots, les pensées critiques, historiques, morales et d'érudition de Monsieur Ménage, receuillis par ses amis,* second edition, vol. II, Paris, Florentin et Pierre Delaulnes, 1694, p. 17.

29 Ole Borch, *Itinerarium, 1660–1665: The Journal of the Danish Polyhistor Ole Borch,* vol. II, edited by H.D. Shepelern, Copenhagen, Danish Society of Language and Literature, 1983, p. 228.

30 *Locke's Travels in France 1675–1679: As Related in his Journals, Correspondence and Other Papers,* edited by John Lough, Cambridge University Press, 1953, p. 50 (quotation) and p. 54 (another example).

31 Louis Sebastien Mercier, *Tableau de Paris,* vol. I, edited by Jean-Claude Bonnet, Paris, Mercure de France, 1994, p. 1412.

32 Bruno Neveu, "L'Eglise et l'Université de France: les facultés de théologie catholique des académies (1808–1885)", doctoral thesis, Paris, 1993, manuscript, p. 404.

33 André Chervel, *Histoire de l'agrégation: contribution à l'étude de la culture scolaire,* Paris, INRP; Editions Kimé, 1993, p. 79.

34 *Pierides sive Latium literatum continens selectum elaborationum a membris Societatis latinae*

exhibitarum ad omnigenam eruditionem facientium Halae Venedum, impensis Societatis, 1736; *Exercitationes Societatis latinae quae Ienae est, publicatae ab ejus directore,* Friderico Andrea Halbauero, Lipsiae, impensis Caspari Henr. Fuchsii, 1741.

35 Antoine de Laval, *Desseins de professions nobles et publiques Dernière édition,* Paris, Claude Cramoisy, 1621, folio 348.

36 Jean Cécile Frey, *Via ad divas scientias artesque, linguarum notitiam, sermones extempora-neos, nova et expeditissima,* Jenae, apud Petrum Brösselin; Arnstadiae, typis Meureri-anis, 1674, pp. 7–8.

37 Daniel Georg Morhof, *Polyhistor . . . Lubecae,* vol. I, P. Böckmann, 1708, p. 461.

38 Pierre Louis Moreau de Maupertuis, *Du devoir de l'académicien,* in *Oeuvres,* Dresden, George Conrad Walther, 1752, p. 290; *Lettre sur le progrès des sciences,* in *ibid.,* p. 339.

39 (La Condamine), *Lettre critique sur l'éducation,* Paris, Prault, 1751, pp. 35–6.

40 Jozef Ijsewijn and Dirk Sacré, "The Ultimate Efforts to save Latin as the Means of International Communication", in *History of European Ideas,* 16 (January 1993), pp. 51–66.

41 Ibid., p. 57; Eskil Källquist, "Jacob Rudbeckius Latinstad: Ett pedagogiskt doku-ment från Gustav II Adolfs tid", in *Lychnos* (1936), pp. 151–79.

42 Jacques Fontaine, *Mémoires d'une famille huguenote victime de la révocation de l'édit de Nantes,* edited by Bernard Cottret, Montpellier, Les Presses du Languedoc, 1992, p. 75.

43 John Durkan and James Kirk, *The University of Glasgow, 1451–1577,* Glasgow Uni-versity Press, 1977, pp. 312–3.

44 Vittorio Alfieri, *Vita scritta da esso,* vol. I, edited by Luigi Fassò, Asti, Casa d'Alfieri, 1951, pp. 39, 44.

45 Fausto Nicolini, *Uomini di spada, di Chiesa, di toga, di studio ai tempi di Giambattista Vico,* Milan, Hoepli, 1942, pp. 395–6.

46 Françoise Waquet, "Elites intellectuelles et reproduction du savoir: le témoignage de la génération des pré-Lumières", in *Problèmes d'histoire de l'éducation: actes des sem-inaires organisés par l'Ecole française de Rome et l'Università di Roma-La Sapienza (janvier-mai 1985),* Rome, Ecole française de Rome, 1988, pp. 9–10.

47 Anna Maria Bernardinis, "Una riforma di due secoli fa (G. Gozzi e il problema del latino)", in *Rassegna di pedagogia,* 23 (October–December 1965), pp. 355, 357.

48 J.-F. La Harpe, "Extrait d'un plan sommaire d'éducation publique et d'un nouveau cours d'étude publié en janvier 1791 dans le *Mercure d France*", in *Lycée,* vol. XIV, part 2, p. 399. See also F. Brunot, *Histoire de la langue française,* vol. VII, p. 104.

49 Jean-Pierre Borle, *Le Latin à l'Académie de Lausanne du XVIe. au XXe. Siècle,* Lausanne University, 1987, p. 55.

50 i.e. *Caesarea Majestas bene gaudet videre vos et orationem vestram libenter audiuit* ("His Impe-rial Majesty is delighted to see you and has heard your address with pleasure").

51 Quotation from Jacques Chomarat's translation, *Oeuvres choisies d'Erasme,* Paris, Le Livre de Poche, 1991, pp. 920–21.

52 *L'esprit de Guy Patin tiré de ses conversations, de son cabinet et de ses ouvrages,* Amsterdam, Schelten, 1709, p. 205.

53 Samuel Sorbière, *Relation d'un voyage en Angleterre où sont touchées plusieurs choses qui regardent l'état des sciences et de la religion et autres matières curieuses,* Saint-Etienne, Presses de l'Université, 1980 (original edition Cologne, 1666), pp. 72–3.

54 Utrecht, University Library, ms. 995 III 6K12, folios 67–8 and 69–70. Theodorus Johannes van Ameloveen to Johann Reiske and Heinrich Meibom, 17 and 18

December 1691. I am grateful to Saskia Stegeman for bringing this text to my attention.

55 From the biography of Bochart by Etienne Morin, in Samuel Bochart, *Opera omnia: Lugduni Batavorum, apud Cornelium Boutesteyn et Samuelem Luchtmans; Trajecti ad Rhenum, apud Guilielmum vande Water*, 1712, p. 3.

56 Florence, Archivio di Stato, ms. 684. "Giornale del viaggio fatto dagli Ecc.mi sigg.ri principi D. Bartolomeo e gran priore Don Lorenzo Corsini", 1752–55. I am grateful to Jean Boutier for bringing this text to my attention.

57 John Bowle, *John Evelyn and His World*, London, Routledge & Kegan Paul, 1981, p. 105.

58 *The Gentleman's Magazine*, LV (1785), p. 362; LXXXVIII (1818), p. 224; for further examples, see *Notes and Queries*, 10th series, vol. IX, pp. 81–3, 131, 175, 251, 314, 351, 511.

59 Christopher Stray, *Grinders and Grammars: A Victorian Controversy*, Reading, The Text Book Colloquium, 1995, p. 44.

60 Published in his *Grammatica philosophica Amstelodami, apud Judocum* Pluymer, 1664, p. 166, where this author provides many other examples. On Chinese pronunciation, see also pp. 53–5.

61 See for example Jacques du Roure, *Essai sur le renouvellement du latin changé depuis plusieurs siècles, où et notre nation et toutes les autres qui de leurs paroles dépendent et usent de cette même langue latine, peuvent avec la manière de la rétablir, voir la différence et l'éloignement de leurs façons de s'énoncer et d'écrire* Paris, published by the author, 1683, ch. 1: "Etat où est présentement la langue latine".

62 Saint-Simon, *Mémoires* vol. 40, edited by Alain de Boislisle, Paris, Hachette, 1928, p. 129.

63 Geoffroy Tory, *Champ Fleury*, Introduction by J.W. Joliffe, Paris, La Haye, Mouton, 1970 (original edition 1574), p. 15.

64 (Johannes Casellius), *Libellus novus de pronunciatione latini sermonis . . . Helmaestadii, Jacobus Lucius*, 1661, no page numbers.

65 John Caius, *De pronunciatione graecae et latinae linguae*, edited and translated by J.B. Gabel, Leeds, University of Leeds, 1968 (original edition 1574), p. 15.

66 Patricia Ranum, *Méthode de la prononciation latine dite vulgaire ou à la française: petite méthode à l'usage des chanteurs et des récitants d'après le manuscrit de Dom Jacques Le Clerc*, Arles, Actes Sud, 1991, p. 34.

67 *Ibid.*, p. 38.

68 *Scaligerana, Thuana, Perroniana, Pithoeiana et Colomesiana ou remarques historiques, critiques, morales et littéraires de Jos. Scaliger, J. Aug. de Thou, le cardinal du Perron, Fr. Pithou et P. Colomiès, Avec les notes de plusieurs savants*, Amsterdam, Covens et Mortier, 1740, vol. II, *Scaligerana II*, p. 380.

69 Augustin Renaudet, "Erasme et la prononciation des langues antiques", in *Bibliothèque d'Humanisme et Renaissance*, 18 (1956), p. 194.

70 Christopher Stray, *Classics Transformed: Schools, Universities and Society in England, 1830–1960*, Oxford University Press, 1998. I am grateful to C. Stray for access to the manuscript passages of this work related to pronunciation.

71 G. Tory, *Champ Fleury*, folio 49.

72 See A. Renaudet,"Erasme"; Maria Cytowoka's introduction to the edition of *De recta pronunciatione* appearing in Erasmus's *Opera omnia* (Amsterdam, North Holland Publishing Company, 1973, vol. 1, p. 4).

73 Charles Beaulieux, "Essai sur l'histoire de la prononciation du latin en France",

in *Revue des études latines*, V (1927), pp. 68–82; Pierre Damas, *La prononciation française du latin depuis le XVIe siècle*, Paris, Les Belles Lettres, 1934; Jules Marouzeau, *La prononciation du latin (histoire, théorie, pratique)*, Paris, Les Belles Lettres, 1955; P. Ranum, *Méthode*, This last pronunciation changed little until the beginning of the twentieth century, apart from the articulation of certain vowels and the debate on accentuation – for quantity, stress or both – which finally resulted in accentuation being dropped.

74 J. Caius, *De pronunciatione*; W. Sidney Allen, "Some Observations on the Pronunciation of Latin", in *Didaskalos*, 1 (1963), pp. 45–63; Frederick Brittain, *Latin in Church: Episodes in the History of its Pronunciation Particularly in England*, Cambridge University Press, 1934, pp. 31–6.

75 William Riley Parker, *Milton: A Biography*, Oxford, Clarendon Press, 1969, p. 920.

76 J. Casellius, *Libellus*; C. Scioppius, *De orthopeia*, pp. 168 ff.; Charles Rollin, *De la manière d'enseigner et d'étudier les belles-lettres par rapport à l'esprit et au coeur*, Paris, Jacques Estienne, 1720, pp. 239 ff.

77 John Milton, *Of Education*, in *Complete Prose Works*, vol. II: *1643–1648*, New Haven, Yale University Press, 1959, p. 383.

78 See texts cited in note 63 above; and Maria Bonioli, *La pronuncia del latino nelle scuole dall'Antichità al Rinascimento*, Turin, Giappichelli, 1962, pp. 25–6.

79 P. Ranum, *Méthode*, p. 60.

80 Charles Perrault, *Parallèle des Anciens et des Modernes en ce qui regarde les arts et les sciences: dialogue*, vol. II, second edition, Geneva, Slatkine, 1971 (reprint of 1692 Paris edition), pp. 8–9.

81 C. Scioppius, *De orthopeia*, pp. 166–7; J. Casellius, *Libellus*, no page numbers.

82 C. Scioppius, *De orthopeia*, p. 166; same idea in J. du Roure, *Essai*, p. 3.

83 *Encyclopédie ou Dictionnaire universel raisonné des connaissances humaines*, ed. M. de Felice, *Supplément*, vol. IV, Yverdon, 1776, p. 104, under "Latinité".

84 J. Caius, *De pronunciatione*, pp. 12–23 (pp. 12, 17, 20, 19).

85 James Boswell, *Life of Johnson*, vol. II, edited by George Birbeck Hill, revised and enlarged by L.F. Powell, Oxford, Clarendon Press, 1979, p. 104.

86 Le Cerf de La Viéville, *Comparaison de la musique italienne et de la musique française*, second edition, Brussels, François Foppens, 1705–06, pp. 175–6.

87 J. Marouzeau, *La prononciation*; Edmond Farral and Jules Marouzeau, "La réforme de la prononciation du latin", in *Revue des études latines*, V (1927), pp. 82–90.

88 On the adoption of Roman pronunciation by the French clergy, see in particular J. Brugerette, *Le prêtre français et la société contemporaine. Sous le régime de la Séparation: la reconstitution catholique (1908–1936)*, Paris, Lethielleux, 1938, pp. 628–32 (p. 631); Camille Couillaut, *La réforme de la prononciation latine*, Paris, Bloud et Cie, 1910; Alcide Macé, "La prononciation du latin dans l'Eglise catholique", in *Revue des cours et conférences*, 21 (1912–13), pp. 62–6 (p. 64).

89 J. Marouzeau, *La prononciation*; Edmond Farral and Jules Marouzeau, "La réforme de la prononciation du latin", in *Revue des études latines*, V (1927), pp. 82–90.

90 Lucien Sausy and Robert France, *Grammaire latine abrégée*, revised and augmented sixth edition, Paris, Librairie Fernand Lanore, undated (c. 1959), p. 1.

91 C. Stray, *Classics Transformed*; "Ideology and Institution: English Classical Scholarship in Transition", in *Annals of Scholarship*, 10 (1993), pp. 115–16.

92 W. Sidney Allen, "Some Observations", pp. 49–52; there were also numerous errors due to mistaking the quantities of syllables.

93 F. Brittain's book (*Latin in Church*,) is an excellent historical demonstration of this point.

94 Alfonso Traina and Giorgio Bernardi Perini, *Propeudetica al latino universitario*, fifth edition, revised and edited by Claudio Marangoni, Bologna, Pàtron, 1995, pp. 66–9, 72–3; Antonio Traglia, "Problemi di grammatica latina (fonetica, accento, pronuncia, aspetto verbale)", in Biagio Amata (ed.), *Cultura e lingue classiche: convegno di aggiornamento e di didattica, Roma, 1–2 novembre 1985*, Rome, LAS, 1986, pp. 12–14. For the debate during the 1960s, see "La pronuncia del latino nelle scuole", in *MAIA*, 18 (1966), pp. 254–62; 19 (1967), pp. 255–78.

95 L. Dehon, *Diario*, pp. 43–4; M. Maccarone, *Il concilio Vaticano I e il giornale di Mons. Arrigoni*, p. 12; V. Marchese, *Le mie impressioni*, pp. 112–3; V. Tizzani, *Il Concilio Vaticano I*, pp. 73–4, 110, 169.

96 *Premier congrès international pour le latin vivant: Avignon, 3–6 septembre 1956*, Avignon, Edouard Aubanel, 1956, pp. 13, 17, 21, 25, 58–65, 153; *Deuxième congrès international pour le latin vivant: Lyon, Villeurbanne du 8 au 10 septembre 1959*, Avignon, Edouard Aubanel, 1960, pp. 29, 46; A. Traina and G. Bernardi Perini, *Propedeutica*, p. 72.

97 There are circles that try to maintain the use of spoken Latin, but they have few participants and very limited influence (for an initial survey, see Biagio Amata (ed.), *Cultura e lingue classiche, 2: 20 convegno di aggiornamento e di didattica, Roma, 31 ottobre–1 novembre 1987*, Rome, LAS, 1988, p. 240, 265–8, 269–73).

Part III What Latin Meant: Introduction

1 Johannes Fredericus Noltenius, *Lexicon latinae linguae antibarbarum. Praemittitur ejusdem oratio de hodierno linguae latinae cultu negligentiori. Helmstadii, impensis Christiani Frider. Weygandi*, 1730, pp. 1–9 (of the *Oratio*).

2 Ferdinand Brunot, *Histoire de la langue française des origines à nos jours*, vol. VII: *La propagation du français en France jusqu'à la fin de l'Ancien Régime*, Paris, Librairie Armand Colin, 1967, p. 95.

3 Denis Diderot, *Plan d'une université*, in *Oeuvres*, vol. III, edited by Laurent Versini, Paris, Robert Laffont, 1995, pp. 449 and 450.

4 Anna Maria Bernardinis, "Una riforma di due secoli fa (G. Gozzi e il problema del latino)", in *Rassegna di pedagogia*, 23 (October–December 1965), pp. 307–68; Meyer Reinhold, *Classica Americana: The Greek and Roman Heritage in the United States*, Detroit, Wayne State University Press, 1984, pp. 60–63, 120, 130–31 (p. 130).

5 D. Diderot, *Plan*, p. 450.

6 M. Reinhold, *Classica Americana*, pp. 30–31 and 46 (footnote 52).

7 Helvetius, *De l'esprit*, Verviers, Editions Gérard & Co., 1973, p. 493; the same viewpoint is expressed by Franklin, Hopkinson and Rush (M. Reinhold, *Classica Americana*, pp. 121, 125, 130). This argument had been explained and refuted by Noltenius in 1730 (*Lexicon*, pp. 10–12).

8 M. Reinhold, *Classica Americana*, pp. 30–32, 37–9, 301.

9 Adeline Daumard, *La bourgeoisie parisienne de 1815 à 1848*, Paris, SEVPEN, 1963, pp. 351–3; second edition, Paris, Albin Michel, 1996. Latin editions were found only in the libraries of academics and the very rich bourgeoisie.

10 Jean Guéhenno, "La querelle du latin", in *La table ronde*, March 1959, p. 27; "La querelle des humanités", in *ibid.*, p. 16; similarly, M. Cabanis: "The aim of Latin teaching at secondary level is not to impart Latin to the pupils for its own sake" ("Pour enseigner le français, la logique, la civilisation", in *L'éducation nationale*, 10

(15 December 1954), p. 235). More generally, on the change of objective in Latin teaching and the reduction in the importance of grammar, see George E. Ganss, *Saint Ignatius' Idea of a Jesuit University: A Study in the History of Catholic Education*, Milwaukee, Marquette University Press, 1954, pp. 219 ff.

11 Quotation from Eugène de Saint-Denis, "Assisterons-nous à l'agonie des études latines?", in *Bulletin de l'Association Guillaume-Budé* (June 1954), p. 26.

12 "Latin: the Basic Language", in *The Classical Journal*, 64 (1969), p. 164. Also on this point, see remarks by Guido Calogero, "Il panlatinismo", in *Scuola sotto inchiesta: nuova edizione accresciuta*, Turin, Einaudi, 1965, p. 42.

7 Making the Man

1 Eugenio Garin, *L'educazione in Europa, 1400/1600: problemi e programmi*, Bari, Laterza, 1976, pp. 3–29 and 87–145 (pp. 83, 95 and 98). Published in French as *L'éducation de l'homme moderne: la pédagogie de la Renaissance*, Paris, Hachette, 1995.

2 Anthony Grafton and Lisa Jardine, *From Humanism to Humanities: Education and the Liberal Arts in Fifteenth- and Sixteenth-Century Europe*, London, Duckworth, 1986 (pp. xv, 22).

3 Meyer Reinhold, *Classica Americana: The Greek and Roman Heritage in the United States*, Detroit, Wayne State University Press, 1984, chs II, IV and VI (pp. 131, 136); for arguments for and against Latin, pp. 176–8.

4 Dominique Julia, "Livres de classe et usages pédagogiques", in Henri-Jean Martin and Roger Chartier (eds), *Histoire de l'édition française*, vol. II: *Le livre triomphant 1660–1830*, Paris, Promodis, 1984, p. 486.

5 Helvetius, *De l'esprit*, Verviers, Editions Gérard et Co., 1973, p. 493.

6 Diderot, *Plan d'une université*, in *Oeuvres*, vol. III: *Politique*, edited by Laurent Versini, Paris, Robert Laffont, 1995, pp. 447–50, 458–9.

7 Dominique Julia, *Les trois couleurs du tableau noir: la Révolution*, Paris, Belin, 1981, p. 252.

8 *Ibid.*, pp. 252–5, which notes that Mirabeau, in his *Travail sur l'éducation publique* (1790–91) used the same reasoning, while still favouring teaching in French.

9 Ferdinand Brunot, *Histoire de la langue française des origines à nos jours*, vol. VII: *La propagation du français en France jusqu'à la fin de l'Ancien Régime*, Paris, Librairie Armand Colin, 1967, pp. 122–3. Brunot notes: "This was the first time that I saw a clear formulation of this argument, which is still used".

10 Jean-François La Harpe, "Extrait d'un plan sommaire d'éducation publique et d'un nouveau cours d'étude publié en janvier 1791 dan le *Mercure de France*", in *Lycée ou Cours de littérature ancienne et moderne*, part II: *Philosophie du dix-huitième siècle*, vol. XVI, part two, Paris, Agasse, Year XIII, pp. 389–90.

11 Examples from Italy could also have been cited (Furio Murru and Giuseppe Pessolano Filos, *Alla riscoperta della didattica del latino in Italia nel Settecento e nell'Ottocento*, Rome, Edizioni Nuova Rivista Pedagogica, 1980, pp. 19–20; Anna Maria Bernardinis, "Una riforma di due secoli fa (G. Gozzi e il problema del lationo)", in *Rassegna di pedagogia*, 23 (October–December 1965), p. 324).

12 Harry N. Rivlin (ed.), *Encyclopaedia of Modern Education*, Port Washington, NY, Kennikat Press, 1943, under "Latin, teaching of"; Torsten Husen and T. Neville Postlethwaite (eds), *The International Encyclopaedia of Education, Research and Studies*, Oxford, Pergamon Press, 1985, under "Classical languages: educational programs".

13 Lucien Sausy and Robert France, *Grammaire latine abrégée*, revised and augmented sixth edition, Paris, Librairie Fernand Lanore, undated (c. 1959), pp. vii–viii.

14 *Studi romani*, 8 (1960), p. 251.

15 Peter Wülfing, "L'enseignement des langues anciennes en Europe", in *L'Athénée* 69 (March–April 1980), pp. 22–6 (pp. 23–5); "Come legitimare l'insegnamento del latino?", in *Aufidus: rivista di scienza e didattica della cultura classica*, 20 (1993), pp. 111–21 (p. 113).

16 As suggested by Maurice Testard, "Réflexions sur la 'Defense et illustration de Latin'", in *Bulletin de l'Association Guillaume-Budé*, 1971, p. 185.

17 See, for one example among thousands, the evidence of Professor Etienne Wolff (in Jacqueline de Romilly, *Lettre aux parents sur les choix scolaires*, Paris, Editions de Fallois, 1994, p. 87): "Myocardial infarct! One of these words from the medical vocabulary is of Latin origin . . . the other of Greek origin. Most current French words, and not only the scientific ones, are of Latin origin; most medical terms are of Greek origin. The study of these two languages is thus indispensable not just to culture, but to everyday speech."

18 Josette Lallemont, "A propos des mesures prises contre les études classiques", in *Bulletin de l'Association Guillaume-Budé*, 1969, p. 177.

19 Guy Serbat, "Latin linguistique française", in *ibid.*, 1976, p. 116.

20 See notably J. de Romilly's book *Lettre aux parents*; a letter from Michel Zink, general administrator of this association, entitled "To learn Latin in fifth grade is to ensure mastery of French", insists, given the urgent situation of French, that Latin should be taught, and links "a renewal of Latin" with "a renewal of literary education in general"; and the minutes of a "colloquy on the future of the humanities" (1995) from which we have taken the title of this development.

21 Martha Hanna, *The Mobilization of Intellect: French Scholars and Writers During the Great War*, Cambridge, Harvard University Press, 1996, pp. 48, 170–74, 231; for the quotation, Louis Bérard, *Pour la réforme de l'enseignement secondaire*, Paris, A. Colin, 1923, p. 90.

22 For a "simple" development of this explanation, see *Lycée* de Foix Section, "Latin ou pas latin?", in *Revue de la Franco-Ancienne*, 164 (June 1969), p. 780; H. Pouzin, *Le latin, pour quoi faire?* Paris, Téqui, 1983.

23 Paul Crouzet and G. Berthet, *Nouvelle méthode latine et exercices illustrés (classes de 6e. et 5e.)*, Toulouse, Privat; Paris, Marcel Didier, 1951.

24 Corinne Saminadayar, "Du latin comme langue naturelle de l'écriture", in Georges Cesbron and Laurence Richer (eds), *La réception du latin du XIXe. siècle à nos jours: actes du colloque d'Angers des 23 et 24 septembre 1994*, Angers, Presses de l'Université, 1996, pp. 161–8 (see p. 15). On this point, see also remarks by Ernest Lavisse in his *Souvenirs* (Paris, Calmann-Lévy, 1912, p. 214).

25 George E. Ganss, *Saint Ignatius' Idea of a Jesuit University: A Study in the History of Catholic Education*, Milwaukee, Marquette University Press, 1954, pp. 219–26; F. Campbell, "Latin and the Elite Tradition in Education", in P.W. Musgrave (ed.), *Sociology, History and Education: A Reader*, London, Methuen & Co., 1970, p. 256.

26 Clément Falcucci, *L'humanisme dans l'enseignement secondaire en France au XIXe. siècle*, Toulouse, Privat; Paris, Didier, 1939, pp. 103, 181, 316, 327, 350, 415, 533–4.

27 Augustin Sicard, *Les études classiques avant la Révolution*, Paris, Librairie Académique Didier, Perrin et Cie, 1887, pp. 113–19.

28 Fritz Ringer, *Fields of Knowledge: French Academic Culture in Comparative Perspective, 1800–1920*, Cambridge University Press; Paris, Editions de la Maison des Sciences de l'Homme, 1992, p. 121, ch. 3; M. Hanna, *The Mobilization of Intellect*, pp. 45–6, 173, 231–2.

29 M.L. Clarke, *Classical Education in Britain, 1500–1900*, Cambridge University Press, 1959, p. 79; W.H.G. Armytage, *Four Hundred Years of English Education*, Cambridge University Press, 1964, pp. 127–8; for the public schools in general, Rupert Wilkinson, *The Prefects: British Leadership in the Public School Tradition. A Comparative Study in the Making of Rulers*, Oxford University Press, 1964, pp. 67–8.

30 Rupert Wilkinson, "Political Leadership and the Late Victorian Public School", in *The British Journal of Sociology*, 13 (1962), p. 324.

31 Jean-Pierre Borle, *Le latin à l'Académie de Lausanne du XVIe. au XXe. siècle*, Lausanne University, 1987, p. 80.

32 Quotation from Marie-Madeleine Martin, *Le latin immortel*, Chiré-en-Montreuil, Diffusion de la Pensée Française, 1971, p. 248.

33 M. Reinhold, *Classica Americana*, pp. 338–41 (p. 339).

34 Wladimir Berelowitch, *La sovietisation de l'école russe, 1917–1931*, Lausanne, L'Age d'Homme, 1990, p. 38.

35 Alexander Vucinich, *Science in Russian Culture: A History to 1860*, Stanford University Press, 1963, pp. 254–5; *Science in Russian Culture, 1861–1917*, Stanford University Press, 1970, pp. 59–61 (p. 60); Alain Besançon, *Education et société en Russie dans le second tiers du XIXe. siècle*, Paris, La Haye, Mouton, 1974, pp. 17–18; James C. McClelland, *Aristocrats and Academics: Education, Culture and Society in Tsarist Russia*, University of Chicago Press, 1979, pp. 13–14.

36 *Encyclopaedia of Modern Education*, under "Latin, teaching of".

37 George Frederick Kneller, *The Educational Philosophy of National Socialism*, New Haven, Yale University Press, 1941, p. 214.

38 And after the war too: see Guido Calogero, "Il panlatinismo" (1955), in *Scuola sotto inchiesta: nuova edizione accresciuta*, Turin, Einaudi, 1965, pp. 36–42 (pp. 36–7).

39 Albert Noirfalise, "Les auteurs anciens et l'homme d'aujourd'hui", in *Les études classiques*, XXI (October 1953), pp. 310–12.

40 José Jimenez Delgado, "Testimonios en favor de la educación classica", in *Rivista de educación*, XLIX (February 1962), p. 57.

41 Léopold Sédar Senghor, "Allocution", in *Revue de la Franco-Ancienne*, 169 (December 1970), p. 22; Institutum Romanis Studiis Provehendis, *Acta omnium gentium ac nationum conventus latinis litteris linguaeque fovendis* (13–16 April 1977), Rome, L'Erma, 1979, p. 29 (commencement address by the Rector of Dakar University) and pp. 429–30 (interview with President Senghor).

42 Generally, see an article by Jacques Perret, a professor at the Sorbonne, "Langue latine et formation de l'esprit", in *Revue de la Franco-Ancienne*, 107 (October 1953), pp. 17–22.

43 Maurice Lacroix, "Lettre", in *Revue de la Franco-Ancienne*, 162 (October–December 1968), p. 647.

44 "Deux questions de M. Hippolyte Ducos", in *Revue de la Franco-Ancienne*, 161 (June 1968), p. 587.

45 M. Lacroix, "Lettre", p. 647. The same argument, almost word for word, is used in a speech to the National Assembly by Hippolyte Ducos (28 October 1968) published in *Revue de la Franco-Ancienne*, 163 (March 1969), p. 732. See also a motion in 1972 moved by various associations co-operating on the defence of classical

studies, demanding "an initiation in Latin for all from the 6th grade" (in *Bulletin de l'Association Guillaume-Budé* (1972), p. 255).

46 Jacqueline de Romilly, "Intervention à la table ronde du 18 mars 1992 (Sorbonne)", in *Bulletin de l'Association Guillaume-Budé* (1993), p. 44; in greater detail from H. Pouzin, *Le latin*, p. 67: "Learning Latin is, above all, learning to reason: Latin is a school of reflection where all the faculties of the mind are put to work: rigour in analysis, subtlety in intuition, perseverance in attention, the memory with its riches."

47 Acknowledgements to Thomas Rütten for this information.

48 J. de Romilly, *Lettre aux parents*, pp. 82–3.

49 This, for example, was one of the arguments advanced in the depositions to the Ribot Commission in 1899 (F. Ringer, *Fields of Knowledge*, p. 143).

50 C. Falcucci, *L'humanisme*, pp. 318–31.

51 Sydney Smith, *Selected Writings*, edited by W.H. Auden, London, Faber and Faber, 1955, p. 262.

52 R. Wilkinson, "Political Leadership", p. 325; Christopher A. Stray, "Culture and Discipline: Classics and Society in Victorian England", in *International Journal of the Classical Tradition*, 3 (1996), pp. 84–5.

53 F. Campbell, "Latin and the Elite Tradition", p. 257.

54 Ibid., p. 258; *Cahiers pédagogiques*, 12 (October 1956), special issue devoted to "Education of the character" (see in particular the article by M. Palinq).

55 See p. 15 and, in general, C. Falcucci, *L'humanisme*.

56 François Arago, *Discours sur l'enseignement*, in *Oeuvres*, vol. 12: *Mélanges*, Paris, Gide; Leipzig, Weigel, 1859, pp. 692–715 (pp. 697, 700, 706); Alphonse de Lamartine, *Sur l'enseignement*, in *France parlementaire (1834–1851): oeuvres oratoires et écrits politiques*, vol. I, Paris, Lacroix, Verbroeckoven et Cie, 1864, pp. 310–21 (pp. 311 and 317).

57 John H. Weiss, "Bridges and Barriers: Narrowing Access and Changing Structure in the French Engineering Profession, 1800–1850", in Gerald L. Gerson (ed.), *Profession and the French State, 1700–1900*, Philadelphia, University of Pennsylvania Press, 1984, pp. 20–28. More generally, see also R.D. Anderson, *Education in France, 1848–1870*, Oxford, Clarendon Press, 1975, p. 27.

58 Maurice Jacob, "Etude comparative des systèmes universitaires et place des études classiques au XIXe. siècle en Allemagne, en Belgique et en France", in M. Bollack, H. Wismann and Theodor Lindken (eds), *Philologie und Hermeneutik im 19. Jahrhundert*, vol. II, Göttingen, Vandenbroeck & Ruprecht, 1983, p. 123.

59 Robert Schilling, "La situation des langues classiques dans l'enseignement français", in *Didaskalos*, 1 (1963), p. 37.

60 Jean Bayet, *Le latin conciliateur entre l'humanisme et la technique: conférence faite aux élèves ingénieurs de 4e. année*, Paris, Ecole Nationale des Arts et Métiers 1952.

61 See various articles attacking the measure taken by Edgar Faure, as well as the text of Hippolyte Ducos' speeches to the National Assembly in *Revue de la Franco-Ancienne*, 161 (June 1968), 162 (October 1968), 163 (March 1969), 164 (June 1969), p. 791, and 165 (October 1969); and in the *Bulletin de l'Association Guillaume-Budé* 2 (1968), 1 (1969). The same idea of complementarity between Latin and mathematics in training the mind has been advanced in Italy (G. Calogero, "Il panlatinismo", pp. 37–8).

62 Charles Lacroix, in *De l'emploi des classiques grecs et romains dans l'enseignement*, Lyon, 1852, quotation from M. Jacob, "Etude comparative", p. 139.

63 Frédéric Bastiat, *Baccalauréat et socialisme*, Paris, Guillaumin et Cie, 1850, pp. 1–12;

R.D. Anderson, *Education in France*, pp. 64–5; Sylvie Ballestra-Puech, "La 'question du latin' en France dans la seconde moitié du XIXe. siècle", in *La réception du latin*, pp. 235–6.

64 Paolo Fedeli, "Studio e uso del latino nella scuola fascista", in *Matrici culturali del fascismo*, Bari, SIE, 1977, p. 220; see also, more generally, Luciano Canfora, "Classicismo e fascismo", in *ibid.*, pp. 85–110.

65 Guido Calogero, "Latinisti in crisi" (1956), in *Scuola sotto inchiesta*, p. 106.

66 Epistémon, "La mort du latin", in *Revue des deux mondes* (January 1969), p. 35.

67 Robert Sautel, "*De antiquis litteris*", in *Quatrième congrès international du latin vivant, Avignon du 1er. au 3 avril 1969*, Avignon, Aubanel, 1969, p. 153.

68 G. Calogero, "Latinisti in crisi", p. 106; "I boati dell'Antiroma e la logica del latino" (1955), in *Scuola sotto inchiesta*, p. 90; "La bataille des humanités", in *Esprit* (1954), p. 831; Roger Ikor, "Plaidoyer pour le latin", in *Le Figaro littéraire* (7–13 October 1968), pp. 14–15; F. Vian, "Rapport moral" (congrès de l'APLAES, Toulouse, 1969), in *Caesarodunum* 4 (1969), p. 17; *Lycée* de Foix section, "Latin ou pas latin?", p. 781; Fernand Robert, "Chronique de la lutte pour nos études", in *Bulletin de l'Association Guillaume-Budé* (1976), p. 248; Edmond Petit, "*O fortunatos nimium agricolas*", in *ibid.*, 1969, p. 183; on Latin as a "soul supplement", see also, for Belgium in the 1950s, A. Noirfalise, "Les auteurs anciens", p. 305.

69 Pierre Grimal, "Allocution d'ouverture", in *Quatrième congrès international pour le latin vivant*, pp. 33–4.

70 C. Falcucci, *L'humanisme*, p. 103.

71 P. Campbell, "Latin and the Elite Tradition", p. 253.

72 C. Falcucci, *L'humanisme*, p. 241.

73 F. Ringer, *Fields of Knowledge*, pp. 142–3.

74 M. Hanna, *The Mobilization of Intellect*, ch. 5.

75 Henri Massis, "Avant-postes. Chronique d'un redressement (1910–1914)", in *Cahiers d'Occident*, II, 4 (1928), pp. 17–19 ("Défendons-nous contre la culture allemande"), 20–24 (M. Gustave Lanson"), 25–32 ("M. Landon contre les humanités"; p. 32), 33–6 ("M. Ferdinand Brunot"); M. Hanna, *The Mobilization of Intellect*, ch. 1.

76 J. de Romilly, *Lettre aux parents*, pp. 105–6.

77 It was in these terms that Luigi Settembrini's father encouraged him to study classics (*Ricordanze della mia vita*, vol. 1, edited by Adolfo Omodeo, Bari, Laterza, 1934, p. 9).

78 J. de Romilly, *Lettre aux parents*, p. 82.

79 C. Falcucci, *L'humanisme*, pp. 182 and 327.

80 J.C. McClelland, *Aristocrats and Academics*, p. 11.

81 John Armstrong, *The European Administrative Elite*, Princeton University Press, 1973, pp. 128–48.

82 R. Wilkinson, *The Prefects*, pp. 67–9.

83 F. Ringer, *Fields of Knowledge*, p. 157.

84 H. Dietz, *Les études classiques sans latin: essai pédagogique*, Paris, L. Cerf, 1886 (pp. 50, 38).

85 Michel Espagne, Françoise Lagier and Michael Werner, *Philologiques* II: *Le maître de langues. Les premiers enseignants d'allemand en France (1830–1850)*, Paris, Edition de la Maison des Sciences de l'Homme, 1991, pp. 23–9, 72–6.

86 A. Sicard, *Les études classiques*, p. 121.

87 H. Pouzin, *Le latin, pour quoi faire?*, p. 30.

88 P. Martin, "Le latin dans l'enseignement secondaire: rien ne va plus", in *Caesarodunum*, 3 (1969), p. 39.

89 Translator's note: *honnête homme* is a French concept without an exact English equivalent. "Gentleman" is probably closest but the French term is less pivoted on social class and more on individual accomplishment and learning. However, both terms convey the same solidity or "bottom", agreeable manners, personal probity and (unspoken but important) the respect of peers, and therefore by implication a certain conventionality or conservatism.

90 M. Hanna, *The Mobilization of Intellect*, ch. 1; Pascale Hummel, *Humanités normaliennes: l'enseignement classique et l'érudition philologique dans l'Ecole normale supérieur du XIXe. siècle*, Paris, Les Belles Lettres, 1995, ch. VI.

91 *Le role des études classiques et humanistes dans l'éducation: réponses de la commission de la République française pour l'éducation, la science et la culture à une enquête de l'Unesco*, in *La documentation française: notes et études documentaires*, no. 2543 (28 May 1959), pp. 7 and 35.

92 P. Campbell, "Latin and the Elite Tradition", p. 252; *Le rôle des études classiques*, pp. 12, 20–21; R. Schilling, "La situation", pp. 41–2.

93 M. Hanna, *The Mobilization of Intellect*, pp. 156–7.

94 C. Falcucci, *L'humanisme*, pp. 317, 350; A. Sicard, *Les études classiques*, pp. 121–2.

95 Epistémon, "La mort du latin", pp. 35 and 37; taking the same line and often using the same words, "Conférence de presse du comité de liaison pour la défense du latin en 6e.", in *Revue de la Franco-Ancienne*, 162 (October–December 1968), pp. 644–5; M. Lacroix, "Lettre", in *ibid.*, pp. 646–8; speeches by Hippolyte Ducos to the National Assembly and by Louis Gros to the Senate, in *ibid.*, 163 (March 1959), pp. 731, 742; again, "Le latin devant l'assemblée nationale", in *ibid.*, 166 (January 1970), pp. 21, 26; Joseph Moreau, "*Obliti sunt Romae*", in *Bulletin de l'Association Guillaume-Budé* (1968), pp. 501–6.

96 Among many other examples, generally Peter Wülfing, "L'enseignement", pp. 1–14 and 31–2; for Germany, information supplied by Thomas Rütten, to whom many thanks; for France, Alain Michel, "La tradition classique et sa mise en question par la critique contemporaine", in *Quatrième congrès international pour le latin vivant*, esp. p. 151; account of the "Colloque sur l'avenir des humanités" (March 1995) organized by the SEL association.

97 Ernest Lavisse, *Souvenirs*, pp. 218–20 and 223–4 (pp. 219 and 224); the same idea from Jules Simon (C. Falcucci, *L'humanisme*, pp. 314–15).

98 See for example, Suzanne Durand, "Les véritables raisons d'étudier les langues anciennes", in *L'éducation nationale*, 10 (15 December 1954); Pierre Chambon, "Esquisse d'une méthode mieux adaptée aux conditions actuelles", in *ibid.*, pp. 313–21; Paul Martin, "Pour gagner au latin at au grec les défenseurs qu'ils méritent", in *ibid.*, p. 333.

99 P. Wülfing, "L'enseignement", pp. 21–6 and 31–2.

100 Colette Mercier-Nast, "L'enseignement vivant du latin, son rôle dans l'affirmation de la personnalité de l'adolescent", in *Quatrième congrès international pour le latin vivant*, pp. 88–95.

101 William F. Train, "Reappraise Classics Teaching Now", in *The Scottish Educational Journal* 49 (9 December 1966), p. 1174.

102 On this point, in a polemical context, see remarks by Jean-Louis Nicolet, *L'affaire du latin: réquisitoires et plaidoiries*, Lausanne, F. Rouge et Cie, 1954, pp. 11–27.

103 Quote taken from M.-M. Martin, *Le latin immortel*, pp. 248–9.

104 Institut National de Recherche et de Documentation Pédagogique, "Controverses

autour du latin: eléments bibliographiques", Paris, 1974, manuscript; François-Xavier Druet, "Cinquante ans de 'disparition' des langues anciennes dans l'enseignement secondaire", in *Les études classiques*, LII (1984), pp. 291–9.

105 M. Reinhold, *Classica Americana*, pp. 340–41; *Value of the Classics: Conference on Classical Studies in Liberal Education, Princeton, 1917*, Princeton University Press (p. v); for "witnesses" not educated in the classics, see pp. 154, 164, 260, 265, etc.

106 "Latin, the Basic Language", in *The Classical Journal*, 64 (1969), pp. 163–6.

107 J. de Romilly, *Lettre aux parents*, p. 20.

108 "The Value of Humanistic, Particularly Classical Studies as a Preparation for the Study of the Law, from the Point of View of the Profession: A Symposium from the Proceedings of the Classical Conference Held at Ann Arbor, Michigan, March 27, 1907", in *School Review*, 1907, pp. 409–35; "The Value of Humanistic, Particularly Classical Studies as a Preparation for the Study of Theology, from the Point of View of the Profession: A Symposium from the Proceedings of the Classical Conference Held at Ann Arbor, Michigan, April 1, 1908", in *School Review*, 1908, pp. 3–47; "The Value of Humanistic, Particularly Classical Studies as a Training for Men of Affairs: A Symposium from the Proceedings of the Classical Conference Held at Ann Arbor, Michigan, April 3, 1909", in *School Review*, 1909 (separate publication).

109 For examples see, apart from the works cited in notes 104 and 106, Léon Bérard, *Pour la réforme classique de l'enseignement secondaire*, Paris, A. Colin, 1923, pp. 90, 108 ("Des savants, tels que MM. Henri Poincaré et Henri Le Châtelier, nous ont dit"); Eugène de Saint-Denis, "Assisterons-nous à l'agonie des études latines?", in *Bulletin de l'Association Guillaume-Budé* (1954), p. 24; "Une trentaine de personnalités lancent un appel pour le maintien du latin en sixième", in *Revue de la Franco-Ancienne*, 161 (June 1968), pp. 589–92; F. Robert, "Chronique", pp. 240–41; F.-X. Druet, "Cinquante ans", p. 299; etc.

110 L. Sausy and R. France, *Grammaire latine abrégée*, p. viii.

111 Pierre Boyancé, "Le latin, discipline de base", in *Revue de la Franco-Ancienne*, 105 (April 1953), p. 129.

112 Michel Delon, "*Homo sum* Un vers de Térence comme devise des Lumières", in *Dix-huitième siècle*, 16 (1984), pp. 279–96.

113 See for example C. Abastardo, "Présence des humanités anciennes", in *Revue de la Franco-Ancienne*, 120 (January 1957), p. 18; *Premier congrès international pour le latin vivant, Avignon, 3–6 septembre 1956*, Avignon, Edouard Aubanel, 1956, p. 144; *Quatrième congrès pour le latin vivant*, pp. 172, 210; "Défense et illustration des études classiques", p. 42; etc.

114 "Latin, the Basic Language", pp. 163–6.

115 "Les parents pour ou contre le latin", in *L'éducation nationale*, 12 (18 October 1956), pp. 5–6.

116 In *Revue de la Franco-Ancienne*, 165 (October 1969), pp. 867 and 868.

117 See on this point remarks by Emile Zola, *Chroniques*, in *Oeuvres complètes*, vol. XIII, edited by Henri Mitterrand, Paris, Cercle du Livre Précieux, 1969, pp. 136, 237–9; see also Raoul Frary, *La question du latin*, Paris, Léopold Cerf, 1887 (first edition 1885), conclusion.

118 Antonio Gramsci, *Selections from the Prison Notebooks*, edited and translated by Quintin Hoare and Geoffrey Nowell Smith, London, Lawrence & Wishart, 1971, pp. 38, 39.

8 Class

1 Speech to the general conference of Unesco, 18 October 1968 (quote from *Revue de la Franco-Ancienne*, 163 (March 1969), p. 712).

2 For some examples, Maurice Lacroix, "Lettre", in *Revue de la Franco-Ancienne*, 162 (October–December 1968), pp. 647–8; various papers in the same issue, esp. pp. 641, 649; *ibid.*, 164 (June 1969), pp. 781, 783, 789–90; Josette Lallemant, "A propos des mesures prises contre les études classiques", in *Bulletin de l'Association Guillaume-Budé* (1969), pp. 176–87; "La question du latin devant le Parlement", in *Revue de la Franco-Ancienne*, 163 (March 1969), pp. 734–5, 742; "Le latin devant l'Assemblée nationale", in *ibid.*, 166 (January 1970), pp. 19, 24–5; Epistémon, "La mort du latin", in *Revue des deux mondes* (January 1969), pp. 31–2; M. Rambaud, "A propos de l'initiation au latin dans les classes de 5e.", in *L'information littéraire*, 21, no. 5 (November–December 1969), p. 230.

3 Pierre Boyancé, "Le latin, discipline de base", in *Revue de la Franco-Ancienne*, 105 (April 1953), p. 128.

4 I have drawn extensively on Pierre Bourdieu's classic work *La distinction: critique sociale du jugement*, Paris, Editions de Minuit, 1979, when analysing the historical documents used here.

5 Anthony Grafton and Lisa Jardine, *From Humanism to the Humanities: Education and the Liberal Arts in Fifteenth- and Sixteenth-Century Europe*, London, Duckworth, 1986, pp. 23–4.

6 *Ibid.*, ch. 4.

7 Eugenio Garin, *L'educazione in Europa. 1400/1600: problemi e programmi*, Bari, Laterza, 1976, pp. 99–100; Antonio Staüble, *"Parlare per lettera". Il pedante nella commedia del Cinquecento e altri saggi sul teatro rinascimentale*, Rome, Bulzoni, 1991, pp. 14–115; Peter Burke, "The Jargons of the Schools", in Peter Burke and Roy Porter (eds), *Languages and Jargons: Contributions to a Social History of Language*, Cambridge, Polity Press, 1995, pp. 35–6; P. Albert Duhamel, "The Ciceronianism of Gabriel Harvey", in *Studies in Philology* (1952), pp. 168–70; Molière, *Les femmes savantes*, in *Oeuvres complètes*, vol. II, edited by Georges Couton, Paris, Gallimard, Pléiade, 1971, pp. 609, 650, 690–91, 1346; Antoine de Furetière, *Dictionnaire universel*, The Hague, Husson, Johnson, Swart, Le Vier, Dole, 1727, under "pédant, pédantesque, pédanterie".

8 Montaigne, *Essais*, in *Oeuvres complètes*, book I, edited by Albert Thibaudet and Maurice Rat, Paris, Gallimard, Pléiade, 1962, ch. XXV, pp. 140–41.

9 Charles Sorel, *Histoire comique de Francion*, in *Romanciers du XVIIe. siècle*, ed. Antoine Adam, Paris, Gallimard, Pléiade, 1958, pp. 183–4.

10 Bernard Beugnot, "Debats autour du latin dans la France classique", in P. Tuynman, G.C. Kuyper and E. Kessler (eds), *Acta conventus neo-latini amstelodamensis: Proceedings of the Second International Congress of Neo-Latin Studies, Amsterdam 19–24 August 1973*, Munich, Wilhelm Fink Verlag, 1979, p. 97.

11 Henry Bardon, *En lisant le Mercure Galant: essai sur la culture latine en France au temps de Louis XIV*, Rome, Edizioni dell'Ateneo, 1962.

12 Apposite suggestions on this very point in P. Bourdieu, *La distinction*, pp. 79–80.

13 Generally, see Hans Bots and Françoise Waquet, *La Republique des Lettres*, Paris, Belin-De Boeck, 1997, pp. 111–15; on the comportment of Paris scholars, see Françoise Waquet, *Le modèle français et l'Italie savante: conscience de soi et perception de l'autre dans la Republique des Lettres, 1660–1750*, Rome, Ecole française de Rome, 1989, pp. 100–105 (p. 103).

14 Mark Motley, *Becoming a French Aristocrat: The Education of the Court Nobility, 1580–1750*, Princeton University Press, 1990, ch. 2.

15 Isabelle Flandrois, *L'institution du prince au debut du XVIIe. siècle*, Paris, PUF, 1992, pp. 137–9. For two concrete examples, see Jill Bepler, *Ferdinand Albrecht duke of Braunschweig-Lüneburg (1636–1687): A Traveller and his Travelogue*, Wiesbaden, Otto Harrassowitz, 1988, pp. 87, 99–100, 106; Derek Beales, *Joseph II: In the Shadow of Maria Theresa, 1741–1780*, Cambridge University Press, 1987, pp. 45–6.

16 Example and quotation from Vittorio Alfieri, *Vita scritta da esso*, vol. I, edited by. Luigi Fassò, Asti, Casa d'Alfieri, 1951, p. 13.

17 See p. 198; John A. Armstrong, *The European Administrative Elite*, Princeton University Press, 1973, p. 143.

18 George Eliot, *The Mill on the Floss*, ed. Gordon S. Haight, Oxford, Clarendon Press, 1980 (original edition 1860), p. 143.

19 Raoul Frary, *La question du latin*, Paris, Léopold Cerf, 1887 (first edition 1885), pp. 162 and 163. On this individual and his book, see Sylvie Ballestra-Puech, "La 'question du latin' en France dans la seconde moitié du XIXe. siècle", in Georges Cesbron and Laurence Richer (eds), *La réception du latin du XIXe. siècle à nos jours: actes du colloque d'Angers des 23 et 24 septembre 1994*, Angers, Presses de l'Université, 1996, pp. 235.

20 Quote from Antoine Prost, *Histoire de l'enseignement en France, 1800–1967*, Paris, Armand Colin, 1968, p. 332.

21 Thorstein Veblen, *Théorie de la classe de loisir*, Paris, Gallimard, 1970 (first edition 1899), pp. 259–64. For an illustration, see G. Pire, "Faut-il bannir les langues anciennes de la République moderne?", in *Bulletin de l'Association Guillaume-Budé* (1972), pp. 313–15.

22 See François Lebrun, Marc Venard and Jean Quéniart, *Histoire générale de l'enseignement et de l'éducation en France*, vol. II: *De Gutenberg aux Lumières*, Paris, Nouvelle Librairie Française, 1981, part III, chs 1 and 2; the entries under "Ecoles, petites écoles" (by Bernard Groperrin) and esp. "Collèges" (by Marie-Madeleine Compère) in Lucien Bély (ed.), *Dictionnaire de l'Ancien Régime: royaume de France, XVIe.–XVIIIe. siècle*, Paris, PUF, 1996. "Fully-functioning colleges" were those teaching the complete cycles of grammar, humanities and rhetoric, and philosophy.

23 J.A. Armstrong, *The European Administrative Elite*, pp. 143–4.

24 Figures from Fritz Ringer, *Education and Society in Modern Europe*, Bloomington, London, Indiana University Press, 1979, p. 330.

25 Pierre Bourdieu and Jean-Claude Passeron, *Les héritiers: les étudiants et la culture*, Paris, Editions de Minuit, 1985, pp. 26–7. See also "Rapport Lallor", in *Caesarodunum*, 4 (1969), pp. 54–5.

26 Louis Legrand, Inspecteur d'Académie, "Où en est l'enseignement du latin?", in *L'éducation nationale*, 9 May 1963, pp. 9–10.

27 Benjamin Franklin, *Observations Relative to the Intentions of the Original Founders of the Academy in Philadelphia, June 1789*, in *Writings*, vol. X, *1789–1790*, edited by Albert Henry Smyth, London, Macmillan and Co., 1907, p. 31. The expression "chapeau bras" is in French in the original.

28 R. Frary, *La question du latin*, p. 162.

29 Jean B. Neveux, *"Cur et quomodo usus sit Sienkiewicz polonus lingua latina in opere suo polonice scripto cui titulus est 'Triloja'"*, in *Troisième congrès international pour le latin vivant, Strasbourg du 2 au 4 septembre 1963*, Avignon, Aubanel, 1964, p. 81.

30 See also the reactions of the Bishop of Salisbury (Goffrey Holmes, *Augustean England: Professions, State and Society, 1680–1730*, London, George Allen & Unwin, 1982, p. 49) and Daniel Defoe, *The Compleat English Gentleman* (1728–9), edited by Karl D. Bülbung, London, David Nutt, 1890, pp. 196 ff.

31 John Locke, *Of Education*, in *Works A New Edition Corrected*, vol. X, Aalen, Scientia Verlag, 1963 (first edition 1823), p. 152.

32 John Chandos, *Boys Together: English Public Schools 1800–1864*, Yale University Press, 1984, p. 33.

33 J.A. Armstrong, *The European Administrative Elite*, p. 130.

34 Christopher Stray, *Grinder and Grammars: A Victorian Controversy*, Reading, The Text Book Colloquium, 1995, pp. 71–3 (p. 71).

35 Christopher Stray, "Ideology and Institution: English Classical Scholarship in Transition", in *Annals of Scholarship*, 10 (1993), p. 125.

36 Used by Matthew Arnold in a report to the School Inquiry Commission (1865–7), published in R.H. Super (ed.), *Schools and Universities on the Continent*, Ann Arbor, University of Michigan Press, 1964, p. 126.

37 A. Prost, *Histoire de l'enseignement*, pp. 331–2.

38 R. Frary, *La question du latin*, pp. 162–3.

39 Emile Zola, *Causerie* (15 August 1869), in *Chroniques et polémiques*, in *Oeuvres complètes*, vol. XIII, edited by Henri Mitterrand, Paris, Cercle du Livre Précieux, 1969, p. 239.

40 Paul Valéry, *Cahiers*, vol. II, edited by Judith Robinson, Paris, Gallimard, Pléiade, 1974, p. 1674; the italics are present in the original.

41 Quote from Georges Gusdorf, *Les sciences humaines et la conscience occidentale*, VI: *L'avènement des sciences humaine au siècle des Lumières*, Paris, Payot, 1973, p. 205; "la parole" is in French in the text.

42 Christopher Stray, *Classics Transformed: Schools, Universities and Society in England, 1830–1960*, Oxford University Press, 1998.

43 Jürgen Schlumbohm, "'Weder Neigung noch Affection zu meiner Frau' und doch 'zehn Kinder mit ihr gezeugt': zur Autobiographie eines Nürnberger Schneiders aus dem 18. Jahrhundert", in Axel Lubinski, Thomas Rudert and Martina Schattkowsky (eds), *Historie und Eigen-Sinn: Festschrift für Jan Peters zum 65 Geburstag*, Weimar, Verlag Hermann Böhlaus Nachfolger, 1997, p. 495.

44 Christopher Stray, "Culture and Discipline: Classics and Society in Victorian England", in *International Journal of the Classical Tradition*, 3 (1996), p. 80.

45 Pierre Larousse, *Flore latine des dames et des gens du monde, ou clef des citations latines que l'on rencontre frequemment dans les ouvrages des écrivains français*, Paris, Larousse et Boyer, 1861, pp. xxix–xxx.

46 M.L. Clarke, *Classical Education in Britain 1500–1900*, Cambridge University Press, 1959, p. 170.

47 T.W. Bamford, *Rise of the Public Schools: A Study of Boys' Public Boarding Schools in England and Wales from 1837 to the Present Day*, London, Nelson, 1967, pp. 170–71.

48 *Encyclopédie pratique de l'éducation en France, publiée sous le patronage et avec le concours de l'Institut pédagogique national*, Paris, IPN et SEDE, 1960, p. 631.

49 For an example see Raymond Brun et Pierre-Bernard Marquet, "Le latin à sa place", in *Esprit*, 22 (1954), p. 845.

50 F. Campbell, "Latin and the Elite Tradition in Education", in P.W. Musgrave (ed.), *Sociology, History and Education: A Reader*, London, Methuen & Co., 1970, p. 250.

51 Christopher Stray, "Beyond Classification: Bernstein and the Grammarians. A Note on Classics in Swansea Schools", in *History of Education* (November 1990), pp. 267–8.

52 Joseph Moreau, "*Obliti sunt Romae*", in *Bulletin de l'Association Guillaume-Budé* (1968), p. 506.

53 Pierre Chessex, "Le latin et la réforme de l'enseignement secondaire", in *L'affaire du latin: réquisitoire et plaidoiries*, Lausanne, F. Rouge et Cie, 1954, p. 51.

54 François Joachim Pierre, Cardinal de Bernis, *Mémoires et lettres*, vol. I, edited by Frédéric Masson, Paris, E. Plon et Cie, 1878, p. 20.

55 Richard L. Kagan, "Il latino nella Castiglia del XVII e del XVIII secolo", in *Rivista storica italiana*, LXXXV (1973), pp. 297–320.

56 James van Horn Melton, *Absolutism and the Eighteenth Century of Compulsory Schooling in Prussia and Austria*, Cambridge University Press, 1988, pp. 114–19 and 184–9.

57 Rétif de la Bretonne, *Monsieur Nicolas*, vol. I, edited by Pierre Testud, Paris, Gallimard, Pléiade, 1989, p. 192.

58 Louis Sebastien Mercier, *Tableau de Paris*, vol. I, edited by Jean-Claude Bonnet, Paris, Mercure de France, 1994, pp. 1146–50 (pp. 1146–8) from the chapter entitled "Latiniste" introduced by Mercier with the words: "I have never, I aver, made any chapter more important than this one"; Harvey Chisick, *The Limits of Reform in the Enlightenment: Attitudes Towards the Education of the Lower Classes in Eighteenth-Century France*, Princeton University Press, 1981, pp. 135–53.

59 Piero Lucchi, "La prima istruzione. Idee, metode, libri", in Gian Paolo Brizzi (ed.), *Il catechismo e la grammatica*, vol. I, Bologna, Il Mulino, 1985, pp. 39–52 and 78–80.

60 Maria Teresa Cigolini, "L'istruzione primaria in Lombardia nell'età delle Riforme", in Aldo De Maddalena, Ettore Rotelli, Gennaro Barbarisi (eds), *Economia, istituzioni, cultura in Lombardia nell'età di Maria Teresa*, vol. III: *Istituzioni e società*, Bologna, Il Mulino, 1982, pp. 1027–9.

61 Marina Roggero, *Insegnar lettere: ricerche di storia dell'istruzione nell'età moderna*, Piacenza, Edizioni dell'Orso, 1992, pp. 144–5.

62 *Ibid.*, p. 145.

63 André Chervel, *Histoire de l'agrégation: contribution à l'étude de la culture scolaire*, Paris, INRP, Editions Kimé, 1993, pp. 39–40.

64 Clément Falcucci, *L'humanisme dans l'enseignement secondaire en France au XIXe. siècle*, Toulouse, Privat; Paris, Didier, 1939, p. 163.

65 Adeline Dumard, *La bourgeoisie parisienne de 1815 à 1848*, Paris, SEVPEN, 1963, pp. 351–2; R.D. Anderson, *Education in France, 1848–1870*, Oxford, Clarendon Press, 1975, pp. 59–60.

66 Albert Léonard, "La formation au latin dans le souvenir de Vallès (*L'enfant*) et de Stendhal (*Vie de Henri Brulard*), in *La réception du latin*, pp. 143–53 (p. 152).

67 Fritz Ringer, *Fields of Knowledge: French Academic Culture in Comparative Perspective, 1890–1920*, Cambridge University Press; Paris, Edition de la Maison des Sciences de l'Homme, 1992, pp. 141–60.

68 In response to a survey on education conducted by the review *Esprit* and published in issue no. 22 (1954), p. 818.

69 Robert Ricard, *La "conquête spirituelle du Mexique": Essai sur l'apostolat et les méthodes missionnaires des ordres mendiants en Nouvelle-Espagne de 1523–4 à 1572*, Paris, Institut d'Ethnologie, 1933, ch. VII; Ignacio Osorio-Romero, "La enseñanza del latín a los Indios", in Alexander Dalzell, Charles Fantazzi, Richard J. Schoeck (eds), *Acta conventus neo-latini torontonensis: Proceedings of the Seventh International Congress of Neo-Latin*

Studies, Toronto, 8 August to 13 August 1988, Binghamton, Mediaeval and Renaissance Texts and Studies, 1991, pp. 865–9.

70 N.C., *Les femmes savantes ou Bibliothèque des dames qui traite des sciences qui conviennent aux dames, de la conduite de leurs études, des livres qu'elles peuvent lire et de l'histoire de celles qui ont excellé dans les sciences*, Amsterdam, Michel Charles Le Cene, 1718, ch. V (proverb: p. 28).

71 Charles Rollin, *Supplément au Traité de la manière d'enseigner et d'étudier les belles-lettres*, Paris, Veuve Estienne, 1734, pp. 53–60. On women's education under the Ancien Régime in general, see Martine Sonnet, "Une fille à éduquer", in Natalie Zemon Davies and Arlette Farge (eds), *Histoire des femmes en Occident, 3: XVIe.–XVIIIe. siècles*, Paris, Plon, 1991, pp. 111–39.

72 Anthony Fletcher, *Gender, Sex and Subordination in England. 1500–1800*, New Haven, Yale University Press, 1995, p. 375.

73 M. Sonnet, "Une fille à éduquer", p. 119.

74 Richard W. Bailey, *Images of English: A Cultural History of the Language*, Ann Arbor, University of Michigan Press, 1991, p. 254. The work mentioned is attributed to Judith Drake. In a similar order of ideas, Erasmus Darwin, after emphasizing the length of time devoted to learning Latin and its difficulty, advised against it all the more strongly for girls in that it was useless for worldly conversation and life; French or Italian would be much more useful, and were also easier and more fashionable (*A Plan for the Conduct of Female Education in Boarding Schools*, Wakefield, S.R. Publishers; New York, Johnson Reprint Corporation, 1968; first edition 1797), pp. 17–18.

75 M. Sonnet, "Une fille à éduquer, pp. 133–7 (p. 133).

76 Marie-Claire Hoock-Demarle, "Lire et écrire en Allemagne", in Geneviève Fraisse and Michelle Perrot (eds), *Histoire des femmes en Occident*, vol. 4, Paris, Plon, 1991, pp. 149–52 (p. 152).

77 James C. Albisetti, *Schooling German Girls and Women: Secondary Education in the Nineteenth Century*, Princeton University Press, 1988, pp. 18 and 19.

78 Anne Digby and Peter Searby, *Children, School and Society in Nineteenth-Century England*, London, Macmillan Press, 1981, pp. 238–9. We should note that the two weekly algebra lessons – the other "noble" subject – received by the boys were replaced with needlework for girls.

79 In the United States, optional Latin courses were introduced for girls in the 1850s (Barbara Miller Solomon, *In the Company of Educated Women: A History of Women and Higher Education in America*, New Haven, Yale University Press, 1985, pp. 23, 78–80). For an example of a school intended for an elite and offering Latin, see the prospectus for Wycombe Abbey (1896) reproduced in A. Digby and P. Searby, *Children, School and Society*, pp. 212–3. The Victoria Lyceum in Berlin, one of the most famous of the institutions offering further education without any profession in mind, introduced a Latin grammar course into its syllabus in 1874 (J.C. Albisetti, *Schooling German Girls*, pp. 120–21).

80 Françoise Mayeur, *L'enseignement secondaire de jeunes filles sous la 3me. République*, Paris, Presses de la Fondation Nationale des Sciences Politiques, 1977, ch. 1.

81 *Lycées et collèges de jeunes filles: documents, rapports et discours à la Chambre des Députés et au Sénat. Décrets, arrêtés, circulaires, etc.*, Paris, L. Cerf, 1900, p. 477.

82 C. Maritan, *De l'étude du latin en général et par les femmes en particulier: diverses méthodes d'enseignement. Cours en dix mois. Résultats définis et garantis*, Paris, published by the author and Delaunay, 1838, pp. 2–3.

83 *Lycées de jeunes filles: 25 ans de discours*, Paris, L. Cerf, 1907, p. 147.

84 *Lycées et collèges de jeunes filles*, p. 477.

85 André Chervel, *Les auteurs français, latins et grecs au programme d'enseignement secondaire de 1800 à nos jours*, Paris, INRP, Publications de la Sorbonne, 1986, p. 5.

86 P. Boyancé, "Le latin, discipline de base", p. 129.

87 "Enquête de l'Unesco", in *Revue de la Franco-Ancienne*, 122 (July 1957), p. 134 (my emphasis).

88 In the US, where Latin was introduced for girls much earlier, complaints about the feminization of classical studies were heard from the beginning of the century (B. Miller Solomon, *In the Company of Educated Women*, pp. 80–81).

89 One would like to have had access to a study on Latin similar to the one conducted by Kim Thomas on English and the sciences for the contemporary period (*Gender and Subject in Higher Education*, Buckingham, The Society for Research into Higher Education & Open University Press, 1990).

90 Quote from A. Prost, *Histoire de l'enseignement*, p. 332.

91 F. Lebrun, M. Venard, J. Quéniart, *Histoire générale de l'enseignement*, p. 431.

92 Matthew Ramsey, *Professional and Popular Medicine in France, 1770–1830*, Cambridge University Press, 1989, pp. 29 and 54.

93 Ferdinand Brunot, *Histoire de la langue française des origines à nos jours*: vol. IX, *La Révolution et l'Empire*, Paris, Librairie Armand Colin, 1967, p. 446.

94 John H. Weiss, "Bridges and Barriers: Narrowing Access and Changing Structures in the French Engineering Profession, 1800–1850", in Gerald L. Gerson (ed.), *Professions and the French State, 1700–1900*, Philadelphia, University of Pennsylvania Press, 1984, p. 28.

95 F.K. Ringer, *Education and Society in Modern Europe*, p. 19.

96 Quote from A. Léonard, "La formation au latin", p. 145.

97 Samuel Bamford, *The Autobiography*, vol. I: *Early Days*, edited by W.H. Chaloner (new edition), New York, Augustus M. Kelley, 1967, pp. 91–3.

98 *Encyclopédie pratique de l'éducation*, p. 631.

99 J. Locke, *Of Education*, p. 153.

100 Thomas Hardy, *Jude the Obscure*, London, Macmillan, 1974 (first edition 1896).

101 David Nasaw, *Schooled to Order: A Social History of Public Schooling in the United States*, Oxford University Press, 1979, pp. 134–9, 145.

102 *Encyclopédie pratique de l'éducation*, p. 631.

103 As reported by Etiemble in his article "Contre le latin", in *Le Figaro littéraire* (14–20 October 1968), p. 16.

9 The Power to Say and to Conceal

1 The autobiography of Pedro Gonzalez (1582) is a manuscript in the Lessing Rosenwald collection, kept at the National Gallery of Arts in Washington. I am greatly indebted to Roberto Zapperi for drawing it to my attention. On Pedro Gonzalez and his son, and more generally on the status of "furry" men as "curiosities", see Roberto Zapperi, "Arrigo le velu, Pietro le fou, Amon le nain et autres bêtes: autour d'un tableau d'Agostino Carrache" ("Arrigo the furry man, Pietro the madman, Amon the dwarf and other creatures: a painting by Agostino Carrache"), in *Annales ESC*, 40 (1985), pp. 307–27.

2 I refer mainly here to Pierre Bourdieu's book *Ce que parler veut dire: l'économie des échanges linguistiques*, Paris, Fayard, 1982.

3 Alessandro Manzoni, *Les fiancés*, translated by Yves Branca, Paris, Gallimard, 1995,

pp. 342–3, 92, 806, 347, 317, 218–19; on this use of Latin by Manzoni, see Michele Feo, "Tradizione latina", in Alberto Asor Rosa (ed.) *Letteratura italiana*, vol. V: *Le questioni*, Turin, Einaudi, 1986, pp. 372–4.

4 *Spectator*, 221 (13 November 1711), p. 360; very generally, on tags and their function, see Gérard Genette, *Seuils*, Paris, Seuil, 1987, pp. 134–41.

5 Vittorio Coletti, *L'éloquence de la chaire: victoires et défaites du latin entre Moyen Age et Renaissance*, Paris, Editions du Cerf, 1987 (first published Casale Monferrato, 1983), p. 61.

6 Isabelle Pantin, "Latin et langues vernaculaires dans la littérature scientifique européenne au début de l'époque moderne (1550–1635)", in Roger Chartier and Pietro Corsi (eds), *Sciences et langues en Europe*, Paris, Ecole des Hautes Etudes en Sciences Sociales, 1996, p. 53.

7 Ferdinand Brunot, *Histoire de la langue française des origines à nos jours*, vol. V: *Le français en France et hors de France au XVIIe. siècle*, Paris, Librairie Armand Colin, 1966, p. 24.

8 M. Feo, "Tradizione latina", p. 370.

9 Carlo Ginzburg, *Il formaggio e i vermi: il cosmo di un mugnaio del '500*, Turin, Einaudi, 1976, p. 12 (French translation: *Le fromage et les vers: l'univers d'un meunier du XVIe. siècle*, Paris, Aubier, 1993).

10 Molière, *Le médecin malgré lui* (1666), in *Oeuvres complètes*, vol. II, edited and annotated by Georges Couton, Paris, Gallimard, Pléiade, 1971, act II, scene 4 (p. 246).

11 Roy Porter, "'Perplex't with Tough Names': The Uses of Medical Jargon", in Peter Burke and Roy Porter (eds), *Languages and Jargons: Contributions to a Social History of Language*, Cambridge, Polity Press, 1995, pp. 44–5; Elizabeth McCutcheon, "Latin and its Uses in William Bullein's Dialogue Against the Fever Pestilence", in Rhoda Schnur *et al.* (eds), *Acta conventus neo-latini hafniensis: Proceedings of the Eighth International Congress of Neo-Latin Studies (1991)*, Binghamton, Medieval and Renaissance Texts and Studies, 1994, pp. 637–9.

12 Silvia Scotti Morgagni, "Latino e italiano nel primo Settecento: Note in margine a una lettera inedita di A. Vallisnieri a L.A. Muratori", in *Rendiconti dell'Istituto lombardo: classe di lettere e scienze morali e storiche*, 110 (1976), p. 158.

13 Bernard Quemada, *Introduction à l'étude du vocabulaire médical (1600–1710)*, Besançon, Faculté des Lettres, 1955, p. 13.

14 Maria Luisa Altieri Biagi, "Lingua della scienza fra Seicento e Settecento", in *Lettere italiane*, 28 (1976), p. 449.

15 Mary E. Fissell, "Readers, Texts and Contexts: Vernacular Medical Works in Early Modern England", in Roy Porter (ed.), *The Popularization of Medicine, 1650–1850*, London, New York, Routledge, 1992, p. 85; on this individual, see Roy Porter, "Spreading Medical Enlightenment: The Popularization of Medicine in Georgian England", in *ibid.*, pp. 219–20.

16 Mary E. Fissell, *Patients, Power and the Poor in Eighteenth-Century Bristol*, Cambridge University Press, 1991, pp. 156–9; "The Disappearance of the Patient's Narrative and the Invention of Hospital Medicine", in Roger French and Andrew Wear (eds), *British Medicine in an Age of Reform*, London, New York, Routledge, 1991, pp. 92–109 (p. 106).

17 Roy Porter, *Health for Sale: Quackery in England, 1660–1850*, Manchester University Press, 1989, p. 107.

18 Matthew Ramsey, *Professional and Popular Medicine in France, 1770–1830*, Cambridge University Press, 1989, p. 136.

19 R. Porter, *Health for Sale*, p. 107.

20 M. Ramsey, *Professional and Popular Medicine*, p. 349.

21 Joseph Connors and Louise Rice (eds), *Specchio di Roma barocca: una guida inedita del XVII secolo*, Rome, Edizioni dell'Elefante, 1991, pp. 76–7.

22 Armando L. De Gaetano, *Giambattista Gelli and the Florentine Academy: The Rebellion Against Latin*, Florence, Olschki, 1976, ch. 3 (p. 81); V. Coletti, *L'éloquence de la chaire*, ch. VIII (p. 166).

23 Giovanni Battista De Luca, *Il dottor volgare, overo il compendio di tutta la legge civile, canonica, feudale e municipale nelle cose più ricevute in pratica; moralizato in lingua italiana per istruzione e comodità maggiore di questa provincia*, Rome, Giuseppe Corvo, 1673, vol. I, pp. 16–27 (pp. 22–3). On De Luca, see entry in the *Dizionario biografico degli Italiani*.

24 See pp. 49–50.

25 Bruce Tolley, *Pastors and Parishioners in Württemberg During the Late Reformation, 1581–1621*, Stanford University Press, 1995, ch. 2; Bernard Vogler, *Le clergé protestant rhénan au siècle de la Réforme (1555–1619)*, Paris, Editions Orphys, 1976, pp. 227–8, 293; Anthony J. La Vopa, *Grace, Talent and Merit: Poor Students, Clerical Careers and Professional Ideology in Eighteenth Century Germany*, Cambridge University Press, 1988, pp. 81–2.

26 *Spectator*, 221 (13 November 1711), pp. 359–60.

27 See pp. 93–4; Ann B. Shteir, *Cultivating Women, Cultivating Science: Flora's Daughters and Botany in England, 1760 to 1860*, Johns Hopkins University Press, 1996, ch. 1 and p. 41.

28 E. Mc.Cutcheon, "Latin and its Uses", p. 639.

29 Stephen Leacock, *The Arrested Philanthropy of Mr. Tomlinson*, in *Laugh Parade*, New York, Dodd, Mead & Company, 1940, pp. 264–90 (p. 265); the Latin quotations are from Virgil (*Aeneid*, I, 94) and Horace (*Odes*, I, 1, 2).

30 See, notably, F. Brunot, *Histoire de la langue française*, vol. V, pp. 10–20; Hubert Gillot, *La querelle des Anciens et des Modernes en France: de la défense et illustration de la langue française aux Parallèles des Anciens et des Modernes*, Paris, Honoré Champion, 1914, ch. V; Bernard Magne, "Crise de la littérature française sous Louis XIV: humanisme et nationalisme", doctoral thesis, Toulouse, 1974, Lille III, 1976, pp. 409–34; Bernard Beugnot, "Débats autour du latin dans la France classique", in P. Tuynman, G.C. Kuiper and E. Kessler (eds), *Acta conventus neo-latini amstelodamensis: Proceedings of the Second International Congress of Neo-Latin Studies, Amsterdam 19–24 August 1973*, Munich, Wilhelm Fink Verlag, 1979, pp. 93–106.

31 Armando Petrucci, *Jeux de lettres: formes et usages de l'inscription en Italie, 11e.–20e. siècles*, Paris, Editions de l'Ecole des Hautes Études en Sciences Sociales, 1993 (original edition Turin, 1980).

32 Jean Lucas, *De monumentis publicis latine inscribendis oratio habita Parisiis VII Cal. Decemb. Anno 1676 in collegio Claromontano*, Parisiis, apud Simonem Bernard, 1677 (pp. 44, 51–2).

33 See (among others) the attitudes of Charpentier and Desmarets de Saint-Sorlin in the writings of B. Magne and F. Brunot cited in note 30, and in Marc Fumaroli, "L'apologétique de la langue française classique", in *Rhetorica* (1984), p. 154.

34 F. Brunot, *Histoire de la langue française*, vol. V, pp. 19–20.

35 Louis Sebastien Mercier, *Tableau de Paris*, ed. Jean-Claude Bonnet, Paris, Mercure de France, 1994, vol. II, ch. entitled "Inscriptions", pp. 43–7 and 993–5.

36 Henri Grégoire, *Convention nationale: rapport sur les inscriptions des monuments publics*

Séance du 22 nivôse l'an II, in *Oeuvres*, vol. II, Nendeln, KTO, 1977, pp. 141–54 (originally published 1794).

37   Petit-Radel, *Fastes. Fasti*, Paris, Didot l'Aîné, 1804 (p. 2).

38   A. Ronesse, *Réflexions d'un Français sur cette question: les inscriptions des monuments français doivent-ils être mises en latin ou en français?* Paris, Lecoudey, Delaunay, 1818 (pp. 28–9, 35, 41).

39   John H. Dirckx, *The Language of Medicine: Its Evolution, Structure and Dynamics*, New York, Praeger, 1983, p. 130.

40   John Henry Newman, *Autobiographical Writings*, edited by Henry Tristram, London, New York, Sheed and Ward, 1956, p. 151; in the same area of ideas, see Elisabeth Bourcier, "Les journaux privés en Angleterre de 1600 à 1660", Lille III, 1977, pp. 74–5.

41   E. Bourcier, "Les journaux privés", p. 74.

42   I am grateful to Thomas Rütten for this information.

43   Jean de Palacio, "Parler latin en français: ou l'écolier limousin à la fin du XIXe. siècle", in Georges Cesbron and Laurence Richer (eds), *La réception du latin du XIXe siècle à nos jours: actes du colloque d'Angers des 23 et 24 septembre 1994*, Angers, Presses de l'Université, 1996, p. 251.

44   Ernst Wirckersheimer, *La médecine et les médecins en France à l'époque de la Renaissance*, Geneva, Slatkine, 1970 (originally published Paris, 1905), pp. 501–3 (pp. 502–3).

45   Agostino Coltellini, *L'instituzioni dell'anatomie del corpo umano*, parts 1 and 2, Florence, Amadore Massi, 1651, note to readers, unnumbered, and pp. 9–16.

46   Charles Webster, *The Great Instauration: Science, Medicine and Reform, 1626–1660*, London, Duckworth, 1975, pp. 264–73; Patricia Crawford, "Sexual Knowledge in England, 1500–1750", in Roy Porter and Mikulás Teich (eds), *Sexual Knowledge, Sexual Science: The History of Attitudes to Sexuality*, Cambridge University Press, 1994, pp. 84–7.

47   Jean Astruc, *De morbis venereis libri sex*, Lutetiae Parisiorum, apud Guillelmum Cavelier, 1736, p. x.

48   Margarita Torremocha Hernández, *Ser estudiante en el siglo XVIII: la universidad vallisoletana de la Ilustración*, Valladolid, Junta de Castilla y León, 1991, p. 97.

49   Quoted from seventh edition, Paris, J.-B. Baillière, 1878, pp. 3, 206.

50   Richard von Krafft-Ebing, *Psychopathia sexualis*, Stuttgart, Ferdinand Enke, 1889 (first edition 1886), pp. 28, 159, 160, 169, 170, 194, 195, etc.; Renate Hauser, "Krafft-Ebing's Psychological Understanding of Sexual Behaviour", in *Sexual Knowledge*, pp. 210–12.

51   Roger Thompson, *Unfit for Modest Ears: A Study of Pornography, Obscene and Bawdy Works Published in England in the Second Half of the Seventeenth Century*, London, Macmillan, 1979, pp. 161–2 and 164–6; see similarly Peter Wagner, "The Discourse on Sex, or Sex as a Discourse: Eighteenth-Century Medical and Para-Medical Erotica", in G.S. Rousseau and Roy Porter (eds), *Sexual Underworlds of the Enlightenment*, Manchester University Press, 1987, pp. 46–68.

52   Abbé Dinouart, *Abrégé de l'embryologie sacrée ou Du traité du devoir des prêtres, des médecins et autres, sur le salut éternel des enfants qui sont dans le ventre de leur mère*, Paris, Nyon, 1762, pp. xx–xxii, 33.

53   I am most grateful to Geneviève Guilleminot-Chrétien for drawing these texts to my attention. I would add that in the *Grande Encyclopédie*, which cannot be accused of prudishness, the passage on "sins against nature" (in the entry on "sin") is in Latin, the author explaining: "It seems quite out of the question to

print these things in French . . . We will present them here veiled in scholastic Latin."

54 Tito Casini, *La tunique déchirée*, Paris, Nouvelles Editions Latines, 1968, pp. 50–55 (p. 55).

55 Joan Lane, "'The Doctor Scolds Me': The Diaries and Correspondence of Patients in Eighteenth Century England", in *Patients and Practitioners: Lay Perceptions of Medicine in Pre-Industrial Society*, Cambridge University Press, 1985, p. 245.

56 Chevalier de Solignac, *Histoire générale de Pologne*, vol. I, Paris, Jean-Thomas Hérissant, 1750, pp. 77–8. The *Bibliothèque raisonnée des ouvrages des savants de l'Europe*, which listed this book, was itself in Latin for the same reasons (Bruno Larrigue, *Un temple de la culture européenne (1728–1753): l'histoire externe de la Bibliothèque raisonnée des ouvrages des savants de l'Europe*, Nijmegen, 1993, pp. 203–4).

57 John Clive, "Gibbon's Humor", in Glen W. Bowerstock, John Clive, Stephen R. Graubard (eds), *Edward Gibbon and the Decline and Fall of the Roman Empire*, Harvard University Press, 1977, p. 183; Edward Gibbon, *My Life and Writings: Illustrated from his Letters, with Occasional Notes and Narrative by John Lord Sheffield*, bicentenary edition edited by A.O. Cockshut and Stephen Constantine, Keele University Press, 1994, p. 211.

58 Pierre de Bourdeille, Seigneur de Brantôme, *Des dames*, in *Oeuvres complètes*, vol. IX, edited by Ludovic Lalanne, Paris, Vve Jules Renouard, 1876, pp. 51–2.

59 Rétif de la Bretonne, *Monsieur Nicolas*, vol. I, edited by Pierre Testud, Paris, Gallimard, Pléiade, 1989, pp. 23, 36, 40, 46–7, 54, 55, 66.

60 See pp. 36–7; Kenneth J. Dover, "Expurgation of Greek Literature", in Willem den Boer (ed.), *Les études classiques aux XIXe. et XXe. siècles: leur place dans l'histoire des idées*, Geneva, Fondation Hardt, 1980, pp. 68–70.

61 W.R. Paton, *The Greek Anthology with an English Translation*, London, William Heinemann; New York, G.P. Putnam's Sons, 1963, *Satirical Epigrams*, nos. 223–5, 328, 339; *Musa Puerilis*, nos. 3, 7, 22, 30, 95, 210, 216, 222, 225, 232, 238, 240, 243 and 245.

62 Enno Littmann (ed.), *Die Erzählungen aus den Tausendundein Nächten*, Wiesbaden, Insel, 1953, p. 365.

63 Karl Heinrich Menges (ed.), *Volkundliche Texte aus Ost-Türkistan, Aus der Nachlass von N. Th. Katanov*, Leipzig, Zentralantiquariat der deutschen Demokratischen Republik, 1976, pp. 39–43. I am greatly indebted to Idikó Hann for drawing this text to my attention.

64 See, generally, pp. 222–5; Linda Timmermans, *L'accès des femmes à la culture (1598–1715): un débat d'idées de Saint François de Sales à la marquise de Lambert*, Paris, Champion, 1994, p. 137.

65 Brantôme, *Des dames*, pp. 570–73; for the sixteenth century, see similar ideas of the humanists including Erasmus (François Lebrun, Marc Venard, Jean Quéniart, *Histoire générale de l'enseignement et de l'éducation en France*, vol. II: *De Gutenberg aux Lumières*, Paris, Nouvelle Librairie de France, 1981, pp. 373–4).

66 N.C., *Les femmes savantes ou Bibliothèque des dames qui traite des sciences qui conviennent aux dames, de la conduite de leurs études, des livres qu'elles peuvent lire et l'histoire de celles qui ont excellé dans les sciences*, Amsterdam, Michel Charles Le Cene, 1718, pp. 27–9.

67 Pierre Bayle, "Eclaircissement que s'il y a des obscenités dans ce livre, elles sont de celles qu'on ne peut censurer avec raison", in *Dictionnaire historique et critique*, Amsterdam, la Compagnie des Libraires, 1734, p. 776.

68 P.V. Delaporte, *L'Art poétique de Boileau commenté par Boileau et ses contemporains*, vol.

II, Geneva, Slatkine, 1970, pp. 143–6. It is interesting to note that when Gibbon was defending himself against accusations that his *Decline and Fall of the Roman Empire* contained obscenities, he used this argument among others, quoting Boileau himself (E. Gibbon, *Memoirs*, p. 211).

69 Antoine Arnauld and Pierre Nicole, *La logique ou l'art de penser*, Paris, Gallimard, 1992 (first edition 1662), pp. 86–91 (pp. 86–7).

70 (Pierre Bayle), *Nouvelles lettres de l'auteur de la Critique générale de l'Histoire du calvinisme de Mr. Maimbourg*, Ville-franche, Pierre Blanc, 1685, pp. 168–70; Bayle used similar arguments in a text written following attacks on his *Dictionnaire* and his subsequent undertaking to the Amsterdam Consistory (*Eclaircissement*, pp. 751–81). For another example, see the (unpaginated) Preface to the *Satyrs* of Juvenal and Persius, *Traduction nouvelle* (by La Valterie), Paris, Claude Barbin, 1681.

71 R. de la Bretonne, *Monsieur Nicolas*, vol. I, p. 23.

72 Jean-Claude Boulogne, *Histoire de la Pudeur*, Paris, Olivier Orban, 1986.

73 Michel Foucault, *Histoire de la sexualité*, 1: *La volonté de savoir*, Paris, Gallimard, 1976 (pp. 25, 26, 45, 47).

74 See pp. 114–16.

75 Gustave Flaubert, *Dictionnaire des idées reçues*, in *Oeuvres*, vol. II, edited by A. Thibaudet and R. Dumesnil, Paris, Gallimard, Pléiade, 1952, p. 1016.

76 Nicolas Chorier, *Les dialogues de Luisa Sigea ou Satire sotadique . . . Prétendue écrite en espagnol par Luisa Sigea et traduite en latin par Jean Mersius. Edition mixte franco-latine*, Paris, Isidore Liseux, 1881, four vols. On this work, see Lynn Hunt, "Introduction", in Lynn Hunt (ed.), *Obscenity and the Origins of Modernity, 1500–1800*, New York, Zone Books, 1993, pp. 19–23; Margaret C. Jacob, "The Materialist World of Pornography", in *ibid.*, pp. 167–72; on its bibliographic career, Pascal Pia, *Les livres de l'Enfer: bibliographie critique des ouvrages érotiques dans leurs différentes éditions du XVIe. siècle à nos jours*, Paris, Coulet et Faure, 1978, pp. 28, 96, 143, 257–70, 1256.

77 J. de Palacio, "Parler latin", p. 251.

78 Charles Baudelaire, *Oeuvres complètes*, vol. I, edited by Claude Pichois, Paris, Gallimard, Pléiade, 1975, p. 940; Louis Forestier, "Rimbaud et le latin", in *La réception*, p. 27.

79 For an example of the first, see the title of Richard Morgiève's novel *Sex vox dominam*, Paris, Calmann-Lévy, 1995; and of the second, see Pierre Klossowski, *Roberte ce soir*, Paris, Editions de Minuit, 1953, pp. 80, 85, 86, 87. On Latin borrowings in erotic writing, see Nicolas Blondeau, *Dictionnaire érotique latin-français . . . Edité pour la première fois sur le manuscrit original avec des notes et des additions de François Noël . . . Précédé d'un essai sur la langue érotique par le Traducteur du Manuel d'érotologie de Forberg*, Paris, Isidore Liseux, 1885; Pierre Guiraud, *Dictionnaire historique, stylistique, rhétorique, étymologique de la littérature érotique: précédé d'une introduction sur les structures étymologiques du vocabulaire érotique*, Paris, Payot, 1975.

80 Derek Jarman, *Dancing Ledge*, edited by Shaun Allen, London, Quartet Books, 1993, ch. VI: "St Sebastiane", and specifically on the inability of certain actors to remember Latin, p. 148; on Jarman's claim to a decadent aesthetic, see David L. Hirst (ed.), *The Last of England*, London, Constable, 1987, p. 47; on the Latin used in the film, see Michael O'Pray, *Derek Jarman: Dream of England*, London, British Film Institute, 1996, p. 82.

81 Edmond and Jules de Goncourt, *Charles Demailly*, in *Oeuvres complètes*, Geneva, Paris, Slatkine Reprints, 1986 (original edition entitled *Les hommes de lettres*, Paris, 1854), p. 136.

10 Yearning for the Universal

1 Jorge Luis Borges, *El congreso* (*Le congrès*), in *El libro de arena* (*Le livre de sable*), translated by Françoise Rosset, Preface and notes by Jean-Pierre Bernès, Paris, Gallimard, 1990, pp. 53–107 (pp. 89, 91). On this text, see Roger Chartier, "Introduction", in Roger Chartier and Pietro Corsi (eds), *Sciences et langues en Europe*, Paris, Ecole des Hautes Etudes en Sciences Sociales, 1996, pp. 11–13.

2 Johannes Vorstius, *De latinitate falso suspecta deque latinae linguae cum germanica con venientis liber . . . Editio secunda . . . Berolini, sumptibus Danielis Richelii*, 1678, unpaginated dedication.

3 An expression originating from Justus Christophorus Böhmer, *Oratio II dicta publice die XII Martii 1701. De latinarum litterarum atque eloquentiae studiis negligenter hodie cultis et diligentius colendis*, in *Orationes tres docendi in Academia Julia muneribus ordinariis praemissae*, Helmstedii, typis Georg. Wolfgangi Hammii, 1715, unpaginated. This was generally one of the arguments in favour of Latin in competition with vernaculars, for example in the quarrel of the inscriptions.

4 Richard Foster Jones, *The Triumph of Language: A Survey of Opinion Concerning the Vernacular from the Introduction of Printing to the Restoration*, Stanford University Press, 1953, p. 313; James Knowlson, *Universal Language Schemes in England and in France, 1600–1800*, University of Toronto Press, 1975, p. 33.

5 J. Knowlson, *Universal Language Schemes*, esp. pp. 7–9, 30–33; Louis Couturat and Léopold Léau, *Histoire de la langue universelle*, Paris, Hachette, 1903–07, p. 515; Umberto Eco, *La ricerca della lingua perfetta nella cultura europea*, Bari, Laterza, 1993, chs 10–14.

6 Quotation from Michele Feo, "Tradizione latina", in Alberto Asor Rosa (ed.), *Letteratura italiana*, vol. V: *Le questioni*, Turin, Einaudi, 1986, pp. 361–2.

7 Vittorio Cian, "Contro il volgare", in *Studi letterari e linguistici dedicati a Pio Rajna*, Florence, Ariani, 1911, pp. 251–97 (p. 296); Maurizio Vitale, *La questione della lingua*, Palermo, Palumbo, 1984, pp. 40 ff.

8 Jerzy Axer, "Latin in Poland and East-Central Europe: Continuity and Discontinuity", in *European Review*, 2 (1994), pp. 305–9 (p. 309).

9 See pp. 22, 28–9, 188–90; Alain Besançon, *Education et société en Russie dans le second tiers du XIXe. siècle*, Paris, The Hague, Mouton, 1974, p. 28.

10 Peter Burke, *Lingua, società e storia*, Bari, Laterza, 1990, p. 50.

11 *The Gentleman's Magazine*, LXXXIV (1814), p. 533.

12 A.-F. Frangulis (ed.), *Dictionnaire diplomatique*, Paris, Académie Diplomatique Internationale, 1933, entry under "Langue internationale".

13 Georges Gusdorf, *Les sciences humaines et la conscience occidentale*, IV: *L'avènement des sciences humaines au siècle des Lumières*, Paris, Payot, 1973, pp. 203–4 (quotation), 309–14; Bernard Colombat, "La description du latin à l'épreuve de la montée des vernaculaires", in Sylvain Auroux (ed.), *Histoire des idées linguistiques*, vol. 2: *Le développement de la grammaire occidentale*, Liège, Mardage, 1992, pp. 509–21.

14 Richard W. Bailey, *Images of English: A Cultural History of the Language*, Ann Arbor, The University of Michigan Press, 1991, pp. 54–5 (quotation), 183; R. Foster Jones, *The Triumph of Language*, ch. 5, "The Misspelled Language".

15 Arne Juul and Hans F. Nielsen, *Otto Jesperson: Facets of his Life and Work*, Amsterdam, Philadelphia, John Benjamin Publishing Company, 1989, p. 7.

16 Ferdinand Brunot, *Histoire de la langue française des origines à nos jours*, vol. V: *Le*

XVIIIe. Siècle, part II: *La langue post-classique* (by Alexis François), Paris, Librairie Armand Colin, 1966, pp. 1159–61.

17 Roland Desné, "Introduction" to *Histoire de Grèce*, in Denis Diderot, *Le modèle anglais*, Paris, Hermann, 1975, pp. 54–5. Acknowledgements to Anne Saada for drawing this text to my attention.

18 Jacques Proust, "Diderot, l'Académie de Pétersbourg et le projet d'une Encyclopédie russe", in *Diderot Studies*, XII (1969), pp. 105–6.

19 Quotation from Marie-Madeleine Martin, *Le latin immortel*, Chiré-en-Montreuil, Diffusion de la Pensée Française, 1971, p. 247; similarly, see the Swiss historian Gonzague de Reynold, in *ibid.*, p. 255.

20 See pp. 239–42; Amedeo Maiuri, "La mostra augustea della Romanità", in *Nuova antologia*, 72 (1937), p. 266.

21 Giovanni Gorini, *Guido Baccelli: la vita, l'opera, il pensiero*, Turin, S. Lattes, 1916, p. 173.

22 The choice of language for book titles has hardly attracted any attention from researchers; a few remarks can be found nevertheless in Christian Moncelet, *Essai sur le titre en littérature et dans les arts*, Le Cendre, BOF, 1972, pp. 96–9; Alain Vaillant, "La latinité hugolienne: bouche d'ombre et langue morte", in Georges Cesbron and Laurence Richer (eds), *La réception du latin du XIXe. siècle à nos jours: actes du colloque d'Angers des 23 et 24 septembre 1994*, Angers, Presses de l'Université, 1996, pp. 79–85.

23 Marie-France David, "De la stèle à la tablette: l'inscription latine dans la littérature antiquisante au tournant du siècle", in *La réception du latin au XIXe. siècle*, pp. 269–77 (pp. 271, 273).

24 See Chapter 2.

25 See pp. 84–8.

26 Marin Mersenne, *Correspondance XI: janvier 1642–27 décembre 1642*, edited by Cornélis de Waard, Paris, Editions du CNRS, 1970, p. 420.

27 D'Alembert, *Discours préliminaire de l'Encyclopédie, publié intégralement d'après l'édition de 1763 par F. Picavet*, Paris, Vrin, 1984, pp. 113–14. The same idea appears in the entry under "Langue" in the *Encyclopédie*, an article written by the grammarian Beauzée: after presenting Latin as "the common language of all the scholars of Europe", he continues: "it is to be hoped perhaps that the practice will become still more general and widespread, to facilitate further communication of the respective enlightenments of the various nations now cultivating the sciences; for how many excellent works are there, in all areas of knowledge, of which we are deprived by our inability to understand the languages in which they are written".

28 Anne Rasmussen, "A la recherche d'une langue internationale de la science 1880–1914", in Roger Chartier and Pietro Corsi (eds), *Sciences et langues en Europe*, Paris, Ecole des Hautes Études en Sciences Sociales, 1996, pp. 139–44.

29 G. Gorrini, *Guido Baccelli*, pp. 171–2, 177.

30 A. Rasmussen, "A la recherche d'une langue internationale", p. 145; L. Couturat and L. Léau, *Histoire de la langue universelle*, pp. 515–23.

31 L. Couturat and L. Léau, *Histoire de la langue universelle*, pp. 523–5 (p. 525); Otto Jesperson, *A Linguist's Life: An English Translation*, edited by Arne Juul, Hans F. Nielsen and Jørgen Erik Nielsen, Odense University Press, 1995, p. 175 (on Diels).

32 "L'histoire aux congrès de 1900", in *Revue de synthèse historique*, I, 2 (October 1900), pp. 207–8; *Atti del Congresso internazionale di scienze storiche (Roma, 1–9 aprile 1903)*, vol.

II: *Atti della sezione I: storia antica e filologia classica*, Rome, Tipografia della R. Accademia dei Lincei, 1905, pp. xxxiv, 269–77, 279–86. Acknowledgements to Edoardo Tortarolo for drawing these texts to my attention.

33 *Cronache della civiltà elleno-latina*, II, nos. 1–3 (April–May 1903), pp. 7–15 (p. 11); the italics are in the original.

34 Roland G. Kent, "Latin as the International Auxiliary Language", in *The Classical Journal*, XVIII (October 1922), pp. 38–44.

35 Gabriella Klein, *La politica linguistica del fascismo*, Bologna, Il Mulino, 1986, pp. 62, 179–81.

36 L. Couturat and L. Léau, *Histoire de la langue universelle*, pp. 526–42.

37 *Ibid.*, pp. 520–21; A. Rasmussen, "A la recherche d'une langue internationale", p. 146.

38 Jean Capelle, "Le latin ou Babel", in *L'éducation nationale* (23 October 1952), pp. 7–8. Four years later he described Latin as "a means of communication inoffensive to national susceptibilities and practically usable in all countries" ("A propos d'un congrès: le latin doit revivre", in *ibid.* (18 October 1956), p. 169.

39 *Premier congrès international pour le latin vivant, Avignon, 3–6 septembre 1956*, Avignon, Edouard Aubanel, 1960 (p. 169).

40 *Deuxième congrès international pour le latin vivant, Lyon, Villeurbanne du 8 au 10 septembre 1959*, Avignon. Edouard Aubanel, 1956 (p. 11).

41 *Ibid.*, p. 25.

42 For an example, see Biagio Amata (ed.), *Cultura e lingue classiche: convegno di aggiornamento e di didattica, Roma, 1–2 novembre 1985*, Rome, LAS, 1986, p. 138.

43 A. Rasmussen, "A la recherche d'une langue internationale", pp. 147–8; Daniel Baggioni, *Langues et nations en Europe*, Paris, Payot, 1997, pp. 319–20.

44 This information is derived from Paolo Albani and Berlinghiero Buonarroti, *Aga magéra difúra. Dizionario delle lingue imaginarie*, Bologna, Zanichelli, 1994, pp. 123, 262, 373–4.

45 L. Couturat and L. Léau, *Histoire de la langue universelle*, pp. 123, 262, 373–4.

46 *Ibid.*, p. 507.

47 *Ibid.*, pp. 415, 449, 457 and (for other examples) pp. 408, 421, 436 and 480; L. Couturat and L. Léau, *Les nouvelles langues internationales: suite à l'histoire de la langue universelle*, Hachette, Paris, 1903–07, pp. 70, 81, 99 and (for other examples) pp. 45, 63, 77.

48 *Ibid.*, p. 285.

49 J.L. Borges, *El congreso*, p. 54.

50 U. Eco, *La ricerca*, pp. 376–7; R. Chartier, "Introduction", p. 13.

Conclusion

1 Quoted in "Le temps des dragonnades", in *Revue de la Franco-Ancienne*, 163 (March 1969), p. 713.

2 See p. 179; see similarly, but in a strongly polemical context, Jean-Louis Nicolet, "Le latin, langue morte et faux savoir", in *L'affaire du latin: réquisitoires et plaidoieries*, Lausanne, F. Rouge et Cie, 1954, p. 25: "The teaching of Latin is a gigantic mystification which has lasted more than 1,000 years".

3 Pierre Grimal, "Le rôle des études classiques et humanistes dans l'éducation et le développement de la vie culturelle des collectivités", in *Le rôle des études classiques et*

humanistes dans l'éducation: réponses à une enquête de l'Unesco, published in *La documentation française: notes et études documentaires*, no. 2543 (28 May 1959).

4 Paul Crouzet, "L'enseignement justifié", in *Pédagogie*, 5 (May 1952), p. 265.

5 See apposite remarks by Daniel Baggioni, *Langues et nations en Europe*, Paris, Payot, 1997, pp. 329–30.

6 See, among others, Peter Burke, *Lingua, società e storia*, Bari, Laterza, 1990, p. 34 (quotation); Ferdinand Brunot, *Histoire de la langue française des origines à nos jours*, vol. VIII: *Le français hors de France au XVIIIe. Siècle*, Paris, Librairie Armand Colin, 1967, pp. 983–4; Jacques Chomarat, "Les études néo-latines en France (et un peu hors de France) 1983–1993", in *Nouvelle revue du seizième siècle*, 12 (1994), pp. 92–3.

7 Alain Bosquet, "A bas le latin", in *Combat* (9 October 1968), p. 1.

8 Acknowledgements to M. Gavrilov and Reinhart Meyer-Kalkus for passing on this information.

9 For the *Janus* collages in *Prospero's Books* and *Europa, Juno, Jupiter, The Library Urchin, The Pedant*, etc., in *Cent allégories pour représenter le monde*, Paris, Adam Biro, 1998.

10 Jean-Luc Godard, *JLG/JLG*, Paris, POL, 1996, pp. 78–9.

11 *Le Monde* (4 April 1998), p. 19.

12 According to an Italian pedagogue, G.D. Pisceria, author of a method for acquiring the rudiments of Latin, 1755 (Furio Murru and Giuseppe Pessolano Filos, *Alla riscoperta della didattica del latino in Italia nel Settecento e nell'Ottocento*, Rome, Edizioni Nuova Rivista Pedagogica, 1980, p. 109).

13 The expression is used by Antonio Gramsci in *Prison Notebooks*.

14 Alfonso Traina and Giorgio Bernardi Perini, *Propedeutica al latino universitario*, fifth edition, revised and edited by Claudio Marangoni, Bologna, Pàtron, 1995, appendix: "Latino perche? Latino per chi?", pp. 433, 436.

Index